I0077282

Final Report of the Thirty-ninth Antarctic Treaty Consultative Meeting

ANTARCTIC TREATY
CONSULTATIVE MEETING

Final Report
of the Thirty-ninth
Antarctic Treaty
Consultative Meeting

Santiago, Chile
23 May - 1 June 2016

Volume II

Secretariat of the Antarctic Treaty
Buenos Aires
2016

Published by:

Secretariat of the Antarctic Treaty
Secrétariat du Traité sur l' Antarctique
Секретариат Договора об Антарктике
Secretaría del Tratado Antártico

Maipú 757 piso 4
C1006ACI Ciudad Autónoma
Buenos Aires - Argentina
Tel: +54 11 4320 4260
Fax: +54 11 4320 4253

This book is also available from: www.ats.aq (digital version)
and online-purchased copies.

ISSN 2346-9897
ISBN (vol. I): 978-987-4024-26-8
ISBN (complete work): 978-987-4024-18-3

Contents

VOLUME I

Acronyms and Abbreviations

PART I. FINAL REPORT

1. ATCM XXXIX Final Report

2. CEP XIX Report

3. Appendices

Appendix 1: Santiago Declaration on the 25th Anniversary of the signing of the Protocol on Environmental Protection to the Antarctic Treaty

Appendix 2: Preliminary Agenda for ATCM XL, Working Groups and Allocation of Items

Appendix 3: Host Country Communique

Appendix 4: Conclusions of the ATCM on Information Exchange

PART II. MEASURES, DECISIONS AND RESOLUTIONS

1. Measures

Measure 1 (2016): Antarctic Specially Protected Area No 116 (New College Valley, Caughley Beach, Cape Bird, Ross Island): Revised Management Plan

Measure 2 (2016): Antarctic Specially Protected Area No 120 (Pointe-Géologie Archipelago, Terre Adélie): Revised Management Plan

Measure 3 (2016): Antarctic Specially Protected Area No 122 (Arrival Heights, Hut Point Peninsula, Ross Island): Revised Management Plan

Measure 4 (2016): Antarctic Specially Protected Area No 126 (Byers Peninsula, Livingston Island, South Shetland Islands): Revised Management Plan

Measure 5 (2016): Antarctic Specially Protected Area No 127 (Haswell Island): Revised Management Plan

Measure 6 (2016): Antarctic Specially Protected Area No 131 (Canada Glacier, Lake Fryxell, Taylor Valley, Victoria Land): Revised Management Plan

Measure 7 (2016): Antarctic Specially Protected Area No 149 (Cape Shirreff and San Telmo Island, Livingston Island, South Shetland Islands): Revised Management Plan

Measure 8 (2016): Antarctic Specially Protected Area No 167 (Hawker Island, Princess Elizabeth Land): Revised Management Plan

Measure 9 (2016): Revised List of Antarctic Historic Sites and Monuments: Incorporation of a historic wooden pole to Historic Site and Monument No 60

(Corvette Uruguay Cairn), in Seymour Island (Marambio), Antarctic Peninsula

Annex: Revised List of Historic Sites and Monuments

2. Decisions

Decision 1 (2016): Observers to the Committee for Environmental Protection

Decision 2 (2016): Revised Rules of Procedure for the Antarctic Treaty Consultative Meeting

Annex: Revised Rules of Procedure for the Antarctic Treaty Consultative Meeting (2016)

Decision 3 (2016): Secretariat Report, Programme and Budget

Annex 1: Audited Financial Report for 2014/2015

Annex 2: Provisional Financial Report for 2015/16

Annex 3: Secretariat Programme for 2016/17

Decision 4 (2016): Procedure for Selection and Appointment of the Executive Secretary of the Secretariat of the Antarctic Treaty

Annex 1: Draft Advertisement

Annex 2: Standard Application Form

Decision 5 (2016): Exchange of Information

Annex: Information Exchange Requirements

Decision 6 (2016): Multi-Year Strategic Work Plan for the Antarctic Treaty Consultative Meeting

Annex: ATCM Multi-Year Strategic Work Plan

3. Resolutions

Resolution 1 (2016): Revised Guidelines for Environmental Impact Assessment in Antarctica

Annex: Revised Guidelines for Environmental Impact Assessment in Antarctica

Resolution 2 (2016): Site Guidelines for Visitors

Annex: List of Sites Subject to Site Guidelines

Resolution 3 (2016): Code of Conduct for Activity within Terrestrial Geothermal Environments in Antarctica

Annex: SCAR Code of Conduct for Activity within Terrestrial Geothermal Environments in Antarctica

Resolution 4 (2016): Non-native Species Manual

Annex: Non-native Species Manual

Resolution 5 (2016): Revised Guide to the Presentation of Working Papers Containing Proposals for Antarctic Specially Protected Areas, Antarctic Specially Managed Areas or Historic Sites and Monuments

Annex: Guide to the presentation of Working Papers containing proposals for Antarctic Specially Protected Areas, Antarctic Specially Managed Areas or Historic Sites and Monuments

Resolution 6 (2016): Confirming ongoing commitment to the prohibition on Antarctic mineral resource activities, other than for scientific research; support for the Antarctic Mining Ban

Heads of Delegation picture

VOLUME II

Acronyms and Abbreviations

ACAP	Agreement on the Conservation of Albatrosses and Petrels
ASMA	Antarctic Specially Managed Area
ASOC	Antarctic and Southern Ocean Coalition
ASPA	Antarctic Specially Protected Area
ATS	Antarctic Treaty System or Antarctic Treaty Secretariat
ATCM	Antarctic Treaty Consultative Meeting
ATME	Antarctic Treaty Meeting of Experts
BP	Background Paper
CCAMLR	Convention on the Conservation of Antarctic Marine Living Resources and/or Commission for the Conservation of Antarctic Marine Living Resources
CCAS	Convention for the Conservation of Antarctic Seals
CCRWP	Climate Change Response Work Programme
CEE	Comprehensive Environmental Evaluation
CEP	Committee for Environmental Protection
COMNAP	Council of Managers of National Antarctic Programs
EIA	Environmental Impact Assessment
EIES	Electronic Information Exchange System
HSM	Historic Site and Monument
IAATO	International Association of Antarctica Tour Operators
ICAO	International Civil Aviation Organization
ICG	Intersessional Contact Group
IEE	Initial Environmental Evaluation
IHO	International Hydrographic Organization
IMO	International Maritime Organization
IOC	Intergovernmental Oceanographic Commission
IOPC Funds	International Oil Pollution Compensation Funds
IP	Information Paper
IPCC	Intergovernmental Panel on Climate Change
IUCN	International Union for Conservation of Nature
MPA	Marine Protected Area
NCA	National Competent Authority
RCC	Rescue Coordination Centre
SAR	Search and Rescue

SCAR	Scientific Committee on Antarctic Research
SC-CAMLR	Scientific Committee of CCAMLR
SGMP	Subsidiary Group on Management Plans
SOLAS	International Convention for the Safety of Life at Sea
SOOS	Southern Ocean Observing System
SP	Secretariat Paper
UAV	Unmanned Aerial Vehicle
UNEP	United Nations Environment Programme
UNFCCC	United Nations Framework Convention on Climate Change
WMO	World Meteorological Organization
WP	Working Paper
WTO	World Tourism Organization

PART II

Measures, Decisions and Resolutions (Cont.)

4. Management Plans

Management Plan For
Antarctic Specially Protected Area No. 116
NEW COLLEGE VALLEY, CAUGHLEY BEACH, CAPE BIRD, ROSS ISLAND

1. Description of values to be protected

An area at Cape Bird, Ross Island was originally designated as Site of Special Scientific Interest (SSSI) No. 10, Caughley Beach by Recommendations XIII-8 (1985) and Specially Protected Area (SPA) No. 20, New College Valley by Recommendation XIII-12 (1985) after proposals by New Zealand on the grounds that the area contains some of the richest stands of moss and associated microflora and fauna in the Ross Sea region of Antarctica. This is the only area on Ross Island where protection is specifically given to plant assemblages and associated ecosystems.

SPA No. 20 was originally enclosed within SSSI No. 10 in order to provide more stringent access conditions to this part of the Area. SSSI No. 10 was incorporated into SPA No. 20 by Measure 1 (2000), with the former Area of SPA No. 20 becoming a Restricted Zone within the SPA. The boundaries of the Area were revised from the boundaries in the original recommendations, in view of improved mapping and to follow more closely the ridges enclosing the catchment of New College Valley. Caughley Beach itself was adjacent to, but never a part of, the original Area, and for this reason the entire Area was renamed as New College Valley, which was within both of the original sites. The Area was redesignated by Decision 1 (2002) as Antarctic Specially Protected Area (ASPA) No. 116 and a revised Management Plan was adopted through Measure 1 (2006) and Measure 1 (2011).

The boundaries of the Area closely follow the ridges enclosing the catchment of New College Valley and cover approximately 0.33 km^2. Moss in this Area is restricted to localised areas of water-flushed ground, with cushions and carpets up to 20 m^2 in area. A diverse range of algal species also inhabit streams in the Area, and springtails, mites and nematodes are plentiful on water surfaces and underneath rocks. The absence of lichens makes the species assemblage in this Area unique on Ross Island.

The susceptibility of mosses to disturbance by trampling, sampling, pollution or introductions of non-native species is such that the Area requires long-term special protection. Designation of this Area is intended to ensure examples of this habitat type are adequately protected from visitors and overuse from scientific investigations. The ecosystem at this site remains of exceptional scientific value for ecological investigations and the Restricted Zone is valuable as a reference site for future comparative studies.

2. Aims and objectives

Management of New College Valley, Caughley Beach, Cape Bird aims to:

- avoid degradation of, or substantial risk to, the values of the Area by preventing unnecessary human disturbance to the Area;
- preserve a part of the natural ecosystem of the Area as a reference area for the purpose of future comparative studies;

- allow scientific research on the ecosystem, in particular on mosses, algae and invertebrates in the Area, while ensuring protection from over-sampling;
- allow other scientific research in the Area provided it is for compelling reasons which cannot be served elsewhere;
- prevent or minimise the introduction to the Area of alien plants, animals and microbes;
- allow visits for management purposes in support of the aims of the Management Plan.

3. Management activities

The following management activities are to be undertaken to protect the values of the Area:

- Copies of this Management Plan including maps of the Area shall be made available at adjacent operational research/field stations.
- Rock cairns or signs illustrating the location and boundaries, with clear statements of entry restrictions, shall be placed at appropriate locations on the boundary of the Area and the Restricted Zone to help avoid inadvertent entry.
- Markers, signs or structures erected within the Area for scientific or management purposes shall be secured and maintained in good condition, and removed when no longer required.
- Visits shall be made as necessary (preferably at least once every five years) to assess whether the Area continues to serve the purposes for which it was designated and to ensure management and maintenance measures are adequate.
- National Antarctic Programmes operating in the Area shall consult together with a view to ensuring the above management activities are implemented.

4. Period of designation

Designated for an indefinite period.

5. Maps

Map A: New College Valley, Caughley Beach, Cape Bird, Ross Island, Regional Topographic Map. Map specifications: Projection - Lambert conformal conic. Standard parallels - 1st 76° 40' 00" S; 2nd 79° 20' 00"S. Central Meridian - 166° 30' 00" E. Latitude of Origin - 78° 01' 16. 211" S. Spheroid - WGS84.

Map B: New College Valley, Caughley Beach, Cape Bird, Ross Island, Vegetation Coverage Map. Map specification: Projection - Lambert conformal conic. Standard parallels – 1st -76.6° S; 2nd - 79.3° S. Spheroid - WGS84. Map includes vegetation coverage and streams.

6. Description of the Area

6(i) Geographical coordinates, boundary markers and natural features
Cape Bird is at the northwest extremity of Mount Bird (1,800 m), an inactive volcanic cone which is probably the oldest on Ross Island. New College Valley is located south of Cape Bird on ice-free slopes above Caughley Beach, and lies between two Adélie penguin colonies known as the Cape Bird Northern and Middle Rookeries (Map A). The Area, comprising veneered glacial moraines at

the foot of the Cape Bird Ice Cap, consists of seaward dipping olivine-augite basalts with scoriaceous tops erupted from the main Mount Bird cone.

The northwest corner of the north boundary of the Area is approximately 100 m south of the Cape Bird hut (New Zealand) and is marked by an ASPA sign post (77° 13.128'S, 166° 26.147'E) (Map B). The north boundary of the Area extends upslope and eastward toward a prominent terminal moraine ridge, approximately 20 m from the Cape Bird Ice Cap and is marked with a rock cairn (77° 13.158'S, 166° 26.702'E).

The eastern boundary follows the terminal moraine ridge from the rock cairn (77° 13.158'S, 166° 26.702'E) southeast until the ridge disappears where it joins the Cape Bird Ice Cap. The boundary continues southeast following the glacier edge to the southern boundary.

The southern boundary is a straight line crossing the broad southern flank of New College Valley, and is marked with rock cairns at the south-western corner of the Area (77° 13.471'S, 166° 25.832'E) and the south-eastern corner of the area on the hilltop 100 m from the Cape Bird Ice Cap glacier edge (77° 13.571'S, 166° 27.122'E).

The west boundary of the Area follows the top of the coastal cliffs of Caughley Beach from the south-western corner rock cairn (77° 13.471'S, 166° 25.832'E) for a distance of 650 m to the northwest corner of the Area (77° 13.128'S, 166° 26.147'E) where the ASPA signpost is.

New College Valley, Caughley Beach is located within Environment S – McMurdo – South Victoria Land geologic based on the Environmental Domains Analysis for Antarctica (Resolution 3 (2008)) and in Region 9 – South Victoria Land based on the Antarctic Conservation Biogeographic Regions (Resolution 6 (2012))

Northwest-facing New College Valley drains meltwater from the Cape Bird Ice Cap during the summer. Streams in the Area are fed by melt from persistent summer snow drifts and have eroded their own shallow gullies and channels. The ground is largely covered by stones and boulders of volcanic origin which have been reworked by glacial action.

The Area contains the most extensive ephemeral stream course distributions of the moss *Hennediella heimii* on Ross Island. Surveys have shown that this moss, together with much lower occurrences of two other species – *Bryum subrotundifolium* and *Bryum pseudotriquetrum* – are confined almost entirely to the stream courses across the steep till and scoria covered slopes (Map B). The mosses are generally associated with algal growths, namely rich, red-brown oscillatorian felts and occasional reddish-black growths of *Nostoc commune*. The Area includes the full course of three stream systems that contain significant growths of algae, together with the mosses.

The Area supports a terrestrial invertebrate community including populations of springtails *Gomphiocephalus hodgsonii* (Collembola: Hypogastruridae), mites *Nanorchestes antarcticus* and *Stereotydeus mollis* (Acari: Prostigmata) and nematodes (*Panagrolaimus davidi, Plectus antarcticus, Plectus frigophilus, Scottnema lindsayae and Eudorylaimus antarcticus*) with the presence of rotifers, tardigrades, and ciliate and flagellate protozoa noted. The distribution of terrestrial invertebrates at this site is related to the abiotic environment with most arthropod species being associated with macroscopic vegetation or soil algal biomass level, although this relationship does not describe the distribution of all taxa.

Skuas (*Catharacta maccormicki*) frequently rest on Caughley Beach and overfly, land and nest within the Area. Adélie penguins (*Pygoscelis adeliae*) from the nearby rookeries do not nest in the Area, but have been observed occasionally to traverse across New College Valley.

6(ii) Special zones within the Area

An area of New College Valley is designated as a Restricted Zone in order to preserve part of the Area as a reference site for future comparative studies, while the remainder of the Area (which is similar in biology, features and character) is more generally available for research programmes and sample collection. The Restricted Zone encompasses ice-free slopes within New College Valley above Caughley Beach some of which are north-facing with snow drifts which provide a ready supply of melt water to foster moss and algal growth.

The northwest corner (77° 13.164'S, 166° 26.073'E) of the Restricted Zone is 60 m to the south and across a small gully from the northwest corner of the Area. The north boundary of the Restricted Zone extends 500 m upslope from the northwest corner to a cairn (77° 13.261'S, 166° 26.619'E), then following a faint but increasingly prominent ridge southeast to a point in the upper catchment of New College Valley marked by a cairn approximately 60 m from the ice terminus of the Cape Bird Ice Cap (77° 13.368'S, 166° 26.976'E). The Restricted Zone boundary extends 110 m southwest across the valley to a cairn marking the southeast corner of the Restricted Zone (77° 13.435'S, 166° 26.865'E). The south boundary of the Restricted Zone extends in a straight line from this cairn (77° 13.435'S, 166° 26.865'E) 440 m northwest down a broad and relatively featureless slope to the southwest corner of the Area (77° 13.328'S, 166° 26.006'E). A cairn is placed on the southwest boundary of the Restricted Zone to mark the lower position of the south boundary (77° 13.226'S, 166° 25.983'E).

Access to the Restricted Zone is allowed only for compelling scientific and management purposes that cannot be served by visits elsewhere in the Area.

6(iii) Location of structures within and adjacent to the Area

Structures known to exist within the Area include a United States Navy Astrofix marker, cairns marking the boundaries of the Area and the Restricted Zone, a signpost situated at the northwest corner of the Area and an approximately one meter square wooden frame marking the site of an experimental oil spill from 1982.

A field hut (New Zealand), stores hut and toilet are located north of the northwest corner of the Area (Map B).

6(iv) Location of other protected areas in the vicinity

The nearest protected areas are:

- Lewis Bay, Mount Erebus, Ross Island (ASPA No. 156), approximately 25 km SE;
- Tramway Ridge, Mount Erebus, Ross Island (ASPA No. 175) 30 km SSE;
- Cape Crozier, Ross Island (ASPA No. 124) 75 km SE;
- Cape Royds, Ross Island (ASPA No. 121 and No. 157) and Cape Evans, Ross Island (ASPA No. 155) 35 km and 45 km south on Ross Island respectively; and
- Beaufort Island, McMurdo Sound, Ross Sea (ASPA No. 105) 40 km to the north.

7. Terms and conditions for entry Permits

Entry into the Area is prohibited except in accordance with a Permit issued by an appropriate national authority. Conditions for issuing a Permit to enter the Area are that:

- outside of the Restricted Zone, it is issued only for scientific study of the ecosystem, or for compelling scientific reasons that cannot be served elsewhere, or for essential management purposes consistent with the Management Plan objectives such as inspection or review;
- access to the Restricted Zone is allowed only for compelling scientific or management reasons that cannot be served elsewhere in the Area;
- the actions permitted are not likely to jeopardise the ecological or scientific values of the Area or other permitted activities;
- any management activities are in support of the objectives of the Management Plan;
- the actions permitted are in accordance with the Management Plan;
- the Permit, or a copy, shall be carried within the Area;
- a visit report shall be supplied to the authority named in the Permit;
- the Permit shall be issued for a stated period.

7(i) Access to and movement within or over the Area

Helicopters are prohibited from landing within the Area. Two helicopter landing sites are located outside the Area. Between October to February, the preferred landing site is below the cliffs on Caughley Beach, 100 m west of the west boundary of the Area 77° 13.221'S, 166° 25.812'E (Maps A and B). Between March and September, an alternative helicopter landing site is located adjacent to the Cape Bird field hut (New Zealand), above Caughley Beach 77° 13.093S, 166° 26.168' E (Map B).

Between October and February the preferred flight path is an approach from the south above Middle Rookery (Map A). Flights north of the helicopter pad may be necessary under certain wind conditions but should follow the recommended aircraft approach and departure routes, and to maximum extent possible, follow the 'Guidelines for the Operation of Aircraft Near Concentrations of Bird in Antarctica' (Resolution 2, 2004). See Map A for the recommended aircraft approach routes into and out of Cape Bird.

Overflight of the Area lower than 50 m (~150 ft) above ground level is prohibited. Hovering over the Area is not permitted lower than 100 m (~300 ft) above ground level. Use of helicopter smoke grenades within the Area is prohibited.

Vehicles are prohibited within the Area and all movement within the Area should be on foot. Access into the Area should preferably follow the track from the Cape Bird Hut (New Zealand). Visitors should avoid areas of visible vegetation and care should be exercised walking in areas of moist ground, particularly the stream course beds, where foot traffic can easily damage sensitive soils, plant and algal communities, and degrade water quality. Avoid walking on such areas by walking on ice or rocky ground. Pedestrian traffic should be kept to the minimum necessary consistent with the objectives of any permitted activities and every reasonable effort should be made to minimise effects.

Access to regions south of the Area from the Cape Bird Hut should be made by a route below the cliffs along Caughley Beach.

7(ii) Activities which may be conducted in the Area
- Compelling scientific research which cannot be undertaken elsewhere and which will not jeopardise the ecosystem or values of the Area or interfere with existing scientific studies;

- Essential management activities, including monitoring and inspection.

7(iii) Installation, modification or removal of structures
No structures are to be erected within the Area, or scientific equipment installed, except for compelling scientific or management reasons, as specified in a Permit. All markers, structures or scientific equipment installed in the Area must be authorised by Permit and clearly identified by country, name of the principal investigator or agency, year of installation and date of expected removal. All such items should be free of organisms, propagules (e.g. seeds, eggs) and non-sterile soil, and be made of materials that pose minimal risk of contamination of the Area. Removal of specific structures or equipment for which the Permit has expired shall be a condition of the Permit.

7(iv) Location of field camps
Camping within the Area is prohibited. A field hut (New Zealand), stores hut and toilet are located north of the northwest corner of the Area (Map B).

7(v) Restrictions on materials and organisms which may be brought into the Area
No living animals, plant material or microorganisms shall be deliberately introduced into the Area and precautions listed in 7(ix) shall be taken against accidental introductions. No poultry products shall be brought into the Area. No herbicides or pesticides shall be brought into the Area. Any other chemicals, including radio-nuclides or stable isotopes, which may be introduced for scientific or management purposes specified in the Permit, shall be removed from the Area at or before the conclusion of the activity for which the Permit was granted. Fuel or other chemicals shall not be stored in the Area, unless required for essential purposes connected with the activity for which the Permit has been granted, and must be contained within an emergency cache authorized by an appropriate authority. All materials introduced shall be for a stated period only, shall be removed at or before the conclusion of that stated period, and shall be stored and handled so that risk of their introduction into the environment is minimised.

7(vi) Taking or harmful interference with native flora or fauna
Taking of, or harmful interference with native flora or fauna is prohibited, except in accordance with a separate Permit issued in accordance with Annex II of the Protocol on Environmental Protection to the Antarctic Treaty. Where taking or harmful interference with animals is involved this should, as a minimum standard, be in accordance with the SCAR Code of Conduct for the Use of Animals for Scientific Purposes in Antarctica.

7(vii) The collection or removal of materials not imported by the Permit holder
Material may be collected or removed from the Area only in accordance with a permit and should be limited to the minimum necessary to meet scientific or management needs. Similarly, sampling is to be carried out using techniques which minimise disturbance to the Area as well as duplication. Material of human origin likely to compromise the values of the Area, which was not brought into the Area by the Permit holder or otherwise authorised and is not an historical artefact or abandoned relic, may be removed from any part of the Area, including the Restricted Zone, unless the environmental impact of removal is likely to be greater than leaving the material *in situ*. If this is the case the appropriate national authority must be notified and approval obtained.

7(viii) Disposal of waste
All wastes, including all human wastes, shall be removed from the Area.

7(ix) Measures that may be necessary to continue to meet the aims and objectives of the Management Plan

Permits may be granted to enter the Area to:

- carry out biological monitoring and Area inspection activities, which may involve the collection of a small number of samples or data for analysis or review;
- to erect or maintain signposts, structures or scientific equipment; or
- for management activities.

Any specific sites of long-term monitoring shall be appropriately marked.

To help maintain the ecological and scientific values of the isolation and relatively low level of human impact at the Area, visitors shall take special precautions against introductions. Of particular concern are microbial or vegetation introductions sourced from soils at other Antarctic sites, including stations, or from regions outside Antarctica. To minimise the risk of introductions, visitors shall thoroughly clean footwear and any equipment to be used in the area particularly sampling equipment and markers before entering the Area.

7(x) Requirements for reports
The principal permit holder for each visit to the Area shall submit a report to the appropriate national authority as soon as practicable, and no later than six months after the visit has been completed. Such visit reports should include, as applicable, the information identified in the recommended visit report form [contained in Appendix 4 of the Guide to the Preparation of Management Plans for Antarctic Specially Protected Areas appended to Resolution 2 (1998)] [available from the website of the Secretariat of the Antarctic Treaty www.ats.aq].

If appropriate, the national authority should also forward a copy of the visit report to the Party that proposed the Management Plan, to assist in managing the Area and reviewing the Management Plan. Parties should maintain a record of such activities and report them in the Annual Exchange of Information. Parties should, wherever possible, deposit originals or copies of such original visit reports in a publicly accessible archive to maintain a record of usage, for the purposes of any review of the management plan and in organising the scientific use of the Area.

8. Bibliography

Ainley, D.G., Ballard, G., Barton, K.J., Karl, B.J., Rau, G.H., Ribic, C.A. and Wilson, P.R. 2003. Spatial and temporal variation of diet within a presumed metapopulation of Adelie penguins. Condor 105: 95-106.

Ainley, D.G., Ribic, C.A., Ballard, G., Heath, S., Gaffney, I., Karl, B.J., Barton, K.J., Wilson, P.R. and Webb, S. 2004. Geographic structure of Adelie penguin populations: overlap in colony-specific foraging areas. Ecological monographs 74(1): 159- 178.

Block, W. 1985. Ecological and physiological studies of terrestrial arthropods in the Ross Dependency 1984-85. British Antarctic Survey Bulletin 68: 115-122.

Broady, P.A. 1981. Non-marine algae of Cape Bird, Ross Island and Taylor Valley, Victoria Land, Antarctica. Report of the Melbourne University Programme in Antarctic Studies No. 37.

Broady, P.A. 1983. Botanical studies at Ross Island, Antarctica, in 1982-83; preliminary report. Report of the Melbourne University Programme in Antarctic Studies.

Broady, P.A. 1985. The vegetation of Cape Bird, Ross Island, Antarctica. Melbourne University Programme in Antarctic Studies, No. 62.

Broady, P.A. 1985. A preliminary report of phycological studies in northern Victoria Land and on Ross Island during 1984-85. Report of the Melbourne University Programme in Antarctic Studies, Report No. 66.

Broady, P.A. 1989. Broadscale patterns in the distribution of aquatic and terrestrial vegetation at three ice-free regions on Ross Island, Antarctica. Hydrobiologia 172: 77-95.

Butler, E.R.T. 2001. Beaches in McMurdo Sound, Antarctica. Unpublished PhD, Victoria University of Wellington, New Zealand. (pg 219)

Cole, J.W. and Ewart, A. 1968. Contributions to the volcanic geology of the Black Island, Brown Peninsula, and Cape Bird areas, McMurdo Sound, Antarctica. New Zealand Journal of Geology and Geophysics 11(4): 793-823.

Dochat, T.M., Marchant, D.R. and Denton, G.H. 2000. Glacial geology of Cape Bird, Ross Island, Antarctica. Geografiska Annaler 82A (2-3): 237-247.

Duncan, K.W. 1979. A note on the distribution and abundance of the endemic collembolan *Gomphiocephalus hodgsonii* Carpenter 1908 at Cape Bird, Antarctica. Mauri Ora 7: 19-24.

Hall, B.L., Denton, G.H. and Hendy, C.H. 2000. Evidence from Taylor Valley for a Grounded Ice Sheet in the Ross Sea, Antarctica. Geografiska annaler 82A(2-3): 275-304.

Konlechner, J.C. 1985. An investigation of the fate and effects of a paraffin-based crude oil in an Antarctic terrestrial ecosystem. New Zealand Antarctic Record 6(3): 40-46.

Lambert, D.M., Ritchie, P.A., Millar, C.D., Holland, B., Drummond, A.J. and Baroni, C. 2002. Rates of evolution in ancient DNA from Adélie penguins. Science 295: 2270-2273.

McGaughran, A., Convey, P, Redding, G.P. and Stevens, M.I. 2010. Temporal and spatial metabolic rate variation in the Antarctic springtail Gomphiocephalus hodgsoni. Journal of Insect Physiology 56: 57-64.

McGaughran, A., Convey, P. and Hogg, I.D. 2011. Extended ecophysiological analysis of Gomphiocephalus hodgsoni (Collembola): flexibility in life history strategy and population response. Polar Biology 34: 1713-1725.

McGaughran, A., Hogg, I.D. and Stevens, M.I. 2008. Patterns of population genetic structure for springtails and mites in southern Victoria Land, Antarctica. Molecular phylogenetics and evolution 46: 606-618.

McGaughran, A., Redding, G.P., Stevens, M.I. and Convey, P. 2009. Temporal metabolic rate variation in a continental Antarctica springtail. Journal of Insect Physiology 55: 130-135.

Nakagawa, S., Möstl, E. and Waas, J.R. 2003. Validation of an enzyme immunoassay to measure faecal glucocorticoid metabolites from Adelie penguins (*Pygoscelis adeliae*): a non-invasive tool for estimating stress? Polar biology 26: 491-493.

Peterson, A.J. 1971. Population studies on the Antarctic Collembolan *Gomphiocephalus hodgsonii* Carpenter. Pacific Insects Monograph 25: 75-98.

Ritchie, P.A., Millar, C.D., Gibb, G.C., Baroni, C., Lambert, D.M. 2004. Ancient DNA enables timing of the Pleistocene origin and Holocene expansion of two Adelie penguin lineages in Antarctica. Molecular biology and evolution 21(2): 240-248.

Roeder, A.D., Marshall, R.K., Mitchelson, A.J., Visagathilagar, T., Ritchie, P.A., Love, D.R., Pakai, T.J., McPartlan, H.C., Murray, N.D., Robinson, N.A., Kerry, K.R. and Lambert, D.M. 2001. Gene flow on the ice: genetic differentiation among Adélie penguin colonies around Antarctica. Molecular Ecology 10: 1645-1656.

Seppelt, R.D. and Green, T.G.A. 1998. A bryophyte flora for Southern Victoria Land, Antarctica. New Zealand Journal of Botany 36: 617-635.

Sinclair, B.J. 2000. The ecology and physiology of New Zealand Alpine and Antarctic arthropods. Unpublished PhD, University of Otago, New Zealand. (pg 231)

Sinclair, B. J. 2001. On the distribution of terrestrial invertebrates at Cape Bird, Ross Island, Antarctica. Polar Biology 24(6): 394-400.

Sinclair, B. J. and Sjursen, H. 2001. Cold tolerance of the Antarctic springtail *Gomphiocephalus hodgsonii* (Collembola, Hypogastruridae). Antarctic Science 13(3): 271-279.

Sinclair, B.J. and Sjursen, H. 2001. Terrestrial invertebrate abundance across a habitat transect in Keble Valley, Ross Island, Antarctica. Pedobiologia 45: 134-145.

Smith, D.J. 1970. The ecology of *Gomphiocephalus hodgsonii* Carpenter (Collembola, Hypogastuidae) at Cape Bird, Antarctica. Unpublished MSc Thesis, University of Canterbury, Christchurch, New Zealand.

Stevens, M.I. and Hogg, I.D. 2003. Long-term isolation and recent expansion from glacial refugia revealed for the endemic springtail *Gomphiocephalus hodgsonii* from Victoria Land, Antarctica. Molecular ecology 12: 2357-2369.

Wilson, P.R., Ainley, D.G., Nur, N., Jacobs, S.S., Barton, K.J., Ballard, G. and Comisco, J.C. 2001. Adélie penguin population change in the Pacific sector of Antarctica: relation to sea-ice extent and the Antarctic Circumpolar Current. Marine ecology progress series 213: 301-309.

Wharton, D.A. and Brown, I.M. 1989. A survey of terrestrial nematodes from the McMurdo Sound region, Antarctica. New Zealand Journal of Zoology 16: 467-470.

Map A - New College Valley, Caughley Beach, Cape Bird, Ross Island
Antarctic Specially Protected Area 116: Regional Topographic Map

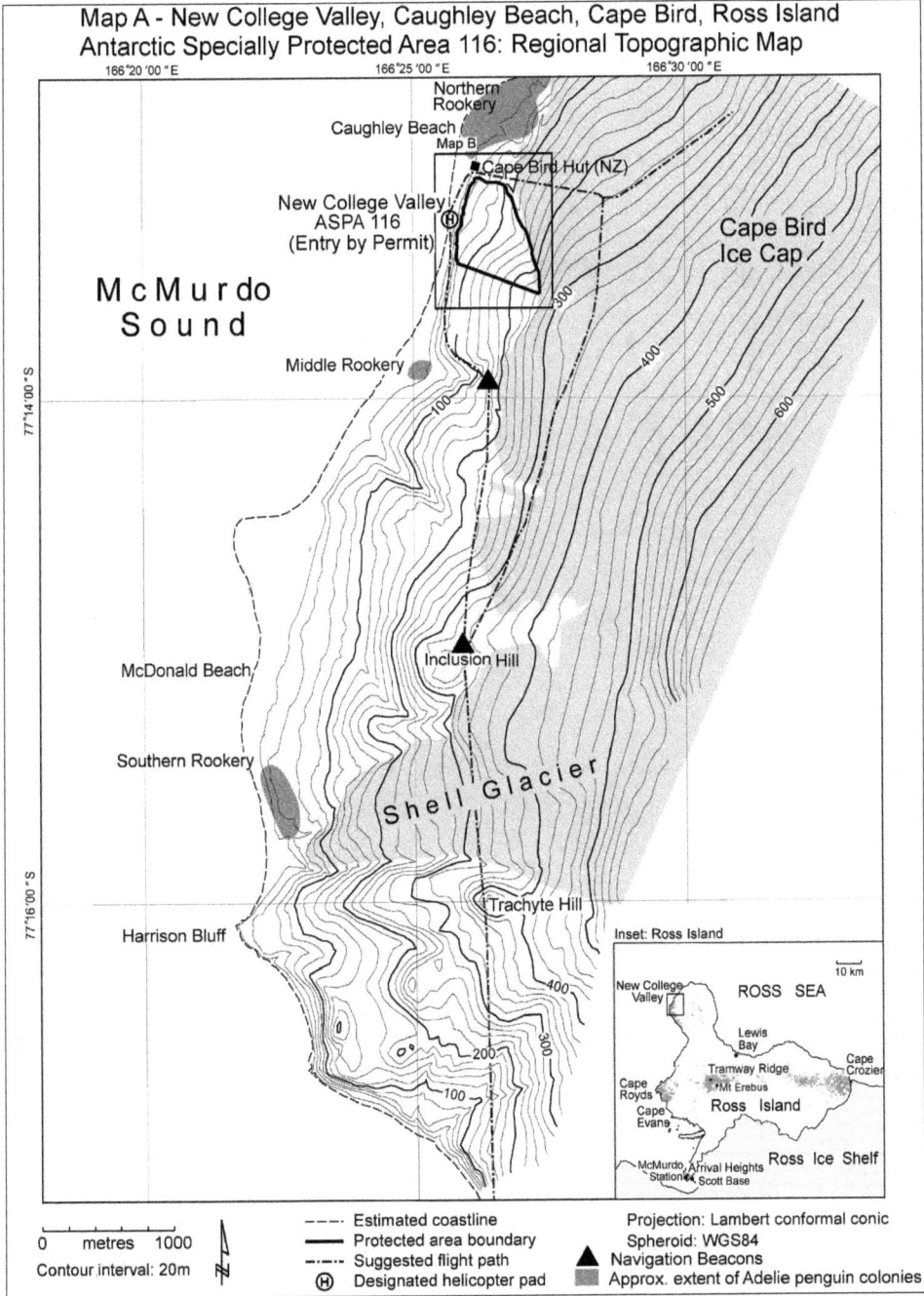

Map B - New College Valley, Caughley Beach, Cape Bird, Ross Island
Antarctic Specially Protected Area 116: Vegetation Coverage Map

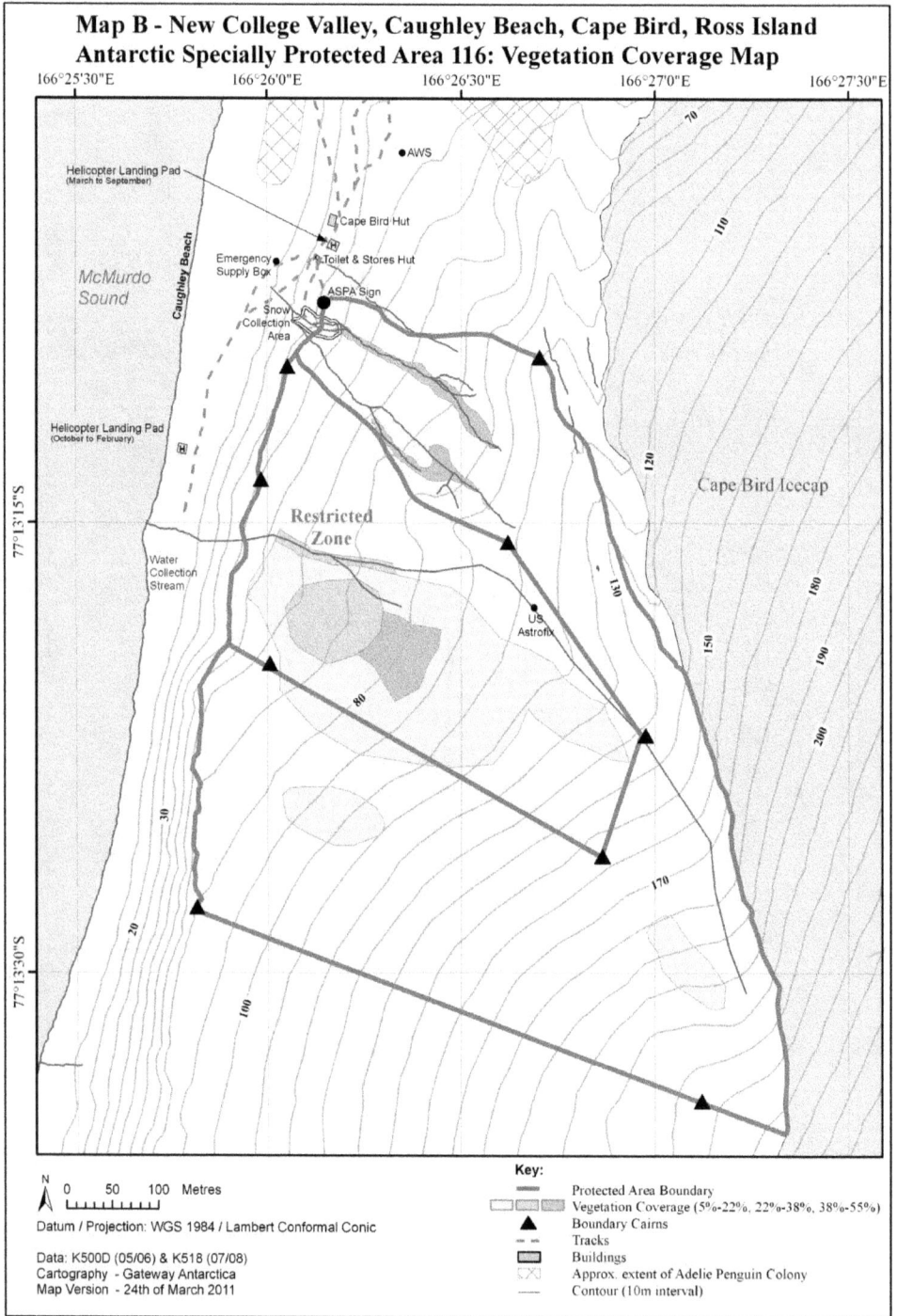

166°25'30"E   166°26'0"E   166°26'30"E   166°27'0"E   166°27'30"E

AWS

Helicopter Landing Pad
(March to September)

Cape Bird Hut

Caughley Beach

Emergency
Supply Box

Toilet & Stores Hut

McMurdo
Sound

ASPA Sign

Snow
Collection
Area

Helicopter Landing Pad
(October to February)

77°13'15"S

Cape Bird Icecap

Restricted
Zone

Water
Collection
Stream

US
Astrofix

80

30

170

20

100

77°13'30"S

N

0   50   100 Metres

Datum / Projection: WGS 1984 / Lambert Conformal Conic

Data: K500D (05/06) & K518 (07/08)
Cartography - Gateway Antarctica
Map Version - 24th of March 2011

Key:

— Protected Area Boundary
▭▭▭ Vegetation Coverage (5%-22%, 22%-38%, 38%-55%)
▲ Boundary Cairns
-- Tracks
▭ Buildings
⊠ Approx. extent of Adelie Penguin Colony
— Contour (10m interval)

26

Management Plan for Antarctic Specially Protected Area No. 120

POINTE-GÉOLOGIE ARCHIPELAGO, TERRE ADÉLIE

Jean Rostand, Le Mauguen (formerly Alexis Carrel),
Lamarck and Claude Bernard Islands, The Good Doctor's Nunatak
And breeding site of Emperor Penguins

Introduction

The Pointe-Géologie Archipelago, in Terre Adélie, comprises 8 principal islands grouped over less than 2.4 km², about 5 km from the Antarctic continent. Petrel Island, the largest of these islands, is the site of the Dumont d'Urville French scientific station (66°39′46″S 140°0′07″E). In the 1980s, important work was undertaken in order to connect the Buffon, Cuvier and Lion Islands with a view to establishing a runway for large aircraft. This project was never completed, essentially because the sea destroyed part of the platform created.

This archipelago is distinctive in that it hosts breeding grounds for eight of the nine species of birds that breed on the coasts of the Antarctic. Among these eight species of birds, four belong to the Procellariidae family, two to the Spheniscidae family, one to the Stercorariidae family and lastly, one belongs to the Hydrobatidae family. Two species which are emblematic of the Antarctic are noticeably present: giant petrels and emperor penguins; the winter colony of the latter being a few hundred metres from the Dumont d'Urville base.

In 1995, four islands, a nunatak and a breeding ground for emperor penguins were classified as an Antarctic Specially Protected Area (Measure 3 (1995), ATCM XIX) because they were a representative example of terrestrial Antarctic ecosystems from a biological, geological and aesthetics perspective.

Resolution 3 (2008) recommended that "Environment Domains Analysis for the Antarctic Continent" should serve as a dynamic model for the identification of Antarctic Specially Protected Areas (see also Morgan *et al.*, 2007). According to this model, ASPA No. 120 is part of environmental domain L (Continental coastal-zone ice sheet).

Also, Resolution 6 (2012) recommended that "the Antarctic Conservation Biogeographic Regions be used in conjunction with the Environmental Domains Analysis... [to identify] areas that could be designated as ASPAs" and to thereby respond to the idea of the systematic environmental-geographic framework referred to in Article 3 Paragraph 2 of Annex V of the Protocol on Environmental Protection to the Antarctic Treaty. Consequently, Pointe-Géologie is part of Conservation Biogeographic Region n°13, "Terre Adélie" (see Terauds *et al.* 2012), one of the smallest Conservation Biogeographic Regions (178 km²).

1. Description of Values to be Protected

The area contains exceptional environmental and scientific values due to the diversity of the species of birds and marine mammals that breed there:
- The Weddell seal *(Leptonychotes weddellii)*
- The emperor penguin *(Aptenodytes forsteri)*
- The Antarctic skua *(Catharacta maccormicki)*
- The Adélie penguin *(Pygoscelis adeliae)*
- The Wilson's petrel *(Oceanites oceanicus)*
- The Southern giant petrel *(Macronectes giganteus)*
- The snow petrel *(Pagodroma nivea)*
- The cape petrel *(Daption capense).*

Long-term research and monitoring programmes of birds and marine mammals have been going on for a long time already (since 1952 or 1964 according to the species), currently supported by the French *Institut Polaire Français Paul-Emile Victor (IPEV)* and the French *Centre National de la Recherche scientifique (CNRS).*

This has enabled the implementation of a population database of exceptional value, by time-scale of observation. It is maintained and used by the *Centre d'Etudes Biologiques de Chizé (CEBC-CNRS)*. Within this context, human scientific presence in the protected area is currently estimated at four people for a few hours, three times a month between the 1st November and the 15th February, and, inside the emperor penguin colony itself, at two people for a few hours between the 1st April and the 1st November.

Among the 46 emperor penguin breeding sites on record (Fretwell *et al.* 2012), Pointe-Géologie is one of the only ones, along with that near the Mirny station, located adjacent to a permanent station. It is therefore a providential spot to study this species and its environment.

2. Aims and Objectives

Management of the Pointe-Géologie Specially Protected Area aims at:

- Preventing disturbance in the area due to the proximity of the Dumont d'Urville station;
- Limiting disturbance in the area by preventing any unjustified human intervention;
- Avoiding any major changes to the structure and composition of flora and fauna and in particular the different species of marine vertebrates, birds and mammals harboured in the area, which is one of the most representative for both faunistic and scientific interest on the Adélie Coast;
- Permitting scientific research which can not be undertaken elsewhere, in particular in the life sciences (ethology, ecology, physiology and biochemistry, demographic studies of birds and sea mammals, impact assessment of surrounding human activities etc) and earth sciences (geology, geomorphology etc);
- Controlling logistical operations related to the activities of the nearby Dumont d'Urville station, which may require temporary access to the ASPA.

3. Management Activities

The following management activities will be undertaken to protect the values of the area:

- The present management plan is kept under periodical review to ensure that the values of the ASPA are wholly protected.
- Any activity - be it scientific or management in nature - carried out in the area must undergo an environmental impact assessment before being undertaken, in accordance with the requirements stipulated in Annex 1 of the Protocol on Environmental Protection to the Antarctic Treaty.
- In accordance with Annex 3 of the Protocol on Environmental Protection to the Antarctic Treaty, abandoned material(s) will be removed, as far as possible, provided that this removal does not damage the environment or the values of the area.
- All members of staff staying at or in transit at the Dumont d'Urville base will be duly informed of the existence of the ASPA, of its geographical boundaries, of the entry restrictions in place and, more generally of the current management plan. To this end, a sign displaying a map of the area and listing the restrictions and relevant management measures shall be displayed prominently at the Dumont d'Urville station.
- Copies of this management plan shall also be available in each of the four Treaty languages at the Dumont d'Urville station.
- Information related to each incursion into the ASPA, namely *a minima*: activity undertaken or reason for presence, number of people involved, duration of stay, is recorded by the Head of the Dumont d'Urville station.

4. Period of Designation

The Area is designated as an Antarctic Specially Protected Area (ASPA) for an indefinite period.

5. Maps

Map 1 shows the geographical location of Terre Adélie in the Antarctic and the location of the Pointe-Géologie Archipelago on the Terre Adélie coast.
Map 2 of the Pointe-Géologie Archipelago shows the location of the main bird colonies and the dotted line indicates the boundary of ASPA No. 120 within the archipelago.

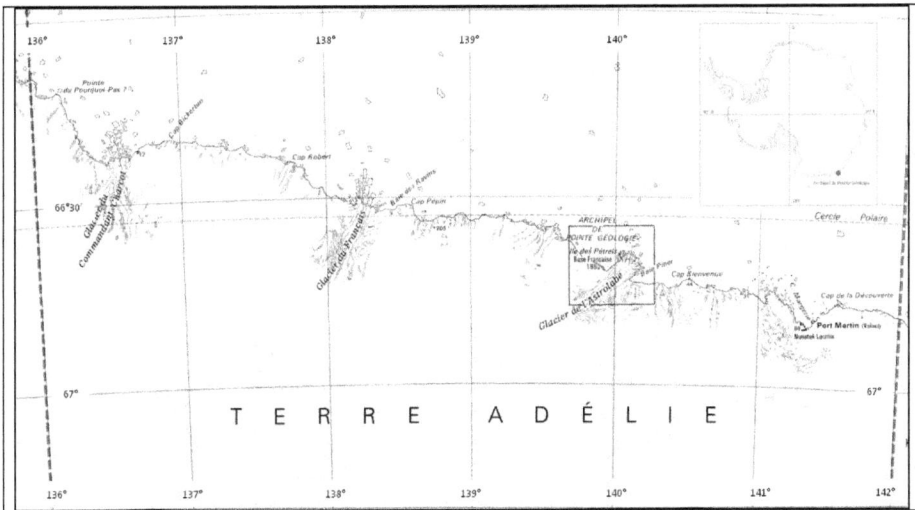

Map 1 - Location of the Pointe-Géologie Archipelago, Terre Adélie (Antarctica).

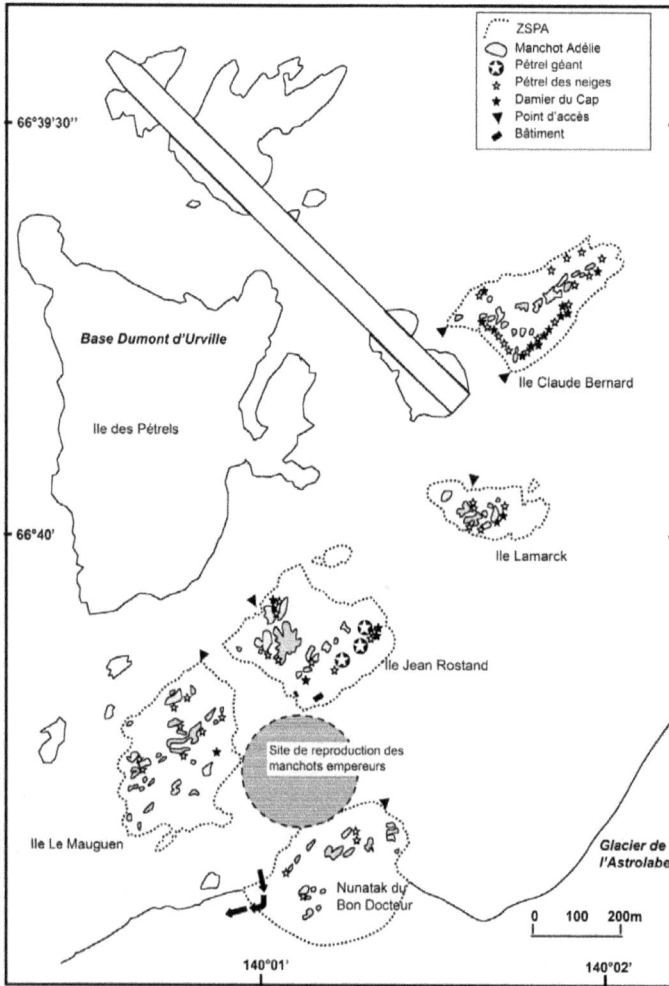

Map 2 - Location of bird colonies (except skua territories and Wilson's petrels nests) within the Pointe-Géologie Archipelago ASPA. The dotted lines show the ASPA boundary. The emperor penguins, present from March to mid-December, establish their colony on the pack ice between the islands and their location is variable. Possible access of land vehicles to the continent via the Good Doctor's Nunatak is shown by means of arrows.

6. Description of the Area and Identification of Sectors

6 (i) Geographic coordinates, boundary markers and natural features
Boundaries and Coordinates

ASPA No. 120 is located along the Terre Adélie coast, in the heart of the Pointe-Géologie Archipelago (140° - 140°02'E; 66°39'30'' - 66°40'30'' S). It comprises the following territories:

- Jean Rostand Island,
- Le Mauguen (formerly Alexis Carrel) Island,
- Lamarck Island,
- Claude Bernard Island,
- the 'Good Doctor' Nunatak,
- and the Emperor penguins breeding grounds, on the pack ice which surrounds the islands in winter.

As a whole, the surface of the rock outcrops does not exceed 2 km². The highest points are distributed along North-East-South-West ridges (C. Bernard Island: 47.6 m; J.Rostand Island: 36.39 m; Le Mauguen (formerly Alexis Carrel) Island: 28.24 m; 'Good Doctor' Nunatak: 28.50 m).

During the summer, the pack ice between the islands disappears, and only the Southern flanks of the islands are still covered by firns. The ASPA is then clearly limited by natural markers (island outlines and rocky outcrops).

No tracks or roads exist in the area.

GENERAL DESCRIPTION OF THE AREA

Geology

Well-marked hills display asymmetrical transverse profiles with gently dipping northern slopes compared to the steeper southern ones. The terrain is affected by numerous cracks and fractures leading to very rough surfaces. The basement rocks consist mainly of sillimanite, cordierite and garnet-rich gneisses which are intruded by abundant dikes of pink anatexites. The lowest parts of the islands are covered by morainic boulders with a heterogeneous granulometry (from a few centimetres to more than a metre across).

Terrestrial biological communities

No vascular plants and no macro-arthropods live in the area. Only the *Prasiola crispa* cosmpolitan algae is present and can have significant coverage locally depending on the supply of bird droppings.

Vertebrate Fauna

Seven species of birds and one marine mammal (the Weddell seal) use the Pointe-Géologie Archipelago. They have all been monitored populations since the 1950s-1960s. Table 1 provides information about the number of seabirds observed, Table 2 about periods of presence of the different species and Table 3 about the estimated sensitivity of each species.

The establishment of the Dumont d'Urville station has resulted in a drastic decrease in the populations of southern giant petrels in the Pointe-Géologie Archipelago. The breeding colony on Petrel Island disappeared completely at the end of the 1950s during the early years when the base was being set up in close proximity to this colony (building extensions, increase in helicopter flights, installation and replacement of fuel storage tanks). Currently, 100% of the southern giant petrels population breeds inside the ASPA, in the South-Eastern part of Rostand Island.

The work undertaken between 1984 and 1993 to connect the Buffon, Cuvier and Lion Islands with a view to establishing a runway resulted in the destruction of the breeding sites of approximately 3,000 Adélie penguin pairs, 210 snow petrel pairs, 170 cape petrel pairs, 180 Wilson's petrel pairs and 3 Antarctic skua pairs (Micol & Jouventin 2001). Quite a significant proportion of the Adélie penguin pairs moved to the ASPA, unlike the other species (Micol & Jouventin 2001, CEBC data not published).

The significant decrease in emperor penguins by the end of the 1970s seems to have been due to long weather anomalies between 1976 and 1982 which caused a significant decrease in the surface area of thepack ice (Barbraud & Weimerskirch 2001, Jenouvrier *et al.* 2012). For the last fifteen years, the emperor penguin breeding population has been slightly increasing in parallel with an increase in pack ice surface area in the Terre Adélie sector (Table 3).

Among the bird species present on the Pointe-Géologie Archipelago, the emperor penguin and the southern giant petrel breed only inside the ASPA. Since the ASPA was established in 1995, the populations of these two species have been stable or slightly increasing (Table 3). However, long-term forecasts suggest that the high protection status should be maintained through the current management plan.

Table 1 Number of sea bird breeding pairs within ASPA No. 120 (count done during the 2014/2015 breeding cycle). The population breeding within the ASPA compared to that of the Pointe-Géologie (PG) population as a whole is also mentioned (Source: unpublished data CEBC-CNRS on the 2014/2015 breeding cycle except for Wilson's storm petrels, data from 1986 in Micol & Jouventin 2001)

Site	Emperor penguin	Adélie penguin	South polar skua	Snow petrel	Cape petrel	Wilson's storm petrel*	Southern giant petrel
C. Bernard	--	3,682	4	152	204	178	--
Lamarck	--	1,410	1	31	26	45	--
J. Rostand	--	5,441	8	54	57	35	19
Le Mauguen (formerly Alexis Carrel)	--	4,271	18	14	1	72	
Nunatak	----	1793	1	5	--	41	--
Winter pack ice between islands	3,772	--	--	--	--	--	--
ASPA TOTAL	3,772	16,597	32	256	288	371	19
PG TOTAL	3,772	42,757	74	691	492	1,200	19
ASPA/PG %	100	39	43	37	59	31	100

Table 2 Presence of birds on breeding grounds

	Emperor penguin	Adélie penguin	South Polar skua	Snow petrel	Cape petrel	Wilson's storm petrel	Southern giant petrel
First arrival	March	October	October	September	October	November	July
First egg laying	May	November	November	December	December	December	October
Last departure	End of December	March	March	March	March	March	April

Table 3 Sensitivity to disturbance caused by human beings and changes in populations of the Pointe-Géologie Archipelago (Sources: unpublished CEBC-CNRS data, Thomas 1986, and Micol & Jouventin 2001 for data on Wilson's storm petrels)

	Emperor penguin	Adélie penguin	South polar skua	Snow petrel	Cape petrel	Wilson's storm petrel	Southern giant petrel
Sensitivity	High	Medium	Medium	Medium	High	High	High
Trend 1952-1984	Diminishing	Stable	Stable	?	?	?	Diminishing
Trend 1984-2000	Stable	Increasing	Increasing	Stable	Stable	?	Stable
Trend 2000/15	Slightly increasing	Increasing	Increasing	Increasing	Stable	?	Slightly increasing

6(ii) Identification of restricted or prohibited zones

- Entry restrictions to different sites within the ASPA are determined according to the distribution of bird species (Table 1), the timing of their presence on breeding grounds (Table 2) and their specific sensitivity (Table 3). The location of breeding colonies and points of access to the islands are shown on map 2. Birds are mainly present during the austral summer, except for the emperor penguins, which breed in winter.

The case of Rostand Island

The Southern giant petrels are present in an area defined by the NE-SW ridgegoing through the 33.10 m and the 36.39 m marks North West of the colony, marked on the ground with stakes. Access to this breeding area is strictly prohibited, except to ornithologists holding a Permit allowing access once a year when southern giant petrel chicks are being banded. Access to the rest of Rostand Island is authorised throughout the year to Permit Holders.

The case of the emperor penguin colony

The emperor penguin colony is not always at the same site and moves about on the pack ice during winter. The protection zone for these animals is therefore defined by the sites where birds are present (colony or groups of individuals), with an additional 40 m buffer zone.

No one, except Permit Holders, is allowed to approach or to disturb the emperor penguin colony in any manner during the period when they are present at the breeding grounds, from March to mid-December when the chicks fledge. It is recommended that the minimum distance between authorised observers and the colony be 20 m.

6(iii) Structures in the Area

Prévost hut and a shelter are located on Rostand Island. There are no other buildings anywhere else in the Area.

6 (iv) Location of other protected Areas nearby

The closest protected area to APSA No. 120 is ASPA No. 166, "Port Martin", located 60 km to the east.

6 (v) Special Areas within the ASPA

None.

7. Permit Conditions

- Entry into the Area is subject to obtaining a Permit issued by an appropriate national authority designated under Article 7 of Annex 5 of the Protocol on Environmental Protection to the Antarctic Treaty. The Head of the Dumont d'Urville station is kept informed regarding Permit-holders.
- Permits can be issued for the activities envisaged in Paragraph 7(ii). Permits will authorise the scope of the tasks to be undertaken, their time-span and the maximum number of people commissioned to enter the Area (Permit Holders and any accompanying persons who may be needed forprofessional or safety reasons).

7(i) Access to and movement within the Area

- Access to the Area is permitted by foot or by light watercraft (in summer) only.

- No helicopters are authorised within the Area and overflights of the Area by all unauthorised aircraft are prohibited (except in the event of emergency procedures).

- The use of leisure drones within the ASPA is prohibited.

- The use of drones or helicopter overflights for scientific research, population monitoring or logistical purposes, must be specifically requested along with the request to access the ASPA. Access authorisations issued by the appropriate authorities must mention the authorisation, as required, of the use of drones in the area or the helicopter overflight by specifying the flying conditions of these aircraft.

- The transit traffic of land vehicles between the Dumont d'Urville station, on Petrel Island, and the Cap Prudhomme station on the continent, will normally take place in winter, following a straight line across the pack ice. During the very rare occasions when sea-ice conditions do not allow thesetransits to be made safely, a route along the western edge of the 'Good Doctor' Nunatak can be permitted exceptionally, as indicated on Map 2.

- In any case, terrestrial vehicles obliged to drive close to colonies of emperor penguins must be remain outside the ASPA, respecting a minimum distance of 40 m.

- The movement of authorised persons within the Area shall, in any case, be limited, in order to avoid unnecessary disturbance to birds, and to ensure that breeding areas and their access are not damaged or endangered.

- Although the base situated on Petrel Island is not included in the ASPA, particular care should also be taken when the emperor penguins move there (an exceptional circumstance which, in the main, involves only adults or thermally emancipated young). In this case, it is recommended that a minimum approach distance of 20 m be maintained, except for ornithologists who can be brought in, taking all necessary precautions, to move the animals in order to allow essential logistical activities to be undertaken around the base.

7(ii) Activities which are or may be conducted within the Area, including restrictions on time and place

- Compelling scientific activities which cannot be conducted elsewhere.

- Conservation activities pertaining to the species present.

- Essential management and logistical activities.

- Educational and scientific outreach activities (filming, photography, sound recording etc) which cannot be conducted elsewhere.

7(iii) Installation, modification or removal of structures

- No structures are to be erected or scientific equipment installed in the Area except for compelling scientific reasons or management or conservation activities as authorised by an appropriate national authority.

- Permanent structures or facilities are prohibited.

- The possible modification or dismantling of installations currently on Rostand Island can proceed only after authorisation.

7(iv) Location of field camps

Camping in the Area is prohibited. An exception can be made only for security reasons. In such an event, tents should be set up in such a way that they disturb the environment as little as possible.

7(v) Restriction on materials and organisms which may be brought into the Area

- According to the provisions set forth in Annex II to the Protocol on Environmental Protection to the Antarctic Treaty, no living animals or plant materials shall be introduced into the Area.
- Special precautions shall be taken against accidentally introducing microbes, invertebrates or plants from other Antarctic sites, including stations, or from regions outside Antarctica. All sampling equipment or markers brought into the Area shall be cleaned or sterilised. To the maximum extent practicable, footwear and other equipment used or brought into the Area (including bags or backpacks) shall be thoroughly cleaned before entering the Area. The CEP's Non-native Species Manual (current edition published on the website of the Secretariat of the Antarctic Treaty) and the COMNAP/SCAR Checklists for Supply Chain Managers of National Antarctic Programmes for the Reduction in the Risk of Transfer of Non-native Species provide additional guidance on this matter.
- No poultry products, including waste associated with these products and products containing egg powder, shall be introduced into the Area.
- No chemicals shall be brought into the Area, except chemicals which may be introduced for a compelling scientific purpose as specified in the Permit. Any chemical introduced shall be removed from the Area at or before the conclusion of the activity for which the Permit was granted.
- Fuel, food and other materials are not to be stored in the Area, unless required for compelling purposes connected with the activity for which the Permit has been granted. Such materials are to be removed when no longer required. Permanent storage is not permitted.

7(vi) The taking of or harmful interference with flora and fauna

Taking of or harmful interference with native flora and fauna is prohibited except in accordance with a specific Permit. In the case of authorised taking or interference, SCAR's Code of Conduct for the Use of Animals for Scientific Purposes in Antarctica (ATCM XXXIV-CPE XIV IP53) must be used as a minimum standard.

7 (vii) The collection or removal of anything not brought into the Area by the Permit Holder

- Collection or removal of anything not brought into the Area by a Permit Holder is prohibited unless specifically mentioned in the Permit.
- Debris of man-made origin may be removed from the Area and dead or pathological specimens of fauna or flora cannot be removed unless explicitly mentioned in the Permit.

7(viii) Disposal of waste

All waste produced must be removed from the Area after each visit in accordance with Annex II of the Protocol on Environmental Protection to the Antarctic Treaty, which acts as a minimum standard.

7(ix) Measures that may be necessary to ensure that the aims and objectives of the Management Plan can continue to be met

- Visits to the Area shall be restricted to the activities referred to in paragraph 7 (ii) and duly authorised.
- Scientific activities will be undertaken in accordance with SCAR's Code of Conduct for Terrestrial Scientific Field Research in Antarctica (ATCM XXXII-CPE XII IP004) and SCAR's Code of Conduct for the Use of Animals for Scientific Purposes in Antarctica (ATCM XXXIV-CPE XIV IP53).

7(x) Reports of visits to the Area

Parties should ensure that the principal Holder of each Permit issued submits to the appropriate authority a report describing the activities undertaken in the Area. Such reports, to be submitted no later than six months after the visit to the Area, should include, as appropriate, the information identified in the visit report form contained in the "Guide to the Preparation ofManagement Plans for Antarctic Specially Protected Areas" (Resolution 2, 2011).

Parties should, wherever possible, deposit original or copies of such original reports in a publicly accessible archive to maintain a record of usage, to be taken into consideration both when reviewing the Management Pland when organising the scientific manipulation of the Area.

8. References

Barbraud, C. and Weimerskirch. H. 2001. Emperor penguins and climate change. *Nature*, 411: 183-186

Fretwell, P.T., LaRue, M.A., Morin, P., Kooyman, G.L., Wienecke, B., Ratcliffe, N., Adrian, J.F., Fleming, A.H., Porter, C. and Trathan, P.N. 2012. An Emperor Penguin Population Estimate: The First Global, Synoptic Survey of a Species from Space. *PLoS ONE*, 7(4), e33751.

Jenouvier, S., Holland, M., Stroeve, J., Barbraud, C., Weimerskirch, H., Serreze, M. and Caswell, H. 2012. Effects of climate change on an emperor penguin population: analysis of coupled demographic and climate models. *Global Change Biology*, 18, 2756-2770.

Micol, T. and Jouventin, P. 2001. Long-term population trends in seven Antarctic seabirds at Pointe Géologie (Terre Adélie). *Polar Biology*, 24, 175-185.

Morgan, F., Barker, G., Briggs, C., Price, R. and Keys, H. 2007. Environmental Domains of Antarctica Version 2.0 Final Report, Manaaki Whenua Landcare Research New Zealand Ltd. 89 pp.

ATCM XXXIV-CPE XIV IP53 2011. SCAR's Code of Conduct for the Use of Animals for Scientific Purposes in Antarctica

Terauds, A., Chown, S.L., Morgan, F., Peat, H.J., Watts, D.J., Keys, H., Convey, P. and Bergstrom, D. 2012. Conservation biogeography of the Antarctic. *Diversity and Distributions*, 18, 726-741.

Thomas, T. 1986. L'effectif des oiseaux nicheurs de l'archipel de Pointe Géologie (Terre Adélie) et son évolution au cours des trente dernières années. *L'oiseau RFO*, 56, 349-368.

Management Plan for
Antarctic Specially Protected Area No. 122
ARRIVAL HEIGHTS, HUT POINT PENINSULA, ROSS ISLAND

Introduction

The Arrival Heights Antarctic Specially Protected Area (ASPA) is situated near the south-western extremity of Hut Point Peninsula, Ross Island, at 77° 49' 41.2" S, 166° 40' 2.8" E, with an approximate area 0.73 km². The primary reason for designation of the Area is its value as an electromagnetically 'quiet' site for the study of the upper atmosphere and its close proximity to logistical support. The Area is used for a number of other scientific studies, including trace gas monitoring, auroral and geomagnetic studies and air quality surveys. As an example, the longevity and quality of the numerous atmospheric datasets makes the Area of high scientific value. Since, its designation in 1975, numerous projects have been located in or near the Area with a potential to degrade the electromagnetically quiet conditions at Arrival Heights. The interference generated by these activities appears to have an acceptably low impact on scientific experiments, although a detailed review of the level of interference is currently being undertaken. The continued use of the Area is favored by its geographical characteristics, unobstructed low viewing horizon, clean air and its proximity to logistical support and high costs associated with relocation. The Area was proposed by the United States of America and adopted through Recommendation VIII-4 [1975, Site of Special Scientific Interest (SSSI) No. 2]; date of expiry was extended through Recommendations X-6 (1979), XII-5 (1983), XIII-7 (1985), and XIV-4 (1987), Resolution 3 (1996) and Measure 2 (2000). The Area was renamed and renumbered through Decision 1 (2002); a revised management plan was adopted through Measure 2 (2004) and Measure 3 (2011). The degradation of electromagnetically 'quiet' conditions within the Area was recognized by SCAR Recommendation XXIII-6 (1994).

The Area lies within 'Environment S – McMurdo – South Victoria Land geologic', as defined in the Environmental Domains Analysis for Antarctica (Resolution 3 (2008)). Under the Antarctic Conservation Biogeographic Regions classification (Resolution 6 (2012)) the Area lies within ACBR9 – South Victoria Land.

1. Description of values to be protected

An area at Arrival Heights was originally designated in Recommendation VIII-4 (1975, SSSI No. 2), after a proposal by the United States of America on the grounds that it was "an electromagnetic and natural 'quiet site' offering ideal conditions for the installation of sensitive instruments for recording minute signals associated with upper atmosphere programs." For example, electromagnetic recordings have been carried out at Arrival Heights as part of long term scientific studies, yielding data of outstanding quality because of the unique characteristics of the geographic location with respect to the geomagnetic field combined with relatively low levels of electromagnetic interference. The electromagnetically quiet conditions and the longevity of data collection at Arrival Heights make the data obtained of particularly high scientific value.

In recent years, however, increases in science and support operations associated with Scott Base and McMurdo Station have raised the levels of locally generated electromagnetic noise at Arrival Heights and it has been recognized that the electromagnetically 'quiet' conditions have to some degree been degraded by these activities, as identified in SCAR Recommendation XXIII-6 (1994).

Scientific research within the Area appears to operate within an acceptably low level of electromagnetic interference (EMI) from other activities in the vicinity and the aims and objectives set out in the management plan for Arrival Heights therefore remain relevant. However, recent site visits and deployment of new instruments have shown that there is some elevated very-low frequency (VLF) noise in the 50 Hz – 12 kHz range from sources located outside of the Area (most likely wind turbines installed ~1 km from the Area). There is also evidence of increased VLF noise in the 12 - 50 KHz frequency range, which probably arises inside of the Area from, for example, the electrical power grid configuration and grounding, and the proliferation of units such as uninterruptable power supplies (UPS). The US and NZ scientific communities that run projects at Arrival Heights are currently undertaking a detailed analysis of the possible causes of EMI with the goal of providing practical recommendations for mitigating potential effects.

Notwithstanding these observations, the original geographical characteristics of the site, such as its elevated position and thus broad viewing horizon, the volcanic crater morphology, and the close proximity to the full logistic support of nearby McMurdo Station (US) 1.5 km south and Scott Base (NZ) 2.7 km SE, continue to render the Area valuable for upper atmospheric studies and boundary layer air sampling studies. Moreover, there are scientific, financial and practical constraints associated with any proposed relocation of the Area and the associated facilities. Thus, the current preferred option for management is to minimize sources of EMI to the maximum extent practicable, and to monitor these levels routinely so that any significant threat to the values of the site can be identified and addressed as appropriate.

Since original designation the site has been used for several other scientific programs that benefit from the restrictions on access in place within the Area. In particular, the broad viewing horizon and relative isolation from activities (e.g. vehicle movements, engine exhausts) has been valuable for measurement of greenhouse gases, trace gases such as ozone, spectroscopic and air particulate investigations, pollution surveys, and auroral and geomagnetic studies. It is important that these values are protected by maintenance of the broad and unobstructed viewing horizon and that anthropogenic gas emissions (in particular long-term gaseous or aerosol emissions from sources such as internal combustion engines) are minimised and where practicable avoided.

In addition, the protected status of Arrival Heights has also had the effect of limiting the extent and magnitude of physical disturbance within the Area. As a result, soils and landscape features are much less disturbed than is the case in the surrounding areas of Hut Point where station developments have taken place. In particular, sand-wedge polygons are far more extensive than elsewhere in the Hut Point vicinity, covering an area of approximately 0.5 km^2. The relatively undisturbed nature of the environment at Arrival Heights makes the Area valuable for comparative studies of impacts associated with station developments, and valuable as a reference against which to consider changes. These additional values are also important reasons for special protection at Arrival Heights.

The Area continues to be of high scientific value for a variety of high quality and long-term atmospheric data sets that have been collected at this site. Despite the acknowledged potential for interference from local and surrounding sources, the long-term data series, the accessibility of the site for year-round observations, its geographical characteristics, and the high cost of relocation, warrant that the site receive ongoing and strengthened protection. The vulnerability of this research to disturbance through chemical and noise pollution, in particular electromagnetic interference, and potential changes to the viewing horizon and/or shadowing of instrumentation is such that this Area requires continued special protection.

2. Aims and objectives

Management at Arrival Heights aims to:

- avoid degradation of, or substantial risk to, the values of the Area by preventing unnecessary human disturbance to the Area;
- allow scientific research in the Area, in particular atmospheric research, while ensuring protection from incompatible uses and uncontrolled equipment installation that may jeopardize such research;
- minimize the possibility of generation of excessive electromagnetic noise interference within the Area through regulating the types, quantity and use of equipment that can be installed and operated in the Area;
- Avoid degradation of the viewing horizon and shadowing effects by installations on instrumentation reliant on solar and sky viewing geometries;
- Avoid / mitigate as far as practicable anthropogenic gaseous or aerosol emissions from sources such as internal combustion engines to the atmosphere within the Area;
- encourage the consideration of the values of the Area in the management of surrounding activities and land uses, in particular to monitor the levels, and encourage the minimization of sources of electromagnetic radiation that may potentially compromise the values of the Area;
- allow access for maintenance, upgrade and management of communications and scientific equipment located within the Area;
- allow visits for management purposes in support of the aims of the management plan; and

- allow visits for education or public awareness purposes associated with the scientific studies being conducted in the Area that cannot be fulfilled elsewhere.

3. Management activities

The following management activities are to be undertaken to protect the values of the Area:

- Signs showing the location and boundaries of the Area with clear statements of entry restrictions shall be placed at appropriate locations at the boundaries of the Area to help avoid inadvertent entry. The signs should include instructions to make no radio transmissions and to turn vehicle headlights off within the Area, unless required in an emergency.

- Signs showing the location of the Area (stating the special restrictions that apply) shall be displayed prominently, and a copy of this management plan shall be kept available, in the principal research hut facilities within the Area and at McMurdo Station and Scott Base.

- Markers, signs or structures erected within or near the boundary of the Area for scientific or management purposes shall be secured and maintained in good condition, and removed when no longer necessary.

- Visits shall be made as necessary (no less than once every five years) to assess whether the Area continues to serve the purposes for which it was designated and to ensure management and maintenance measures are adequate.

- Electromagnetic noise surveys shall be undertaken within the Area bi-annually to detect equipment faults and to monitor levels of interference that may have potential to compromise the values of the Area unacceptably, for the purposes of identification and mitigation of their sources.

- Potentially disruptive activities that are planned to be conducted outside of but close to the Area, such as blasting or drilling, or the operation of transmitters or other equipment with the potential to cause significant electromagnetic interference within the Area, should be notified in advance to the appropriate representative(s) of national authorities operating in the region, with a view to coordinating activities and / or undertaking mitigating actions in order to avoid or minimize disruption to scientific programs.

- National Antarctic Programs operating in the region shall appoint an Activity Coordinator who will be responsible for inter-program consultation regarding all activities within the Area. The Activity Coordinators shall keep a log of visits to the Area by their programs, recording number of personnel, time and duration of visit, activities, and means of travel into the Area, and shall exchange this information to create a consolidated log of all visits to the Area annually.

- National Antarctic Programs operating in the region shall consult together with a view to ensuring the conditions in this management plan are implemented, and take appropriate measures to detect and enforce compliance where the conditions are not being followed.

4. Period of designation

Designated for an indefinite period.

5. Maps

Map 1: ASPA No. 122 Arrival Heights – Regional overview, showing Hut Point Peninsula, nearby stations (McMurdo Station, US; and Scott Base, NZ), installations (SuperDARN, satellite receptors and wind turbines) and routes (roads and recreational trails). Projection Lambert Conformal Conic: Standard parallels: 1st 77° 40' S; 2nd 78° 00' S; Central Meridian: 166° 45' E; Latitude of Origin: 77° 50' S; Spheroid WGS84; Datum McMurdo Sound Geodetic Control Network. Data sources: Topography: contours (10 m interval) derived from digital orthophoto and DEM from aerial imagery (Nov 1993); Permanent ice extent digitized from orthorectified Quickbird satellite image (15 Oct 05) (Imagery © 2005 Digital Globe, provided through the NGA Commercial Imagery Program); Infrastructure: station layout CAD data USAP (Feb 09 / Mar 11), ERA (Nov 09) and USAP (Jan 11) field survey; Recreational trails PGC field survey (Jan 09 / Jan 11).

Inset 1: The location of Ross Island in the Ross Sea. ***Inset 2:*** The location of Map 1 on Ross Island and key topographic features.

Map 2: Arrival Heights, ASPA No. 122 topographic map, showing protected area boundaries, site facilities, nearby installations (SuperDARN, satellite receptors) and routes (access roads and recreational trails). Projection details and data sources are the same as for Map 1.

6. Description of the Area

6(i) Geographical coordinates, boundary markers and natural features

Boundaries and coordinates

Arrival Heights (77° 49' 41.2" S, 166° 40' 2.8" E; Area: 0.73 km²) is a small range of low hills located near the southwestern extremity of Hut Point Peninsula, Ross Island. Hut Point Peninsula is composed of a series of volcanic craters extending from Mount Erebus, two of which, namely First Crater and Second Crater, respectively form part of the southern and northern boundaries of the Area. The Area is predominantly ice-free and elevations range from 150 m to a maximum of 280 m at Second Crater. Arrival Heights is located approximately 1.5 km north of McMurdo Station and 2.7 km northwest of Scott Base. The Area has a broad viewing horizon and is comparatively isolated from activities at McMurdo Station and Scott Base, with the majority of McMurdo Station being hidden from view.

The southeastern boundary corner of the Area is defined by Trig T510 No.2, the center of which is located at 77° 50' 08.4" S, 166° 40' 16.4" E at an elevation of 157.3 m. Trig T510 No.2 replaced and is 0.7 m from the former boundary survey marker (T510), which no longer exists. The replacement T510 No.2 marker is an iron rod (painted orange) installed into the ground approximately 7.3 m west of the access road to Arrival Heights, and is surrounded by a small circle of rocks. The boundary of the Area extends from Trig T510 No.2 in a straight line 656.0 m northwest over First Crater to a point located at 77° 49' 53.8" S, 166° 39' 03.9" E at 150 m elevation. The boundary thence follows the 150 m contour northward for 1186 m to a point (77° 49' 18.6" S, 166° 39' 56.1" E) due west of the northern rim of Second Crater. The boundary thence extends 398 m due east to Second Crater, and around the crater rim to a US Hydrographic Survey marker (a stamped brass disk) which is installed near ground level at 77° 49' 23.4" S, 166° 40' 59.0" E and 282 m elevation, forming the northeastern boundary of the Area. The boundary thence extends from the US Hydrographic Survey marker southward for 1423 m in a straight line directly to Trig T510 No.2.

Geology, geomorphology and soils

Hut Point Peninsula is 20 km long and is formed by a line of craters that extend south from the flanks of Mt. Erebus (Kyle 1981). The basaltic rocks of Hut Point Peninsula constitute part of the Erebus volcanic province and the dominant rock types are alkali basanite lavas and pyroclastics, with small amounts of phonolite and occasional outcrops of intermediate lavas (Kyle 1981). Aeromagnetic data and magnetic models indicate that the magnetic volcanic rocks underlying Hut Point Peninsula are likely to be <2 km in thickness (Behrendt *et al*. 1996) and dating studies suggest that the majority of basaltic rocks are younger than ~ 750 ka (Tauxe *et al*. 2004).

The soils at Arrival Heights consist mostly of volcanic scoria deposited from the eruptions of Mount Erebus, with particle size ranging from silt to boulders. The thickness of surface deposits ranges from a few centimetres to tens of metres, with permafrost underlying the active layer (Stefano, 1992). Surface material at Arrival Heights also includes magma flows from Mount Erebus, which have been weathered and reworked over time. Sand-wedge polygons cover an area of approximately 0.5 km² at Arrival Heights and, because physical disturbance has been limited by the protected status of the Area, are far more extensive than elsewhere in the southern Hut Point Peninsula vicinity (Klein *et al*. 2004).

Climate

Arrival Heights is exposed to frequent strong winds and conditions are generally colder and windier than at nearby McMurdo Station and Scott Base (Mazzera *et al*. 2001). During the period February 1999 to April 2009, the maximum temperature recorded within the Area was 7.1°C (30 Dec 2001) and the minimum was -49.8°C (21 July 2004). During this period, December was the warmest month, with mean monthly air temperatures of -5.1°C, and August was the coolest month, averaging –28.8°C (data sourced from National Institute of Water and Atmospheric Research (NIWA), New Zealand, http://www.niwa.co.nz, 21 May 2009).

The mean annual wind speed recorded at Arrival Heights between 1999 and 2009 was 6.96 ms-1, with June and September being the windiest months (data sourced from NIWA, http://www.niwa.co.nz, 21 May 2009). The highest recorded gust at Arrival Heights between 1999-2011 was 51 m/s (~184 km/h) on 16 May 2004. The prevailing wind direction at Arrival Heights is north-easterly, as southern air masses are deflected by the surrounding topography (Sinclair 1988). Hut Point Peninsula lies at the confluence of three dissimilar air masses, predisposing the area to rapid onset of severe weather (Monaghan *et al.* 2005).

Scientific research

Numerous long-term scientific investigations are conducted at Arrival Heights, with the majority of research focusing on the earth's atmosphere and magnetosphere. Research areas include extremely low and very low radio frequencies, auroral events, geomagnetic storms, meteorological phenomena and variations in trace gas levels, particularly ozone, ozone precursors, ozone destroying substances, biomass burning products and greenhouse gases. The Area has good access and logistical support from nearby McMurdo Station and Scott Base, which helps to facilitate research within the Area.

The extremely-low-frequency and very-low-frequency (ELF/VLF) data have been continuously collected at Arrival Heights since the austral summer of 1984/1985 (Fraser-Smith *et al.* 1991). The ELF/VLF noise data are unique in both length and continuity for the Antarctic and were recorded concurrently with ELF/VLF data at Stanford University, allowing for comparison between polar and mid-latitude time series. The lack of electromagnetic interference and remote location of Arrival Heights allow researchers to measure background ELF/VLF noise spectra and weak ELF signals, such as Schumann resonances, which are associated changes in the magnetosphere and ionosphere (Füllekrug & Fraser-Smith 1996). ELF/VLF and Schumann resonance data collected within the Area have been studied in relation to fluctuations in sun spots, solar particle precipitation events, and planetary-scale meteorological phenomenon (Anyamba *et al.* 2000; Schlegel & Füllekrug 1999; Fraser-Smith & Turtle 1993). Furthermore, ELF data have been used as a proxy measure of global cloud-to-ground lightning activity and thunderstorm activity (Füllekrug *et al.* 1999) and VLF data provide input to global networks which monitor lightning activity and conditions in the ionosphere (Clilverd *et al.* 2009; Rodger *et al.* 2009). High quality electromagnetic data from Arrival Heights has enabled determination of an upper limit for the photon rest mass of ~10^{-52} kg (Füllerkrug 2004) based on detection of minute global ionospheric reflection height measurements (Füllerkrug *et al.* 2002), and it has also provided a critical link between lightning at mid- and tropical latitudes and surface temperature variations in moderate and tropical climates (Füllerkrug & Fraser-Smith 1997). Recent research has developed novel measurement technologies with a sensitivity of μV/m over the broad frequency range from ~4 Hz to ~400 kHz (Füllerkrug 2010), which has promising scientific potential requiring conditions of electromagnetic quiescence such as are present at Arrival Heights.

The southerly location of Arrival Heights results in several weeks of total darkness during the austral winter, allowing low intensity auroral events and dayside emissions to be observed (Wright *et al.* 1998). Data recorded at Arrival Heights have been used to track the motion of polar cap arcs, a form of polar aurora, and results have been related to solar wind and interplanetary magnetic field conditions. Auroral observations made at Arrival Heights by researchers for the University of Washington have also been used to calculate the velocity and temperature of high altitude winds by analyzing the Doppler shift of auroral light emissions. In addition to auroral research, optical data collected within the Area have been used to monitor the response of the thermosphere to geomagnetic storms (Hernandez & Roble 2003) and medium frequency radar has been used to measure middle atmospheric (70-100 km) wind velocities (McDonald *et al.* 2007).

A range of trace gas species are measured at Arrival Heights, including carbon dioxide, ozone, bromine, methane, nitrogen oxides, hydrogen chloride and carbon monoxide, with records commencing as early as 1982 (Zeng *et al.* 2012, Kolhepp *et al.* 2012). Arrival Heights represents a key site in the Network of the Detection of Atmospheric Composition (NDACC) and the Global Atmospheric Watch (GAW), with data being used to monitor changes in the stratosphere and troposphere, including long-term evolution of the ozone layer, Southern Hemisphere greenhouse gas concentrations and changes in overall atmospheric composition. The measurements made at Arrival Heights are vital for Southern Hemisphere and Antarctic satellite comparison (Vigouroux *et al.* 2007) and atmospheric chemistry model validation (Risi *et al.* 2012). Arrival Heights has also been used as one of several Antarctic reference stations for intercomparisons of surface air measurements (Levin *et al.* 2012).

Ozone levels have been recorded at Arrival Heights since 1988 and are used to monitor both long-term and seasonal variations in ozone (Oltmans *et al.* 2008; Nichol *et al.* 1991), as well as in estimations of Antarctic ozone loss (Kuttippurath *et al.* 2010). In addition to longer-term trends, sudden and substantial ozone depletion events have been recorded during spring-time at Arrival Heights, which occur over a period of hours and thought to result from the release of bromine compounds from sea salt (Riedel *et al.* 2006; Hay *et al.* 2007). Tropospheric bromine levels have been continuously recorded since 1995 within the Area and have been studied in relation to ozone depletion, stratospheric warming and changes in the polar vortex, as well as being used in validation of satellite measurements (Schofield *et al.* 2006). Nitrogen oxide (NO_2) data collected at Arrival Heights have also been used to investigate variations in ozone levels and results show substantial variations in NO_2 at daily to interannual timescales, potentially resulting from changes in atmospheric circulation, temperature and chemical forcing (Struthers *et al.* 2004, Wood et al., 2004). In addition, ground-based Fourier transform spectroscopy has been used at Arrival Heights to monitor atmospheric carbonyl sulfide levels and to record HCl fluxes from Mount Erebus (Kremser *et al.* 2015; Keys *et al.* 1998).

Vegetation

Lichens at Arrival Heights were surveyed in 1957 by C.W. Dodge and G.E. Baker, with species recorded including: *Buellia alboradians, B. frigida, B. grisea, B. pernigra, Caloplaca citrine, Candelariella flava, Lecanora expectans, L. fuscobrunnea, Lecidella siplei, Parmelia griseola, P. leucoblephara* and *Physcia caesia*. Moss species recorded at Arrival Heights include *Sarconeurum glaciale* and *Syntrichia sarconeurum* (BAS Plant Database, 2009), with *S. glaciale* documented within drainage channels and disused vehicle tracks (Skotnicki *et al.* 1999).

Human activities and impact

The Arrival Heights facilities are used year-round by personnel from McMurdo Station (US) and Scott Base (NZ). In addition to two laboratory buildings, numerous antenna arrays, aerials, communications equipment, and scientific instruments are located throughout the Area, along with associated cabling.

The scientific instruments used for atmospheric research in the Area are sensitive to electromagnetic noise and interference, with potential local noise sources including VLF radio transmissions, powerlines, vehicle emission systems and also laboratory equipment. Noise sources generated outside of the Area that may also affect electromagnetic conditions at Arrival Heights include radio communications, entertainment broadcast systems, ship, aircraft, or satellite radio transmissions, or aircraft surveillance radars. A site visit report from 2006 suggested that levels of interference at that time were acceptably low, despite activities operating out of McMurdo Station and Scott Base. In order to provide some degree of protection from local radio transmissions and station noise, some of the VLF antennas at Arrival Heights are located within Second Crater.

Unauthorised access to the Area, both by vehicle and on foot, is thought to have resulted in damage to cabling and scientific instruments, although the extent of damage and impact upon scientific results is unknown. A camera was installed at the USAP building in early 2010 to monitor traffic entering the Area via the road leading to the laboratories.

Recent installations within and close to the Area include an FE-Boltzmann LiDAR in the New Zealand Arrival Heights Research Laboratory in 2010, the Super Dual Auroral RADAR Network (SuperDARN) Antenna Array (2009-10) and two satellite earth station receptors (Map 2). The SuperDARN Antenna Array transmits at low frequencies (8 – 20 MHz), with the main transmission direction to the southwest of the Area, and its location was selected in part to minimize interference with experiments at Arrival Heights. Two satellite earth station receptors (Joint Polar Satellite System (JPSS) and MG2) are located nearby. One of the receptors has the ability to transmit (frequency range 2025 – 2120 Hz) and measures have been taken to ensure that any irradiation of the Area is minimal.

Three wind turbines were constructed approximately 1.5 km east of the Area and close to Crater Hill during austral summer 2009-10 (Map 1). EMI emissions from the turbines should comply with accepted standards for electrical machinery and utilities. However, EMI originating from the new wind turbines has been detected in very low frequency datasets at Arrival Heights, with potential sources of EMI including turbine transformers, generators and power lines. Interference in the VLF range has been sufficient to render Arrival Heights unsuitable for scientific studies measuring radio pulses from lightning (e.g. the AARDVARK experiment), and for this reason a second antenna was established at Scott Base where disturbance in the VLF range is much lower.

Air quality monitoring has been regularly carried out at Arrival Heights since 1992 and recent studies suggest that air quality has been reduced, most likely due to emissions originating from McMurdo or Scott Base (Mazzera *et al.* 2001), for example from construction and vehicle operations. Investigations found that air quality samples contained higher concentrations of pollution derived species (EC, SO_2, Pb, Zn) and PM_{10} (particles with aerodynamic diameters less than 10 μm) aerosols than other coastal and Antarctic sites.

6(ii) Access to the Area

Access to the Area may be made over land by vehicle or on foot. The access road to the Area enters at the south-east and extends to the research laboratories. Several vehicle trails are present within the Area and run from the Satellite Earth Station in First Crater to the foot of Second Crater. Pedestrian access may be made from the access road.

Access by air and overflight of the Area are prohibited, except when specifically authorized by permit, in which case the appropriate authority supporting research programs within the Area must be notified prior to entry.

6(iii) Location of structures within and adjacent to the Area

Both New Zealand and United States maintain research and living facilities within the Area. New Zealand opened a new research laboratory at Arrival Heights on 20 January 2007, replacing an old building which has been removed from the Area. The United States maintains one laboratory within the Area. A range of antenna arrays and aerials designed to meet scientific needs are located throughout the Area (Map 2), and a new VLF antenna was installed at Arrival Heights in December 2008. A Satellite Earth Station (SES) is located several meters inside the boundary of the Area on First Crater (Map 2).

The SuperDARN Antenna Array is located approximately 270 m SW of the Area, while two satellite earth station receptors are installed approximately 150 m SW of the Area (Map 2).

6(iv) Location of other protected areas in the vicinity

The nearest protected areas to Arrival Heights are on Ross Island: Discovery Hut, Hut Point (ASPA No.158), is the closest at 1.3 km southwest; Cape Evans (ASPA No. 155) is 22 km north; Backdoor Bay (ASPA No. 157) is 32 km north; Cape Royds (ASPA No. 121) is 35 km NNW; High Altitude Geothermal sites of the Ross Sea region (ASPA No. 175) near the summit of Mt. Erebus is 40 km north; Lewis Bay (ASPA No. 156) the site of the 1979 DC-10 passenger aircraft crash is 50 km NE; New College Valley (ASPA No. 116) is 65 km north at Cape Bird; and Cape Crozier (ASPA No. 124) is 70 km to the NE. NW White Island (ASPA No. 137) is 35 km to the south across the Ross Ice Shelf. Antarctic Specially Managed Area No. 2 McMurdo Dry Valleys is located approximately 50 km to the west of the Area.

6(v) Special zones within the Area

None.

7. Terms and conditions for entry permits

7(i) General permit conditions

Entry into the Area is prohibited except in accordance with a permit issued by an appropriate national authority. Conditions for issuing a permit to enter the Area are that:

- it is issued only for scientific study of the atmosphere and magnetosphere, or for other scientific purposes that cannot be served elsewhere; or

- it is issued for operation, management and maintenance of science support facilities (including safe operations), on the condition that movement within the Area be restricted to that necessary to access those facilities; or

- it is issued for educational or public awareness activities that cannot be fulfilled elsewhere and which are associated with the scientific studies being conducted in the Area, on the condition that visitors are accompanied by permitted personnel responsible for the facilities visited; or

- it is issued for essential management purposes consistent with plan objectives such as inspection or review;

- the actions permitted will not jeopardize the scientific or educational values of the Area;

- any management activities are in support of the objectives of the Management Plan;

- the actions permitted are in accordance with the Management Plan;

- the Permit, or a copy, shall be carried within the Area;

- a visit report shall be supplied to the authority or authorities named in the Permit;

- permits shall be valid for a stated period.

7(ii) Access to, and movement within or over, the Area

Access to the Area is permitted by vehicle and on foot. Landing of aircraft and overflight within the Area is prohibited unless specifically authorized by permit. Prior written notification must be given to the appropriate authority or authorities supporting scientific research being conducted in the Area at the time of the proposed aircraft activity. The location and timing of the aircraft activity should be coordinated as appropriate in order to avoid or minimize disruption to scientific programs.

Vehicle and pedestrian traffic should be kept to the minimum necessary to fulfil the objectives of permitted activities and every reasonable effort should be made to minimize potential impacts on scientific research: e.g. personnel entering the Area by vehicle should coordinate travel so vehicle use is kept to a minimum.

Vehicles shall keep to the established vehicle tracks as shown on Map 2, unless specifically authorized by permit otherwise. Pedestrians should also keep to established tracks wherever possible. Care should be taken to avoid cables and other instruments when moving around the Area, as they are susceptible to damage from both foot and vehicle traffic. During hours of darkness, vehicle headlights should be switched off when approaching the facilities, in order to prevent damage to light-sensitive instruments within the Area.

7(iii) Activities which may be conducted in the Area

- scientific research that will not jeopardize the scientific values of the Area or interfere with current research activities;

- essential management activities, including the installation of new facilities to support scientific research;

- Activities with educational aims (such as documentary reporting (photographic, audio or written) or the production of educational resources or services) that cannot be served elsewhere;

- use of hand-held and vehicle radios by visitors entering the Area is allowed; however, their use should be minimized and shall be restricted to communications for scientific, management or safety purposes;

- surveys of electromagnetic noise to help ensure that scientific research is not significantly compromised.

7(iv) Installation, modification or removal of structures

- No structures are to be erected within the Area except as specified in a permit.

- All structures, scientific equipment or markers installed within the Area, outside of research hut facilities, must be authorized by permit and clearly identified by country, name of the principal investigator and year of installation. Removal of such structures, equipment or markers upon expiration of the permit shall be the responsibility of the authority which granted the original permit, and shall be a condition of the permit.

- Installation (including site selection), maintenance, modification or removal of structures shall be undertaken in a manner that minimizes environmental disturbance and installations should not jeopardize the values of the Area, particularly the electromagnetically 'quiet' conditions and the current viewing horizon. Installations should be made of materials that pose minimal risk of environmental contamination of the Area. The time period for removal of equipment shall be specified in the permit.

- No new Radio Frequency (RF) transmitting equipment other than low power transceivers for essential local communications may be installed within the Area. Electromagnetic radiation produced by equipment introduced to the Area shall not have significant adverse effects on any on-going investigations unless specifically authorized. Precautions shall be taken to ensure that electrical equipment used within the Area is adequately shielded to keep electromagnetic noise to a minimum.

- Installation or modification of structures or equipment within the Area is subject to an assessment of the likely impacts of the proposed installations or modifications on the values of the Area, as required according to national procedures. Details of proposals and the accompanying assessment of impacts shall, in addition to any other procedures that may be required by appropriate authorities, be submitted by investigators to the activity coordinator for their national program, who will exchange documents received with other activity coordinators for the Area. Activity coordinators will assess the proposals in consultation with national program managers and relevant investigators for the potential impacts on the scientific or natural environmental values of the Area. Activity coordinators shall confer with each other and make recommendations (to proceed as proposed, to proceed with revisions, to trial for further assessment, or not to proceed) to their national program within 60 days of receiving a proposal. National programs shall be responsible for notifying investigators whether or not they may proceed with their proposals and under what conditions.

- The planning, installation or modification of nearby structures or equipment outside the Area that emit EMR, obstruct the viewing horizon or emit gases to the atmosphere should take into account their potential to affect the values of the Area.

- Removal of structures, equipment or markers for which the permit has expired shall be the responsibility of the authority which granted the original permit, and shall be a condition of the permit.

7(v) Location of field camps

Camping within the Area is prohibited. Overnight visits are permitted in buildings equipped for such purposes.

7(vi) Restrictions on materials and organisms which may be brought into the Area

- anthropogenic gaseous or aerosol emissions to the atmosphere from sources such as internal combustion engines within the Area shall be minimised or where practicable avoided. Long-term or permanent anthropogenic gaseous or aerosol emissions within the Area would jeopardize scientific experiments and are prohibited.

7(vii) Taking of, or harmful interference with, native flora or fauna

Taking or harmful interference with native flora and fauna is prohibited, except in accordance with a separate permit issued by the appropriate national authority specifically for that purpose under Article 3 of Annex II to the Protocol.

7(viii) Collection or removal of materials not brought into the Area by the permit holder

- Material may be collected or removed from the Area only in accordance with a permit and should be limited to the minimum necessary to meet scientific or management needs.
- Material of human origin likely to compromise the values of the Area, which was not brought into the Area by the permit holder or otherwise authorized, may be removed from any part of the Area unless the impact of removal is likely to be greater than leaving the material *in situ*. If this is the case the appropriate authority should be notified.
- The appropriate national authority should be notified of any items removed from the Area that were not introduced by the permit holder.

7(ix) Disposal of waste

All wastes, including human wastes, shall be removed from the Area.

7(x) Measures that may be necessary to continue to meet the aims of the Management Plan

1) Permits may be granted to enter the Area to carry out scientific monitoring and site inspection activities, which may involve the collection of data for analysis or review, or for protective measures.

2) Any specific sites of long-term monitoring shall be appropriately marked.

3) Electromagnetic bands of particular scientific interest and that warrant special protection from interference should be identified by parties active within the Area. As far as practically possible, the generation of electromagnetic noise should be limited to frequencies outside of these bands.

4) The intentional generation of electromagnetic noise within the Area is prohibited, apart from within agreed frequency bands and power levels or in accordance with a permit.

7(xi) Requirements for reports

- Parties should ensure that the principal holder for each permit issued submits to the appropriate authority a report describing the activities undertaken. Such reports should include, as appropriate, the information identified in the visit report form contained in the Guide to the Preparation of Management Plans for Antarctic Specially Protected Areas.

- Parties should maintain a record of such activities and, in the annual Exchange of Information, should provide summary descriptions of activities conducted by persons subject to their jurisdiction, which should be in sufficient detail to allow evaluation of the effectiveness of the Management Plan. Parties should, wherever possible, deposit originals or copies of such original reports in a publicly accessible archive to maintain a record of usage, to be used both for review of the management plan and in organizing the scientific use of the Area.

- The appropriate authority should be notified of any activities / measures undertaken, and / or of any materials released and not removed, that were not included in the authorized permit. All spills shall be reported to the appropriate authority.

8. Supporting documentation

Anyamba, E., Williams, E., Susskind, J., Fraser-Smith, A. & Fullerkrug, M. 2000. The Manifestation of the Madden-Julian Oscillation in Global Deep Convection and in the Schumann Resonance Intensity. *American Meteorology Society* **57**(8): 1029–44.

Behrendt, J. C., Saltus, R., Damaske, D., McCafferty, A., Finn, C., Blankenship, D.D. & Bell, R.E. 1996. Patterns of Late Cenozoic volcanic tectonic activity in the West Antarctic rift system revealed by aeromagnetic surveys. *Tectonics* **15**: 660–76.

Clilverd, M.A., Rodger, C.J., Thomson, N.R., Brundell, J.B., Ulich, Th., Lichtenberger, J., Cobbett, N., Collier, A.B., Menk, F.W., Seppl, A., Verronen, P.T., & Turunen, E. 2009. Remote sensing space weather events: the AARDDVARK network. *Space Weather* **7** (S04001). DOI: 10.1029/2008SW000412.

Connor, B.J., Bodeker, G., Johnston, P.V., Kreher, K., Liley, J.B., Matthews, W.A., McKenzie, R.L., Struthers, H. & Wood, S.W. 2005. Overview of long-term stratospheric measurements at Lauder, New Zealand, and Arrival Heights, Antartica. *American Geophysical Union, Spring Meeting 2005.*

Deutscher, N.M., Jones, N.B., Griffith, D.W.T., Wood, S.W. and Murcray, F.J. 2006. Atmospheric carbonyl sulfide (OCS) variation from 1992-2004 by ground-based solar FTIR spectrometry. *Atmospheric Chemistry and Physics Discussions* **6**: 1619–36.

Fraser-Smith, A.C., McGill, P.R., Bernardi, A., Helliwell, R.A. & Ladd, M.E. 1991. Global Measurements of Low-Frequency Radio Noise *in* Environmental and Space Electromagnetics (Ed. H. Kikuchi). Springer-Verlad, Tokyo.

Fraser-Smith, A.C. & Turtle, J.P.1993. ELF/VLF Radio Noise Measurements at High Latitudes during Solar Particle Events. Paper presented at the 51st AGARD-EPP Specialists meeting on *ELF/VLF/LF Radio Propagation and Systems Aspects.* Brussels, Belgium; 28 Sep – 2 Oct, 1992.

M. Füllekrug, M. 2004. Probing the speed of light with radio waves at extremely low frequencies. *Physical Review Letters* **93**(4), 043901: 1-3.

Füllekrug, M. 2010. Wideband digital low-frequency radio receiver. *Measurement Science and Technology,* **21**, 015901: 1-9. doi:10.1088/0957-0233/21/1/015901.

Füllekrug , M. & Fraser-Smith, A.C.1996. Further evidence for a global correlation of the Earth-ionosphere cavity resonances. *General Assembly of the International Union of Geodesy and Geophysics No. 21, Boulder, Colorado, USA.*

Füllekrug, M. & Fraser-Smith, A.C. 1997. Global lightning and climate variability inferred from ELF magnetic field variations. *Geophysical Research Letters* **24**(19): 2411.

Füllekrug, M., Fraser-Smith, A.C., Bering, E.A. & Few, A.A. 1999. On the hourly contribution of global cloud-to-ground lightning activity to the atmospheric electric field in the Antarctic during December 1992. *Journal of Atmospheric and Solar-Terrestrial Physics* **61**: 745-50.

Füllekrug, M., Fraser-Smith, A.C. & Schlegel, K. 2002. Global ionospheric D-layer height monitoring. *Europhysics Letters* **59**(4): 626.

Hay, T., Kreher, K., Riedel, K., Johnston, P., Thomas, A. & McDonald, A. 2007. Investigation of Bromine Explosion Events in McMurdo Sound, Antarctica. *Geophysical Research Abstracts.* Vol. 7.

Hernandez, G. & Roble, R.G. 2003. Simultaneous thermospheric observations during the geomagnetic storm of April 2002 from South Pole and Arrival Heights, Antarctica. *Geophysical Research Letters* **30** (10): 1511.

Keys, J.G., Wood, S.W., Jones, N.B. & Murcray, F.J. 1998. Spectral Measurements of HCl in the Plume of the Antarctic Volcano Mount Erebus. *Geophysical Research Letters* **25** (13): 2421–24.

Klein, A.G., Kennicutt, M.C., Wolff, G.A., Sweet, S.T., Gielstra, D.A. & Bloxom, T. 2004. Disruption of Sand-Wedge Polygons at McMurdo Station Antarctica: An Indication of Physical Disturbance. *61st Eastern Snow Conference*, Portland, Maine, USA.

Kohlhepp, R., Ruhnke, R., Chipperfield, M.P., De Mazière, M., Notholt, J., & 46 others 2012. Observed and simulated time evolution of HCl, ClONO2, and HF total column abundances, *Atmospheric Chemistry & Physics* **12**: 3527-56.

Kremser, S., Jones, N.B., Palm, M., Lejeune, B., Wang, Y., Smale, D. & Deutscher, N.M. 2015. Positive trends in Southern Hemisphere carbonyl sulfide, *Geophysical Research Letters* **42**: 9473–80.

Kyle, P. 1981. Mineralogy and Geochemistry of a Basanite to Phonolite Sequence at Hut Point Peninsula, Antarctica, based on Core from Dry Valley Drilling Project Drillholes 1,2 and 3. *Journal of Petrology*. **22** (4): 451 – 500.

Kuttippurath, J., Goutail, F., Pommereau, J.-P., Lefèvre, F., Roscoe, H.K., Pazmiño A., Feng, W., Chipperfield, M.P., & Godin-Beekmann, S. 2010. Estimation of Antarctic ozone loss from ground-based total column measurements. *Atmospheric Chemistry and Physics* **10**: 6569–81.

Levin, C., Veidt, C., Vaughn, B.H., Brailsford, G., Bromley, T., Heinz, R., Lowe, D., Miller, J.B., Poß, C.& White, J.W.C. 2012 No inter-hemispheric δ13CH4 trend observed. *Nature* **486**: E3–E4.

Mazzera, D. M., Lowenthal, D. H., Chow, J, C. & Watson, J. G. 2001. Sources of PM_{10} and sulfate aerosol at McMurdo station, Antarctica. *Chemosphere* **45**: 347–56.

McDonald, A.J., Baumgaertner, A.J.G., Fraser, G.J., George, S.E. & Marsh, S. 2007. Empirical Mode Decomposition of the atmospheric wave field. *Annals of Geophysics* **25**: 375–84.

Monaghan, A.J. & Bromwich, D.H. 2005. The Climate of the McMurdo, Antarctica, Region as Represented by One Year Forecasts from the Antarctic Mesoscale Prediction System. *Journal of Climate*. 18, pp. 1174–89.

Nichol, S.E., Coulmann, S. & Clarkson, T.S. 1991. Relationship of springtime ozone depletion at Arrival Heights, Antarctica, to the 70 HPA temperatures. *Geophysical Research Letters* **18** (10): 1865–68.

Oltmans, S.J., Johnson, B.J. & Helmig, D. 2008. Episodes of high surface-ozone amounts at South Pole during summer and their impact on the long-term surface-ozone variation. *Atmospheric Environment* **42**: 2804–16.

Riedel, K., Kreher, K., Nichol, S. & Oltmans, S.J. 2006. Air mass origin during tropospheric ozone depletion events at Arrival Heights, Antarctica. *Geophysical Research Abstracts* **8**.

Risi, C., Noone, D., Worden, J., Frankenberg, C., Stiller, G., & 25 others 2012. Process-evaluation of tropospheric humidity simulated by general circulation models using water vapor isotopologues: 1. Comparison between models and observations. *Journal of Geophysical Research* **117**: D05303 .

Rodger, C. J., Brundell, J.B., Holzworth, R.H. & Lay, E.H. 2009. Growing detection efficiency of the World Wide Lightning Location Network. American Institute of Physics Conference Proceedings **1118**: 15-20. DOI:10.1063/1.3137706.

Schlegel, K. & Fullekrug, M. 1999. Schumann resonance parameter changes during high-energy particle precipitation. *Journal of Geophysical Research* **104** (A5): 10111-18.

Schofield, R., Johnston, P.V., Thomas, A., Kreher, K., Connor, B.J., Wood, S., Shooter, D., Chipperfield, M.P., Richter, A., von Glasow, R. & Rodgers, C.D. 2006. Tropospheric and stratospheric BrO columns over Arrival Heights, Antarctica, 2002. *Journal of Geophysical Research* **111**: 1–14.

Sinclair, M.R. 1988. Local topographic influence on low-level wind at Scott Base, Antarctica. *New Zealand Journal of Geology and Geophysics*. **31**: 237–45.

Skotnicki, M.L., Ninham, J.A. & Selkirk P.M. 1999. Genetic diversity and dispersal of the moss *Sarconeurum glaciale* on Ross Island, East Antarctica. *Molecular Ecology* **8**: 753-62.

Stefano, J.E. 1992. Application of Ground-Penetrating Radar at McMurdo Station, Antarctica. Presented at the Hazardous Materials Control Research Institute federal environment restoration conference, Vienna, USA, 15-17 April 1992.

Struthers, H., Kreher, K., Austin, J., Schofield, R., Bodeker, G., Johnston, P., Shiona, H. & Thomas, A. 2004. Past and future simulations of NO2 from a coupled chemistry-climate model in comparison with observations. *Atmospheric Chemistry and Physics Discussions* **4**: 4545–79.

Tauxe, L., Gans, P.B. & Mankinen, E.A. 2004. Paleomagnetic and 40Ar/39Ar ages from Matuyama/Brunhes aged volcanics near McMurdo Sound, Antarctica. *Geochemical Geophysical Geosystems* **5** (10): 1029.

Vigouroux, C., De Mazière, M., Errera, Q., Chabrillat, S., Mahieu, E., Duchatelet, P., Wood, S., Smale, D., Mikuteit, S., Blumenstock, T., Hase, F., & Jones, N. 2007. Comparisons between ground-based FTIR and MIPAS N2O and HNO3 profiles before and after assimilation in BASCOE. *Atmospheric Chemistry & Physics* **7**: 377-96. .

Wood, S.W., Batchelor, R.L., Goldman, A., Rinsland, C.P., Connor, B.J., Murcray, F.J., Stephan, T.M. & Heuff, D.N. 2004. Ground-based nitric acid measurements at Arrival Heights, Antarctica, using solar and lunar Fourier transform infrared observations. *Journal of Geophysical Research* **109**: D18307.

Wright, I.M., Fraser, B.J., & Menk F.W. 1998. Observations of polar cap arc drift motion from Scott Base S-RAMP Proceedings of the AIP Congress, Perth, September 1998.

Zeng, G., Wood, S.W., Morgenstern, O., Jones, N.B., Robinson, J., & Smale, D. 2012. Trends and variations in CO, C2H6, and HCN in the Southern Hemisphere point to the declining anthropogenic emissions of CO and C2H6, *Atmospheric Chemistry & Physics* **12**: 7543-55.

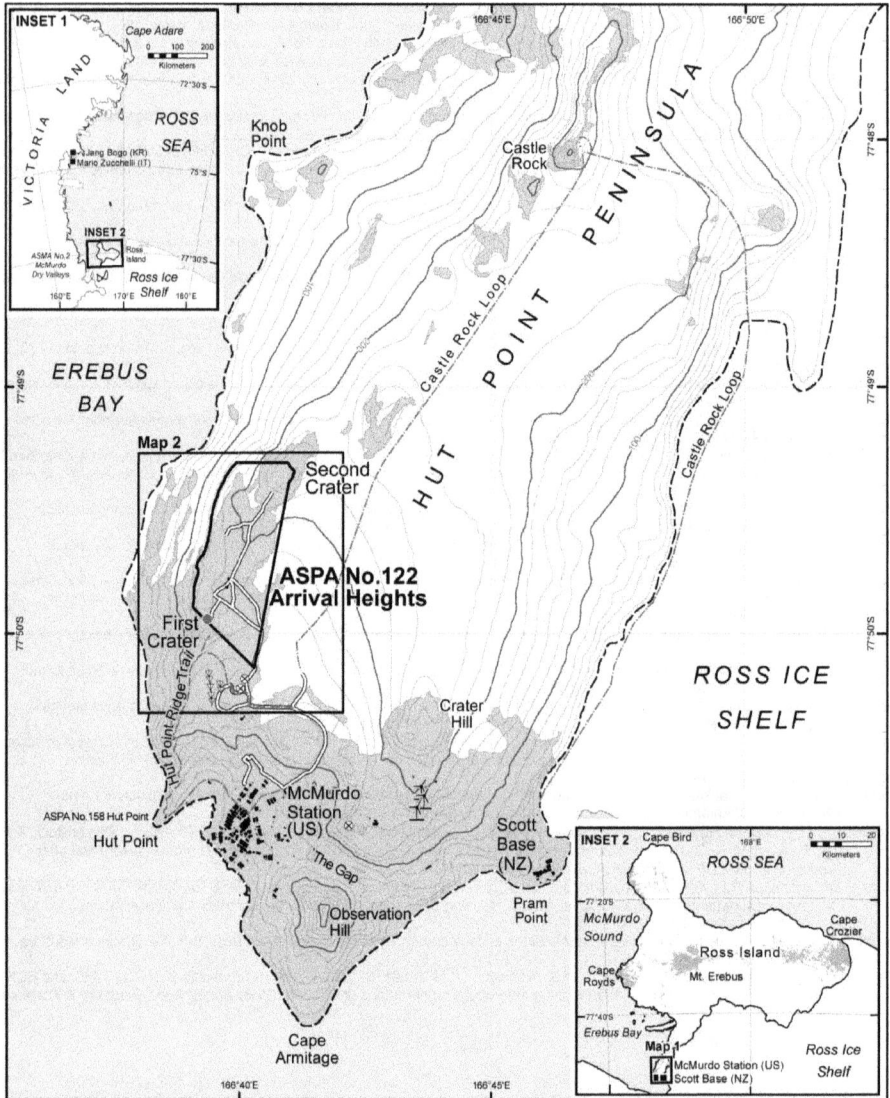

Map 1: ASPA No. 122 - Arrival Heights - Regional overview

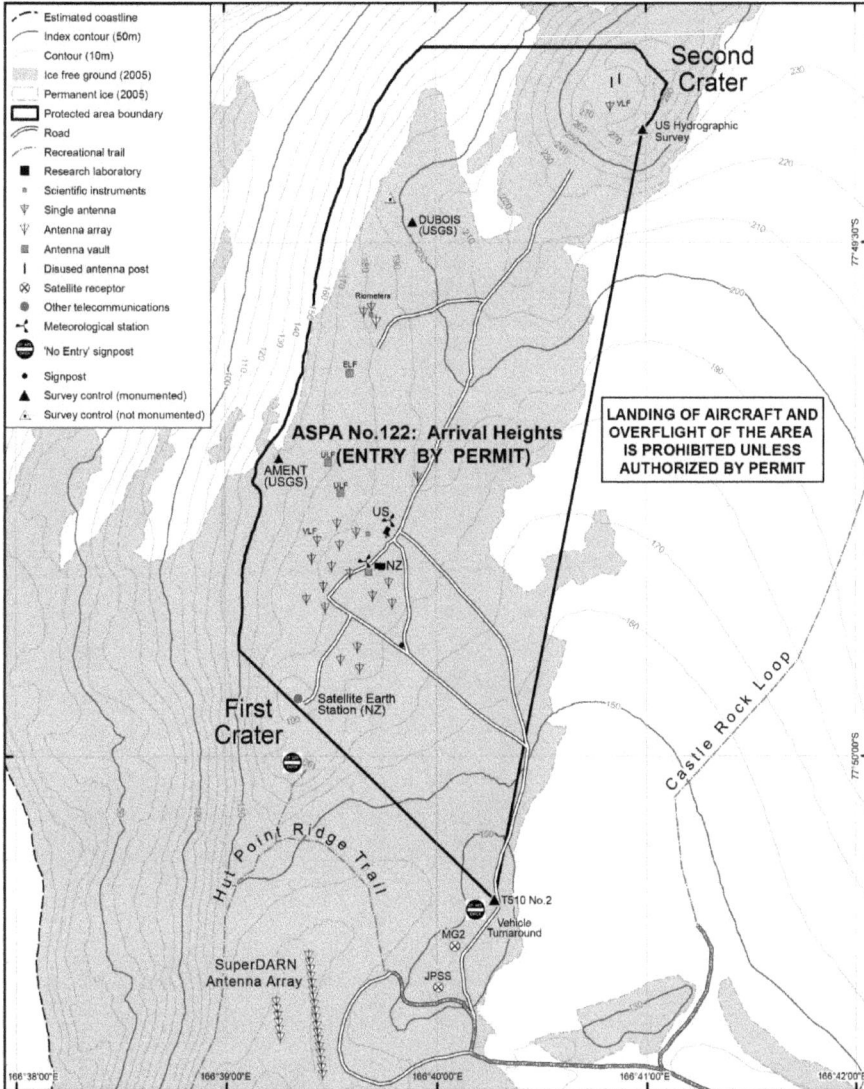

Legend:

- Estimated coastline
- Index contour (50m)
- Contour (10m)
- Ice free ground (2005)
- Permanent ice (2005)
- Protected area boundary
- Road
- Recreational trail
- ■ Research laboratory
- ⱱ Scientific instruments
- Ⱨ Single antenna
- Ⱨ Antenna array
- ▦ Antenna vault
- I Disused antenna post
- ⊗ Satellite receptor
- ● Other telecommunications
- ⤙ Meteorological station
- 'No Entry' signpost
- • Signpost
- ▲ Survey control (monumented)
- ⚬ Survey control (not monumented)

Second Crater

US Hydrographic Survey

DUBOIS (USGS)

Rometers

ELF

ASPA No.122: Arrival Heights
(ENTRY BY PERMIT)

AMENT (USGS)

VLF

US

NZ

LANDING OF AIRCRAFT AND
OVERFLIGHT OF THE AREA
IS PROHIBITED UNLESS
AUTHORIZED BY PERMIT

First Crater

Satellite Earth Station (NZ)

Castle Rock Loop

Hut Point Ridge Trail

TS10 No.2
Vehicle Turnaround
MG2
JPSS

SuperDARN Antenna Array

Map 2: ASPA No. 122 - Arrival Heights - Boundary & topography

11 Mar 2016 (Map ID: 10068.002.03)
United States Antarctic Program
Environmental Research & Assessment

Caution:
Overground cables are present throughout
Arrival Heights and are not shown on this map.
Care should be taken to avoid disturbing these cables.

N

0   100   200
Meters

Projection: Lambert Conic Conformal
Data sources: Contours: Derived from
2m DEM, contour interval 10m; Features: Derived from
USAP (Feb 2009) & ERA (Nov 2009) field surveys;
Recreational trails: PGC field survey 2009; Permanent ice
digitised from orthorectified Quickbird image (15 Oct 05)
(Imagery © Digital Globe; NGA Commercial Imagery Program);
ASPA boundary based on Management Plan (2016).

Management Plan for
Antarctic Specially Protected Area No. 126
BYERS PENINSULA, LIVINGSTON ISLAND,
SOUTH SHETLAND ISLANDS

Introduction

The primary reason for the designation of Byers Peninsula (latitude 62°34'35" S, longitude 61°13'07" W), Livingston Island, South Shetland Islands, as an Antarctic Specially Protected Area (ASPA) is to protect the terrestrial and lacustrine habitats within the Area.

Byers Peninsula was originally designated as Specially Protected Area (SPA) No. 10 through Recommendation IV-10 in 1966. This area included the ice-free ground west of the western margin of the permanent ice sheet on Livingston Island, below Rotch Dome, as well as Window Island about 500 m off the northwest coast and five small ice-free areas on the south coast immediately to the east of Byers Peninsula. Values protected under the original designation included the diversity of plant and animal life, many invertebrates, a substantial population of southern elephant seals (*Mirounga leonina*), small colonies of Antarctic fur seals (*Arctocephalus gazella*), and the outstanding scientific values associated with such a large variety of plants and animals within a relatively small area.

Designation as an SPA was terminated through Recommendation VIII-2 and redesignation as a Site of Special Scientific Interest (SSSI) was made through Recommendation VIII-4 (1975, SSSI No. 6). The new designation as an SSSI more specifically sought to protect four smaller ice-free sites on the peninsula of Jurassic and Cretaceous sedimentary and fossiliferous strata, considered of outstanding scientific value for study of the former link between Antarctica and other southern continents. Following a proposal by Chile and the United Kingdom, the SSSI was subsequently extended through Recommendation XVI-5 (1991) to include boundaries similar to those of the original SPA: i.e. the entire ice-free ground of Byers Peninsula west of the margin of the permanent Livingston Island ice sheet, including the littoral zone, but excluding Window Island and the five southern coastal sites originally included, as well as excluding all offshore islets and rocks. Recommendation XVI-5 noted that in addition to the special geological value, the Area was also of considerable biological and archaeological importance.

While the particular status of designation and boundaries have changed from time to time, Byers Peninsula has in effect been under special protection for most of the modern era of scientific activity in the region. Recent activities within the Area have been almost exclusively for scientific research (Benayas et al. (2013) provide a review of all science conducted in the area that was published between 1957 and 2012). Most visits and sampling within the Area, since original designation in 1966, have been subject to Permit conditions, and some areas (e.g. Ray Promontory) have been rarely visited. During the International Polar Year, Byers Peninsula was established as an 'International Antarctic Reference Site for Terrestrial, Freshwater and Coastal Ecosystems' (Quesada et al 2009, 2013). During this period baseline data relating to terrestrial, limnetic and coastal ecosystems was established, including permafrost characteristics, geomorphology, vegetation extent, limnetic diversity and functioning, marine mammal and bird diversity, microbiology, and coastal marine invertebrate diversity (López-Bueno et al., 2009; Moura et al., 2012; Barbosa et al., 2013; De Pablos et al., 2013; Emslie et al., 2013; Gil-Delgado et al., 2013; Kopalova and van de Vijvier, 2013; Lyons et al., 2013; Nakai et al., 2013; Pla-Rabes et al., 2013; Rico et al., 2013; Rochera et al., 2013a; Rochera et al., 2013b; Toro et al., 2013; Velazquez et al., 2013; Velazquez et al 2016; Vera et al., 2013; Villaescusa et al., 2013). The archaeological values of Byers Peninsula have been described as unique in possessing the greatest concentration of historical sites in Antarctica, namely the remains of refuges, together with contemporary artefacts and shipwrecks of early nineteenth century sealing expeditions (see Map 2).

Byers Peninsula makes a substantial contribution to the Antarctic protected areas system as it (a) contains a particularly wide diversity of species, (b) is distinct from other areas due to its numerous and diverse lakes, freshwater ponds and streams, (c) is of great ecological importance and represents the most significant limnological site in the region, (d) is vulnerable to human interference, in particular, due to the oligotrophic nature of the lakes which are highly sensitive to pollution and (e) is of great scientific interest across a range of disciplines. While some of these quality criteria are represented in other ASPAs in the region, Byers Peninsula is unique in possessing a high number of different criteria within one area. While Byers Peninsula is protected primarily for its outstanding environmental values (specifically its biological diversity and terrestrial and lake ecosystems) the Area contains a combination of other values including scientific (i.e. for terrestrial biology, limnology, ornithology, palaeolimnology, geomorphology and geology), historic (artefacts and refuge remains of early sealers), wilderness (e.g. Ray Promontory) and on-going scientific values that may benefit from the Area's protection.

The ice-free ground of Byers Peninsula is surrounded on three sides by ocean and the Rotch Dome glacier to the east. The Area has been designated to protect values found within the ice-free ground on Byers Peninsula. To fulfil this objective a portion of Rotch Dome has been included within the ASPA to ensure newly exposed ice-free ground, (resulting from any retreat of Rotch Dome), will be within the boundaries of the ASPA. In addition, the northwestern Rotch Dome including adjacent de-glaciated ground and Ray Promontory have been designated as restricted zones to allow microbiological studies that required higher quarantine standards than considered necessary within the rest of the Area. The Area (84.7 km^2) is considered to be of sufficient size to provide adequate protection of the values described below.

Resolution 3 (2008) recommended that the "Environmental Domains Analysis for the Antarctic Continent", be used as a dynamic model for the identification of Antarctic Specially Protected Areas within the systematic environmental-geographical framework referred to in Article 3(2) of Annex V of the Protocol. Using this model, Byers Peninsula is predominantly Environment Domain G (Antarctic Peninsula off-shore islands geologic). The scarcity of Environment G, relative to the other environmental domain areas, means that substantial efforts have been made to conserve the values found within this environment type elsewhere: other protected areas containing Domain G include ASPAs 109, 111, 112, 114, 125, 128, 140, 145, 149, 150, and 152 and ASMAs 1 and 4. The permanent ice of Rotch Dome comes under Environment Domain E. Other protected areas containing Domain E include ASPAs 113, 114, 117, 126, 128, 129, 133, 134, 139, 147, 149, 152 and ASMAs 1 and 4. Resolution 6 (2012) recommended that the Antarctic Conservation Biogeographic Regions (ACBRs) be used for the 'identification of areas that could be designated as Antarctic Specially Protected Areas within the systematic environmental-geographic framework referred to in Article 3(2) of Annex V to the Environmental Protocol. ASPA 126 sits within Antarctic Conservation Biogeographic Region (ACBR) 3 Northwest Antarctic Peninsula. In Resolution 5 (2015) the ATCM recognised the significance of the Important Bird Areas (IBAs) of Antarctica. The boundary of ASPA 126 also marks the extent of Important Bird Area ANT054 Byers Peninsula, Livingston Island. The IBA qualifies on the basis of the Antarctic tern (*Sterna vittata*) and kelp gull (*Larus dominicanus*) colonies although may other bird species, including southern giant petrels (*Macronectes giganteus*) are present.

1.   Description of values to be protected

The Management Plan attached to Measure 1 (2002) noted values considered important as reasons for special protection of the Area. The values recorded in the original Management Plans are reaffirmed. These values are set out as follows:

- With over 60 lakes, numerous freshwater pools and a great variety of often extensive streams, it is the most significant limnological site in the South Shetland Islands – and perhaps the Antarctica Peninsula region – and also one which has not been subjected to significant levels of human disturbance.

- The described terrestrial flora and fauna is of exceptional diversity, with one of the broadest representations of species known in the maritime Antarctic. For example, sparse but diverse flora of calcicolous and calcifuge plants and cyanobacteria are associated with the lavas and basalts, respectively, and several rare cryptogams and the two native vascular plants (*Deschampsia antarctica* and *Colobanthus quitensis*) occur at several sites. The abundance of vegetation is also exceptional with c. 8.1 km^2 of green vegetation contained within the Area, representing over half of the green vegetation protected with all terrestrial ASPAs.

- *Parochlus steinenii* (the only native winged insect in Antarctica) is of limited distribution in the South Shetland Islands. The only other native dipteral, the wingless midge *Belgica antarctica,* has a widespread but sporadic distribution on the Antarctic Peninsula. Both species are abundant at several of the lakes, streams and pools on Byers Peninsula.

- Unusually extensive cyanobacterial mats dominated by *Leptolyngbya* spp. and *Phormidium* spp. and other species, particularly on the upper levels of the central Byers Peninsula plateau, are the best examples so far described in the maritime Antarctic.

- The breeding avifauna within the Area is diverse, including two species of penguin [chinstrap (*Pygoscelis antarctica*) and gentoo (*P. papua*)], Antarctic tern (*Sterna vittata*), Wilson's storm petrels (*Oceanites oceanicus*), cape petrels (*Daption capense*), kelp gulls (*Larus dominicanus*), southern giant petrels (*Macronectes giganteus*), black-bellied storm petrels (*Fregetta tropica*), blue-eyed cormorants (*Phalacrocorax atriceps*), brown skuas (*Catharacta loennbergi*), and sheathbills (*Chionis alba*).

- The lakes and their sediments constitute one of the most important archives for study of the Holocene palaeoenvironment in the Antarctic Peninsula region, as well as for establishing a regional Holocene tephrachronology.

- Well-preserved sub-fossil whale bones are present in raised beaches, which are important for radiocarbon and other heavy isotope dating of beach deposits.

- The ice-free sites on the peninsula with exposed Jurassic and Cretaceous sedimentary and fossiliferous strata, are considered of outstanding scientific value for study of the former link between Antarctica and other southern continents.

- The area has remained largely unaffected by human disturbance, compared to other extensive ice-free areas in the local vicinity, and is thought to be free of non-native plants.

2.   Aims and objectives

Management at Byers Peninsula aims to:

- avoid degradation of, or substantial risk to, the values of the Area by preventing unnecessary human disturbance;

- allow scientific research on the terrestrial and lacustrine ecosystems, marine mammals, avifauna, coastal ecosystems and geology;

- allow other scientific research within the Area provided it is for compelling reasons which cannot be served elsewhere;

- allow archaeological research and measures for artefact protection, while protecting historic artefacts present within the Area from unnecessary destruction, disturbance, or removal;

- prevent or minimise the introduction to the Area of alien plants, animals and microbes;

- minimise the possibility of the introduction of pathogens which may cause disease in fauna within the Area; and

- allow visits for management purposes in support of the aims of the management plan.

3.   Management activities

The following management activities shall be undertaken to protect the values of the Area:

- A map showing the location of the Area and stating the special restrictions that apply, shall be displayed prominently at Base Juan Carlos I (Spain) and St. Kliment Ochridski Station (Bulgaria) on Hurd Peninsula, where copies of this management plan shall be made available.

- Markers, signs, fences or other structures erected within the Area for scientific or management purposes shall be secured and maintained in good condition.

- Visits shall be made as necessary to assess whether the Area continues to serve the purposes for which it was designated and to ensure management and maintenance measures are adequate.

Byers Peninsula has been described as extremely sensitive to trampling impact (Tejedo et al., 2009; Pertierra et al., 2013a). The Area was designated as an ASPA to protect a diverse range of values present within the Area. As a result, it attracts scientists (representing a diverse range of disciplines) and archaeologists from a number of Treaty nations. The high number of people present in the Area at peak times (mid-summer) means there is potential for the environmental values of the area to be negatively impacted upon by human activities, for example by potentially increasing (i) the size and number of camping location, (ii) the trampling of vegetation, (iii) the disturbance of native wildlife (iv) the generation of waste and (v) the need for fuel storage. **Consequently, when making plans for field work within the Area, Parties are strongly encouraged to liaise with other nations likely to be operating in the Area that season and co-ordinate activities to keep environmental impacts, including cumulative impacts, to an absolute minimum** (e.g. fewer than c. 12 people in the International Field Camp at any one time).

All Parties are strongly encouraged to use the established International Field Camp (located on South Beaches, 62°39'49.7" S, 61°05'59.8' W), to reduce the creation of new camping sites that would increase levels of human impacts within the Area. Two melon huts are found within the camp (one set up for scientific research, the other for domestic activities; both huts are managed by Spain). The melon huts are available to all Treaty Parties, should they wish to use them. Parties should liaise with Spain to co-ordinate access to the melon huts. Pertierra et al. (2013b) provides information concerning the challenges and environmental impacts resulting from the running of the camp.

4.   Period of designation
Designated for an indefinite period.

5.   Maps and photographs
Map 1:   Byers Peninsula ASPA No. 126 in relation to the South Shetland Islands, showing the location of Base Juan Carlos I (Spain) and St. Kliment Ochridski Station (Bulgaria), and showing the location of protected areas within 75 km of the Area. Inset: the location of Livingston Island along the Antarctica Peninsula.

Map 2:   Byers Peninsula ASPA No. 126 topographic map. Map specifications: Projection UTM Zone 20S; Spheroid: WGS 1984; Datum: Mean Sea Level. Horizontal accuracy of control: ±0.05 m. Vertical contour interval 50 m.

6.   Description of the Area
6(i) Geographical coordinates, boundary markers and natural features

BOUNDARIES

The Area encompasses:

- Byers Peninsula and all ice-free ground and ice sheet west of longitude 60°53'45'' W, including Clark Nunatak and Rowe Point;
- the near-shore marine environment extending 10 m offshore from the low tide water line; and
- Demon Island and Sprite Island, adjacent to the southern shoreline of Devils Point, but excluding all other offshore islets, including Rugged Island, and rocks (Map 2).

The linear eastern boundary follows longitude 60°53'45'' W to ensure newly exposed ice-free ground resulting from the retreat of Rotch Dome, which may contain scientifically useful opportunities and new habitats for colonization studies, will be within the boundaries of the ASPA.

No boundary markers are in place.

GENERAL DESCRIPTION

Byers Peninsula (between latitudes 62°34'35" and 62°40'35" S and longitudes 60°53'45''" and 61°13'07" W, 84.7 km^2) is situated at the west end of Livingston Island, the second-largest of the South Shetland Islands (Map 1). The ice-free area on the peninsula has a central west-east extent of about 9 km and a NW-SE extent of 18.2 km, and is the largest ice-free area in the South Shetland Islands. The peninsula is generally of low, gently rolling relief, although there are a number of prominent hills ranging in altitude between 80 – 265 m (Map 2). The interior is dominated by a series of extensive platforms at altitudes of up to 105 m, interrupted by isolated volcanic plugs such as Chester Cone (188 m) and Negro Hill (143 m) (Thomson and López-Martínez 1996). There is an abundance of rounded, flat landforms resulting from marine, glacial and periglacial erosional processes. The most rugged terrain occurs on Ray Promontory, a ridge forming the northwest-trending axis of the roughly 'Y'-shaped peninsula. Precipitous cliffs surround the coastline at the northern end of Ray Promontory with Start Hill (265 m) at the NW extremity being the highest point on the peninsula.

The coast of Byers Peninsula has a total length of 71 km (Map 2). Although of generally low relief, the coast is irregular and often rugged, with numerous headlands, cliffs, offshore islets, rocks and shoals. Byers Peninsula is also notable for its broad beaches, prominent features on all three coasts (Robbery Beaches in the north, President Beaches in the west, and South Beaches). The South Beaches are the most extensive; extending 12 km along the coast and up to almost 0.9 km in width, these are the largest in the South Shetland Islands (Thomson and López-Martínez 1996). For a detailed description of the geology and biology of the Area see Annex 1.

6(ii) Access to the Area

- Access shall be by helicopter or small boat.

- There are no special restrictions on boat landings from the sea, or that apply to the sea routes used to move to and from the Area. Due to the large extent of accessible beach around the Area, landing is possible at many locations. Nevertheless, if possible, landing of cargo and scientific equipment should be close to the International Field Camp located at Southern Beaches (62°39'49.7" S, 61°05'59.8' W; see 6(*iii*) for further details). Personnel operating vessels to deliver cargo and/or personnel to the ASPA must not leave the landing area unless in accordance with a permit issued by an appropriate national authority.

- A designated helicopter landing site is located at 62°39'36.4" S, 61°05'48.5' W, to the east of the International Field Camp.

- Under exceptional circumstances necessary for purposes consistent with the objectives of the Management Plan, helicopters may land elsewhere within the Area, although landings should, where practicable, be made on ridge and raised beach crests.

- No helicopter lands shall be made within the restricted zones [see section 6(*v*)].

- Helicopters should avoid sites where there are concentrations of birds (e.g. Devils Point, Lair Point and Robbery Beaches) or well-developed vegetation (e.g. large stands of mosses near President and South Beaches).

- To avoid disturbance of wildlife, aircraft should avoid landing within an over-flight restriction zone extending ¼ nautical mile (c. 460 m) inland from the coast during the period 1 October – 30 April inclusive (see Map 2). The only exception to this is the designated helicopter landing site at 62°39'36.4" S, 61°05'48.5'W.

- Within the over-flight restriction zone the operation of aircraft should be carried out, as a minimum requirement, in compliance with the 'Guidelines for the Operation of Aircraft near Concentrations of Birds' contained in Resolution 2 (2004). In particular, aircraft should maintain a vertical height of 2000 ft (~ 610 m) AGL and cross the coastline at right angles where possible. When conditions require aircraft to fly at lower elevations than recommended in the guidelines, aircraft should maintain the maximum elevation possible and minimise the time taken to transit the coastal zone.

- Use of helicopter smoke grenades is prohibited within the Area unless absolutely necessary for safety. If used all smoke grenades should be retrieved.

6(iii) Location of structures within and adjacent to the Area

An International Field Camp is located at South Beaches, at 62°39'49.7" S, 61°05'59.8' W. It is comprised of two fibreglass 'melon huts'. It is maintained by Spain and is available for use by all Parties. Parties aiming to use the melon huts should communicate their intentions to the Spanish Polar Committee well in advance. The locations of 19th Century sealers remains, including refuges and caves used for shelter are given in Smith and Simpson (1987) (see Map 2). Several cairns marking sites used for topographical survey are also present within the Area, predominantly on high points.

The nearest scientific research stations are 30 km east at Hurd Peninsula, Livingston Island [Base Juan Carlos I (Spain) and St Kliment Ochridski (Bulgaria)].

6(iv) Location of other protected areas within close proximity of the Area

The nearest protected areas to Byers Peninsula are: Cape Shirreff (ASPA No. 149) which lies about 20 km to the northeast, Deception Island (ASMA No. 4), Port Foster and other parts of Deception Island (ASPAs No. 140, 145) which are approximately 40 km SSE and 'Chile Bay' (Discovery Bay) (ASPA No. 144), which is about 70 km to the east at Greenwich Island (Map 1).

6(v) Restricted and managed zones within the Area

Some zones on Byers Peninsula are thought to have been visited only very rarely, or never. New metagenomic techniques are predicted to allow future identification of microbial biodiversity (bacteria, fungi and viruses) to an unprecedented level, allowing many fundamental questions regarding microbial dispersal and distribution to be answered. Restricted zones have been designated that are of scientific importance to Antarctic microbiology and greater restriction is placed on access with the aim of preventing microbial or other contamination by human activity:

- In keeping with this aim, within the restricted zones sterile protective over-clothing shall be worn. The protective clothing shall be put on immediately prior to entering the restricted zones. Spare boots, previously cleaned using a biocide then sealed in plastic bags, shall be unwrapped and put on just before entering the restricted zones. If accessing the restricted zones by boat, protective clothing shall be put on immediately upon landing.

- To the greatest extent possible, all sampling equipment, scientific apparatus and markers brought into the restricted zones shall have been sterilized, and maintained in a sterile condition, before being used within the Area. Sterilization should be by an accepted method, including UV radiation, autoclaving or by surface sterilisation using 70% ethanol or a commercially available biocide (e.g. Virkon®).

- General equipment includes harnesses, crampons, climbing equipment, ice axes, walking poles, ski equipment, temporary route markers, pulks, sledges, camera and video equipment, rucksacks, sledge boxes and all other personal equipment. To the maximum extent practicable, all equipment used or brought into the restricted zones shall have been thoroughly cleaned and sterilized at the originating Antarctic station or ship. Equipment shall have been maintained in this condition before entering the restricted zones, preferably by sealing in sterile plastic bags or other clean containers.

- Scientists from disciplines other than microbiology are permitted to enter the restricted areas, but shall adhere to the quarantine measures detailed above.

- Camping within the restricted zones is not permitted.

- Helicopter landings within the restricted zones are not permitted.

- If access to the restricted zones is required for research or for emergency reasons, a detailed record of where visitation occurred (preferably using GPS technology) and the specific activities, should be submitted to the appropriate national authority and included in the Exchange of Information Annual Report, preferably through the Electronic Information Exchange System (EIES).

The restricted zones are:
1. North-western Rotch Dome and adjacent deglaciated ground. The restricted zone includes all land and ice sheet within an area bordered to the east by longitude 60°53'45"W, to the west by longitude

60°58'48" W, to the south by latitude 62°38'30"S, and the northern boundary follows the coastline (see Map 2).

2. Ray Promontory. The restricted zone includes all land and permanent ice northwest of a straight line crossing the Promontory from 62°37'S, 61°08'W (marked by a small coastal lake) to 62°36'S, 61°06'W. Within the Ray Promontory restricted zone, access to archaeological remains located on the coast is permitted without the need for quarantine precautions required elsewhere within the restricted zone. Access to inland areas beyond the coastal archaeological remains is not permitted without quarantine measures, detailed in this section, in place. Preferably, access to the archaeological remains shall be from the sea using small boats. Access to the archaeological remains on foot is also permitted without the need for the additional quarantine measures, by following the coastline from the unrestricted area of the Byers Peninsula ASPA to the southeast. Access to the archaeological remains shall be solely for archaeological investigations, authorised by the appropriate national authority.

7.   Terms and conditions for entry permits

Entry into the Area is prohibited except in accordance with a Permit issued by an appropriate national authority.

7(i) General permit conditions

Conditions for issuing a Permit to enter the Area are that:

*   it is issued only for scientific study of the ecosystem, geology, palaeontology or archaeology of the Area, or for compelling scientific reasons that cannot be served elsewhere; or
*   it is issued for essential management purposes consistent with management plan objectives such as inspection, maintenance or review;
*   the actions permitted will not jeopardise the ecological, geological, historical or scientific values of the Area;
*   the sampling proposed will not take, remove or damage such quantities of soil, rock, native flora or fauna that their distribution or abundance on Byers Peninsula would be significantly affected;
*   cumulative impacts of geological sampling are taken into consideration in any EIA, as substantial collections have been made at some palaeontological sites with significant negative impacts upon the Area's scientific values.
*   any management activities are in support of the objectives of the management plan;
*   the actions permitted are in accordance with the management plan;
*   the Permit, or an authorised copy, shall be carried within the Area;
*   a visit report shall be supplied to the authority named in the Permit;
*   permits shall be issued for a stated period; and
*   the appropriate authority should be notified of any activities/measures undertaken that were not included in the authorised Permit.

7(ii) Access to and movement within or over the Area

*   Land vehicles are prohibited within the Area.
*   Movement within the Area shall be on foot unless under exceptional circumstances when helicopter may be used.
*   All movement shall be undertaken carefully so as to minimise disturbance to archaeological remains, animals, soils, geomorphological features and vegetated surfaces, walking on rocky terrain or ridges if practical to avoid damage to sensitive plants, patterned ground and waterlogged soils.
*   Pedestrian traffic should be kept to the minimum consistent with the objectives of any permitted activities and every reasonable effort should be made to minimise trampling effects. Where possible, existing tracks should be used to transit the area (Map 2). If no track exists, care should be taken to avoid creation

of new tracks. Research has shown that vegetation on Byers Peninsula can recover if fewer than 200 transits are made over it in a single season (Tejedo et al 2009). Pedestrian routes over vegetated ground should therefore be chosen depending on the forecasted number of transits (i.e. number of people × transits per day × number of days). When the number of transits on the same track is expected to be less than 200 in the same season, the track should be clearly identified and transits always made along the track. When the number is expected to be larger than 200 in a season, then the route should not be fixed along a single track, but transits should be done across a wide belt (i.e. multiple tracks, each with fewer than 200 transits), to diffuse the impact and allow quicker recovery of trampled vegetation.

- Conditions for use of helicopters within the Area are described in section 6(*ii*)
- Overflight of bird colonies within the Area by Unmanned Autonomous Vehicles (UAVs) at an altitude likely to result in harmful interference shall not be permitted unless in accordance with a permit issued by an appropriate national authority.
- Pilots, air and boat crew, or other people on aircraft or boats, are prohibited from moving on foot beyond the immediate vicinity of their landing site unless specifically authorised by Permit.
- Restrictions on access and movement within the restricted zones are described in section 6(*v*)

7(iii) Activities which may be conducted in the Area
- Compelling scientific research which cannot be undertaken elsewhere and that will not jeopardise the ecosystem or values of the Area or interfere with existing scientific studies.
- Archaeological research.
- Essential management activities, including monitoring.

7(iv) Installation, modification or removal of structures

No new structures are to be erected within the Area, or scientific equipment installed, except for compelling scientific or management reasons and for a pre-established period, as specified in a permit. Installation (including site selection), maintenance, modification or removal of structures and equipment shall be undertaken in a manner that minimises disturbance to the values of the Area. All structures or scientific equipment installed in the Area shall be clearly identified by country, name of the principal investigator and year of installation. All such items should be free of organisms, propagules (e.g. seeds, eggs) and non-sterile soil, and be made of materials that can withstand the environmental conditions and pose minimal risk of contamination of the Area. Removal of specific structures or equipment for which the Permit has expired shall be a condition of the Permit. Permanent structures or installations are prohibited.

7(v) Location of field camps

In order to minimise the area of ground within the ASPA impacted by camping activities, camps should be within the immediate vicinity of the International Field Camp (62°39'49.7" S, 61°05'59.8" W). When necessary for purposes specified in the Permit, temporary camping beyond the International Field Camp is allowed within the Area. Camps should be located on non-vegetated sites, such as on the drier parts of the raised beaches, or on thick (>0.5 m) snow-cover when practicable, and should avoid concentrations of breeding birds or mammals. Camping within 50 m of any sealers' refuge or shelter is prohibited. Previously used campsites should be re-used where practical, unless the guidance above suggests that they were inappropriately located. Camping within the restricted zones is not permitted. Due to the high winds often experienced in the area, great care should be taken to ensure all camping and scientific equipment is adequately secured.

7(vi) Restrictions on materials and organisms which can be brought into the Area

The deliberate introduction of animals, plant material, microorganisms and non-sterile soil into the Area shall not be permitted. Precautions shall be taken to prevent the accidental introduction of animals, plant material, micro-organisms and non-sterile soil from other biologically distinct regions (within or beyond the Antarctic

Treaty area). Visitors should also consult and follow, as appropriate, recommendations contained in the *CEP non-native species manual* (CEP, 2011), and in the *Environmental code of conduct for terrestrial scientific field research in Antarctica* (SCAR, 2009). In view of the presence of breeding bird colonies on Byers Peninsula, no poultry products, including wastes from such products and products containing uncooked dried eggs, shall be released into the Area or into the adjacent sea.

No herbicides or pesticides shall be brought into the Area. Any other chemicals, including radio-nuclides or stable isotopes, which may be introduced for scientific or management purposes specified in the Permit, shall be removed from the Area at or before the conclusion of the activity for which the Permit was granted. Release of radio-nuclides or stable isotopes directly into the environment in a way that renders them unrecoverable should be avoided. Fuel or other chemicals shall not be stored in the Area unless specifically authorised by Permit condition. They shall be stored and handled in a way that minimises the risk of their accidental introduction into the environment. Materials introduced into the Area shall be for a stated period only and shall be removed by the end of that stated period. If release occurs which is likely to compromise the values of the Area, removal is encouraged only where the impact of removal is not likely to be greater than that of leaving the material *in situ*. The appropriate authority should be notified of anything released and not removed that was not included in the authorised Permit.

7(vii) Taking of, or harmful interference with, native flora or fauna

Taking of or harmful interference with native flora or fauna is prohibited, except by Permit issued in accordance with Annex II to the Protocol on Environmental Protection to the Antarctic Treaty. Where taking of or harmful interference with animals is involved, the *SCAR Code of Conduct for the Use of Animals for Scientific Purposes in Antarctica* should be used as a minimum standard.

7(viii) The collection or removal of materials not brought into the Area by the Permit holder

Collection or removal of anything not brought into the Area by the permit holder shall only be in accordance with a Permit and should be limited to the minimum necessary to meet scientific, archaeological or management needs.

Unless specifically authorized by permit, visitors to the Area are prohibited from interfering with or from handling, taking or damaging any historic anthropogenic material meeting the criteria in Resolution 5 (2001). Similarly, relocation or removal of artefacts for the purposes of preservation, protection or to re-establish historical accuracy is allowable only by permit. The appropriate national authority shall be informed of the location and nature of any newly identified anthropogenic materials.

Other material of human origin likely to compromise the values of the Area which was not brought into the Area by the permit holder or otherwise authorised, may be removed from the Area unless the environmental impact of the removal is likely to be greater than leaving the material in situ; if this is the case the appropriate Authority must be notified and approval obtained.

7(ix) Disposal of waste

As a minimum standard all waste shall be disposed of in accordance with Annex III to the Protocol on Environmental Protection to the Antarctic Treaty. In addition, all wastes, including all solid human waste, shall be removed from the Area. Liquid human wastes may be disposed of into the sea. Solid human waste should not be disposed of to the sea as the near-shore reefs will prevent dispersal, but shall be removed from the Area. No human waste shall be disposed of inland as the oligotrophic characteristics of the lakes and other water-bodies on the plateau can be compromised by even a small quantity of human waste, including urine.

7(x) Measures that are necessary to ensure that the aims and objectives of the management plan can continue to be met

Permits may be granted to enter the Area to:

- carry out monitoring and site inspection activities, which may involve the collection of data and/or a small number of samples for analysis or review;
- erect or maintain signposts, structures or scientific equipment; or
- carry out protective measures.

Any specific sites of long-term monitoring shall be appropriately marked on site and on maps of the Area. A GPS position should be obtained for lodgement with the Antarctic Data Directory System through the appropriate national authority.

To help maintain the ecological and scientific values of the Area, visitors shall take special precautions against introductions. Of particular concern are microbial, animal or vegetation introductions sourced from soils from other Antarctic sites, including stations, or from regions outside Antarctica. To the maximum extent practicable, visitors shall ensure that footwear, clothing and any equipment – particularly camping and sampling equipment – is thoroughly cleaned before entering the Area. Poultry products and other introduced avian products, which may be a vector of avian diseases, shall not be released into the Area. Visitors accessing the ASPA by helicopter should ensure it is free of seeds, soil and propagules before entering the area. The transfer of species between lakes from outside and within the ASPA presents a substantial threat to these chemically and biologically unique waterbodies. Therefore, every precaution shall be taken to prevent cross-contamination of lakes including the cleaning of sampling equipment between use in different waterbodies.

7(xi) Requirements for reports

The principal permit holder for each visit to the Area shall submit a report to the appropriate national authority as soon as practicable, and no later than six months after the visit has been completed. Such visit reports should include, as applicable, the information identified in the recommended visit report form [contained as an Appendix in the Guide to the Preparation of Management Plans for Antarctic Specially Protected Areas available from the website of the Secretariat of the Antarctic Treaty (www.ats.aq)]. If appropriate, the national authority should also forward a copy of the visit report to the Party that proposed the Management Plan, to assist in managing the Area and reviewing the Management Plan. Wherever possible, Parties should deposit the original or copies of the original visit reports, in a publicly accessible archive to maintain a record of usage, for the purpose of any review of the Management Plan and in organising the scientific use of the Area.

8. Supporting documentation

For a recent list of publication resulting from scientific investigations on Byers Peninsula, see Benayas et al. (2013).

Bañón, M., Justel M. A., Quesada, A. 2006. Análisis del microclima de la península Byers, isla Livingston, Antártida, en el marco del proyecto LIMNOPOLAR. In: *Aplicaciones meteorológicas*. Asociación Meteorológica Española.

Bañón, M., Justel, M. A., Velazquez, D., Quesada, A. 2013. Regional weather survey on Byers Peninsula, Livingston Island, South Shetland Islands, Antarctica. *Antarctic Science* **25**: 146-156.

Barbosa, A., de Mas, E., Benzal, J., Diaz, J. I., Motas, M., Jerez, S., Pertierra, L., Benayas, J., Justel, A., Lauzurica, P., Garcia-Peña, F. J., and Serrano, T. 2013. Pollution and physiological variability in gentoo penguins at two rookeries with different levels of human visitation. *Antarctic Science* **25**: 329-338.

Benayas, J., Pertierra, L., Tejedo, P., Lara, F., Bermudez, O., Hughes, K.A., and Quesada, A. 2013. A review of scientific research trends within ASPA 126 Byers Peninsula, South Shetland Islands, Antarctica. *Antarctic Science* **25**: 128-145.

Birnie, R.V., Gordon, J.E. 1980. Drainage systems associated with snow melt, South Shetland Islands, Antarctica. *Geografiska Annaler* **62A**: 57-62.

Björck, S., Hakansson, H, Zale, R., Karlén, W., Jönsson, B.L. 1991. A late Holocene lake sediment sequence from Livingston Island, South Shetland Islands, with palaeoclimatic implications. *Antarctic Science* **3**: 61-72.

Björck, S., Sandgren, P., Zale, R. 1991. Late Holocene tephrochronology of the Northern Antarctic Peninsula. *Quaternary Research* **36**: 322-28.

Björck, S., Hjort, C, Ingólfsson, O., Skog, G. 1991. Radiocarbon dates from the Antarctic Peninsula - problems and potential. In: Lowe, J.J. (ed.), *Radiocarbon dating: recent applications and future potential. Quaternary Proceedings* 1, Quaternary Research Association, Cambridge. pp 55-65.

Björck, S., Håkansson, H., Olsson, S., Barnekow, L., Janssens, J. 1993. Palaeoclimatic studies in South Shetland Islands, Antarctica, based on numerous stratigraphic variables in lake sediments. *Journal of Paleolimnology* **8**: 233-72.

Björck, S., Zale, R. 1996. Late Holocene tephrochronology and palaeoclimate, based on lake sediment studies. In: López-Martínez, J., Thomson, M. R. A., Thomson, J.W. (eds.) *Geomorphological map of Byers Peninsula, Livingston Island*. BAS GEOMAP Series Sheet 5-A, 43-48. British Antarctic Survey, Cambridge.

Björck, S., Hjort, C., Ingólfsson, O., Zale, R., Ising, J. 1996. Holocene deglaciation chronology from lake sediments. In: López-Martínez, J., Thomson, M. R. A., Thomson, J.W. (eds.) *Geomorphological map of Byers Peninsula, Livingston Island*. BAS GEOMAP Series Sheet 5-A, 49-51. British Antarctic Survey, Cambridge.

Block, W., Starý, J. 1996. Oribatid mites (Acari: Oribatida) of the maritime Antarctic and Antarctic Peninsula. *Journal of Natural History* **30**: 1059-67.

Bonner, W.N., Smith, R.I.L. (Eds) 1985. *Conservation areas in the Antarctic*. SCAR, Cambridge: 147-56.

Booth, R.G., Edwards, M., Usher, M.B. 1985. Mites of the genus Eupodes (Acari, Prostigmata) from maritime Antarctica: a biometrical and taxonomic study. *Journal of the Zoological Society of London (A)* **207**: 381-406.

Carlini, A.R., Coria, N.R., Santos, M.M., Negrete, J., Juares, M.A., Daneri, G.A. 2009. Responses of *Pygoscelis adeliae* and *P. papua* populations to environmental changes at Isla 25 de Mayo (King George Island). *Polar Biology* **32**: 1427-1433.

Committee for Environmental Protection. 2011. CEP non-native species manual. Antarctic Treaty Secretariat, Buenos Aires. (see: http://www.ats.aq/e/ep_faflo_nns.htm)

Convey, P., Greenslade, P. Richard, K.J., Block, W. 1996. The terrestrial arthropod fauna of the Byers Peninsula, Livingston Island, South Shetland Islands - Collembola. *Polar Biology* **16**: 257-59.

Covacevich, V.C. 1976. Fauna valanginiana de Peninsula Byers, Isla Livingston, Antartica. *Revista Geologica de Chile* **3**: 25-56.

Crame, J.A. 1984. Preliminary bivalve zonation of the Jurassic-Cretaceous boundary in Antarctica. In: Perrilliat, M. de C. (Ed.) *Memoria, III Congreso Latinamerico de Paleontologia, Mexico, 1984. Mexico City,* Universidad Nacional Autonoma de Mexico, Instituto de Geologia. pp 242-54.

Crame, J.A. 1985. New Late Jurassic Oxytomid bivalves from the Antarctic Peninsula region. *British Antarctic Survey Bulletin* **69**: 35-55.

Crame, J.A. 1995. Occurrence of the bivalve genus Manticula in the Early Cretaceous of Antarctica. *Palaeontology* **38** Pt. 2: 299-312.

Crame, J.A. 1995. A new Oxytomid bivalve from the Upper Jurassic–Lower Cretaceous of Antarctica. *Palaeontology* **39** Pt. 3: 615-28.

Crame, J.A. 1996. Early Cretaceous bivalves from the South Shetland Islands, Antarctica. *Mitt. Geol-Palaont. Inst. Univ. Hamburg* **77**: 125-127.

Crame, J.A., Kelly, S.R.A. 1995. Composition and distribution of the Inoceramid bivalve genus *Anopaea*. *Palaeontology* **38** Pt. 1: 87-103.

Crame, J.A., Pirrie, D., Crampton, J.S., Duane, A.M. 1993. Stratigraphy and regional significance of the Upper Jurassic - Lower Cretaceous Byers Group, Livingston Island, Antarctica. *Journal of the Geological Society* **150** Pt. 6: 1075-87.

Croxall, J.P., Kirkwood, E.D. 1979. *The distribution of penguins on the Antarctic Peninsula and the islands of the Scotia Sea.* British Antarctic Survey, Cambridge.

Davey, M.C. 1993. Carbon and nitrogen dynamics in a maritime Antarctic stream. *Freshwater Biology* **30**: 319-30.

Davey, M.C. 1993. Carbon and nitrogen dynamics in a small pond in the maritime Antarctic. *Hydrobiologia* **257**: 165-75.

De Pablo, M.A., Blanco, J.J., Molina, A., Ramos, M. Quesada, A., and Vieira G. 2013. Interannual active layer variability at the Limnopolar Lake CALM site on Byers Peninsula, Livingston Island, Antarctica. *Antarctic Science* 25: 167-180.

Duane, A.M. 1994. Preliminary palynological investigation of the Byers Group (Late Jurassic-Early Cretaceous), Livingston Island, Antarctic Peninsula. *Review of Palaeobotany and Palynology* **84**: 113-120.

Duane, A.M. 1996. Palynology of the Byers Group (Late Jurassic-Early Cretaceous) Livingston and Snow Islands, Antarctic Peninsula: its biostratigraphical and palaeoenvironmental significance. *Review of Palaeobotany and Palynology* **91**: 241-81.

Duane, A.M. 1997. Taxonomic investigations of Palynomorphs from the Byers Group (Upper Jurassic-Lower Cretaceous), Livingston and Snow Islands, Antarctic Peninsula. *Palynology* 21: 123-144.

Ellis-Evans, J.C. 1996. Biological and chemical features of lakes and streams. In: López-Martínez, J., Thomson, M. R. A., Thomson, J.W. (eds.) *Geomorphological map of Byers Peninsula, Livingston Island.* BAS GEOMAP Series Sheet 5-A, 20-22. British Antarctic Survey, Cambridge.

Emslie, S. D., Polito, M. J., and Patterson W. P. 2013. Stable isotope analysis of ancient and modern gentoo penguin egg membrane and the krill surplus hypothesis in Antarctica. *Antarctic Science* **25**: 213-218.

Fernández-Valiente, E., Camacho, A., Rochera, C., Rico, E., Vincent, W. F., Quesada, A. 2007 Community structure and physiological characterization of microbial mats in Byers Peninsula, Livingston Island (South Shetland islands, Antarctica). *FEMS Microbiology Ecology* **59**: 377- 385

Gil-Delgado, J.A., Villaescusa, J.A., Diazmacip, M.E., Velazquez, D., Rico, E., Toro, M., Quesada, A., Camacho, A. 2013. Minimum population size estimates demonstrate an increase in southern elephant seals (Mirounga leonina) on Livingston Island, maritime Antarctica *Polar Biology* **36**: 607-610

Gil-Delgado, J.A., González-Solis, J., Barbosa, A. 2010. Breeding birds populations in Byers Peninsula (Livingston Is., South Shetlands Islands. 18th International Conference of the European Bird Census Council. 22-26 March. Caceres. Spain).

González-Ferrán, O., Katsui, Y., Tavera, J. 1970. Contribución al conocimiento geológico de la Península Byers, Isla Livingston, Islas Shetland del Sur, Antártica. *Publ. INACH Serie. Científica* **1**: 41-54.

Gray, N.F., Smith, R.I. L. 1984. The distribution of nematophagous fungi in the maritime Antarctic. *Mycopathologia* **85**: 81-92.

Harris, C.M. 2001. *Revision of management plans for Antarctic protected areas originally proposed by the United States of America and the United Kingdom: Field visit report.* Internal report for the National Science Foundation, US, and the Foreign and Commonwealth Office, UK. Environmental Research and Assessment, Cambridge.

Hansom, J.D. 1979. Radiocarbon dating of a raised beach at 10 m in the South Shetland Islands. *British Antarctic Survey Bulletin* **49**: 287-288.

Hathway, B. 1997. Non-marine sedimentation in an Early Cretaceous extensional continental-margin arc, Byers Peninsula, Livingston Island, South Shetland Islands. *Journal of Sedimentary Research* **67**: 686-697.

Hathway, B., Lomas, S.A. 1998. The Upper Jurassic-Lower cretaceous Byers Group, South Shetland Islands, Antarctica: revised stratigraphy and regional correlations. *Cretaceous Research* **19**: 43-67.

Hernandez, P.J., Azcarate, V. 1971. Estudio paleobotanico preliminar sobre restos de una tafoflora de la Peninsula Byers (Cerro Negro), Isla Livingston, Islas Shetland del Sur, Antartica. *Publ. INACH Serie. Cientifica* **2**: 15-50.

Hjort, C., Ingólfsson, O., Björck, S. 1992. The last major deglaciation in the Antarctic Peninsula region - a review of recent Swedish Quaternary research. In: Y. Yoshida *et al.* (eds.) *Recent Progress in Antarctic Science.* Terra Scientific Publishing Company (TERRAPUB), Tokyo: 741-743.

Hjort, C., Björck, S., Ingólfsson, Ó., Möller, P. 1998. Holocene deglaciation and climate history of the northern Antarctic Peninsula region: a discussion of correlations between the Southern and Northern Hemispheres. *Annals of Glaciology* **27**: 110-112.

Hodgson, D.A., Dyson, C.L., Jones, V.J., Smellie, J.L. 1998. Tephra analysis of sediments from Midge Lake (South Shetland Islands) and Sombre Lake (South Orkney Islands), Antarctica. *Antarctic Science* **10**: 13-20.

Hughes, K. A., Ireland, L. C, Convey, P., Fleming, A. 2015. Assessing the effectiveness of specially protected areas for conservation of Antarctica's botanical diversity. *Conservation Biology* **30**: 113-120.

John, B.S., Sugden, D.E. 1971. Raised marine features and phases of glaciation in the South Shetland Islands. *British Antarctic Survey Bulletin* **24**: 45-111.

Jones, V.J., Juggins, S., Ellis-Evans, J.C. 1993. The relationship between water chemistry and surface sediment diatom assemblages in maritime Antarctic lakes. *Antarctic Science* **5**: 339-48.

Kelly, S.R.A. 1995. New Trigonioid bivalves from the Early Jurassic to Earliest Cretaceous of the Antarctic Peninsula region: systematics and austral paleobiogeography. *Journal of Paleontology* **69**: 66-84.

Kopalova, K., van de Vijver, B. 2013. Structure and ecology of freshwater benthic diatom communities from Byers Peninsula, Livingston Island, South Shetland Islands. *Antarctic Science* **25**: 239-253.

Lindsay, D.C. 1971. Vegetation of the South Shetland Islands. *British Antarctic Survey Bulletin* **25**: 59-83.

López-Bueno, A., Tamames, J. Velazquez, D., Moya, A., Quesada, A., Alcami, A. 2009. Viral Metagenome of an Antarctic lake: high diversity and seasonal variations. *Science* **326**: 858-861.

Lopez-Martinez, J., Serrano, E., Martinez de Pison, E. 1996. Geomorphological features of the drainage system. In: López-Martínez, J., Thomson, M. R. A., Thomson, J.W. (eds.) *Geomorphological map of Byers Peninsula, Livingston Island.* BAS GEOMAP Series Sheet 5-A, 15-19. British Antarctic Survey, Cambridge.

Lopez-Martinez, J., Martínez de Pisón, E., Serrano, E., Arche, A. 1996 *Geomorphological map of Byers Peninsula, Livingston Island.* BAS GEOMAP Series, Sheet 5-A, Scale 1:25 000. Cambridge, British Antarctic Survey.

Lyons, W. B., Welch, K. A., Welch, S. A., Camacho, A. Rochera, C., Michaud, L., deWit, R., Carey, A.E. 2013. Geochemistry of streams from Byers Peninsula, Livingston Island. *Antarctic Science* 25: 181-190.

Martínez De Pisón, E., Serrano, E., Arche, A., Lopez-Martínez, J. 1996. Glacial geomorphology. In: López-Martínez, J., Thomson, M. R. A., Thomson, J.W. (eds.) *Geomorphological map of Byers Peninsula, Livingston Island*. BAS GEOMAP Series Sheet 5-A, 23-27. British Antarctic Survey, Cambridge.

Morgan, F., Barker, G., Briggs, C., Price, R. and Keys, H. 2007. Environmental Domains of Antarctica Version 2.0 Final Report, Manaaki Whenua Landcare Research New Zealand Ltd. 89 pp.

Moura, P.A., Francelino, M.R., Schaefer, C.E.G.R., Simas, F.N.B., de Mendonca, B.A.F. 2012. Distribution and characterization of soils and landform relationships in Byers Peninsula, Livingston Island, Maritime Antarctica. *Geomorphology* **155**: 45-54.

Nakai, R., Shibuya, E., Justel, A., Rico, E., Quesada, A., Kobayashi, F., Iwasaka, Y., Shi, G.-Y., Amano, Y., Iwatsuki, T., Naganuma, T. 2013. Phylogeographic analysis of filterable bacteria with special reference to *Rhizobiales* strains that occur in cryospheric habitats. *Antarctic Science* **25**: 219-228.

Nielsen, U. N., Wall, D. H. W., Li, G., Toro, M., Adams, B. J., Virginia, R. A. 2011. Nematode communities of Byers Peninsula, Livingston Island, maritime Antarctica. *Antarctic Science* 23: 349-357.

Otero, X.L., Fernández, S., De Pablo-Hernández, M.A., Nizoli, E.C., Quesada, A. 2013. Plant communities as a key factor in biogeochemical processes involving micronutrients (Fe, Mn, Co, and Cu) in Antarctic soils (Byers Peninsula, maritime Antarctica). *Geoderma* 195-196: 145-154.

Pankhurst, R.J., Weaver, S.D., Brook, M., Saunders, A.D. 1979. K-Ar chronology of Byers Peninsula, Livingston Island, South Shetland Islands. *British Antarctic Survey Bulletin* **49**: 277-282.

Pertierra, L.R., Lara, F., Tejedo, P., Quesada, A., Benayas, J. 2013a. Rapid denudation processes in cryptogamic communities from Maritime Antarctica subjected to human trampling. *Antarctic Science* 25: 318-328.

Pertierra, L.R., Hughes, K.A., Benayas, J., Justel, A., and Quesada, A. 2013b. Environmental management of a scientific field camp in Maritime Antarctica: reconciling research impacts with conservation goals in remote ice-free areas. *Antarctic Science* 25: 307-317.

Pla-Rabes, S., Toro, M., Van De Vijver, B., Rochera, C., Villaescusa, J. A., Camacho, A., and Quesada, A. 2013. Stability and endemicity of benthic diatom assemblages from different substrates in a maritime stream on Byers Peninsula, Livingston Island, Antarctica: the role of climate variability. *Antarctic Science* 25: 254-269.

Petz, W., Valbonesi, A., Schiftner, U., Quesada, A., Ellis-Evans, C.J. 2007. Ciliate biogeography in Antarctic and Arctic freshwater ecosystems: endemism or global distribution of species? *FEMS Microbiology Ecology* **59**: 396-408.

Quesada, A., Fernández Valiente, E., Hawes, I., Howard.Williams, C. 2008. Benthic primary production in polar lakes and rivers. In: Vincent, W., Leybourn-Parry J. (eds). *Polar Lakes and Rivers – Arctic and Antarctic Aquatic Ecosystems*. Springer. pp 179-196.

Quesada, A., Camacho, A. Rochera, C., Velazquez, D. 2009. Byers Peninsula: a reference site for coastal, terrestrial and limnetic ecosystems studies in maritime Antarctica. *Polar Science* 3: 181-187.

Quesada, A., Camacho, A., Lyons, W.B. 2013. Multidisciplinary research on Byers Peninsula, Livingston Island: a future benchmark for change in Maritime Antarctica. *Antarctic Science* 25: 123-127.

Richard, K.J., Convey, P., Block, W. 1994. The terrestrial arthropod fauna of the Byers Peninsula, Livingston Island, South Shetland Islands. *Polar Biology* 14: 371-79.

Rico, E., Quesada, A. 2013. Distribution and ecology of chironomids (Diptera, Chironomidae) on Byers Peninsula, Maritime Antarctica. *Antarctic Science* 25: 288-291.

Rochera, C., Justel, A., Fernandez-Valiente, E., Bañón, M., Rico, E., Toro, M., Camacho, A., Quesada, A. 2010. Interannual meteorological variability and its effects on a lake from maritime Antarctica. *Polar Biology* **33**: 1615-1628.

Rochera, C., Villaescusa, J. A., Velázquez, D., Fernández-Valiente, E., Quesada, A., Camacho, A. 2013a. Vertical structure of bi-layered microbial mats from Byers Peninsula, Maritime Antarctica. *Antarctic Science* **25**: 270-276.

Rochera, C., Toro, M., Rico, E., Fernández-Valiente, E., Villaescusa, J. A., Picazo, A., Quesada, A., Camacho, A. 2013b. Structure of planktonic microbial communities along a trophic gradient in lakes of Byers Peninsula, South Shetland Islands. *Antarctic Science* **25**: 277-287.

Rodríguez, P., Rico, E. 2008. A new freshwater oligochaete species (Clitellata: Enchytraeidae) from Livingston Island, Antarctica. *Polar Biology* **31**: 1267-1279.

SCAR (Scientific Committee on Antarctic Research). 2009. Environmental code of conduct for terrestrial scientific field research in Antarctica. ATCM XXXII IP4.

SCAR (Scientific Committee on Antarctic Research). 2011. SCAR code of conduct for the use of animals for scientific purposes in Antarctica. ATCM XXXIV IP53.

SGE, WAM and BAS. 1993. *Byers Peninsula, Livingston Island.* Topographic map, Scale 1:25 000. Cartografia Antartica. Madrid, Servicio Geografia del Ejercito.

Serrano, E., Martínez De Pisón, E., Lopez-Martínez, J. 1996. Periglacial and nival landforms and deposits. In: López-Martínez, J., Thomson, M. R. A., Thomson, J.W. (eds.) *Geomorphological map of Byers Peninsula, Livingston Island.* BAS GEOMAP Series Sheet 5-A, 28-34. British Antarctic Survey, Cambridge.

Smellie J.L., Davies, R.E.S., Thomson, M.R.A. 1980. Geology of a Mesozoic intra-arc sequence on Byers Peninsula, Livingston Island, South Shetland Islands. *British Antarctic Survey Bulletin* **50**: 55-76.

Smith, R.I.L., Simpson, H.W. 1987. Early Nineteeth Century sealers' refuges on Livingston Island, South Shetland Islands. *British Antarctic Survey Bulletin* **74**: 49-72.

Starý, J., Block, W. 1998. Distribution and biogeography of oribatid mites (Acari: Oribatida) in Antarctica, the sub-Antarctic and nearby land areas. *Journal of Natural History* **32**: 861-94.

Sugden, D.E., John, B.S. 1973. The ages of glacier fluctuations in the South Shetland Islands, Antarctica. In: van Zinderen Bakker, E.M. (ed.) *Paleoecology of Africa and of the surrounding islands and Antarctica*. Balkema, Cape Town, pp. 141-159.

Tejedo, P., Justel, A., Benayas, J., Rico, E., Convey, P., Quesada, A. 2009. Soil trampling in an Antarctic Specially Protected Area: tools to assess levels of human impact. *Antarctic Science* **21**: 229-236.

Tejedo, P., Pertierra, L.R., Benayas, J., Convey, P., Justel, A., Quesada, A. 2012. Trampling on maritime Antarctica: can soil ecosystems be effectively protected through existing codes of conduct? *Polar Research* **31**: Art. No. UNSP 100888

Thom, G. 1978. Disruption of bedrock by the growth and collapse of ice lenses. *Journal of Glaciology* **20**: 571-75.

Thomson, M.R.A., López-Martínez, J. 1996. Introduction. In: López-Martínez, J., Thomson, M. R. A., Thomson, J.W. (eds.) *Geomorphological map of Byers Peninsula, Livingston Island.* BAS GEOMAP Series Sheet 5-A, 1-4. British Antarctic Survey, Cambridge.

Toro, M., Camacho, A., Rochera, C., Rico, E., Bañón, M., Fernández, E., Marco, E., Avendaño, C., Ariosa, Y., Quesada, A. 2007. Limnology of freshwater ecosystems of Byers Peninsula (Livingston Island, South Shetland Islands, Antarctica. *Polar Biology* **30**: 635-649.

Toro, M., Granados, I., Pla, S., Giralt, S., Antoniades, D., Galán, L., Cortizas, A. M., Lim, H. S., Appleby, P. G. 2013. Chronostratigraphy of the sedimentary record of Limnopolar Lake, Byers Peninsula, Livingston Island, Antarctica. *Antarctic Science* **25**: 198-212.

Torres, D., Cattan, P., Yanez, J. 1981. Post-breeding preferences of the Southern Elephant seal *Mirounga leonina* in Livingston Island (South Shetlands). *Publ. INACH Serie. Cientifica* **27**: 13-18.

Torres, D., Jorquera, D. 1994. Marine debris analysis collected at cape Shirreff, Livingston Island, South Shetland, Antarctica. *Ser. Cient. INACH* **44**: 81-86.

Usher, M.B., Edwards, M. 1986. The selection of conservation areas in Antarctica: an example using the arthropod fauna of Antarctic islands. *Environmental Conservation* **13**: 115-22.

Van der Vijver, J., Agius, T., Gibson, J., Quesada, A. 2009. An unusual spine-bearing Pinnularia species from the Antarctic Livingston Island. *Diatom Research* **24**: 431-441.

Velazquez, D., Lezcano, M.A., Frias, A., Quesada, A. 2013. Ecological relationships and stoichiometry within a Maritime Antarctic watershed. *Antarctic Science* **25**: 191-197.

Vera, M. L., Fernández-Teruel, T., Quesada, A. 2013. Distribution and reproductive capacity of *Deschampsia antarctica* and *Colobanthus quitensis* on Byers Peninsula, Livingston Island, South Shetland Islands, Antarctica. *Antarctic Science* **25**: 292-302.

Villaescusa, J.A., Jorgensen, S.E., Rochera, C., Velazquez, D., Quesada, A., Camacho, A. 2013. Carbon dynamics modelization and biological community sensitivity to temperature in an oligotrophic freshwater Antarctic lake. *Ecological Modelling* **319**: 21-30.

Villaescusa, J.A., Casamayor, E.O., Rochera, C., Velazquez, D., Chicote, A., Quesada, A., Camacho, A. 2010. A close link between bacterial community composition and environmental heterogeneity in maritime Antarctic lakes. *International Microbiology* **13**: 67-77.

Villaescusa, J. A., Casamayor, E. O., Rochera, C., Quesada, A., Michaud L., Camacho, A. 2013. Heterogeneous vertical structure of the bacterioplankton community in a non-stratified Antarctic lake. *Antarctic Science* **25**: 229-238.

White, M.G. Preliminary report on field studies in the South Shetland Islands 1965/66. Unpublished field report in BAS Archives AD6/2H1966/N6.

Woehler, E.J. (Ed.) 1993. *The distribution and abundance of Antarctic and sub-Antarctic penguins*. SCAR, Cambridge.

Zidarova, E., Van de Vijver, B., Quesada, A., de Haan, M. 2010. Revision of the genus *Hantzschia* (Bacillariophyceae) on Livingston Island (South Shetland Islands, Southern Atlantic Ocean). *Plant Ecology and Evolution* **143**: 318-333.

Annex 1

Supporting information

Byers Peninsula has supported scientific investigations for many years and many of the resulting publications up until 2013 are listed in Banayas et al. (2013); however, but numerous new articles have been published since then.

CLIMATE

No extended meteorological records are available for Byers Peninsula before 2001, but the climate is expected to be similar to that at Base Juan Carlos I, Hurd Peninsula (recorded since 1988). Conditions there indicate a mean annual temperature of below -2.8 °C, with temperatures less than 0 °C for at least several months each winter and a relatively high precipitation rate estimated at about 800 mm yr^{-1}, much of which falls as rain in summer (Ellis-Evans 1996; Bañón et al. 2013). The peninsula is snow-covered for much of the year, but is usually mostly snow-free by the end of the summer. The peninsula is exposed to weather from the Drake Passage in the north and northwest, the directions from which winds prevail, and Bransfield Strait to the south. The climate is polar maritime, with a permanently high relative humidity (about 90%), cloud covered skies for most of the time, frequent fogs and regular precipitation events. Mean temperature in summer is 1.1 ° C, but occasionally can be higher than 5 °C. Exceptionally summer temperature has reached 9 °C. Minimum average temperature in summer is close to 0 °C. In winter, temperatures can be lower than -26 °C, although the average value is -6 °C and maximum temperatures in winter can be close to 0 °C. Mean radiation in summer is 14,000 KJ m^{-2}, reaching 30,000 KJ m^{-2} on sunny days close to the solstice. Winds are high and average speed is 24 km h^{-1}, with frequent storms with winds over 140 Km h^{-1}. The predominant winds are from SW and NE.

GEOLOGY

The bedrock of Byers Peninsula is composed of Upper Jurassic to Lower Cretaceous marine sedimentary, volcanic and volcaniclastic rocks, intruded by igneous bodies (see Smellie *et al* 1980; Crame *et al* 1993, Hathway and Lomas 1998). The rocks represent part of a Mesozoic-Cenozoic magmatic arc complex which is exposed throughout the whole of the Antarctic Peninsula region, although most extensively on the Byers Peninsula (Hathway and Lomas 1998). The elevated interior region of the eastern half of the peninsula – surrounded to the north and south by Holocene beach deposits – is dominated by Lower Cretaceous non-marine tuffs, volcanic breccias, conglomerates, sandstones and minor mudstones, with intrusions in several places by volcanic plugs and sills. The western half of the peninsula, and extending NW half-way along Ray Promontory, is predominantly Upper Jurassic-Lower Cretaceous marine mudstones, with sandstones and conglomerates, with frequent intrusions of volcanic sills, plugs and other igneous bodies. The NW half of Ray Promontory comprises mainly volcanic breccias of the same age. Mudstones, sandstones, conglomerates and pyroclastic rocks are the most common lithologies found on the peninsula. Expanses of Holocene beach gravels and alluvium are found in coastal areas, particularly on South Beaches and the eastern half of Robbery Beaches, with less-extensive deposits on President Beaches.

The Area is of high geological value because "the sedimentary and igneous rocks exposed at Byers Peninsula constitute the most complete record of the Jurassic-Early Cretaceous period in the northern part of the Pacific flank of the magmatic arc complex, and they have proved a key succession for the study of marine molluscan faunas (e.g. Crame 1984, 1995, Crame and Kelly 1995) and non-marine floras (e.g. Hernandez and Azcárte 1971, Philippe *et al* 1995)" (Hathway and Lomas 1998).

GEOMORPHOLOGY AND SOILS

Much of the terrain consists of lithosols, essentially a layer of shattered rock, with permafrost widespread below an active layer of 30-70 cm depth (Thom 1978, Ellis-Evans 1996, Serrano *et al* 1996). Stone fields (consisting of silty fines with dispersed boulders and surficial clasts), gelifluction lobes, polygonal ground (both in flooded and dry areas), stone stripes and circles and other periglacial landforms dominate the surface morphology of the upper platforms where bedrock outcrop is absent (Serrano at al 1996). Debris and mudflows are observed in several localities. Beneath some of the moss and grass communities there is a 10-20 cm deep layer of organic matter although, because vegetation is sparse over most of Byers Peninsula, there are no deep accumulations of peat (Bonner and Smith 1985; Moura et al., 2012; Otero et al., 2013). Ornithogenic soils are present especially in the Devils Point vicinity and on a number of knolls along President Beaches (Ellis-Evans 1996).

Parts of the interior of the peninsula have been shaped by coastal processes with a series of raised beaches ranging from 3 to 54 m in altitude, some of which are over 1 km wide. A radiocarbon date for the highest beach deposits suggests that Byers Peninsula was largely free of permanent ice by 9700 yr B.P., while the lowest beach deposits are dated at 300 yr B.P. (John and Sugden 1971, Sugden and John 1973). Lake sediment analyses, however, are contradictory; some suggest a recent general deglaciation of central Byers Peninsula of around 4000-5000 yr B.P. (Björck *et al* 1991a, b), but others provide a deglaciation age about 8000-9000 yr B.P. (Toro et al, 2013). In several places sub-fossil whalebones are embedded in the raised beaches, occasionally as almost entire skeletons. Radiocarbon dates of skeletal material from about 10 m a.s.l. on South Beaches suggest an age of between 2000 and 2400 yr B.P. (Hansom 1979). Pre-Holocene surfaces of Byers Peninsula exhibit clear evidence of a glacial landscape, despite the gentle landforms. Today only three small residual glaciers (comprising less than 0.5 km^2) remain on Ray Promontory. The pre-existing glacially modified landforms, have been subsequently overprinted by fluvial and periglacial processes (Martinez de Pison *et al* 1996).

STREAMS AND LAKES

Byers Peninsula is perhaps the most significant limnological site in the South Shetland Islands/Antarctic Peninsula region, with over 60 lakes, numerous freshwater pools (differentiated from lakes in that they freeze to the bottom in winter) and a dense and varied stream network. The gentle terrain favours water retention and waterlogged soils are common in the summer. The water capacity of the thin soils is limited, however, and many of the channels are frequently dry, with flow often intermittent except during periods of substantial snow melt, rain or where they drain glaciers (Lopez-Martinez *et al* 1996). Most of the streams drain seasonal snowfields and are often no more than 5-10 cm in depth (Ellis-Evans 1996) although snow accumulation in some narrow gorges can reach over 2 m height, and result in ice dams blocking the lake outlet. The larger streams are up to 4.5 km in length, up to 20 m in width and 30-50 cm in depth in the lower reaches during periods of flow. Streams that drain to the west often have sizeable gorges (Lopez-Martinez *et al* 1996) and gullies up to 30 m in depth have been cut into the uppermost, and largest, of the raised marine platforms (Ellis-Evans 1996). Above the Holocene raised beaches the valleys are gentle, with widths of up to several hundred metres.

Lakes are especially abundant on the higher platforms (i.e. at the heads of basins) and on the Holocene raised beaches near the coast. Midge Lake is the largest at 587 × 112 m, and deepest with a maximum depth of 9.0 m. The inland lakes are all nutrient-poor and highly transparent, with extensive sediments in deeper water overlain by a dense aquatic moss carpet [*Drepanocladus longifolius (=D. aduncus)*]. In some lakes, such as Chester Cone Lake about 500 m to the south of Midge Lake, or Limnopolar lake, stands of aquatic moss are found growing at one to several metres in depth and cover most of the lake bottom, which is the habitat for *Parochlus* larvae (Bonner and Smith 1985). Large masses of this moss are sometimes washed up along parts of the shoreline. The lakes are generally frozen to a depth of 1.0 - 1.5 m for 9 - 11 months of the year and overlain by snow (Rochera et al., 2010), although surfaces of some of the higher lakes remain frozen year-round (Ellis-Evans 1996, Lopez-Martinez *et al* 1996). On the upper levels of the central plateau many small, shallow, slow-flowing streams flow between lakes and drain onto large flat areas of saturated lithosol covered with thick cyanobacterial mats of *Phormidium* sp. and *Leptolyngbya* spp. These mats are more extensive than in any other maritime Antarctic site thus far described and reflect the unique geomorphology and relatively high annual precipitation of the Area. With spring melt there is considerable flush through most lakes, but outflow from many lakes may cease late in the season as seasonal snowmelt decreases (Rochera et al., 2010). Most lakes contain some crustaceans such as the copepods *Boeckella poppei* and the fairy shrimp *Branchinecta gainii*. Some of the streams also contain substantial growths of cyanobacterial and green filamentous algae, along with diatoms and copepods (Kopalova and van de Vijver 2013). A number of relatively saline lakes of lagoonal origin occur close to the shore, particularly on President Beaches. Where these are used as southern elephant seal (*Mirounga leonina*) wallows these lakes have been highly organically enriched. Those coastal shallow lakes and pools located behind the first raised beach often have abundant algal mats and crustaceans, including the copepods *B. poppei* and *Parabroteas sorsi*, and occasionally the fairy shrimp *Br. gainii*. Some of these water bodies have high biological diversity, with newly described species of diatoms (van der Vijver et al., 2009), oligochaete (Rodriguez and Rico, 2009) and ciliate protozoa (Petz et al 2008).

VEGETATION

Although much of Byers Peninsula lacks abundant vegetation, especially inland (see Lindsay 1971), the use of satellite technology shows the areas does contain 8.1 km^2 of green vegetation (e.g. vascular plants, algae and some moss species), which represents over 50% of the green vegetation protected within all the terrestrial ASPAs (Hughes et al., 2015) (see http://www.add.scar.org/aspa_vegetation_pilot.jsp). The often sparse communities contain a diverse flora, with at least 56 lichen species, 29 mosses, 5 hepatics and 2 phanerogams having been identified as present within the Area (Vera et al., 2013). Numerous unidentified lichens and mosses have also been collected. This suggests the Area contains one of the most diverse representations of terrestrial flora known in the maritime Antarctic. A number of the species are rare in this part of the maritime Antarctic. For example, of the bryophytes, *Anthelia juratzkana*, *Brachythecium austroglareosum*, *Chorisodontium aciphyllum*, *Ditrichum hyalinum*, *Herzogobryum teres*, *Hypnum revolutum*, *Notoligotrichum trichodon*, *Pachyglossa dissitifolia*, *Platydictya jungermannioides*, *Sanionia* cf. *plicata*, *Schistidium occultum*, *Syntrichia filaris* and *Syntrichia saxicola* are considered rare. For *A. juratzkana*, *D. hyalinum*, *N. trichodon* and *S. plicata*, their furthest-south record is on Byers Peninsula. Of the lichen flora, *Himantormia lugubris*, *Ochrolechia parella*, *Peltigera didactyla* and *Pleopsidium chlorophanum* are considered rare.

Vegetation development is much greater on the south coast than on the north. Commonly found on the higher, drier raised beaches in the south is an open community dominated by abundant *Polytrichastrum alpinum* (=*Polytrichum alpinum*), *Polytrichum piliferum* (=*Polytrichum antarcticum*), *P. juniperinum*, *Ceratodon purpureus*, and the moss *Pohlia nutans* and several crustose lichens are frequent. Some large stands of mosses occur near President and South Beaches, where extensive snowdrifts often accumulate at the base of slopes rising behind the raised beaches, providing an ample source of melt water in the summer. These moss stands are dominated mainly by *Sanionia uncinata* (=*Drepanocladus uncinatus*), which locally forms continuous carpets of several hectares. The vegetation composition is more diverse than on the higher, drier areas. Inland, wet valley floors have stands of *Brachythecium austro-salebrosum*, *Campylium polygamum*, *Sanionia uncinata*, *Warnstorfia laculosa* (=*Calliergidium austro-stramineum*), and *W. sarmentosa* (=*Calliergon sarmentosum*). In contrast, moss carpets are almost non-existent within 250 m of the northern coast, replaced by scant growth of *Sanionia* in hollows between raised beaches of up to 12 m in altitude. Lichens, principally of the genera *Acarospora*, *Buellia*, *Caloplaca*, *Verrucaria* and *Xanthoria*, are present on the lower (2-5 m) raised beach crests, with *Sphaerophorus*, *Stereocaulon* and *Usnea* becoming the more dominant lichens with increasing altitude (Lindsay 1971).

On better drained ash slopes *Bryum* spp., *Dicranoweisia* spp., *Ditrichum* spp., *Pohlia* spp., *Schistidium* spp., and *Tortula* spp. are common as isolated cushions and turves with various liverworts, lichens (notably the pink *Placopsis contortuplicata* and black foliose *Leptogium puberulum*), and the cyanobacterium *Nostoc commune*. *P. contortuplicata* occurs in inland and upland habitats lacking in nitrogen, and is typical of substrata with some degree of disturbance such as solifluction; it is often the only plant to colonise the small rock fragments of stone stripes and frost-heave polygons (Lindsay 1971). It is usually found growing alone, though rarely with species of *Andreaea* and *Usnea*. *N. commune* covers extensive saturated areas on level or gently sloping, gravelly boulder clay from altitudes of between 60-150 m, forming discrete rosettes of about 5 cm in diameter 10-20 cm apart (Lindsay 1971). Scattered, almost spherical, cushions of *Andreaea*, *Dicranoweisia*, and *Ditrichum* are found on the driest soils. In wet, bird- and seal-influenced areas the green foliose alga *Prasiola crispa* is sometimes abundant.

Rock surfaces on Byers Peninsula are mostly friable, but locally colonised by lichens, especially near the coast. Volcanic plugs are composed of harder, more stable rock and are densely covered by lichens and occasional mosses. Usnea Plug is remarkable for its luxuriant growth of *Himantormia lugubris* and *Usnea aurantiaco-atra* (=*U. fasciata*). More generally, *H. lugubris* and *U. aurantiaco-atra* are the dominant lichen species on inland exposed montane surfaces, growing with the moss *Andreaea gainii* over much of the exposed rock with up to 80% cover of the substratum (Lindsay 1971). In sheltered pockets harbouring small accumulations of mineral soil, the liverworts *Barbilophozia hatcheri* and *Cephaloziella varians* (= *C. exiliflora*) are often found, but more frequently intermixed with cushions of *Bryum, Ceratodon, Dicranoweisia, Pohlia, Sanionia, Schistidium,* and *Tortula. Sanionia* and *Warnstorfia* form small stands, possibly correlated with the absence of large snow patches and associated melt streams. *Polytrichastrum alpinum* forms small inconspicuous cushions in hollows, but it may merge with *Andreaea gainii* cushions in favourable situations (Lindsay 1971).

Crustose lichens are mainly species of *Buellia, Lecanora, Lecedella, Lecidea, Placopsis* and *Rhizocarpon* growing on rock, with species of *Cladonia* and *Stereocaulon* growing on mosses, particularly *Andreaea* (Lindsay 1971). On the south coast moss carpets are commonly colonised by epiphytic lichens, such as *Leptogium puberulum, Peltigera rufescens, Psoroma* spp., together with *Coclocaulon aculeata* and *C. epiphorella.* On sea cliffs *Caloplaca* and *Verrucaria* spp. dominate on lower surfaces exposed to salt spray up to about 5 m, with nitrophilous species, such as *Caloplaca regalis, Haematomma erythromma,*and *Xanthoria elegans* often dominant at higher altitudes where seabirds are frequently nesting. Elsewhere on dry cliff surfaces a *Ramalina terebrata* - crustose lichen community is common. A variety of ornithocoprophilous lichens, such as *Catillaria corymbosa, Lecania brialmontii,* and species of *Buellia, Haematomma, Lecanora,* and *Physcia* occur on rocks near concentrations of breeding birds, along with the foliose lichens *Mastodia tessellata, Xanthoria elegans* and *X. candelaria* which are usually dominant on dry boulders.

Antarctic hairgrass (*Deschampsia antarctica*) is common in several localities, mainly on the south coast, and occasionally forms closed swards (e.g. at Sealer Hill); Antarctic pearlwort (*Colobanthus quitensis*) is sometimes associated. Both plants are quite abundant in southern gullies with a steep north-facing slope, forming large, occasionally pure stands with thick carpets of *Brachythecium* and *Sanionia,* although they are rarely found above 50 m in altitude (Lindsay 1971). An open community of predominantly *Deschampsia* and *Polytrichum piliferum* extends for several kilometres on the sandy, dry, flat raised beaches on South Beaches. A unusual growth-form of the grass, forming isolated mounds 25 cm high and up to 2 m across, occurs on the beach near Sealer Hill. *Deschampsia* has been reported at only one locality on the north coast (Lair Point), where it forms small stunted tufts (Lindsay 1971).

INVERTEBRATES

The invertebrate fauna on Byers Peninsula thus far described comprises (Usher and Edwards 1986, Richard *et al* 1994, Block and Stary 1996, Convey *et al* 1996, Rodriguez and Rico, 2008): six Collembola (*Cryptopygus antarcticus, Cryptopygus badasa, Friesea grisea, Friesea woyciechowskii, Isotoma (Folsomotoma) octooculata* (=*Parisotoma octooculata*) and *Tullbergia mixta*; one mesostigmatid mite (*Gamasellus racovitzai*), five cryptostigmatid mites (*Alaskozetes antarcticus, Edwardzetes dentifer, Globoppia loxolineata* (=*Oppia loxolineata*), *Halozetes belgicae* and *Magellozetes antarcticus*); ten prostigmatid mites (*Bakerdania antarcticus, Ereynetes macquariensis, Eupodes minutus, Eupodes parvus grahamensis, Nanorchestes berryi, Nanorchestes nivalis, Pretriophtydeus tilbrooki, Rhagidia gerlachei, Rhagidia leechi,* and *Stereotydeus villosus*); two Dipterans (*Belgica antarctica* and *Parochlus steinenii*), and two oligochaetes (*Lumbricillus healyae* and *Lumbricillus sp.*), one copepod (*Boeckella poppei*), one crustacean (*Branchinecta gainii*) and one cladoceran (*Macrothrix ciliate*).

Larvae of the wingless midge *Belgica antarctica* occur in limited numbers in moist moss, especially carpets of *Sanionia,* although it is of very restricted distribution on Byers Peninsula (found especially near Cerro Negro) and may be near its northern geographical limit. The winged midge *Parochlus steinenii* and its larvae inhabit the margins of inland lakes and pools, notably Midge Lake and another near Usnea Plug, and are also found amongst the stones of many stream beds (Bonner and Smith 1985, Richard *et al* 1994, Ellis-Evans pers comm 1999, Rico et al 2013). During warm calm weather, swarms of adults may be seen above lake margins.

The diversity of the arthropod community described at Byers Peninsula is greater than at any other documented Antarctic site (Convey *et al* 1996). Various studies (Usher and Edwards 1986, Richard *et al* 1994, Convey *et al* 1996) have demonstrated that the arthropod population composition on Byers Peninsula varies significantly with habitat over a small area. *Tullbergia mixta* has been observed in relatively large numbers; it appears to be limited in Antarctic distribution to the South Shetland Islands (Usher and Edwards 1986). Locally, the greatest diversity is likely to be observed in communities dominated by moss cushions such as *Andreaea* spp. (Usher and Edwards 1986). Further sampling is required to establish populations and diversities with greater reliability. While further sampling at other sites may yet reveal the communities described at Byers Peninsula to be typical of similar habitats in the region, available data on the microfauna confirm the biological importance of the Area.

MICROORGANISMS

An analysis of soil samples collected from Byers Peninsula yielded several nematophagous fungi: in soil colonised by *Deschampsia* were found *Acrostalagmus goniodes, A. obovatus, Cephalosporium balanoides* and *Dactylaria gracilis,* while in *Colobanthus*-dominated soil was found *Cephalosporium balanoides* and *Dactylella gephyropaga* (Gray and Smith 1984). The basidiomycete *Omphalina antarctica* is often abundant on moist stands of the moss *Sanionia uncinata* (Bonner and Smith 1985). Thirty seven nematode taxa have been recorded, with samples showing great variation in richness and abundance making Byers Peninsula a nematode biodiversity hotspot (Nielsen et al., 2011).

Some of the water bodies have high microbial biodiversity (Velazquez et al., 2010; Villaescusa et al., 2010) including the largest viral genetic diversity found in Antarctic lakes (López-Bueno et al 2009)

BREEDING BIRDS

The avifauna of Byers Peninsula is diverse, although breeding colonies are generally not large. Two species of penguin, the chinstrap (*Pygoscelis antarctica*) and the gentoo (*P. papua*), breed in the Area.

Adélie penguins (*P. adeliae*) have not been observed to breed on Byers Peninsula or its offshore islets. In the South Shetlands Islands, Adélie penguins only breeds on King George Island where the populations are declining (Carlini et al. 2009).

The principal chinstrap penguin colony is at Devils Point, where a rough estimate of about 3000 pairs was made in 1987; a more accurate count made in 1965 indicated about 5300 pairs in four discrete colonies, of which almost 95% were nesting on Demon Island, 100 m to the south of Devils Point (Croxall and Kirkwood 1979; Woehler 1993). Two colonies of about 25 chinstrap penguin pairs surrounded by a colony of gentoo penguins can be found on the President Beaches close to Devils Point (Barbosa et al., 2013). Small chinstrap penguin colonies have been reported on the northern coast, e.g. on Robbery Beaches (50 pairs in 1958; Woehler 1993), but no breeding pairs were reported there in a 1987 survey. In other locations, Lair Point contained 156 pairs in 1966, declining to 25 pairs in 1987 (Woehler 1993). In a recent visit to the area (January 2009) 20 pairs were counted (Barbosa pers.com).

Gentoo penguins breed at several colonies on Devils Point, with approximately 750 pairs recorded in 1965 (Croxall and Kirkwood 1979, Woehler 1993). Currently three colonies of about 3000 pairs in total can be found (Barbosa pers.com). On the northern coast, a rookery of three colonies with 900 pairs in total is located in Robbery Beaches (Woehler 1993). In a visit to Lair Point in January 2009, about 1200 pairs were counted. Woehler (1993) gives no data on gentoo penguins at this location.

Recent estimations of population size for some species of flying birds were obtained from a survey conducted in December 2008 and January 2009 (Gil-Delgado et al. 2010). The Antarctic tern (*Sterna vittata*) population was estimated at 1873 breeding pairs. Two hundred and thirty eight pairs of southern giant petrels *(Macronectes giganticus)* and 15 pairs of brown skua (*Catharacta lonnbergi*) nest locally. A detailed survey of other breeding birds was conducted in 1965 (White 1965). The most populous breeding species recorded then, with approximately 1760 pairs, was the Antarctic tern (*Sterna vittata*), followed by 1315 pairs of Wilson's storm petrels (*Oceanites oceanicus*), approximately 570 pairs of cape petrels (*Daption capense*), 449 pairs of kelp gulls (*Larus dominicanus*), 216 pairs of southern giant petrels, 95 pairs of black-bellied storm petrels (*Fregetta tropica*), 47 pairs of blue-eyed cormorants (*Phalacrocorax atriceps*) (including those on nearshore islets), 39 pairs of brown skuas, and 3 pairs of sheathbills (*Chionis alba*). In addition, prions (*Pachytilla* sp.) and snow petrels (*Pagodroma nivea*) have been seen on the peninsula but their breeding presence has not been confirmed. The census of burrowing and scree-nesting birds is considered an underestimate (White pers. comm. 1999). The majority of the birds nest in close proximity to the coast, principally in the west and south.

Recently some vagrant waders, probably white-rumped sandpipers (*Calidris fuscicollis*) have been seen frequently foraging in some streams in the southern beaches (Quesada pers. comm. 2009).

BREEDING MAMMALS

Large groups of southern elephant seals (*Mirounga leonina*) breed on the Byers Peninsula coast, with a total of over 2500 individuals reported on South Beaches (Torres *et al.* 1981), which is one of the largest populations of this species recorded in the South Shetland Islands. A estimation made in 2008-2009 showed a population ranging from 4700 to 6300 individuals (Gil-Delgado et al. 2013). Large numbers haul out in wallows and along beaches in summer. Weddell (*Leptonychotes weddellii*), crabeater (*Lobodon carcinophagous*) and leopard (*Hydrurga leptonyx*) seals may be seen around the shorelines. Antarctic fur seals (*Arctocephalus gazella*) were once very abundant on Byers Peninsula (see below), but have not substantially recolonised the Area in high numbers in spite of the recent rapid population expansion in other parts of the maritime Antarctic.

HISTORICAL FEATURES

Following discovery of the South Shetland Islands in 1819, intensive sealing at Byers Peninsula between 1820 and 1824 exterminated almost all local Antarctic fur seals and southern elephant seals (Smith and Simpson 1987). During this period there was a summer population of up to 200 American and British sealers living ashore in dry-stone refuges and caves around Byers Peninsula (Smith and Simpson 1987). Evidence of their occupation remains in their many refuges, some of which still contain artefacts (clothing, implements, structural materials, etc.). Several sealing vessels were wrecked near Byers Peninsula and timbers from these ships may be found along the shores. Byers Peninsula has the greatest concentration of early 19th Century sealers' refuges and associated relics in the Antarctic and these are vulnerable to disturbance and/or removal.

Elephant seal numbers, and to some extent fur seal numbers, recovered after 1860, but were again decimated by a second sealing cycle extending to the first decade of the twentieth century.

HUMAN ACTIVITIES/IMPACTS

The modern era of human activity at Byers Peninsula has been largely confined to science. The impacts of these activities have not been fully described, but are believed to be minor and limited to items such as campsites, trampling (Tejedo et al., 2012; Pertierra et al., 2013a), markers of various kinds, sea-borne litter washed onto beaches (e.g. from fishing vessels) and from human wastes and scientific sampling. More recently the impacts of the field activities originating from the International Field Camp (62°39'49.7" S, 61°05'59.8" W) between 2001-2010 were quantified (Pertierra et al, 2013b). Several wooden stake markers and a plastic fishing float were observed in the southwest of the Area in a brief visit made in February 2001 (Harris 2001). In summer 2009-2010, a beach litter survey was undertaken (L. R. Pertierra pers. comm. 2011). The highest proportion of litter on beaches (averaged over beach length) was found in Robbery Beach (64%) followed by President Beach (28%) and beaches to the southwest of the Area (8%). This is likely to be related to their exposure to the Drake Passage (Torres and Jorquera, 1994). The majority of the litter found on the three beaches was wood (78% by number of items) and plastic (19%) whereas metal, glass and cloth were found more rarely (less than 1%). Several pieces of timber were found, some of them quite large (several meters in length). The plastic items were highly diverse, with bottles, ropes and tape the most numerous items. Floats and glass bottles were also found on the beaches.

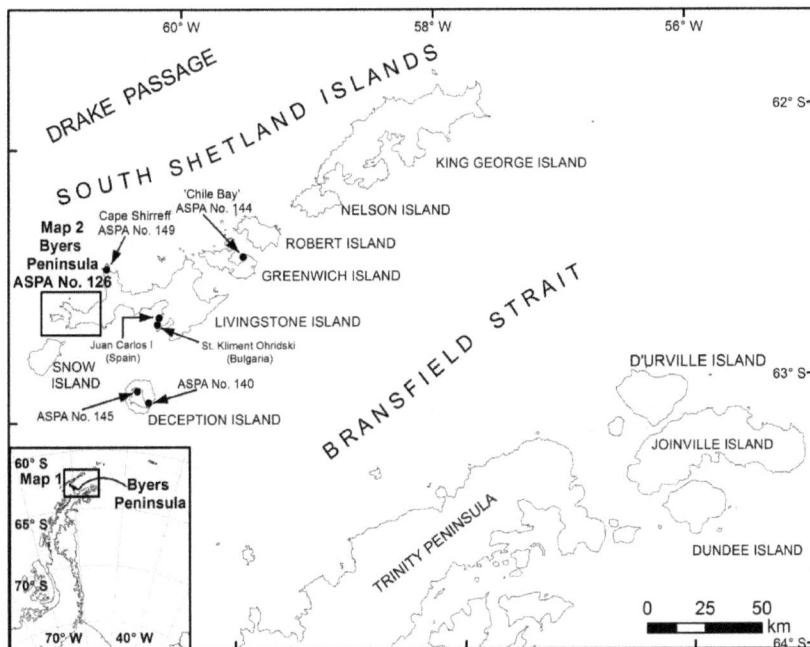

Map 1. Byers Peninsula, ASPA No. 126, Livingston Island, South Shetland Islands, location map. Insert: location of Byers Peninsula on the Antarctic Peninsula.

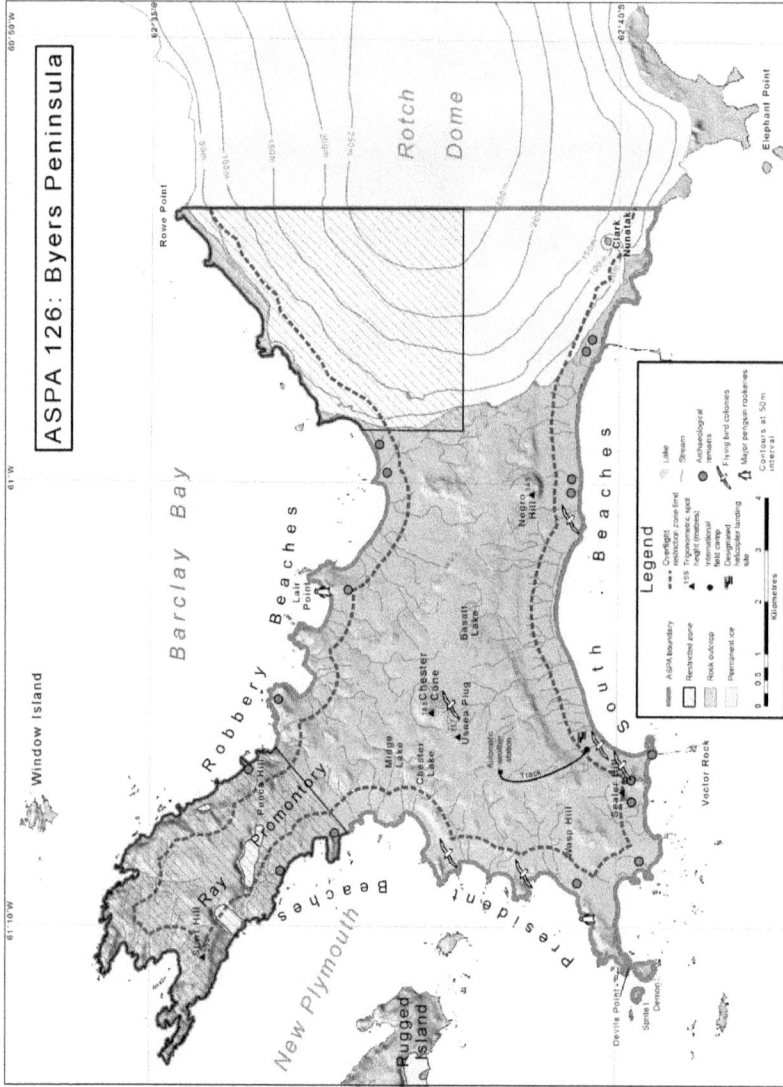

Map 2. ASPA 126: Byers Peninsula topographic map.

Management Plan for Antarctic Specially Protected Area No. 127

Haswell Island (Haswell Island and Adjacent Emperor Penguin Rookery on Fast Ice)

1. Description of values to be protected

The area includes Haswell Island with its littoral zone and adjacent fast ice when present.

Haswell Island was discovered in 1912 by the Australian Antarctic Expedition led by D. Mawson. It was named after William Haswell, professor of biology who rendered assistance to the expedition. Haswell is the biggest island of the same-name archipelago, with a height of 93 meters and 0,82 sq.meters in area. The island is at 2,5 km distance from the Russian Mirny Station operational from 1956.

At East and South-East of the island, there is a large colony of Emperor penguins (*Aptenodytes forsteri*) on fast ice.

The Haswell Island is a unique breeding site for almost all breeding bird species in East Antarctica including the: Antarctic petrel (*Talassoica antarctica*), Antarctic fulmar (*Fulmarus glacioloides*), Cape petrel (*Daption capense*), Snow petrel (*Pagodroma nivea*), Wilson's storm petrel (*Oceanites oceanicus*), South polar skua (*Catharacta maccormicki*), Lonnberg skua *Catharacta antarctica lonnbergi* and Adelie penguin (*Pygoscelis adeliae*).

The Area supports five species of pinnipeds, including the Ross seal (*Ommatophoca rossii*) which falls in the protected species category.

ATCM VIII (Oslo, 1975) approved its designation as SSSI 7 on the aforementioned grounds after a proposal by the USSR. Map 1 shows the location of the Haswell Islands (except Vkhodnoy Island), Mirny Station, and logistic activity sites. It was renamed and renumbered as ASPA No. 127 by Decision 1 (2002).

The boundaries of the ASPA No 127 embrace Haswell Island (66°31'S, 93°00'E), of 0,82 km² in area and the adjacent section of Davis Sea fast ice (when present) of approximately 5 km², that supports a colony of Emperor penguins (Map 2). It is one of a few Emperor penguin colonies in the vicinity of a permanent Antarctic station, and therefore it has advantages for the study of the species and its habitat.

Described by biologists during the first Soviet expeditions, the Area was studied in the 1970s and recent years, providing valuable materials for comparative analyses and monitoring of the long-term environmental impact of a large Antarctic station.

2. Aims and Objectives

Research in the ASPA is conducted to provide a better understanding of how natural and anthropogenic environmental changes affect the status and dynamics of local populations of flora and fauna, and how these changes affect the interaction between key species of the Antarctic ecosystem.

Management at Haswell Island aims to:

- Avoid direct impact of logistic activities on the Area;

- Regulate access to the Area;

- Avoid anthropogenic changes in the structure and abundance of local populations of flora and fauna;

- Allow scientific research, provided it is for compelling scientific reasons that cannot be served elsewhere;

- Facilitate scientific research on the environment in the context of monitoring and assessment of human impact on populations:

- Encourage environmental education and awareness.

3. Management Activities

The following management activities shall be undertaken to protect the values of the Area:

- When the vessel is approaching Mirny Station and upon arrival at the station, all persons arriving shall be informed of the existence and location of the ASPA and the relevant provisions of the Management Plan.
- Copies of the Management Plan and maps of the Area showing its location shall be available at all units engaged in logistic and scientific activities on the Haswell Islands.
- A sign showing directions of the Area boundaries, with clear statements of entry restrictions ("No entry! Antarctic Specially Protected Area"), shall be placed at the crossing point of lines Gorev Island – Fulmar Island and Cape Mabus – eastern extremity of Haswell Island to help avoid inadvertent entry into the Area following the formation of fast ice which is safe for pedestrian and vehicle traffic.
- Information signs shall be installed at the top of Cape Mabus slope, and at station activity sites in the direct vicinity of the Area.
- Markers and signs erected within the Area shall be secured, maintained in good condition, and have no impact on the environment.
- Overflight shall only be allowed under those conditions as set out under *7. Permit Conditions.*

The Management Plan shall be revised periodically to ensure that the values of the Antarctic Specially Protected Area are adequately protected. Any activity in the Area shall be preceded by the environmental impact assessment.

4. Period of Designation

Designated for an indefinite period.

5. Maps

Map 1: Location of the Haswell Islands, Mirny Station, and logistic activity sites.
Map 2: Boundaries of Antarctic Specially Protected Area 127, Haswell Island.
Map 3: Location of breeding seabird colonies.
Map 4: Topographic map of Haswell Island.

6. Description of the Area

6(i) Geographical co-ordinates, boundary markers and natural features

The Area occupies a territory inside polygon ABFEDC (66° 31'10" S, 92° 59'20" E; 66° 31'10" S, 93° 03' E; 66° 32'30" S, 93° 03' E; 66° 32'30" S, 93° 01'E; 66° 31'45" S, 93° 01'E; 66° 31'45" S, 92° 59'20'' E) (Map 2). The marked section of fast ice in the Davis Sea encompasses the most likely routes taken by Emperor penguins during the breeding season.

Topography

The Area boundaries on fast ice closer to the station can be broadly (visually) identified on site as directions EF (Vkhodnoy Island – Fulmar Island) and ED (Cape Mabus – eastern extremity of Haswell Island). A sign showing the directions of the Area boundaries, with clear statements of entry restrictions ("No entry! Antarctic Specially Protected Area"), shall be placed in point E. Information signs showing distance to the Area boundary shall be installed at station activity sites in the direct vicinity of the Area (at the top of Cape Mabus slope, and on Buromsky, Zykov, Fulmar, and Tokarev Islands).

It is highly unlikely that the outlying marine boundaries of the Area will be crossed inadvertently, as presently there is not any station activity. These boundaries have no visual features and shall be identified by the map.

There are no paths or roads within the Area.

Ice conditions

The Area comprises Haswell Island (the largest island in the archipelago), its littoral zone, and the adjacent section of fast ice in the Davis Sea. Russia's Mirny Observatory (now station) on Mirny Peninsula located in coastal nunataks south of the ASPA has been operational since 1956.

For the larger part of the year, the sea within the Area is covered with fast ice, whose width reaches 30-40 km by the end of winter. Fast ice breaks up between December 17 and March 9 (February 3, on average) and freezes between March 18 and May 5 (April 6, on average). The probability that the ice-free period off Mirny Station will last more than 1 month is 85%, more than 2 months 45%, and more than 3 months 25%. The Area is always full of icebergs. In summer, when fast ice disappears, icebergs drift westward along the coast. Seawater temperature is always below zero. The tide has an irregular daily pattern.

Environmental domains analysis

Based on the Environmental Domains Analysis for Antarctica (Resolution 3(2008)) Haswell Island is located within Environment L *Continental coastal-zone ice sheet*.

Biological Features

Coastal waters support a rich benthic fauna. Fish fauna in the Area is dominated by various icefish species, while Antarctic toothfish (*Dissostichus mawsoni*) and Antarctic silverfish (*Pleuragramma antarcticum*) are less abundant. An ample forage base and the availability of suitable nesting sites create a favorable environment for numerous seabirds. According to the records, there are 14 bird species in the vicinity of Mirny Station(Table 1).

The coastal fauna is mainly represented by pinnipeds, among which Weddell seals (*Leptonychotes weddelli*) are most abundant. Other Antarctic seal species can be seen occasionally in very small numbers. Minke whales (*Balaenoptera acutorostrata*) and killer whales (*Orcinus orca*) have frequently been observed near Mirny Station.

Table 1: The avifauna of the Haswell Islands (ASPA 127).

1	Emperor penguin (*Aptenodytes forsteri*)	B, M
2	Adelie penguin (*Pygoscelis adeliae*)	B, M
3	Chinstrap penguin (*Pygoscelis antarctica*)	V
4	Macaroni penguin (*Eudyptes chrysolophus*)	V
5	Southern fulmar (*Fulmarus glacioloides*)	B
6	Antarctic petrel (*Thalassoica antarctica*)	B
7	Cape petrel (*Daption capense*)	B
8	Snow petrel (*Pagodroma nivea*)	B
9	Southern giant petrel (*Macronectes giganteus*)	V
10	Wilson's storm petrel (*Oceanites oceanicus*)	B
11	Pomarine skua (*Stercorarius pomarinus*)	V
12	South-polar skua (*Catharacta maccormicki*)	B
13	Lonnberg skua (*Catharacta Antarctica lonnbergi*)	B
14	Kelp gull (*Larus dominicanus*)	V

Notes: B – breeding species; M – molting sites in the vicinity of the station; V – vagrant species.

At present, seabirds nest on ten out of seventeen archipelago islands. Seven species breed directly on the islands, and one species – the Emperor penguin (Aptenodytes forsteri) – on fast ice. A few vagrant species have also been observed in the Area. In general, core species composition of the aviafauna remains stable during past 60 years, and is characteristic of the East Antarctica coastal areas.

Updates of vagrants to the species list are explained by more extensive ornithological observations. All new species are recorded as vagrants only. At the same time, the Southern giant petrel observed in 2006 for the first time at Mirny, seems to become rare but regular visitor to the Area, and the traced quartering of Lonnberg skua and their recorded breeding at the archipelago suggest the natural expansion of the breeding areas.

Starting from 2012 the cases of hybrid pair nesting by South-polar skua (*Catharacta maccormicki*) and Lonnberg skua (*Catharacta Antarctica*) came to be observed.

Emperor penguin (Aptenodytes forsteri)

The Emperor penguin colony of the Haswell Islands is located on fast ice in the Davis Sea 2 to 3 km north-east of Mirny Station and usually within 1 km of Haswell Island. The colony was discovered and described by the Western Party of the Australasian Antarctic Expedition on November 25, 1912. However, a detailed study of the colony was initiated only after the establishment of Mirny Observatory. Since its foundation in 1956, the Observatory has been conducting periodic monitoring of the size of the breeding population. The first round-the-year observation of the colony was initiated by E.S. Korotkevich in 1956 (Korotkevich, 1958), continued until 1962 (Makushok, 1959; Korotkevich, 1960; Prior, 1968), and was then resumed by V.M. Kamenev in the late 1960s-early 1970s (Kamenev, 1977). After a long break, observations of the avifauna in the area were resumed in 1999-2011 (Gavrilo, Mizin, 2007, Gavrilo, Mizin, 2011, Neelov 2007 et al).

Table 2 shows a schedule of various phenological events in the Emperor penguin colony of the Haswell Islands.

Table 2: Dates of phenological events in the Emperor penguin colony, Haswell Islands.

Penguins arrive at the colony site	Last 10 days in March
Peak of the mating period	Late April – first ten days in May
Commencement of egg laying	First 5 days in May
Commencement of hatching	July 5–15
Chicks start leaving brood pouches	Last 10 days in August
Chicks start getting together in creches	First 10 days in September
Chicks start molting	Late October – early November
Adult birds start molting	Last 10 days in November – first 5 days in December
The colony starts disintegrating	Last 10 days in November – mid-December
Birds abandon the colony site	Last 5 days in December – first 10 days in January

According to the census data obtained during 1956 to 1966 the total population of the emperor penguin colony varied between 14 to 20 thousand (Korotkevich, 1958, Makushok, 1959, Prior, 1964, Kamenev, 1977). After that, during the 1970s and 1980s a population declined by one third, but in the 2000s it has been gradually recovered. At present the colony population is stable with tendency for decrease. The observations of 2010/2011 summer season during egg laying period with maximum concentration of adult birds revealed that the colony population reached 13 thousand and according to chick census in 2015 it could be assumed that the colony population was more than 14 thousand (RAE, unpublished).

Comparative analysis of the emperor penguin population dynamics in two colonies located in the same ecoregion (80°E - 140°E), i.e. Haswell and Pointe Géologie, revealed similar trends during past 50 years (Barbraud et al., 2011). Before the 1970s the penguin population at Pointe-Geologie Archipelago, Terre Adelie (ASPA 120) was stable, and at Haswell it was also stable or slightly decreasing. The population growth rate notably decreased and population numbers declined in both colonies during climatic regime shift in 1970-1980. Magnitude of decline was similar as well, and the numbers of breeding pairs correlated. Given that, one could suggest common large-scale environmental/climatic changes and related ecosystem shifts observed widely over the Southern Ocean might affect penguin populations.

The same string negative factor is likely to impact both populations. The ice cover, which is known to effect emperor penguin ecology, is suggested to be such a factor. In particular, decrease in ice cover and earlier onset of the fast-ice break-up dates negatively impacted penguin survival and further breeding population numbers via changes in food availability as shown previously (Barbraud, Weimerskirch, 2001, Jenouvrier et al., 2009). During the past 20 years both colonies demonstrated positive population dynamics under conditions of increasing extent of the ice cover and shift of fast-ice break-up onset to the later dates.

Table 3: Factors affecting the population of Emperor penguins on the Haswell Islands and relevant mitigation actions.

		Actions to mitigate the impact of anthropogenic factors
Anthropogenic factors	Disturbance by visitors	Visits to the colony should be strictly regulated
	Collection of eggs	The collection of eggs is prohibited, except in accordance with a permit for research issued by a national authority.
	Disturbance by flights	Flight route and height should be selected in accordance with this Management Plan
Natural factors		
	Climate changes and related changes in food resources. Ice conditions affect food availability and survival of adults and chicks. (Decrease in sea ice extent in April – June leads to decline in population growth rate and population numbers decline. An early break-up of fast ice increases chick mortality).	

Data on changes in the size of other populations are less complete (Table 4). Long-term changes may show a negative trend. However, it's not possible to make well-grounded conclusions based just on the three surveys with not full coverage of the populations and which are several decades apart.

Table 4: Long-term changes in the size of bird populations on the Haswell Islands (trend: 1 = positive, 0 = uncertain, -1 = negative, ? = supposed)

Species	1960s-1970s, adults in individuals	1999/2001	2009/10, adults in individuals	Trend
Adelie penguin	41,000-44,500	Ca. 31,000 adults	Ca. 27,000	-1
Southern fulmar	9,500-10000	2300 nests with clutches	Ca. 5,000	-1
Antarctic petrel	900-1050	150-200 nests with clutches	Ca. 500	-1
Cape petrel	750	150 nests with clutches	Ca. 300	-1
Snow petrel	600-700	60-75 nests with clutches	No data	-1 ?
Wilson's storm-petrel	400-500	Min 30 occupied nests	Over 80	-1 ?
South-polar skua	48 (24 pairs)	Min. 38 (19 pairs)	170 (62 pairs)	1

The data from Haswell Island area show possible long-term negative trends in different seabird species including both penguins and flying birds. It is possible that the root cause which determined the population dynamics of not only emperor penguins but other sea birds in the Haswell Island area as well, are climate changes. However no data on population dynamics in the last 10 to 15 years is available .The one exception is represented by the south polar skua which population tripled during the whole observation period.

More research and further monitoring are needed to reveal population trends in the birds of Haswell Island and to understand their causes.

6(ii) Definition of seasons; restricted and prohibited zones within the Area

Entry into any part of the Area is allowed only for holders of a Permit issued by an appropriate National Authority.

Activity in the Area shall be subject to special restrictions during the bird breeding season:

- From mid-April to December in the vicinity of the Emperor penguin colony; and

- From October to March in the vicinity of the nesting sites on Haswell Island.

The location of the breeding colonies is shown in Map 3. Emperor penguins, which are especially sensitive to disturbance, shall also be protected outside the designated breeding site as the breeding site may vary in location.

6(iii) Structures within the Area

A beacon – a metal pole whose base is secured by stones – is located on Haswell Island. There are no other structures on the island.

A heated shack containing an emergency food supply may be located on one of the neighboring islands (but not on Haswell Island).

6(iv) Location of other protected areas within close proximity

HSM No 9 Cemetery on Buromskiy Island is located in 200 m to boundary of the Area.

7. Permit Conditions

7(i) Permit conditions

Entry into the Area is prohibited unless in accordance with a Permit issued by an appropriate national authority. Issue of a Permit to enter the Area must satisfy the following conditions:

- A Permit is issued only for purposes specified in para. 2 of the Management Plan;

- Permits shall be issued for a stated period;

- The actions permitted will not jeopardize the ecosystems of the Area or interfere with existing scientific research;

- Visits to the Area under a Permit shall be allowed to organized groups accompanied by an authorized person. Relevant information shall be entered in the Visit Logbook specifying the date and purpose of the visit and the number of visitors. The leader of Mirny Station keeps the Logbook.

- The authorized person is appointed in accordance with national procedure; and

- A visit report shall be supplied to the authority named in the Permit by the end of stated period or annually.

Permits shall be issued for scientific research, monitoring studies, or inspections that do not require collection of biological materials or fauna samples, or that require collecting in small quantities. A Permit for a visit to or stay in the Area shall specify the scope of tasks to be implemented, the implementation period, and the maximum number of staff allowed to visit the Area.

7(ii) Access to and movement within the Area

Vehicles other than skidoos are prohibited within the Area.

When approaching or moving within the Area, care shall be taken to avoid any disturbance to birds and seals, especially during the breeding season. Deterioration of the conditions of or approaches to the bird nesting sites, or seal haulouts shall be prohibited at all times.

Haswell Island. The western or south-western slopes are most suitable for access (Map 4). Movement shall only be on foot.

Fast ice section. During the formation of fast ice which provides pedestrian and vehicle safety, entry into the section shall be at any suitable place from Mirny Station. The use of any vehicles in the Area shall be prohibited during the nest sitting season (May-July). When using skidoos, visitors shall not approach the Emperor penguin colony closer than 500 m (irrespective of its location).

Overflight of the Area is prohibited during the most sensitive period of the Emperor penguin breeding cycle, from April 15 to August 31.

During the remainder of the year, overflight of the Area shall be conducted according to the following restrictions (Table 5). Direct overflights of the seabird breeding colonies should be avoided whenever it is possible.

Table 5: Minimum overflight heights within the Area according to aircraft type.

Aircraft type	Number of engines	Minimum height above ground	
		Feet	Meters
Helicopter	1	2,460	750
Helicopter	2	3,300	1,000
Fixed-wing	1 or 2	2,460	750
Fixed-wing	4	3,300	1,000

7(iii) Activities that are or may be conducted in the Area, including restrictions on time or place

• Research on avifauna and other environmental studies that cannot be conducted elsewhere;

• Management activities, including monitoring.

• Education visits to the Emperor penguins colony except of the early nesting period (May – July)

7(iv) Installation, modification, or removal of structures

Structures or scientific equipment may be installed in the Area only for compelling scientific or management purposes approved by an appropriate authority pursuant to the effective regulations.

7(v) Location of field camps

Camping shall be allowed only for safety reasons, and every precaution shall be taken to avoid damage to the local ecosystem and disturbance to the local fauna.

7(vi) Restrictions on materials and organisms which can be brought into the Area

No living organisms or chemicals other than chemicals required for scientific purposes specified in the Permit shall be introduced into the Area (chemicals introduced for scientific purposes shall be removed from the Area before the Permit expiry).

Fuel is not to be stored in the Area unless it is required for essential needs relating to the permitted activity. Anything introduced shall be for a stated period only, handled so that the risk to the ecosystem is minimized, and removed at the conclusion of the stated period. No permanent storage facilities shall be established in the Area.

7(vii) Taking of or harmful interference with native flora or fauna

Taking of or harmful interference with native flora or fauna is prohibited, except by Permit. In the case the activity is determined to have less than a minor or transitory impact, it should be conducted in accordance with the *SCAR Code of Conduct for the Use of Animals for Scientific Purposes in Antarctica,* to be used as a minimum standard.

7(viii) Collection or removal of anything not brought into the Area by the Permit holder

Collection or removal of anything not brought into the Area by the Permit holder shall only be for scientific or management purposes specified in the Permit.

However, human waste may be removed from the Area, and dead or pathological samples of fauna and flora may be removed for laboratory analysis.

7(ix) Disposal of waste

All waste shall be removed from the Area.

7(x) Measures that are necessary to ensure that the aims and objectives of the Management Plan continue to be met

Permits to enter the Area may be granted to carry out scientific observation, monitoring, and site inspection activities, which may involve limited collection of fauna samples, eggs, and other biological materials for scientific purposes.

To help maintain the environmental and scientific values of the Area, visitors shall take every precaution against the introduction of alien materials and organisms.

Any long-term monitoring sites shall be appropriately marked on a map and on site. A map showing the boundary of the ASPA shall be displayed at Mirny Station. A copy of the Management Plan shall be displayed at Mirny Station. A copy of the Management Plan shall be freely available at Mirny Station.

Visits to the Area shall be limited to scientific, management and educational purposes.

7(xi) Requirements for reports

Parties should ensure that the principal holder of each Permit issued submits to the appropriate authority a report describing the activities undertaken. Such reports should include, as appropriate, the information identified in the Visit Report form suggested by SCAR. Parties should maintain a record of such activities, and, in the Annual Exchange of Information, should provide summary descriptions of activities conducted by persons subject to their jurisdiction, which should be in sufficient detail to allow evaluation of the effectiveness of the management plan. Parties should, wherever possible, deposit originals or copies of such original reports in a publicly accessible archive to maintain a record of usage, to be used both in any review of the management plan and in organizing the scientific use of the Area.

8. References

Androsova, E.I.. Antarctic and Subantarctic bryozoans // Soviet Antarctic Expedition Newsletter.-1973.-No. 87.-P.65-69. (in Russian)

Averintsev, V.G. Ecology of sublittoral polychaetes in the Davis Sea // Animal Morphology, Systematics and Evolution.-L.,1978.-P.41-42. (in Russian)

Averintsev, V.G. Seasonal variations of sublittoral polychaetes in the Davis Sea // Marine Fauna Studies.-L.,1982.-Vol.. 28(36).-P.4-70. (in Russian)

Barbroud C. & Weimerskirch H. 2001 Emperor Penguins and climate change. Nature, 411: 183 – 185.

Barbroud C., Gavrilo M., Mizin Yu., Weimerskirch H. Comparison of emperor penguin declines between Pointe Géologie and Haswell Island over the past 50 years. Antarctic Science. V. 23. P. 461–468 doi:10.1017/S0954102011000356

Budylenko, G.A., and Pervushin, A.S. The migration of finwhales, sei whales and Minke whales in the Southern Hemisphere // Marine Mammals: Proceedings of VI All-Union Meeting.-Kiev, 1975.-Part.1.-P.57-59. (in Russian)

Bushueva, I.V. A new Acanthonotozommella species in the Davis Sea (East Antarctica) // Zool. Zhurn.-1978.-Vol.57, issue 3.-P.450-453. (in Russian)

Bushueva, I.V. A new Pseudharpinia (Amphipoda) species in the Davis Sea (Antarctica) // Zool. Zhurn.-1982.-Vol.61, issue.8.-P.1262-1265.

Bushueva, I.V. Some peculiarities of off-shore amphipod (Gammaridea) distribution in the Davis Sea (East Antarctica) // Hydrobiology and Biogeography of Cold and Moderate World Ocean Waters in the Off-shore Zone: Report Abstracts.-L.,1974.-P.48-49. (in Russian)

Bushueva, I.V. Some peculiarities of Paramola walkeri ecology in the Davis Sea (East Antarctica) // Off-shore Biology: Abstracts of Reports Presented at the All-Union Conference. - Vladivostok,1975.-P.21-22. (in Russian)

Chernov, A., Mizin, Yu. 2001 Avifauna observations at Mirny Station during RAE 44 (1999-2000) — The State of the Antarctic Environment as Shown by Real-time Data from Russia's Antarctic Stations. — SPb: AARI. (in Russian)

Doroshenko, N.V. The distribution of Minke whales (Balaenoptera acutorostrata Lac) in the Southern Hemisphere // V All-Union Meeting on Marine Mammal Research: Report Abstracts. - Makhachkala, 1972.-Part1.-P.181-185. (in Russian)

Egorova, E.N. Biogeographic composition and possible development of gastropods and bivalves in the Davis Sea, // Soviet Antarctic Expedition Newsletter.-1972.-No. 83.-P.70-76. (in Russian)

Egorova, E.N. Mollusks of the Davis Sea (East Antarctica).- L.:Nauka, 1982.-144 pp. - (Marine Fauna Research; No. 26(34). (in Russian)

Egorova, E.N. Zoogeographic composition of the mollusk fauna in the Davis Sea (East Antarctica) // Mollusks. Major Results of the Study: VI All-Union Mollusk Research Meeting.- L.,1979.-Vol.6.-P..78-79. (in Russian)

Gavrilo, M.V., Chupin, I.I., Mizin, Yu.A., and Chernov A.S. 2002. Study of the Biological Diversity of Antarctic Seabirds and Mammals. – Report on Antarctic Studies and Research under the World Ocean Federal Targeted Program. SPb: AARI (unpublished). (in Russian)

Gavrilo M., Mizin Yu. 2007. Penguin population dynamics in Haswell Archipelago area, ASPA № 127, East Antarctica. – p. 92 in Wohler E.j. (ed.) 2007. Abstracts of oral and poster presentations, 6th International Penguin Conference. Hobart, Australia, 3-7 September 2007

Gavrilo M., Mizin I. Current zoological researches in the area of Mirny station.Russian Polar Researches. Iss. 3. AARI, 2011.

Golubev S.V. 2012. Report on ecological and environmental studies at Mirny station during 57 RAE. St.P.,AARI (in Russian) (unpublished)

Golubev S.V. 2016. Report on ecological and environmental studies at Mirny station during 60 RAE. St.P.,AARI (in Russian) (unpublished)

Gruzov, E.N. Echinoderms in coastal biocenoses of the Davis Sea (Antarctica) // Systematics, Evolution, Biology, and Distribution of Modern and Extinct Echinoderms.-L.,1977.-P.21-23. (in Russian)

Kamenev, V.M. Adaptive peculiarities of the reproduction cycle of some Antarctic birds. - Body Adaptation to Far North Conditions: Abstracts of Reports Presented at the All-Union Meeting. Tallinn, 1984. P. 72-76. (in Russian)

Kamenev, V.M. Antarctic petrels of Haswell Island // Soviet Antarctic Expedition Newsletter.-1979.-No. 99.-P.78-84. (in Russian)

Kamenev, V.M. Ecology of Adelie penguins of the Haswell Islands // Soviet Antarctic Expedition Newsletter. 1971. No. 82. P. 67-71. (in Russian)

Kamenev, V.M. Ecology of Cape and snow petrels. - Soviet Antarctic Expedition Newsletter. 1988. No. 110. P. 117-129. (in Russian)

Kamenev, V.M. Ecology of Emperor penguins of the Haswell Islands. – The Adaptation of Penguins. M., 1977. P. 141-156. (in Russian)

Kamenev, V.M. Ecology of Wilson's storm petrels (Oceanites oceanicus Kuhl) on the Haswell Islands // Soviet Antarctic Expedition Newsletter. 1977. No. 94. P. 49-57. (in Russian)

Kamenev, V.M. Protected Antarctica. – Lecturer's Aid. L.: Znanie RSFSR, 1986. P. 1-17. (in Russian)

Kamenev, V.M. The Antarctic fulmar (Fulmarus glacialoides) of the Haswell Islands // Soviet Antarctic Expedition Newsletter. - 1978. No. 98. P. 76-82. (in Russian)

Korotkevish, E.P. 1959 The bids of East Antarctica. – Arctic and Antarctic Issues. – No. 1. (in Russian)

Korotkevish, E.P. 1960 By radio from Antarctica. — Soviet Antarctic Expedition Newsletter. - № 20-24. (in Russian)

Krylov, V.I., Medvedev, L.P. The distribution of the Ceteans in the Atlantic and South Oceans // Soviet Antarctic Expedition Newsletter.-1971.-No. 82.-P.64-66. (in Russian)

Makushok, V.M. 1959 Biological takings and observations at the Mirny Observatory in 1958. — Soviet Antarctic Expedition Newsletter. – No. 6. (in Russian)

Minichev, Yu.R. Opisthobranchia (Gastropoda, Opisthobranchia) of the Davis Sea // Marine Fauna Research.-L.,1972.-Vol.11(19).-P.358-382. (in Russian)

Mizin, Yu.V. 2004 Report on the Ecological and Environmental Research Program Conducted by RAE 48 at the Mirny Observatory – SPb: AARI, unpublished. (in Russian)

Neelov A.V., Smirnov I.S., Gavrilo M.V. 2007 50 years of the Russian studies of antarctic ecosystems. – Problemy Arktiki I Antarktiki. – № 76. – Pp. 113 – 130

Popov, L.A., Studenetskaya, I.R. Ice-based Antarctic seals // The Use of the World Ocean Resources for Fishery Needs. An overview by the Central Research Institute of Fishery Information and Technical Studies. Series. 1.- M., 1971. Issue 5.-P.3-42. (in Russian)

Prior, M.E. 1964 Observations of Emperor penguins (Aptenodytes forsteri Gray) in the Mirny area in 1962. Soviet Antarctic Expedition Newsletter. – No. 47. (in Russian)

Pushkin, A.F. Some ecological and zoogeographic peculiarities of the Pantopoda fauna in the Davis Sea // Hydrobiology and Biogeography of Cold and Moderate World Ocean Waters in the Off-shore Zone: Report Abstracts.- L.,1974.-P.43-45. (in Russian)

Splettstoesser J.F., Maria Gavrilo, Carmen Field, Conrad Field, Peter Harrison, M. Messicl, P. Oxford, F. Todd 2000 Notes on Antarctic wildlife: Ross seals *Ommatophoca rossii* and Emperor penguins *Aptenodytes forsteri*. New Zealand Journal of Zoology, 27: 137-142.

Stepaniants, R.D. Coastal hydrozoans of the Davis Sea (materials of the 11th Soviet Antarctic Expedition, 1965/66) // Marine Fauna Research.- L.,1972.-Vol.11(19).-P.56-79. (in Russian)

The Final Report of the Twenty Second Antarctic Treaty Consultative Meeting (Tromse, Norway, May 25 – June 5, 1998). [Oslo, Royal Ministry of Foreign Affairs], P. – 93 – 130. (in Russian).

Map 1: Location of the Haswell Islands, Mirny Station, and logistic activity sites.

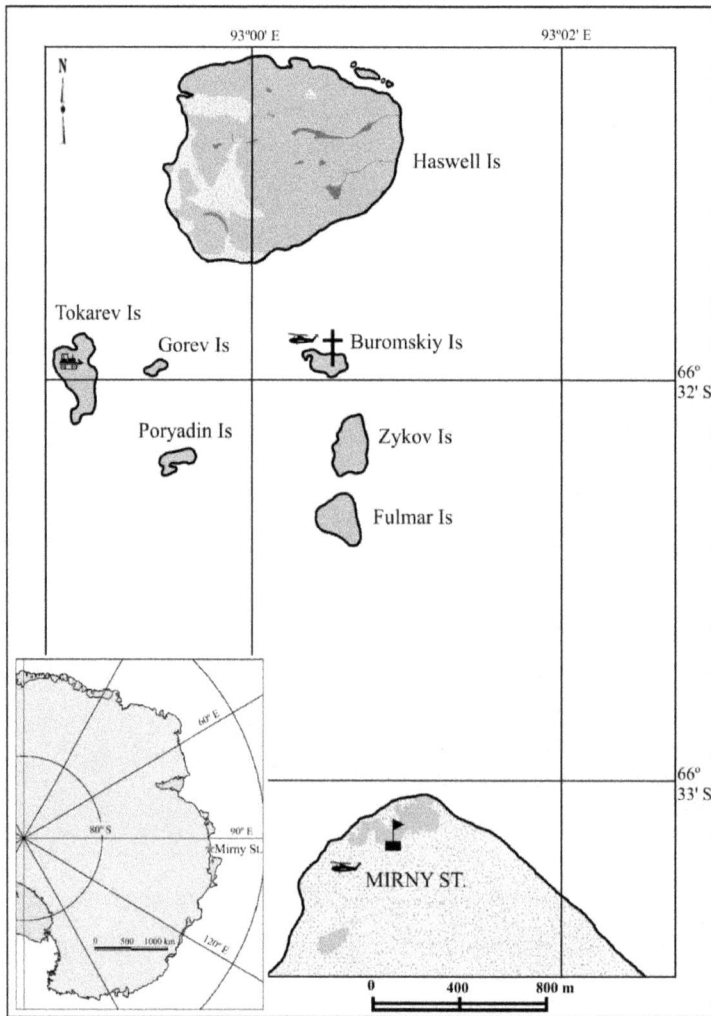

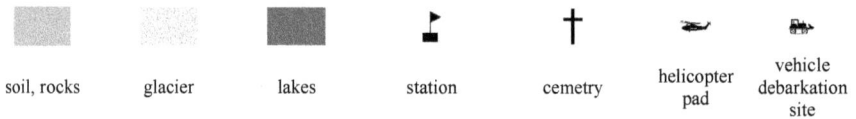

Map 2: Boundaries of Antarctic Specially Protected Area 127, Haswell Island.

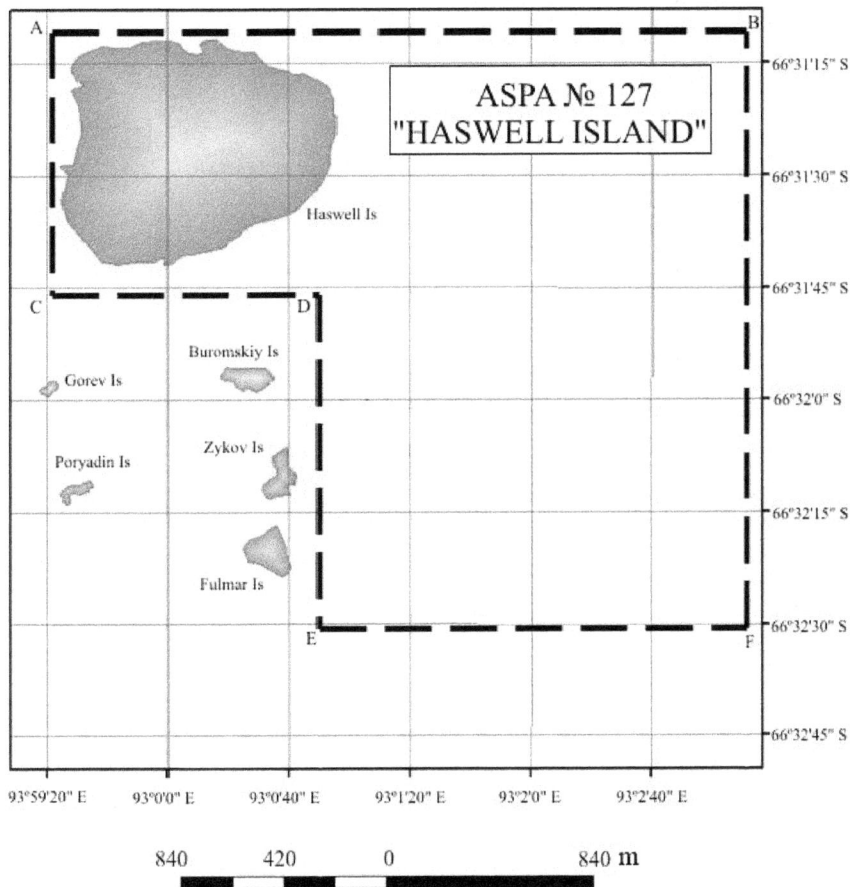

Map 3: Location of breeding seabird colonies.

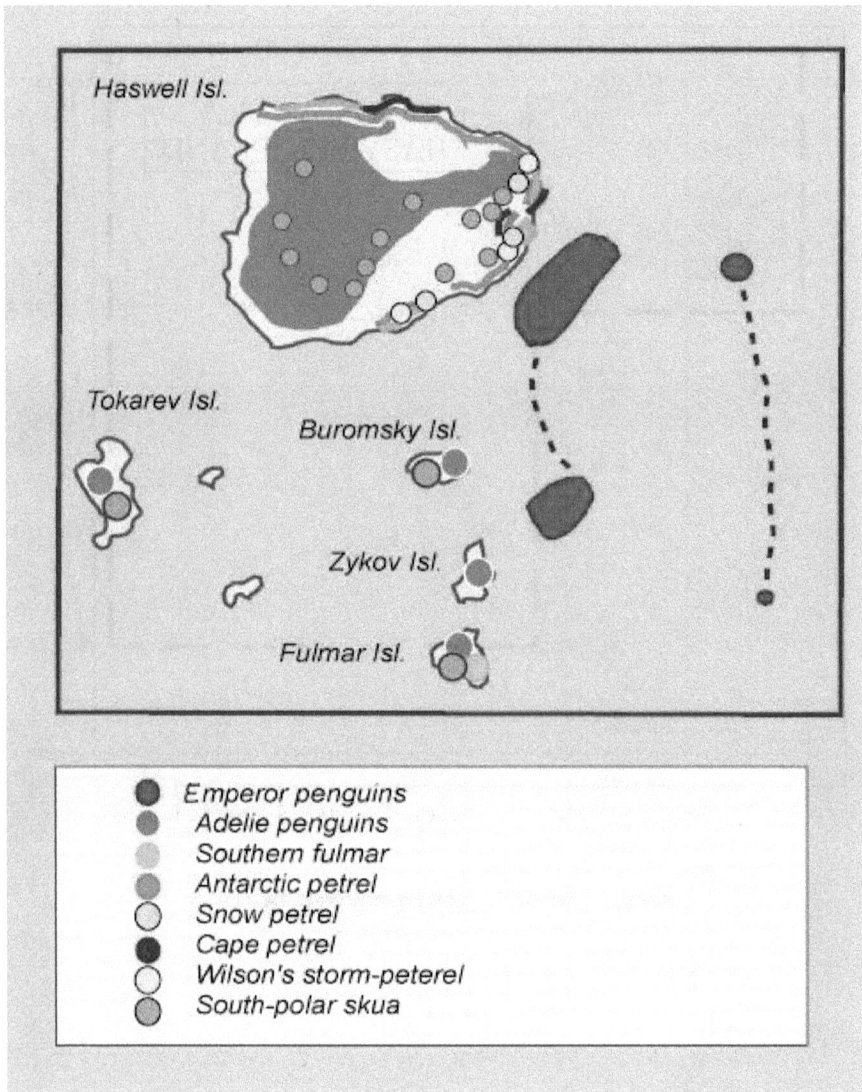

Haswell Isl.

Tokarev Isl.

Buromsky Isl.

Zykov Isl.

Fulmar Isl.

Emperor penguins
Adelie penguins
Southern fulmar
Antarctic petrel
Snow petrel
Cape petrel
Wilson's storm-peterel
South-polar skua

Map 4: Topographic map of Haswell Island.

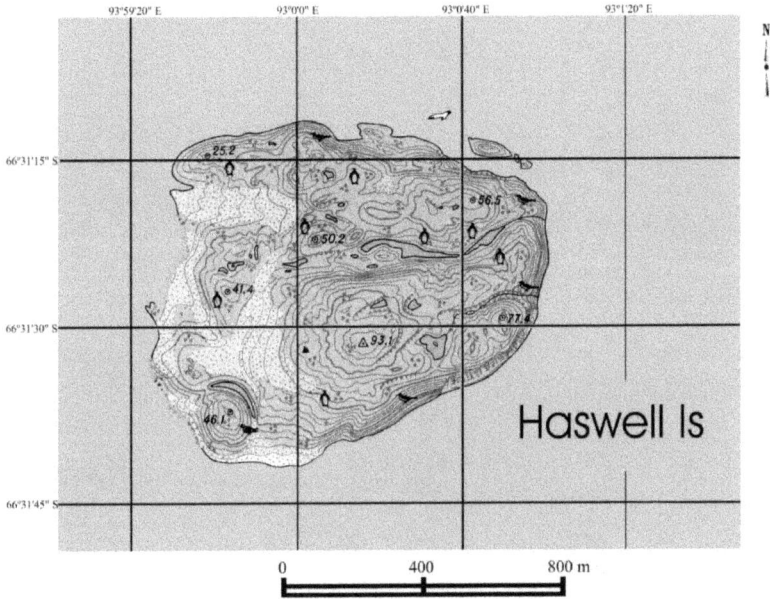

Management Plan For
Antarctic Specially Protected Area No. 131
CANADA GLACIER, LAKE FRYXELL, TAYLOR VALLEY, VICTORIA LAND

1. Description of values to be protected

An area of approximately 1 km^2 between the east side of Canada Glacier and Lake Fryxell was originally designated in Recommendation XIII-8 (1985) as SSSI No. 12 after a proposal by New Zealand on the grounds that it contains some of the richest plant growth (bryophytes and algae) in the McMurdo Dry Valleys. The Area is designated primarily to protect the site's scientific and ecological values.

The boundaries of the Area were increased by Measure 3 (1997) to include biologically rich areas that were previously excluded. The Area was redesignated by Decision 1 (2002) as Antarctic Specially Protected Area (ASPA) No. 131. and a revised Management Plan was adopted through Measure 1 (2006) and Measure 6 (2011).

The Area comprises sloping ice-free ground with summer ponds and small meltwater streams draining from Canada Glacier towards Lake Fryxell. Most of the plant growth occurs in a wet area (referred to as 'the flush') close to the glacier in the central part of the Area. The composition and distribution of the moss, lichen, cyanobacteria, bacteria and algae communities in the Area are correlated closely with the water regime. Thus, hydrology and water quality are important to the values of the site.

The Area has been well-studied and documented, which adds to its scientific value. The vegetation communities, particularly the bryophytes, are vulnerable to disturbance by trampling and sampling. Damaged areas may be slow to recover. Sites damaged at known times in the past have been identified, which are valuable in that they provide one of the few areas in the McMurdo Dry Valleys where the long-term effects of disturbance, and recovery rates, can be measured.

The Area is of regional significance and remains of exceptional scientific value for ecological investigations. Increasing pressure from scientific, logistic and tourist activities in the region coupled with the vulnerability of the Area to disturbance through trampling, sampling, pollution or introduction of non-native species mean the values of the Area continues to require on-going protection.

2. Aims and objectives

Management of Canada Glacier aims to:

- avoid degradation of, or substantial risk to, the values of the Area by preventing unnecessary human disturbance to the Area;
- allow scientific research on the ecosystem and elements of the ecosystem while ensuring protection from over-sampling;
- allow other scientific research in the Area provided it is for compelling reasons which cannot be served elsewhere;

- prevent or minimise the introduction to the Area of alien plants, animals and microbes; and
- allow visits for management purposes in support of the aims of the management plan.

3. Management activities

The following management activities are to be undertaken to protect the values of the Area:

- Copies of this Management Plan, including maps of the Area, shall be made available at adjacent operational research stations and all of the research hut facilities located in the Taylor Valley that are within 20 km of the Area.
- Rock cairns or signs illustrating the location and boundaries, with clear statements of entry restrictions, shall be placed at appropriate locations on the boundary of the Area to help avoid inadvertent entry.
- Markers, signs or other structures erected within the Area for scientific or management purposes shall be secured and maintained in good condition and removed when no longer required.
- The Area shall be visited as necessary, and no less than once every five years, to assess whether it continues to serve the purposes for which it was designated and to ensure that management activities are adequate.
- National Antarctic Programmes operating in the Area shall consult together with a view to ensuring the above management activities are implemented.

4. Period of designation

Designated for an indefinite period.

5. Maps

Map A: ASPA No. 131 Canada Glacier: Regional Map.
Map specifications: Projection - Lambert conformal conic. Standard parallels - 1st 77° 35' 00" S; 2nd 77° 38' 00"S. Central Meridian - 163° 00' 00" E. Latitude of Origin - 78° 00' 00" S. Spheroid - WGS84.

Map B:ASPA 131 Canada Glacier: Vegetation density map.
Map specifications are the same as those for Map A. Contours are derived from combining orthophotograph and Landsat images. Precise areas of moist ground associated with the flush are subject to variation seasonally and inter-annually.

6. Description of the Area

6(i) Geographical coordinates, boundary markers and natural features
Canada Glacier is situated in the Taylor Valley, in the McMurdo Dry Valleys. The designated Area encompasses most of the glacier forefront area on the east side of the lower Canada Glacier, on the north shore of Lake Fryxell (77° 37' S, 163° 03' E: Map A). It comprises gently to moderately sloping ice-free ground at an elevation of 20 m to 220 m with seasonal melt water ponds and streams draining Canada Glacier into Lake Fryxell.

The southern boundary of the Area is defined as the shoreline of Lake Fryxell, to the water's edge. The lake level is currently rising. This boundary extends northeast for approximately 1 km along the shoreline from where Canada Glacier meets Lake Fryxell (77° 37.20' S, 163° 3.64' E) to the southeast corner of the boundary which is marked with a cairn (77° 36.83' S, 163° 4.88' E) adjacent to a small island in Lake Fryxell. The island was once a part of a small peninsula extending into Lake Fryxell but recent lake level rise has turned it into an island (Map B). The peninsula was once marked by a large split rock surrounded by a circle of rocks which was a benchmark for the 1985 NZ survey of the original SSSI, but is no longer visible. A wooden post marking the Dry Valley Drilling Project Site 7 (1973) is still visible on the island.

A moraine ridge extending upslope from the southeast corner of the boundary in a northerly direction defines the eastern boundary of the Area. A cairn (77° 36.68' S, 163° 4.40' E) is located on a knoll on this ridge 450 m from the southeast corner of the boundary. The ridge dips sharply before joining the featureless slope of the main Taylor Valley wall. The northeast boundary corner of the Area is in this dip and is marked by a cairn (77° 36.43' S, 163° 3.73' E).

From the northeast boundary cairn, the northern boundary slopes gently upwards and west for 1.7 km to Canada Glacier, to the point where the stream flows from the glacier and snow field, through a conspicuously narrow gap in the moraine (77° 36.42' S, 162° 59.69' E).

The western boundary follows the glacier edge for about 1 km, down a slope of lateral moraine of fairly even gradient to the southwest corner of the boundary where the glacier meets the lake shore (77° 37.20' S, 163° 3.64' E).

The flush area at Canada Glacier is believed to be the largest high density area of vegetation in the McMurdo Dry Valleys (Map B). The summer water flow, in conjunction with the microtopography, has the greatest influence in determining where mosses, lichens, cyanobacteria, bacteria and algae grow. The glacier face also provides protection from destructive winds which could blow the mosses away in their freeze dry state and from abrasion from wind borne dust.

The flush is located close to the glacier edge. There are two main vegetated areas, separated to the north and south by a small, shallow pond (Map B). The flush area is gently sloping and very moist in summer with areas of wet ground, numerous small ponds and rivulets. The slopes above this area are drier, but vegetation colonises several small stream channels which extend parallel to the glacier from the upper boundary of the Area down to the flush. Undulating moraines assist accumulation of persistent snow patches on this slope, which may also provide moisture for plant growth. Stream channels, and associated vegetation, become less obvious with distance from the glacier (Map B). These slopes and the central flush are drained to the southeast by Canada Stream. Prior to 1983, Canada Stream was informally known as Fryxell Stream.

Four moss species have been identified from the flush area: *Bryum argenteum* (previously referred to as *Bryum subrotundifolium)* and *Hennediella heimii* (previously referred to as *Pottia heimii)* dominate, with rare occurrences of *Bryum pseudotriquetrum* and *Syntrichia sarconeurum* (formerly known as *Sarconeurum glaciale)*. *B. argenteum* occurs mainly in areas of flowing water and seepage. Where water is flowing, a high proportion of this moss has epiphytic *Nostoc* communities associated with it. Towards the edges of the flowing water zones or on higher ground, *Hennediella heimii* dominates. Sporophytes of *Hennediella heimii* are found at this location and may be one of the most southerly recorded fruiting location for a moss.

Lichen growth in the Area is inconspicuous, but the epilithic lichens, *Carbonea vorticosa, Sarcogyne privigna, Lecanora expectans, Rhizoplaca melanophthalma* and *Caloplaca citrina* may be found in a small area near the outflow of the pond near Canada Glacier. Chasmoendolithic lichens also occur in many boulders throughout the flush area.

Over 37 species of freshwater algae and cyanobacteria have been described at the site. The upper part of Canada Stream superficially appears sparse but encrusting communities dominated by cyanobacterium grow on the sides and undersides of stones and boulders. The green alga *Prasiola calophylla* and cyanobacterium *Chamaesiphon subglobosus* have been observed only in this upper part of the stream. *Prasiola calophylla,* growing in dense green ribbons beneath stones in the stream, is generally only apparent when stones are overturned. Cyanobacterial mats, comprising a diverse assemblage of species (including *Oscillatoria, Pseudanabaena, Leptolyngbya, Phormidium, Gloeocapsa, Calothrix* and *Nostoc*) are extensive in the middle and lower reaches of the stream and more diverse than those in the upper stream. Mucilaginous colonies of *Nostoc commune* dominate standing water in the central flush and grow epiphytically on mosses in the wetted margins of water courses, while cyanobacterial mats cover much of the mineral fines and gravels in flowing sections. The filamentous green alga *Binuclearia* is found streaming out in the flow in the middle reaches of the stream. The lower stream is similar in floral composition to the upper, although the algae *Tribonema elegans* and *Binuclearia* have been reported as abundant, but *Prasiola calophylla* is absent. *Tribonema elegans* is rarely encountered in this region of Antarctica.

Invertebrates from six phyla have been described in the Area: the three main groups are Rotifera, Nematoda and Tardigrada, with Protozoa, Platyhelminthes, and Arthropoda also present. There are no records of Collembola found in the Area, though there are records where they have been found nearby outside the Area.

The Canada flush vegetation has been described as profuse but lacking in diversity, when compared to other botanically rich sites in Antarctica. This may be attributable at least in part to the oligotrophic nature of the site. Water flowing through the stream is similar to glacial ice melt, with conductivity in December 2014 of close to 35.32 µS cm^{-1} from the point where it left the glacier to the delta where it enters the lake. The prevalence of nitrogen fixing cyanobacteria (*Nostoc* and *Calothrix* species) further supports the view of a low nutrient status.

Canada Glacier is located within Environment S – McMurdo - South Victoria Land geologic based on the Environmental Domains Analysis for Antarctica (Resolution 3 (2008)) and in Region 9 – South Victoria Land based on the Antarctic Conservation Biogeographic Regions (Resolution 6 (2012).

Evidence of past human activity is noticeable within the Area. Indications of past human activity are likely to be found in the soils adjacent to the original New Zealand hut and helicopter landing site. These may be in the form of localised areas of petrochemical residues and soil nutrients. Within the flush area, damage to the vegetation including paths and footprints and sites of experimental removal of core samples and larger clumps from moss turfs are visible. A number of old markers are also present in the flush area.

A plastic greenhouse was erected within the Area close to the flush from 1979 to 1983 for research and experimental growth of garden vegetables. The structure was removed at the end of each season. In 1983 it was destroyed by a winter storm. Remains of the greenhouse found in the Area have since been removed.

Near the flush area, the first site of the New Zealand hut at Canada Glacier consisted of paths marked by lines of rocks, areas cleared for use as campsites, an old helicopter pad, and several low rock structures. A series of at least four shallow pits (~1 m in depth) were also dug close to the site. This site was relocated to a second site in 1989 and the first hut site was remediated. The second hut site comprised two small buildings, several new campsites, and a helicopter pad. The buildings were removed completely in the 1995–96 season. However, the helicopter pad remains and is the only helicopter landing site in the Area. This camp site area is still the preferred camping site in the Area (Map B) and the paths marked by lines of rocks and areas cleared for use as campsites are still present.

A weir is present on Canada Stream (see Section 6(iii)). Hydrological data collected from this stream measured the average discharge rate of Canada Stream when it was flowing as 22.13 L/s [min = 0.0 L/s and max = 395.76 L/s] from November 2014 to February 2015. The average water temperature over this time was 1.99 °C [min = -1.1 °C and max = 11.34 °C] (http://www.mcmlter.org/).

A path from the Lake Fryxell Camp Facilities Zone is located between the lake shore and the weir on Canada Stream (Map B). Another path exists between the designated camp site and the Canada Glacier edge, crossing a moist area of plant growth, but is not indicated on the map. An access route is also located between the Lake Hoare Camp Facilities Zone and the Lake Fryxell Camp Facilities Zone running just above the northern boundary (Maps A and B).

6(ii) Special zones within the Area
None.

6(iii) Location of structures within and adjacent to the Area
A rock weir was constructed in the constricted part of Canada Stream in the 1981/1982 season and was fully removed at the end of the season. In 1990 a more substantial weir and 9-inch Parshall flume were installed nearby (Maps B). The flume is made of black fibreglass. The weir consists of polyester sandbags filled with alluvium from near the stream channel. Areas disturbed during construction were restored and after one season were not evident. The upstream side of the weir is lined with vinyl-coated nylon. A notch has been built into the weir for relief in case of high flow. Clearance of seasonal snow from the channel has been necessary to prevent water from backing up at the weir. Data logging instrumentation and batteries are stored in a plywood crate located nearby on the north side of the stream. The weir is maintained by the McMurdo Dry Valleys Long Term Ecological Research project.

Three cairns mark the Area boundaries.

The Lake Fryxell Camp Facilities Zone (USA) is located 1.5 km to the east of the Area (20 m asl) midway along Lake Fryxell on the north side of the lake. The F6 Camp Facilities Zone (USA) is located approximately 10 km to the east of the Area on the south side of Lake Fryxell. The Lake

Hoare Camp Facilities Zone (USA) is located 3 km to the west of the Area (65 m asl) on the western side of Canada Glacier at the base of the glacier on the north side of Lake Hoare. The Taylor Valley Visitor Zone is located to the south of the Area at the terminus of Canada Glacier (Map A).

6(iv) Location of other protected areas in the vicinity
The nearest protected areas to Canada Glacier are:

- Lower Taylor Glacier and Blood Falls, Taylor Valley, McMurdo Dry Valley (ASPA No. 172) approximately 23 km west in the Taylor Valley;
- Linnaeus Terrace, Asgard Range (ASPA No. 138) approximately 47 km west in the Wright Valley; and
- Barwick and Balham Valleys, Southern Victoria Land (ASPA No. 123) approximately 50 km to the northwest (Map A, Inset).

7. Terms and conditions for entry Permits

Entry into the Area is prohibited except in accordance with a Permit issued by an appropriate national authority. Conditions for issuing a Permit to enter the Area are that:
- it is issued for compelling scientific reasons that cannot be served elsewhere, or for reasons essential to the management of the Area;
- the actions permitted will not jeopardise the ecological or scientific values of the Area;
- access to any zone marked as possessing medium or higher vegetation density (Map B) should be carefully considered and special conditions to access such areas should be attached to the Permit;
- any management activities are in support of the aims of the Management Plan;
- the actions permitted are in accordance with the Management Plan;
- the Permit, or an authorized copy, shall be carried within the Area;
- a visit report shall be supplied to the authority named in the Permit; and
- Permits shall be issued for a stated period.

7(i) Access to and movement within or over the Area
Access to the Area shall be primarily by foot or for essential scientific reasons, by helicopter. Vehicles are prohibited within the Area and all movement within the Area should be on foot.

Pedestrians travelling up or down the valley shall not enter the Area without a Permit. Permitted visitors entering the Area are encouraged to keep to established paths where possible. Visitors should avoid walking on visible vegetation or through stream beds. Care should be exercised when walking in areas of moist ground, where foot traffic can easily damage sensitive soils, plant, algal and bacteria communities, and degrade water quality: walk around such areas, on ice or rocky ground, and step on larger stones when stream crossing is unavoidable. Care should also be taken around salt-encrusted vegetation in drier areas, which can be inconspicuous. Pedestrian traffic should be kept to the minimum necessary consistent with the objectives of any permitted activities and every reasonable effort should be made to minimise effects.

Where possible, helicopters should land at existing landing sites in nearby Facilities Zones (Lake Hoare and Lake Fryxell) and/or the Taylor Valley Visitor Zone. If requiring access to the Area by helicopter, helicopters should approach the Area from south of the line marked on the accompanying site map (Map B). Helicopters shall land only at the designated landing site (163° 02.88' E, 77°

36.97' S: Map B). Over flight of the Area should generally be avoided. Within the Area overflights less than 100 m Above Ground Level (AGL) north of the line indicated on Map B is prohibited. Exceptions to these flight restrictions will only be granted for an exceptional scientific or management purpose and must be specifically authorised by Permit. Use of helicopter smoke grenades within the Area is prohibited unless absolutely necessary for safety, and then these should be retrieved. Visitors, pilots, air crew, or passengers en route elsewhere on helicopters, are prohibited from moving on foot beyond the immediate vicinity of the designated landing and camping site unless specifically authorised by a Permit.

7(ii) Activities which may be conducted in the Area
- Scientific research that will not jeopardise the ecosystem of the Area;
- Essential management activities, including monitoring and inspection.

In view of the importance of the water regime to the ecosystem, activities should be conducted so that disturbance to water courses and water quality is minimised. Activities occurring outside of the Area (e.g. on the Canada Glacier) which may have the potential to affect water quantity and quality should be planned and conducted taking possible downstream effects into account. Those conducting activities within the Area should also be mindful of any downstream effects within the Area and on endorheic Lake Fryxell.

Activities which cause disturbance to the flush area should take into account the slow recovery rates of the vegetation at this site. In particular, consideration should be given to minimising any required sample sizes and sample numbers and conducting the sampling regime in such a way that full recovery of the vegetation community is likely.

7(iii) Installation, modification or removal of structures
No structures are to be erected within the Area, or scientific equipment installed, except for compelling scientific or management reasons, as specified in a permit. All markers, structures or scientific equipment installed in the Area must be authorised by a Permit and clearly identified by country, name of the principal investigator, year of installation and date of expected removal. All such items should be free of organisms, propagules (e.g. seeds, eggs) and non-sterile soil, and be made of materials that pose minimal risk of contamination of the Area. Removal of specific structures or equipment for which the Permit has expired shall be a condition of the Permit. Permanent structures or installations are prohibited.

7(iv) Location of field camps
Nearby Facilities Zones outside of the Area should be used as a base for work in the Area (Map A). Camping at the designated campsite (Map B) may be permitted to meet specific essential scientific or management needs.

7(v) Restrictions on materials and organisms which may be brought into the Area
No living animals, plant material or microorganisms shall be deliberately introduced into the Area and precautions listed in 7(ix) shall be taken against accidental introductions. No herbicides or pesticides shall be brought into the Area. Any other chemicals, including radio-nuclides or stable isotopes, which may be introduced for scientific or management purposes specified in the Permit, shall be removed from the Area at or before the conclusion of the activity for which the Permit was granted. Fuel or other chemicals shall not be stored in the Area, unless required for essential purposes connected with the activity for which the Permit has been granted, and must be contained within an emergency cache authorized by an appropriate authority. All materials introduced shall be for a stated period only, shall be removed at or before the conclusion of that stated period, and shall be stored and handled so that risk of their introduction into the environment is minimised.

7(vi) Taking or harmful interference with native flora or fauna
Taking of, or harmful interference with, native flora and fauna is prohibited, except in accordance with a separate permit issued in accordance with Annex II to the Protocol on Environmental Protection to the Antarctic Treaty. Where taking or harmful interference with animals is involved this should, as a minimum standard, be in accordance with the SCAR Code of Conduct for the Use of Animals for Scientific Purposes in Antarctica.

Material may be collected or removed from the Area only in accordance with a Permit and should be limited to the minimum number of samples necessary to meet scientific or management needs. Sampling is to be carried out using techniques which minimise disturbance to the Area and from which full recovery of the vegetation from sampling can be expected.

7(vii) The collection or removal of materials not imported by the Permit holder
Material of human origin likely to compromise the values of the Area, and which was not brought into the Area by the Permit holder or otherwise authorised, may be removed unless the impact of removal is likely to be greater than leaving the material in situ: if this is the case the appropriate authority should be notified and approval obtained prior to removal of the items.

7(viii) Disposal of waste
All wastes, including all human wastes, shall be removed from the Area.

7(ix) Measures that may be necessary to continue to meet the aims and objectives of the Management Plan
Permits may be granted to enter the Area to:
- carry out biological monitoring and Area inspection activities, which may involve the collection of a small number of samples or data for analysis or review;
- erect or maintain signposts, structures or scientific equipment;
- carry out protective measures;

Any specific sites of long-term monitoring shall be appropriately marked on site and on maps of the Area. A GPS position should be obtained for lodgement with the Antarctic Master Directory system through the appropriate national authority.

To help maintain the ecological and scientific values of the plant communities found at the Area visitors shall take special precautions against introductions. Of particular concern are microbial or vegetation introductions sourced from soils at other Antarctic sites, including stations, or from regions outside Antarctica. To minimise the risk of introductions, visitors shall thoroughly clean footwear and any equipment to be used in the area particularly camping and sampling equipment and markers before entering the Area.

7(x) Requirements for reports
The principal permit holder for each visit to the Area shall submit a report to the appropriate national authority as soon as practicable, and no later than six months after the visit has been completed. Such visit reports should include, as applicable, the information identified in the recommended visit report form [contained in Appendix 4 of the Guide to the Preparation of Management Plans for Antarctic Specially Protected Areas appended to Resolution 2 (1998)] [available from the website of the Secretariat of the Antarctic Treaty www.ats.aq].

If appropriate, the national authority should also forward a copy of the visit report to the Party that proposed the Management Plan, to assist in managing the Area and reviewing the Management Plan. Parties should maintain a record of such activities and report them in the Annual Exchange of Information. Parties should, wherever possible, deposit originals or copies of such original visit reports in a publicly accessible archive to maintain a record of usage, for the purpose of any review of the management plan and in organising the scientific use of the Area.

8. Bibliography

Broady, P.A. 1982. Taxonomy and ecology of algae in a freshwater stream in Taylor Valley, Victoria Land, Antarctica. Archivs fur Hydrobiologia 32 (Supplement 63 (3), Algological Studies): 331-349.

Conovitz, P.A., McKnight, D.M., MacDonald, L.H., Fountain, A.G. and House, H.R. 1998. Hydrologic processes influencing stream flow variation in Fryxell Basin, Antarctica. Ecosystem Processes in a Polar Desert: The McMurdo Dry Valleys, Antarctica. Antarctic Research Series 72: 93-108.

Downes, M.T., Howard-Williams, C. and Vincent, W.F. 1986. Sources of organic nitrogen, phosphorus and carbon in Antarctic streams. Hydrobiologia 134: 215-225.

Fortner, S.K., Lyons, W.B. and Munk, L. 2013. Diel stream geochemistry, Taylor Valley, Antarctica. Hydrological Processes 27: 394-404.

Fortner, S.K., Lyons, W.B. and Olesik, J.W. 2011. Eolian deposition of trace elements onto Taylor Valley Antarctic glaciers. Applied Geochemistry 26: 1897-1904.

Green, T.G.A., Seppelt, R.D. and Schwarz, A-M.J. 1992. Epilithic lichens on the floor of the Taylor Valley, Ross Dependency, Antarctica. Lichenologist 24(1): 57-61.

Howard-Williams, C., Priscu, J.C. and Vincent, W.F. 1989. Nitrogen dynamics in two Antarctic streams. Hydrobiologia 172: 51-61.

Howard-Williams, C. and Vincent, W.F. 1989. Microbial communities in Southern Victoria Land streams I: Photosynthesis. Hydrobiologia: 172: 27-38.

Howard-Williams, C., Vincent, C.L., Broady, P.A. and Vincent, W.F. 1986. Antarctic stream ecosystems: Variability in environmental properties and algal community structure. Internationale Revue der gesamten Hydrobiologie 71: 511-544.

Lewis, K.J., Fountain, A.G. and Dana, G.L. 1999. How important is terminus cliff melt? A study of the Canada Glacier terminus, Taylor Valley, Antarctica. Global and Planetary Change 22(1-4): 105-115.

Lewis, K.J., Fountain, A.G. and Dana, G.L. 1998. Surface energy balance and meltwater production for a Dry Valley glacier, Taylor Valley, Antarctica. International Symposium on Antarctica and Global Change: Interactions and Impacts, Hobart, Tasmania, Australia, July 13-18, 1997. Papers. Edited by W.F. Budd, et al; Annals of glaciology, Vol.27, p.603-609. United Kingdom.

McKnight, D.M. and Tate, C.M. 1997. Canada Stream: A glacial meltwater stream in Taylor Valley, South Victoria Land, Antarctica. Journal of the North American Benthological Society 16(1): 14-17.

Pannewitz, S., Green, T.G.A., Scheiddegger, C., Schlensog, M. and Schroeter, B. 2003. Activity pattern of the moss *Hennediella heimii* (Hedw.) Zand. in the Dry Valleys, Southern Victoria Land, Antarctica during the mid-austral summer. Polar Biology 26(8): 545-551.

Seppelt, R.D. and Green, T.G.A. 1998. A bryophyte flora for Southern Victoria Land, Antarctica. New Zealand Journal of Botany 36: 617-635.

Seppelt, R.D., Green, T.G.A., Schwarz, A-M.J. and Frost, A. 1992. Extreme southern locations for moss sporophytes in Antarctica. Antarctic Science 4: 37-39.

Seppelt, R.D., Turk, R., Green, T.G.A., Moser, G., Pannewitz, S., Sancho, L.G. and Schroeter, B. 2010. Lichen and moss communities of Botany Bay, Granite Harbour, Ross Sea, Antarctica. Antarctic Science 22(6): 691-702.

Schwarz, A.-M. J., Green, J.D., Green, T.G.A. and Seppelt, R.D. 1993. Invertebrates associated with moss communities at Canada Glacier, southern Victoria Land, Antarctica. Polar Biology 13(3): 157-162.

Schwarz, A-M. J., Green, T.G.A. and Seppelt, R.D. 1992. Terrestrial vegetation at Canada Glacier, South Victoria Land, Antarctica. Polar Biology 12: 397-404.

Sjoling, S. and Cowan, D.A. 2000. Detecting human bacterial contamination in Antarctic soils. Polar Biology 23(9): 644-650.

Skotnicki, M.L., Ninham, J.A. and Selkirk, P.M. 1999. Genetic diversity and dispersal of the moss *Sarconeurum glaciale* on Ross Island, East Antarctica. Molecular Ecology 8(5): 753-762.

Strandtmann, R.W. and George, J.E. 1973. Distribution of the Antarctic mite *Stereotydeus mollis* Womersley and Strandtmann in South Victoria Land. Antarctic Journal of the USA 8:209-211.

Vandal, G.M., Mason, R.P., McKnight, D.M. and Fitzgerald, W. 1998. Mercury speciation and distribution in a polar desert lake (Lake Hoare, Antarctica) and two glacial meltwater streams. Science of the Total Environment 213(1-3): 229-237.

Vincent, W.F. and Howard-Williams, C. 1989. Microbial communities in Southern Victoria Land Streams II: The effects of low temperature. Hydrobiologia 172: 39-49.

Map A: ASPA No. 131 Canada Glacier: Regional map

Environmental Research & Assessment
Issued 24 Mar 2016

Antarctica New Zealand

Map B: ASPA No. 131 Canada Glacier: Vegetation density map

Environmental Research & Assessment
Issued 04 Apr 2016

103

Management Plan for

Antarctic Specially Protected Area (ASPA) No. 149

CAPE SHIRREFF AND SAN TELMO ISLAND, LIVINGSTON ISLAND,

SOUTH SHETLAND ISLANDS

Introduction

The Cape Shirreff Antarctic Specially Protected Area (ASPA) is situated on the northern coast of Livingston Island, South Shetland Islands, at 60°47'17"W, 62°27'30"S, and is approximately 9.7 km² in area. The primary reason for designation of the Area is to protect the biota present within the Area, in particular the large and diverse seabird and pinniped populations which are the subject of long-term scientific monitoring. Krill fishing is carried out within the foraging range of these species. Cape Shirreff is thus a key site for ecosystem monitoring, which helps to meet the objectives of the Convention on the Conservation of Antarctic Marine Living Resources (CCAMLR). The Area contains the largest Antarctic fur seal (*Arctocephalus gazella*) breeding colony in the Antarctic Peninsula region and is the most southerly colony where fur seal reproduction, demography and diet can be monitored. Palynoflora discovered within the Area are of significant scientific interest. The Area also contains numerous items of historical and archaeological value, mostly associated with sealing activities in the 19th Century. The Area was originally designated following proposals by Chile and the United States of America and adopted through Recommendation IV-11 [1966, Specially Protected Area (SPA) No. 11]. The Area was re-designated as Site of Special Scientific

Interest (SSSI) No. 32 through Recommendation XV-7 (1989). The Area was designated as CCAMLR Ecosystem Monitoring Program (CEMP) Site No. 2 through CCAMLR Conservation Measure 82/XIII (1994); protection was continued by Conservation Measure (CM) 91/02 (2004) and boundaries were extended through Measure 2 (2005) to include a larger marine component and to incorporate plant fossil sites. Conservation Measure 91-02 was lapsed in November 2009 and protection of Cape Shirreff continues as ASPA No. 149 (SC-CAMLR-XXVIII, Annex 4, para 5.29). The Management Plan was revised through Measure 7 (2011).

The Area lies within 'Environment E – Antarctic Peninsula, Alexander and other islands and 'Environment G – Antarctic Peninsula offshore islands, as defined in the Environmental Domains Analysis for Antarctica (Resolution 3 (2008)). Under the Antarctic Conservation Biogeographic Regions classification (Resolution 6 (2012)) the Area lies within ACBR3 – North-west Antarctic Peninsula.

1. Description of values to be protected

Cape Shirreff (60°47'17" W, 62°27'30" S, a peninsula of approximately 3.1 km²), Livingston Island, South Shetland Islands, was originally designated as Specially Protected Area (SPA) No. 11 through Recommendation IV-11 (1966). In the light of results from the first census of Pinnipedia carried out in the South Shetland Islands (Aguayo and Torres, 1966), Chile considered special protection for the site was needed. Formal proposal of the SPA was made by the United States (U.S.). The Area included the ice-free ground of the Cape Shirreff peninsula north of the Livingston Island ice cap margin. Values protected under the original designation included the diversity of plant and animal life, many invertebrates, a substantial population of southern elephant seals (*Mirounga leonina*) and a small colony of Antarctic fur seals (*Arctocephalus gazella*).

Following designation, the size of the Cape Shirreff Antarctic fur seal colony increased to a level at which biological research could be undertaken without threatening continued colony growth. A survey of the South Shetland Islands and the Antarctic Peninsula identified Cape Shirreff – San Telmo Island as the most suitable site to monitor Antarctic fur seal colonies potentially affected by fisheries around the South Shetland Islands. In order to accommodate the monitoring program, the SPA was redesignated as Site of Special Scientific Interest (SSSI) No. 32 through Recommendation XV-7 (1989) following a joint proposal by Chile, the United Kingdom and the United States. Designation was on the grounds that the "presence of both Antarctic fur seal and penguin colonies, and of krill fisheries within the foraging ranges of these species, make this a critical site for inclusion in the ecosystem monitoring network being established to help meet the objectives of the Convention on the Conservation of Antarctic Marine Living Resources (CCAMLR). The purpose of the designation is to allow planned research and monitoring to proceed, while avoiding or reducing, to the greatest extent possible, other activities which could interfere with or affect the results of the research and monitoring program or alter the natural features of the Site". The boundaries were enlarged to include San Telmo Island and associated nearby islets. Following a proposal prepared by Chile and the United States, the Area was subsequently designated as CCAMLR Ecosystem Monitoring Program (CEMP) Site No. 2 through CCAMLR Conservation Measure 82/XIII (1994), with boundaries identical to SSSI No. 32. Protection of Cape Shirreff as a CCAMLR Ecosystem Monitoring Program (CEMP) was continued by Conservation Measure (CM) 91/02 (2004).

The boundaries of the Area were further enlarged through Measure 2 (2005) to include a larger marine component and to incorporate two new sites where plant fossils were discovered in 2001 (Maps 1 and 2). The designated Area (9.7 km^2) comprises the entire Cape Shirreff peninsula north of the Livingston Island permanent ice cap, the adjacent part of the Livingston Island permanent ice cap where the fossil discoveries were made in 2001, the San Telmo Island group, and the surrounding and intervening marine area enclosed within 100 m of the coast of the Cape Shirreff peninsula and of the outer islets of the San Telmo Island group. The boundary extends from the San Telmo Island group to the south of Mercury Bluff.

Conservation Measure 91-02 lapsed in November 2009, with the protection of Cape Shirreff continuing under the Management Plan for ASPA No. 149 (SC-CAMLR-XXVIII, Annex 4, para 5.29). The change was made with the aim of harmonizing protection under both CCAMLR and the Protocol on Environmental Protection to the Antarctic Treaty (The Protocol) and to eliminate any potential duplication in management requirements and procedures.

The current Management Plan reaffirms the exceptional scientific and monitoring values associated with the large and diverse populations of seabirds and pinnipeds which breed within the Area, and in particular those of the Antarctic fur seal colony. The Antarctic fur seal colony is the largest in the Antarctic Peninsula region and is the most southerly that is large enough to study growth, survival, diet, and reproduction parameters: it numbered around 21,000 individuals in 2002 (Hucke-Gaete *et al.* 2004). Monitoring of the Antarctic fur seal colony began in 1965 (Aguayo and Torres 1966, 1967) and seasonal data are available from 1991, making this one of the longest continuous Antarctic fur seal monitoring programs. As part of the CCAMLR Ecosystem Monitoring Program (CEMP), monitoring was established to detect and avoid possible adverse effects of fisheries on dependant species such as pinnipeds and seabirds, as well as target species such as Antarctic krill (*Euphausia superba*). Long-term studies are assessing and monitoring the survival, feeding ecology, growth, condition, reproduction, behavior, vital rates, and abundance of pinnipeds and seabirds that breed within the Area. Data from these studies will be evaluated in context with environmental and other biological data and fisheries statistics to help identify possible cause-effect relationships between fisheries and pinniped and seabird populations.

In 2001/02 imprints of megaflora were discovered in rocks incorporated within moraines of the Livingston Island glacier (Palma-Heldt *et al.* 2004, 2007) (Map 2). The fossiliferous rocks were found to contain two distinct palynological assemblages, indicative of different time periods and climatic conditions, and formed part of a study into the geological history of Antarctica and Gondwana. Studies of microbial research were carried out within the Area in 2009/10, to assess the influence of microhabitats on microbial diversity and metabolic capacity (INACH 2010).

The original values of the protected area associated with the plant and invertebrate communities cannot be confirmed as primary reasons for special protection of the Area because there is a lack of data available describing the communities.

The Area contains a number of pre-1958 human artifacts. Historic Site & Monument (HSM) No.59, a rock cairn commemorating those who died when the Spanish ship San Telmo sank in the Drake Passage in 1819, lies within the Area. Remnants of a 19th Century sealing community also can be found within the Area.

2.   Aims and objectives

Management at Cape Shirreff aims to:

- avoid degradation of, or substantial risk to, the values of the Area by preventing unnecessary human disturbance;

- avoid activities that would harm or interfere with CEMP research and monitoring activities;
- allow scientific research on the ecosystem and physical environment in the Area associated with the CEMP;
- allow other scientific research within the Area provided it is for compelling reasons which cannot be served elsewhere and provided it will not compromise the values for which the Area is protected;
- allow archaeological and historical research and measures for artifact protection, while protecting the historic artifacts present within the Area from unnecessary destruction, disturbance, or removal;
- minimize the possibility of introduction of alien plants, animals and microbes to the Area; and
- allow visits for management purposes in support of the aims of the Management Plan.

3. Management activities

The following management activities shall be undertaken to protect the values of the Area:

- Copies of this Management Plan, including maps of the Area, shall be made available at the following locations:
  1. accommodation facilities at Cape Shirreff;
  2. Saint Kliment Ohridski Station (Bulgaria), Hurd Peninsula, Livingston Island;
  3. Arturo Prat Station (Chile), Discovery Bay/Chile Bay, Greenwich Island;
  4. Base Juan Carlos I (Spain), Hurd Peninsula, Livingston Island;
  5. Julio Escudero Station (Chile), Fildes Peninsula, King George Island; and
  6. Eduardo Frei Station (Chile), Fildes Peninsula, King George Island.
- A sign showing the location and boundaries of the Area with clear statements of entry restrictions should be placed at Módulo Beach, Cape Shirreff, to help avoid inadvertent entry;
- Markers, signs or other structures erected within the Area for scientific or management purposes shall be secured and maintained in good condition;
- National Antarctic programs operating within the Area should maintain a record of all new markers, signs and structures erected within the Area;
- Visits shall be made as necessary (no less than once every five years) to assess whether the Area continues to serve the purposes for which it was designated and to ensure management and maintenance measures are adequate;
- National Antarctic programs operating in the region shall consult together for the purpose of ensuring that the above provisions are implemented.

4. Period of designation

Designated for an indefinite period.

5. Maps

Map 1: Cape Shirreff and San Telmo Island, ASPA No. 149, in relation to Livingston Island, showing the location of Base Juan Carlos I (Spain) and Saint Kliment Ohridiski Station (Bulgaria), and the location of the closest protected area, Byers Peninsula (ASPA No. 126), also on Livingston Island. Map specifications: Projection: Lambert Conformal Conic; Standard parallels: 1st 60°00' S; 2nd 64°00' S; Central Meridian: 60°45' W; Latitude of Origin: 62°00' S; Spheroid: WGS84; Horizontal accuracy: < ±200 m. Bathymetric contour interval 50 m and 200 m; vertical accuracy unknown. Data sources: land features from SCAR Antarctic Digital Database v6 (2012); bathymetry supplied by the U.S. Antarctic Marine Living Resources (U.S. AMLR) Program, NOAA (2002) and IBCSO (v1.0 2013) (http://ibcso.org).

Inset: the location of Map 1 in relation to the South Shetland Islands and the Antarctic Peninsula.

Map 2: Cape Shirreff and San Telmo Island, ASPA No. 149, boundary and access guidelines. Map specifications as per Map 1, except the vertical contour interval is 10 m and the horizontal accuracy is expected to be greater than ±5 m. Data source: from digital data supplied by Instituto Antártico Chileno (INACH) (2002) (Torres *et al.* 2001), except small boat landing site supplied by M. Goebel (Dec 2015).

Map 3: Cape Shirreff, ASPA No. 149: breeding wildlife and human features. Map specifications and data source as per Map 2 with the exception of the vertical contour interval, which is 5 m. Seal tracking station and HSM: D. Krause (Dec 2015). Walking routes and fauna: INACH, updated by M. Goebel and D. Krause (Dec 2015).

6. Description of the Area

6(i) Geographical coordinates, boundary markers and natural features

Boundaries and coordinates

Cape Shirreff (60°47'17" W, 62°27'30" S) is situated on the northern coast of Livingston Island, the second largest of the South Shetland Islands, between Barclay Bay and Hero Bay (Map 1). The cape lies at the northern extremity of an ice-free peninsula of low-lying, hilly relief. To the west of the peninsula lies Shirreff Cove, to the east Black Point, and to the south lies the permanent ice cap of Livingston Island. The peninsula has an area of approximately 3.1 km², being 2.6 km from north to south and ranging from 0.5 to 1.5 km from east to west. The interior of the peninsula comprises a series of raised beaches and both rounded and steep-sided hills, rising to a high point at Toqui Hill (82 m) in the central northern part of the peninsula. The western coast is formed by almost continuous cliffs 10 to 15 m high, while the eastern coast has extensive sand and gravel beaches.

A small group of low-lying, rocky islets lie approximately 1200 m west of the Cape Shirreff peninsula, forming the western enclosure of Shirreff Cove. San Telmo Island, the largest of the group, is 950 m in length, up to 200 m in width, and of approximately 0.1 km² in area. There is a sand and pebble beach on the southeastern coast of San Telmo Island, separated from a sand beach to the north by two irregular cliffs and narrow pebble beaches.

The designated Area comprises the entire Cape Shirreff peninsula north of the permanent Livingston Island ice cap, the San Telmo Island group, and the surrounding and intervening marine area (Map 2). The marine boundary encloses an area that extends 100 m from, and parallel to, the outer coastline of the Cape Shirreff peninsula and the San Telmo Island group. In the north, the marine boundary extends from the northwestern extremity of the Cape Shirreff peninsula to the southwest for 1.4 km to the San Telmo Island group, enclosing the intervening sea within Shirreff Cove. The western boundary extends southwards for 1.8 km from 62°28' S to a small island near 62°29' S, passing around the western shore of this small island and proceeding a further 1.2 km south-east to the shore of Livingston Island at 62°29'30" S, which is approximately 300 m south of Mercury Bluff. From this point on the coast, the southern boundary extends approximately 300 m due east to 60°49' W, from where it proceeds in a northeasterly direction parallel to the coast for approximately 2 km to the ice sheet margin at 60°47' W. The southern boundary then extends due east for 600 m to the eastern coast. The eastern boundary is marine, following the eastern coastline 100 m from the shore. The boundary encompasses an area of 9.7 km² (Map 2).

Climate

Meteorological records for Cape Shirreff have been collected for a number of years by Chilean and U.S. scientists and are currently recorded by instruments mounted on the Cape Shirreff Field Station buildings. During recent summer seasons (Nov – Feb inclusive, 2005/06 to 2009/10) the mean air temperature recorded at Cape Shirreff was 1.84°C (U.S. AMLR Program data, 2005-2010). The maximum air temperature recorded during this period was 19.9°C and the minimum was -8.1°C. Wind speed averaged 5.36 m/s and the maximum recorded wind speed reached 20.1 m/s. Wind direction over the data collection period was predominantly from the west, followed by WNW and ENE. Meteorological data are available for two recent winters, with mean daily temperature for Jun-Aug 2007 of -6.7°C with a minimum of -20.6°C and a maximum of +0.9°C, and a mean daily temperature for Jun-Sep 2009 of -5.8°C with a minimum of -15.2°C and a maximum of +1.9°C.

Precipitation recorded in summer seasons (21 Dec – 24 Feb, 1998-2001) ranged from 56.0 mm (recorded on 36 days in 2000/01) to 59.6 mm (recorded on 43 days in 1998/99) (Goebel *et al.* 2000; 2001). The peninsula is snow-covered for much of the year, but is mostly snow-free by the end of the summer.

Geology, geomorphology and soils

Cape Shirreff is composed of porphyritic basaltic lavas and minor volcanic breccias of approximately 450 m in thickness (Smellie *et al.* 1996). The rocks at Cape Shirreff are deformed into open folds, which trend in a NW-SE direction, and subvertical axial surfaces that are intruded by numerous dykes. A rock sample obtained from the southern side of Cape Shirreff was identified as fresh olivine basalt and was composed of approximately 4% olivine and 10% plagioclase phenocrysts in a groundmass of plagioclase, clinopyroxene and opaque oxide. Rock samples at Cape Shirreff have been K-Ar dated as of late Cretaceous age with a minimum age of 90.2± 5.6 million years old (Smellie *et al.* 1996). The volcanic sequences at Cape Shirreff form part of a broader group of relatively fresh basalt and andesite lavas covering eastern-central Livingston Island that are similar to basalts found on Byers Peninsula.

The Cape Shirreff peninsula is predominantly a raised marine platform, 46 to 53 m above sea level, (Bonner and Smith 1985). The bedrock is largely covered by weathered rock and glacial deposits. Two lower platforms, covered with rounded water-worn pebbles, occur at elevations of approximately 7-9 m and 12-15 m above Mean Sea Level (MSL) (Hobbs 1968).

There is little information on the soils of Cape Shirreff. They are mainly fine, highly porous, ash and scoria. The soils support a sparse vegetation and are enriched by bird and seal colonies which inhabit the Area.

Paleontology

A fossilized wood specimen belonging to the Araucariaceae family (*Araucarioxylon* sp.) was recorded from Cape Shirreff (Torres, 1993). It is similar to fossils found at Byers Peninsula (ASPA No. 126), a site with rich fossil flora and fauna 20 km to the southwest. Several fossil specimens have also been found at the northern extremity of the Cape Shirreff peninsula. In 2001/02 fossiliferous rocks of two different ages were discovered incorporated within frontal and lateral moraines of the Livingston Island permanent ice cap (Map 2). Study of the palynomorphs found within the moraines identified two distinct palynological assemblages, arbitrarily named 'Type A' and 'B' (Palma-Held *et al.* 2004, 2007). The 'Type A' association was dominated by Pteridophyta, mainly Cyatheaceae and Gleicheniaceae, and by *Podocarpidites* spp. and also contained *Myrtaceidites eugenioides* and epiphyllous fungal spores. The assemblage is believed to be indicative of warm and humid conditions of Early Cretaceous in age (Palma-Heldt *et al.* 2007). The 'Type B' assemblage was characterized by a subantarctic flora with *Nothofagidites, Araucariacites australis, Podocarpidites otagoensis, P. marwickii, Proteacidites parvus* and also epiphyllous fungal spores, which indicate a cold and humid temperate climate (Palma-Heldt *et al.* 2007). The age of the assemblage is estimated to be Late Cretaceous-Paleogene (Palma-Heldt *et al.* 2004; Leppe *et al.* 2003). Palynological investigations were undertaken at Cape Shirreff in order to investigate the evolution of the southern Pacific margin of Gondwana and to develop a model of the Mesozoic-Cenozoic evolution of the Antarctic Peninsula. It has been noted that other fossils may be revealed by further recession of the Livingston Island permanent ice cap (D. Torres, A. Aguayo and J. Acevedo, pers. comm. 2010).

Streams and lakes

There is one permanent lake on Cape Shirreff, located north and at the base of Toqui Hill (Map 3). The lake is approximately 2-3 m deep and 12 m long at full capacity, diminishing in size after February (Torres 1995). Moss banks grow on surrounding slopes. There are also several ephemeral ponds and streams on the peninsula, fed by snow-melt, especially in January and February. The largest of the streams is found draining southwestern slopes toward the coast at Yamana Beach.

Vegetation and invertebrates

Although a comprehensive survey of the vegetation communities at Cape Shirreff has not been undertaken, Cape Shirreff appears to be less well vegetated than many other sites in the South Shetland Islands. Observations to date have recorded one grass, five species of moss, six of lichen, one fungi and one nitrophilous macroalgae (Torres 1995).

Patches of Antarctic hairgrass (*Deschampsia antarctica*) can be found in some valleys, often growing with mosses. Mosses are predominantly found inland from the coast. In a valley running northwest from Half Moon Beach, there is a moderately well-developed wet moss carpet of *Warnstorfia laculosa* (=*Calliergidium austro-stramineum*, also =*Calliergon sarmentosum*) (Bonner 1989, in Heap 1994). In areas with better drainage, *Sanionia uncinata* (=*Drepanocladus uncinatus*) and *Polytrichastrum alpinum* (=*Polytrichum alpinum*) are found. The raised beach areas and some higher plateaus have extensive stands of the foliose nitrophilous macroalga *Prasiola crispa*, which is characteristic of areas enriched by animal excreta and has been observed to replace moss-lichen associations damaged by fur seals (Bonner 1989, in Heap 1994).

The six lichen species thus far described at Cape Shirreff are *Caloplaca spp, Umbilicaria antarctica, Usnea antarctica, U. fasciata, Xanthoria candelaria* and *X. elegans*. The fruticose species *Umbilicaria antarctica, Usnea antarctica* and *U. fasciata* form dense growths on cliff faces and on the tops of steep rocks (Bonner 1989, in Heap 1994). The bright yellow and orange crustose lichens *Caloplaca spp, Xanthoria candelaria* and *X. elegans* are common beneath bird colonies and are also present with the fruticose species. The identity of the single recorded fungal species is unknown.

The invertebrate fauna at Cape Shirreff has not been described.

Microbial ecology

Field studies of the microbial ecology at Cape Shirreff were carried out 11-21 January 2010 and results were compared with the bacterial communities present at Fildes Peninsula, King George Island. The study aimed to evaluate the influence of the different microhabitats on the biodiversity and metabolic capacities of bacterial communities found at Cape Shirreff and Fildes Peninsula (INACH, 2010).

Breeding birds

The avifauna of Cape Shirreff is diverse, with ten species known to breed within the Area, and several non-breeding species present. Chinstrap (*Pygoscelis antarctica*) and gentoo (*P. papua*) penguins breed within the Area; Adélie penguins (*P. adeliae*) have not been observed to breed on Cape Shirreff or San Telmo Island, although are widely distributed throughout the region. Both chinstrap and gentoo penguins are found in small colonies on the northeastern and northwestern coasts of Cape Shirreff peninsula (Map 3). Data have been collected on the chinstrap and gentoo penguin colonies every summer season since 1996/97, including reproductive success, demography, diet, foraging and diving behaviour (e.g. Hinke *et al.* 2007; Pietrzak *et al.* 2009, Polito *et al.* 2015). During the 2009/10 summer season, chinstrap and gentoo penguins at Cape Shirreff were tagged with satellite transmitters, in order to study their over-winter behaviour.

Data available on penguin numbers are presented in Table 1. In 2015/16 there were 19 active breeding sub-colonies at Cape Shirreff, with a total of 655 gentoo and 3302 chinstrap penguin nests (U.S. AMLR unpublished data), although the number of the sub-colonies and their composition show some inter-annual variation. From the late 1990's to 2004, the numbers of chinstrap penguins at Cape Shirreff declined significantly, whilst gentoo populations showed no discernible trend (Hinke *et al.* 2007). The negative trend in chinstrap numbers has continued and nest counts for both penguin species reached their lowest for 11 years in 2007/08, due to poor weather conditions (Chisholm *et al.* 2008; Miller and Trivelpiece 2008). In 2008/09 the population and reproductive success of both gentoos and chinstraps at Cape Shirreff increased significantly in comparison to the previous season but numbers of chinstrap nests remained 30% below average for the site (Pietrzak *et al.* 2009). The differing trends in chinstrap and gentoo populations at Cape Shirreff have been attributed to the higher winter juvenile mortality rate experienced by chinstraps (Hinke *et al.* 2007) and a greater flexibility in feeding patterns exhibited by gentoos (Miller *et al.* 2009).

In general, the chinstrap penguins nest on higher escarpments at Cape Shirreff, although they are also found breeding on small promontories near the shore. Gentoo penguins tend to breed on more gentle slopes and rounded promontories. During the period of chick rearing, foraging by both species of penguin is confined to the shelf region, approximately 20 to 30km offshore of Cape Shirreff (Miller and Trivelpiece 2007). During the 2010/11 and 2012/13 seasons unmanned aerial systems were tested to aid in estimating penguin abundance (Goebel *et al.* 2015).

Several other species breed within the Area (Map 3), although data on numbers are patchy. Kelp gulls (*Larus domincanus)* and brown skuas (*Catharacta antarctica*) nest in abundance along the entire coastline of the Area. In 2000 there were 25 and 22 breeding pairs of these species respectively (U.S. AMLR, pers. comm. 2000). In 2007/08, 24 pairs of skuas were identified at Cape Shirreff and near Mercury Bluff, of which 23 were brown skuas (*Catharacta antarctica*) and one pair was a hybrid of brown-south polar skuas (*C. maccormicki*). Fifty-six kelp gull nests were observed at Cape Shirreff during the 2006/07 season. Reproductive success of skuas and kelp gulls has been regularly monitored during recent summer seasons at nesting sites around Cape Shirreff (Chisholm *et al.* 2008; Pietrzak *et al.* 2009).

Sheathbills (*Chionis alba*) nest in two places: one pair has been recorded nesting on the western coast of the Cape Shirreff peninsula; a second pair has been observed breeding among rocks at the northern beach on San Telmo Island, near an Antarctic fur seal breeding site (Torres, pers. comm. 2002). Antarctic terns (*Sterna vittata*) breed in several locations, which have been observed to vary from year to year. Since 1990/91 a small colony of approximately 11 pairs of Antarctic shag (*Phalacrocorax* [atriceps] *bransfieldensis*) has been observed breeding on Yeco Rocks, on the western coast of the peninsula (Torres, 1995). Cape petrels (*Daption capense*) breed on cliffs on the western coast of the Area; 14 pairs were recorded in January 1993, nine in January 1994, three in January 1995 and eight in 1999. Wilson's storm petrel (*Oceanites oceanicus*) also breed on the western coast of the Area. Black-bellied storm petrel (*Fregetta tropica*) have been observed to breed near the field camp on the eastern coast. A large number of non-breeding southern giant petrels (*Macronectes giganteus*) frequent the Area in the summer, but a report of a breeding colony on the peninsula (Bonner 1989, in Heap 1994) is incorrect (Torres, pers. comm. 2002). Other bird species recorded but not breeding within the Area include macaroni penguin (*Eudyptes chrysolophus*), king penguin (*Aptenodytes patagonicus*), emperor penguin (*Aptenodytes forsteri*), snow petrel (*Pagadroma nivea*), white-rumped sandpiper (*Calidris fuscicollis*), black-necked swan (*Cygnus melanocoryphus*), and the cattle egret *Bubulcus ibis* (Torres 1995; Olavarría *et al.* 1999). Additional bird species recorded as foraging close to Cape Shirreff include the black-browed albatross (*Thalassarche melanophris*) and gray-headed albatross (*T. chrysostoma*), although neither species has yet been recorded within the Area (Cox *et al.* 2009).

Table 1: Chinstrap (*Pygoscelis antarctica)* and gentoo (*P. papua*) penguin numbers at Cape Shirreff.

Year	Chinstrap (pairs)	Gentoo (pairs)	Source
1958	2000 (N3[1])	200-500 (N1[1])	Croxall and Kirkwood, 1979
1981	2164 (A4)	843 (A4)	Sallaberry and Schlatter, 1983 [2]
1987	5200 (A3)	300 (N4)	Woehler, 1993
1997	6907 (N1)	682 (N1)	Hucke-Gaete *et al.* 1997a
1999/00	7744 (N1)	922 (N1)	U.S. AMLR data, Carten *et al.* 2001
2000/01	7212 (N1)	1043 (N1)	U.S. AMLR data, Taft *et al.* 2001
2001/02	6606	907	U.S. AMLR data, Saxer *et al.* 2003
2002/03	5868 (A3)	778 (A3)	U.S. AMLR data, Shill *et al.* 2003
2003/04	5636 (N1)	751 (N1)	U.S. AMLR data, Antolos *et al.* 2004
2004/05	4907 (N1)	818 (N1)	U.S. AMLR data, Miller *et al.* 2005
2005/06	4849 (N1)	807 (N1)	U.S. AMLR data, Leung *et al.* 2006
2006/07	4544 (N1)	781 (N1)	U.S. AMLR data, Orben *et al.* 2007
2007/08	3032 (N1)	610 (N1)	U.S. AMLR data, Chisholm *et al.* 2008
2008/09	4026 (N1)	879 (N1)	U.S. AMLR data, Pietrzak *et al.* 2009

Year	Chinstrap (pairs)	Gentoo (pairs)	Source
2009/10	4339 (N1)	802 (N1)	U.S. AMLR data, Pietrzak *et al.* 2011
2010/11	4127 (N1)	834 (N1)	U.S. AMLR data, Mudge *et al.* 2014
2011/12	4100 (N1)	829 (N1)	U.S. AMLR unpublished data
2012/13	4200 (N1)	853 (N1)	U.S. AMLR unpublished data
2013/14	3582 (N1)	839 (N1)	U.S. AMLR unpublished data
2014/15	3464 (N1)	721 (N1)	U.S. AMLR unpublished data
2015/16	3302 (N1)	655 (N1)	U.S. AMLR unpublished data

1. Alphanumeric code refers to the type of count, as in Woehler (1993).
2. Reported data did not specify species. It has been assumed that the higher number referred to chinstrap penguins. Data were reported as individuals, which have been halved to derive 'pairs' in the table.

Breeding mammals

Cape Shirreff (including San Telmo Island) is presently the site of the largest known breeding colony of the Antarctic fur seal in the Antarctic Peninsula region. Antarctic fur seals were once abundant throughout the South Shetland Islands but were hunted to local extinction between 1820 and 1824. The next observation of Antarctic fur seals at Cape Shirreff was on 14 January 1958, when 27 animals were recorded, including seven juveniles (Tufft 1958). The following season, on 31 January 1959, a group of seven adult males, one female and one male pup were recorded, along with one dead male pup (O'Gorman, 1961). A second female arrived three days later, and, by mid-March, 32 Antarctic fur seals were present. By 2002, the estimated Antarctic fur seal population at Cape Shirreff (excluding San Telmo Island) increased to 14,842 animals (including 6,453 pups), with the total population (including San Telmo Island) being 21,190 animals (including 8,577 pups) (Hucke-Gaete *et al.* 2004). More recent data on Antarctic fur seal numbers have yet to be published. However, the present number of Antarctic fur seals at Cape Shirreff remains an order of magnitude lower than pre-exploitation populations, and it is unclear whether numbers will recover to their previous levels (Hucke-Gaete *et al.* 2004).

Antarctic fur seal breeding sites at Cape Shirreff are concentrated around the coastline of the northern half of the peninsula (Map 3). At San Telmo Island, breeding is concentrated at both ends of the island, with juveniles commonly found near the middle (Torres 1995). Long-term monitoring of Antarctic fur seals has been carried at Cape Shirreff since 1991, with the primary objective of studying breeding success in relation to prey availability, environmental variability and human impacts (Osman *et al.* 2004). Researchers have studied various aspects of the fur seal colony, including pup production, predation and growth, female attendance behavior, seal diet and diving and foraging (Goebel et al. 2014).. Genetic analysis to investigate the recolonization of Antarctic fur seals at Cape Shirreff from the putative source population at South Georgia has been conducted and highly significant genetic differences have been found, which indicates that even relict populations can recover without losing genetic diversity (Bonin *et al.* 2013). The Antarctic fur seal colony at Cape Shirreff has also been used to study the genetic analysis of twin pups, which are rare among pinnipeds (Bonin *et al.* 2012).

During the 2010/11 season, the U.S. AMLR program reported a 14% reduction in pup production from the previous summer season (Goebel *et al.* 2014). Pup production at Cape Shirreff was particularly low during the 2007/08, 2008/09, 2009/10 and 2010/11 seasons, with all of them showing a double-digit decline, most likely as a result of unfavorable winter conditions and a change in demography with an increase in older female seals, leading to lower reproductive rates and higher mortality (Goebel *et al.* 2008, 2009, 2011, 2014). During recent seasons, growth rates of fur seal pups within the Area have been studied in relation to sex, breeding season and maternal foraging and attendance (Vargas *et al.* 2009, McDonald *et al.* 2012a, 2012b). Studies on population dynamics have also been undertaken, with results showing that without the top-down impact from predation the Antarctic fur seal colony would most likely increase, despite the bottom-up effects of climate change (Schwarz *et al.* 2013).

A small number of southern elephant seals breed in October on several eastern beaches (U.S. AMLR, pers. comm. 2000; Torres, pers. comm. 2002). On 2 Nov 1999 34 pups were counted on beaches south of Condor Hill (U.S. AMLR, unpublished data). During the 2008/09 season, a total of 40 southern elephant seal pups were born near Cape Shirreff (Goebel *et al.* 2009). During the 2010/11 season a total of 31 pups were born near Cape Shirreff pups (Goebel *et al.* 2014).

Groups of non-breeding southern elephant seals are also present, while isolated animals, mainly juveniles, may be found on various beaches. The maximum number of southern elephant seals during the 2010/11 season at Cape Shirreff was 221 individuals (Goebel *et al.* 2014). The foraging behavior of southern elephant seals has been studied using satellite tracking of animals tagged at Cape Shirreff and analyzed in relation to the physical properties of the water column (Huckstadt *et al.* 2006; Goebel *et al.* 2009). Seals were found to forage as far afield as the Amundsen Sea and one animal was observed travelling 4,700 km due west of the Antarctic Peninsula.

Weddell seals, leopard seals and crabeater seals have been observed, although do not breed, on the Cape Shirreff peninsula and are the subject of monitoring programs (O'Gorman 1961; Bengtson *et al.* 1990; Oliva *et al.* 1988; Torres 1995; Goebel, pers. comm. 2015). During the 2010/11 season the maximum recorded number of Weddell seals was 48 individuals, 19 individuals of leopard seals and 2 individuals of crabeater seals (Goebel *et al.* 2014). Monitoring of leopard seal predation on the Antarctic fur seal population was initiated in 2001/02 and was recorded during the 2003/04 Antarctic season (Vera *et al.* 2004). Leopard seals hauling out at Cape Shirreff have been fitted with HD video cameras, GPS and time-depth recorders to monitor their foraging range, and hunting strategies (Krause *et al.* 2015). Observations of leopard seal feeding behaviour and pup survival studies suggest that they consume up to half of all Antarctic fur seal pups born within the Area each year (Goebel *et al.* 2008, 2009). In addition to fur seal pups and penguins, leopard seals were found to take two species of demersal fish (*Gobionotothen gibberifrons and Notothenia coriiceps*), and scavenge carcasses of fur seals and penguins (Krause et al. *in press*). DNA samples are frequently collected from four seal species at Cape Shirreff and stored in the Southwest Fisheries Science Center DNA archives (Goebel *et al.* 2009). During the 2009/10, 2010/11, 2011/12, and 2014/15 summer seasons, researchers deployed archival tags on Antarctic fur seals, along with Weddell seals and leopard seals, to monitor their behavior over the winter period (Goebel et al. 2014). Unmanned aerial system (UAS) surveys were conducted in 2010/11 and 2012/13 which were successful in estimating the abundance and size of seals (Goebel *et al.* 2015).

A number of extremely rare color patterns in fur seal pups have been recorded within the Area. Antarctic fur seals with pie-bald or light colorings were documented for the first time and an albino Weddell seal represented the first confirmed case of albinism in Weddell, leopard, Ross or crabeater seals (Acevedo *et al.* 2009a, 2009b). In December 2005 an adult male subantarctic fur seal was observed among Antarctic fur seals at Cape Sherriff, which is more than 4000 km from the nearest subantarctic fur seal breeding colony (Torres *et al.* 2012).

Humpback whales (*Megaptera novaeangliae*) have been observed in the offshore area immediately to the north-east of the Area (Cox *et al.* 2009).

Marine environment and ecosystem

The seafloor surrounding the Cape Shirreff peninsula slopes relatively gently from the coast, reaching depths of 50 m approximately 2-3 km from the shore and 100 m at about 6-11 km (Map 1). This relatively shallow and broad submarine ridge extends to the NW for about 24 km before dropping more steeply at the continental shelf edge. The ridge is about 20 km in width and flanked on either side by canyons reaching depths of around 300-400 m. There is abundant macroalgae present in the intertidal zone. The limpet *Nacella concinna* is common, as elsewhere in the South Shetland Islands.

The waters offshore from Cape Shirreff have been identified as one of three areas of consistently high krill biomass density in the South Shetland Islands area, although absolute krill populations fluctuate significantly over time (Hewitt *et al.* 2004; Reiss *et al.* 2008). The spatial distribution, demography, density and size of krill and krill swarms have been studied in the nearshore region at Cape Shirreff, primarily using acoustic surveys and also using an Autonomous Underwater Vehicle (AUV) (Reiss *et al.* 2008; Warren *et al.* 2005). Acoustic surveys of the nearshore environment indicate that krill in this area are most abundant to the south and SE of

Cape Shirreff and at the margins of the two submarine canyons, which are believed to be a source of nutrient-rich water that may increase productivity in the nearshore area surrounding Cape Shirreff (Warren *et al.* 2006, 2007). Nearshore net tows indicated that the organisms identified in acoustic surveys were primarily the euphausiids, *Euphausia superba*, *Thysanoessa macrura* and *Euphausia frigida*, and may also include chaetognaths, salps, siphonophores, larval fish, myctophids and amphipods (Warren *et al.* 2007).

The nearshore environment surrounding Cape Shirreff has been identified as a primary feeding ground for penguins resident at the site, particularly during the breeding season when chick provisioning limits foraging range (Cox *et al.* 2009). Fur seals and penguins at Cape Shirreff depend strongly upon krill for prey. Predator foraging ranges are known to overlap with areas of commercial krill fisheries and changes in the abundance of both predators and krill have been linked to climatic change. Research at Cape Shirreff therefore aims to monitor krill abundance in combination with predator populations and breeding success, in order to assess the potential effects of commercial fishing, as well as environmental variability and climatic change on the ecosystem.

Numerous studies of the marine environment have been conducted in the region offshore from Cape Shirreff as part of research carried out within the U.S. AMLR survey grid. These studies include investigations into various aspects of the marine environment, including physical oceanography, environmental conditions, phytoplankton distribution and productivity, krill distribution and biomass and the distribution and density of seabirds and marine mammals (U.S. AMLR 2008, 2009).

Historical features

Following discovery of the South Shetland Islands in 1819, intensive sealing at Cape Shirreff between 1820 and 1824 exterminated almost the entire local populations of Antarctic fur seals and southern elephant seals (Smith and Simpson 1987). In January 1821, 60–75 British sealers were recorded living ashore at Cape Shirreff and 95,000 skins were taken during the 1821/22 season (O'Gorman 1963). Evidence of the sealers' occupation remains, with ruins of at least one sealers' hut in the northwestern region of the peninsula and remains of sealer's settlements recorded on a number of the beaches (D. Torres, A. Aquayo and J. Acevedo, pers. comm. 2010). The shoreline of several bays is also littered with timbers and sections of wrecked sealers' vessels. Other evidence of sealing activity includes the remains of stoves, pieces of glass bottles, a wooden harpoon, and a handcrafted bone figure (Torres and Aguayo 1993). Fildes (1821) reported that sealers found spars and an anchor stock from the Spanish ship San Telmo on Half Moon Beach around the time she was lost. The ship sank in the Drake Passage at around 62°S on 4 September 1819, with 644 persons aboard (Headland 1989; Pinochet de la Barra 1991). These were possibly the first people to die in Antarctica, and the event remains the greatest single loss of life yet to occur south of 60°S. A cairn has been erected on the northwestern coast of Cape Shirreff peninsula to commemorate the loss, which is designated as Historic Monument No. 59 (Map 3).

The remains of a camp were found close to the site of present camp facilities (Torres and Aguayo 1993). On the evidence of the script on items found at the site, the camp is believed to be of Russian origin and date from the 1940-50s, although its exact origins have yet to be determined. Items found include parts of an antenna, electrical wires, tools, boots, nails, battery cells, canned food, ammunition and a wooden box covered by a pyramid of stones. Several notes in Russian, dating from later visits, were found in this box (Torres 2007).

In January 1985 a human skull was found at Yamana Beach (Torres 1992), determined to be that of a young woman (Constantinescu and Torres 1995). In January 1987 part of a human femur was found on the ground surface nearby, inland from Yamana Beach. After a careful surface survey, no other remains were evident at that time. However, in January 1991, another part of a femur was found in close proximity to the site of the earlier (1987) find. In January 1993 an archaeological survey was carried out in the area, although no further human remains were found. The original samples were dated as from approximately 175 years BP, and it was hypothesised they belong to a single individual (Torres 1999).

Human activities / impacts

The modern era of human activity at Cape Shirreff has been largely confined to science. During the past three decades, the population of Antarctic fur seals in the South Shetland Islands grew to a level at which tagging and other research could be undertaken without threatening the existence and growth of the local population.

Chilean studies on Cape Shirreff began in 1965 (Aguayo and Torres 1966, 1967), with a more intensive program initiated by Chilean scientists in 1982, including an ongoing Antarctic fur seal tagging program (Cattan *et al.* 1982; Torres 1984; Oliva *et al.* 1987). United States investigators have conducted pinniped and seabird surveys at Cape Shirreff and San Telmo Island since 1986/87 (Bengtson *et al.* 1990).

CEMP studies at Cape Shirreff began in the mid-1980s, initiated by Chilean and U.S. scientists. Cape Shirreff was designated as a CEMP Site in 1994 to protect the site from damage or disturbance that could adversely affect long-term CEMP monitoring. As part of the CEMP, long-term studies are assessing and monitoring the feeding ecology, growth and condition, reproductive success, behavior, vital rates, and abundance of pinnipeds and seabirds that breed in the Area. The results of these studies will be evaluated in context with environmental data, offshore sampling data, and fishery statistics to identify possible cause-effect relationships between krill fisheries and pinniped and seabird populations.

Brucella and herpes virus antibodies were detected in tissue samples taken from Antarctic fur seals at Cape Shirreff over summer seasons from 1998-2001, and Brucella antibodies were also detected in Weddell seal tissue (Blank *et al.* 1999; Blank *et al.* 2001a & b). Studies on the mortality of Antarctic fur seal pups from diseases began in the 2003/04 Antarctic season (Torres and Valdenegro 2004). Enteropathogenic *Escherichia coli* (EPEC) has been recorded in swabs from Antarctic fur seals at Cape Shirreff, with two out of 33 pups sampled testing positive for the pathogen. The findings were the first reports of EPEC in Antarctic wildlife and in pinnipeds, and the effects of the pathogen on Antarctic wildlife is unknown (Hernandez *et al.* 2007).

Plastic rubbish was first reported at Cape Shirreff by Torres and Gajardo (1985), and marine debris monitoring studies have been carried out regularly since 1992 (Torres and Jorquera 1995). Debris remains an ongoing problem at the site, with over 1.5 tons of material removed from the area by Chilean scientists to date (D. Torres, A. Aquayo and J. Acevedo, pers. comm., 2010). Recent surveys have yielded large numbers of articles, mostly made of plastic, but have also included vegetable waste from ships, metal oil drums, rifle shells and an antenna. For example, the 2000/01 season survey recorded a total of 1,774 articles, almost 98% of which were made of plastic and the remainder made of glass, metal and paper. It is significant that 34% of the plastic items found in 2000/01 were packing bands, representing approximately 589 bands. Of these, 40 were uncut and another 48 had been knotted into a loop. Several articles found in this survey were oiled, and some plastic articles were partially burnt. Antarctic fur seal entanglement in marine debris has been recorded frequently at Cape Shirreff (Torres 1990; Hucke-Gaete *et al.* 1997c; Goebel *et al.* 2008, 2009), primarily in fishing equipment such as nylon ropes, net fragments and packing bands. Between 1987-1997 a total of 20 Antarctic fur seals were recorded with 'neck collars' from such debris. Plastic fibers are also found in kelp gull and chinstrap penguin nests (Torres and Jorquera 1992), as well as those of sheathbills (Torres and Jorquera 1994).

The waters surrounding Cape Shirreff represent an important krill fishing area. Catch data specifically for Cape Shirreff are unavailable, but fishing statistics are published for CCAMLR Statistical Subarea 48.1, within which the Area lies. In 2008/09 33,970 tonnes (t) of Antarctic krill (*Euphausia superba*) were caught in Subarea 48.1 compared with an average of 32993 tonnes per year caught during the period 1999-00 to 2008/09 (CCAMLR 2010). On 10 October 2010, the krill fishery in Subarea 48.1 was closed for the remainder of the 2009/10 fishing season (1 December 2009 - 30 November 2010) because the catch reached 99.9% of the annual limit for the Subarea (155 000 t). In 2012/13, 2013/14 and 2014/15 (data provisional) respectively, 153,830, 146,191 and 153,946 t were caught, and the fishery was closed in each of these years in view of the catch limit (CCAMLR 2015; 2015b). Nations recorded as fishing for krill within the Subarea during the recent past included Chile, China, Germany, Japan, Korea, Norway, Poland, Ukraine, Uruguay, the United States and Vanuatu. Krill fishing generally occurred between December and August, with the highest catches usually occurring between March and May. Catches of other species occurred in very much smaller quantities and included *Champsocephalus gunnari*, *Champsocephalus gunnari*, *Nototheniops nybelini*, *Notothenia coriiceps*, *Notolepis* spp, *Notothenia gibberifrons*, *Notothenia neglecta*, *Notothenia rossii*, *Pseudochaenichthys georgianus* and *Chaenocephalus aceratus* (CCAMLR 2010).

6(ii) Access to the Area

Access to the Area may be made by small boat, by aircraft or across sea ice by vehicle or on foot. Historically seasonal sea ice formation in the South Shetlands area generally began in early April and persisted until early

December, although more recently the South Shetland Islands can be ice-free year round as a result of regional warming.

Air access is discouraged, and restrictions apply to routes and landing sites for the period 01 November – 31 March inclusive. Details of these restrictions are given in Section 7(ii) below, and of the Helicopter Access Zone in Section 6(v).

Two anchorages have been identified close to the Area (Map 2) and when access to the Area is made from the sea, small boats should land at one of the locations defined in Section 7(ii). Sea states are generally between 1 and 4 m, decreasing closer to shore or in lea of Cape Shirreff (Warren *et al.* 2006, 2007).

When sea-ice conditions allow, the Area may be accessed over sea ice on foot or by vehicle. However, vehicle use on land within the Area is restricted to the coastal zone between Módulo Beach and the Chilean / U.S. camp facilities and to following the access route shown on Map 3 to allow re-supply of the bird blind / emergency hut (see Section 7(ii) for more details).

6(iii) Location of structures within and adjacent to the Area

A semi-permanent summer-only research camp has been established on the eastern coast of the Cape Shirreff peninsula, located at the base of Condor Hill (62°28.249' S, 60°46.283' W) (Map 3). Buildings for the camp remain *in situ* year-round. In 2015, the field camp known as Cape Shirreff Field Station (U.S.), consisted of four small buildings and an outhouse (Krause pers. comm. 2015). The camp 'Dr Guillermo Mann-Fischer' (Chile) is located around 50 m from the U.S. camp and comprised of a main hut, laboratory, store house, a fiberglass igloo, an outhouse and a wind-powered generator (D. Torres, A. Aquayo and J. Acevedo, pers. comm., 2010)). The Chilean fiberglass igloo was originally installed in 1990/91, while the U.S. camp was established in 1996/97. Storage areas are also present, and tents are erected seasonally nearby as required. An All-Terrain Vehicle (ATV) shed, with secondary containment for summer use and winter storage of the ATV, was constructed at the U.S. camp in 2009/10. The site was selected to remain within the existing station footprint and to avoid interference with seal movements. A 'Weatherport' is stored at Cape Shirreff as additional accommodation for visiting scientists and is erected within 10 m of the south side of the U.S. camp when needed.

Two automatic weather stations are mounted on the exterior of existing buildings at Cape Shirreff. Two remote receiving station used for seal tracking studies are stored within a box (90x60x100cm) located to the east of helicopter landing site A on the northeastern slopes of Condor Hill and northeast of Toqui Hill (see Map 3).

A boundary sign stating that the Area is protected and that access is prohibited is located at Módulo Beach, close to the Chilean and U.S. camps. In the 2015/16 season, the sign was in need of repair, and it is intended that a new sign will be installed during the 2016/17 season (Krause, pers. comm. 2015). The boundaries of the Area are not otherwise marked.

The remains of a camp, believed to be of Russian origin, are present near the Chilean and U.S. camps. In other parts of the peninsula, sparse evidence may be found of 19th Century sealers' camps (Smith and Simpson 1987; Torres 1993; Stehberg and Lucero 1996). A cairn (Historic Monument No. 59) has been erected on Gaviota Hill on the northwestern coast to commemorate the loss of those aboard the *San Telmo* in 1819 (Map 3). In 1998/99 a 5x7 m bird observation / emergency hut (62°27.653' S, 60°47.404' W) was installed by U.S. scientists on the northern slopes of Enrique Hill above Bahamonde Beach, close to the penguin colonies (Map 3).

6(iv) Location of other protected areas in the vicinity

The nearest protected areas to Cape Shirreff are Byers Peninsula (ASPA No. 126), which lies about 20 km to the southwest; Port Foster (ASPA No. 145, Deception Island) and other parts of Deception Island (ASPA No. 140), which are approximately 30 km to the south; and 'Chile Bay' (Discovery Bay) (ASPA No. 144), which lies about 30 km to the east at Greenwich Island (Map 1).

6(v) Special zones within the Area

A zone in the north and west of the Area is designated as a Restricted Zone, due to its high concentrations of wildlife. Restrictions apply to air access only and prohibit overflight below 2000 ft (~610m), unless specifically authorized by permit. The Restricted Zone is defined as the area north of 62°28' S (Map 2), and west of 60°48' W and north of 62°29' S.

A Helicopter Access Zone (Map 2) has been defined which applies to aircraft entering the Area and accessing the designated landing sites. The Helicopter Access Zone extends from the Livingston Island permanent ice cap northward following the main ridgeline of the peninsula for 1200 m (~ 0.65 n. mi.) towards Selknam Hill. The Helicopter Access Zone then extends east by 300 m (~0.15 n. mi) (to helicopter landing site B at Ancho Pass and a further 400 m (~0.23 n. mi) east to the summit of Condor Hill close to helicopter landing site. The southern boundary of the Helicopter Access Zone is coincident with the southern boundary of the Area.

7.   Terms and conditions for entry permits

7(i) General permit conditions

Entry into the Area is prohibited except in accordance with a Permit issued by an appropriate national authority. Conditions for issuing a Permit to enter the Area are that:

- it is issued only for scientific study associated with the CEMP, or for compelling scientific, educational, archaeological or historic purposes that cannot be served elsewhere; or
- it is issued for essential management purposes consistent with plan objectives such as inspection, maintenance or review;
- the actions permitted will not jeopardize the ecological, scientific, educational archaeological or historic values of the Area;
- any management activities are in support of the objectives of the Management Plan;
- the actions permitted are in accordance with the Management Plan;
- the Permit, or a copy, shall be carried within the Area;
- a visit report shall be supplied to the authority named in the Permit;
- permits shall be issued for a stated period.

7(ii) Access to, and movement within or over, the Area

Access to the Area shall be by small boat, by helicopter, on foot or by vehicle. Persons entering the Area may not move beyond the immediate vicinity of their landing site unless authorised by Permit.

Boat access

Access by small boats should be at one of the following locations (Map 2):

1. the eastern coast of the peninsula at El Módulo Beach, 300 m north of the camp facilities, where a deep channel enables relatively easy access;
2. the northern end of Half Moon Beach, on the eastern coast of the peninsula;
3. the northern end of Yámana Beach, on the western coast (suitable at high tide only);
4. the north coast at Alcazar Beach near the bird blind / emergency hut;
5. the southern end of the northern beach on San Telmo Island.

Access by small boat at other locations around the coast is allowed, provided this is consistent with the purposes for which a Permit has been granted. Two anchorages have been identified close to the Area; 1,600 m north-east of the main camp facilities and approximately 800 m north of San Telmo Island (Map 2). Visitors should, where practicable, avoid landing where pinniped or seabird colonies are present on or near the coast.

Aircraft access and overflight

Due to the widespread presence of pinnipeds and seabirds over the Cape Shirreff peninsula during the breeding season (01 November – 31 March), access to the Area by aircraft in this period is strongly discouraged. Where possible and by preference, access should be by small boat. All restrictions on aircraft access and overflight apply between 01 November – 31 March inclusive, when aircraft shall operate and land within the Area according to strict observance of the following conditions:

1) It is recommended that aircraft maintain a horizontal and vertical separation distance 2000 ft (~610 m) from the Antarctic Specially Protected Area boundary (Map 2), unless accessing the designated landing sites through the Helicopter Access Zone or otherwise authorized by permit;

2) Overflight of the Restricted Zone is prohibited below 610 m (2,000 ft) unless authorized by permit. The Restricted Zone is defined as the area north of 62°28' S, or north of 62°29' S and west of 60°48' W (Map 2), and includes the areas of greatest wildlife concentration;

3) Helicopter landing is permitted at two designated sites (Map 2). The landing sites with their coordinates are described as follows:

   (A) on a small area of flat ground, ~150 m northwest of the summit of Condor Hill (50 m, or ~150 ft) (60°46.438'W, 62°28.257'S), which is the preferred landing site for most purposes; and

   (B) on the wide flat area on Ancho Pass (25 m), situated between Condor Hill and Selknam Hill (60°46.814'W, 62°28.269'S).

4) Aircraft accessing the Area should follow the Helicopter Access Zone to the maximum extent practicable. The Helicopter Access Zone allows access from the south across the Livingston Island permanent ice cap and extends along the main ridgeline of the peninsula for 1,200 m (~ 0.65 n. mi.) towards Selknam Hill (elevation = 50 m, or ~150 ft). The Helicopter Access Zone then extends east by 300 m (~ 0.15 n. mi) to Ancho Pass, where helicopter landing site B is situated, and a further 400 m (~0.23 n. mi) east to the summit of Condor Hill (elevation = 50 m, or ~150 ft), close to helicopter landing site A. Aircraft should avoid overflight of the hut and beach areas on the eastern side of Condor Hill.

5) The preferred approaches to the Helicopter Access Zone are from the south across the Livingston Island permanent ice cap, from the southwest from the direction of Barclay Bay, and from the southeast from the direction of Hero Bay (Maps 1 and 2).

6) Weather with a low cloud ceiling often prevails at Cape Shirreff, particularly in the vicinity of the permanent ice cap, which can make snow/ice ground definition difficult to discern from the air. On-site personnel who may be advising on local conditions before aircraft approaches should be aware that a minimum cloud base of 150 m (500 ft) AMSL over the approach zone of the Livingston Island ice cap is necessary in order for access guidelines to be followed;

7) Use of smoke grenades to indicate wind direction is prohibited within the Area unless absolutely necessary for safety, and any grenades used should be retrieved.

Vehicle access and use

Access by vehicle over land may be made to the boundary to the Area. Access by vehicle over sea ice may be made to the shore within the Area. Vehicles are permitted to operate on snow-covered land only:

- in the coastal zone between Módulo Beach and the Chilean / U.S. camp facilities (Map 3); and

- in support of annual re-supply of the bird blind / emergency hut following the designated route (see Map 3), which should be undertaken prior to 15 November in a given season and only if the entire route is snow-covered to a depth of at least 40 cm, to minimise the possibility of damage to underlying soil and vegetation (Felix & Raynolds 1989). A journey after 15 November should be considered carefully, due to potential disturbance to adult female fur seals, which tend to arrive around that time of the year. No more than two re-supply journeys by vehicle to the emergency hut are allowed per season. An inspection of the route should be undertaken when it is snow-free to check for any evidence that vehicle use has caused damage to soils or vegetation. Should any damage be observed, use of vehicles for the purpose of re-supply shall be suspended until such time as a review of this policy has been completed.

The use of vehicles elsewhere within the Area is prohibited.

Foot access and movement within the Area

With the exception of the restricted use of vehicles described above, movement on land within the Area shall be on foot. Pilots, air, boat or vehicle crew, or other people in aircraft, boats, or vehicles are prohibited from moving on foot beyond the immediate vicinity of their landing site or the hut facilities unless specifically authorised by Permit. Visitors should move carefully so as to minimize disturbance to flora, fauna, and soils, and should walk on snow or rocky terrain if practical, but taking care not to damage lichens. Pedestrian traffic should be kept to the minimum consistent with the objectives of any permitted activities and every reasonable effort should be made to minimize effects.

7(iii) Activities which may be conducted in the Area

- Scientific research that will not jeopardize the values of the Area, in particular those associated with the CEMP;
- Essential management activities, including monitoring;
- Activities with educational aims (such as documentary reporting (photographic, audio or written) or the production of educational resources or services) that cannot be served elsewhere.
- Activities with the aim of preserving or protecting historic resources within the Area.
- Archaeological research that will not threaten the values of the Area.

7(iv) Installation, modification or removal of structures

- No structures are to be erected within the Area except as specified in a permit;
- The principal camp facilities shall be limited to the area within 200 m of the existing Chilean and U.S. field camps (Map 3). Small temporary hides, blinds or screens may be constructed for the purpose of facilitating scientific study of the fauna;
- All structures, scientific equipment or markers installed in the Area must be authorized by permit and clearly identified by country, name of the principal investigator and year of installation. All such items should be made of materials that pose minimal risk of harm to fauna or of contamination of the Area;
- Installation (including site selection), maintenance, modification or removal of structures shall be undertaken in a manner that minimizes disturbance to flora and fauna, preferably avoiding the main breeding season (1 November – 31 March);
- Removal of structures, equipment, hides or markers for which the permit has expired shall be the responsibility of the authority which granted the original Permit, and shall be a condition of the Permit;

7(v) Location of field camps

Camping is permitted within 200 m of the facilities of the Chilean and U.S. field camps, on the eastern coast of the Cape Shirreff peninsula (Map 3). Temporary camping is permitted at the northern extremity of Yamana beach to support fieldwork on the San Telmo Islets (Map 3). The U.S. bird observation hut on the northern slopes of Enrique Hill (60°47'28" W, 62°27'41" S) may be used for temporary overnight camping for research purposes, although should not be used as a semi-permanent camp. Camping is permitted on San Telmo Island when necessary for purposes consistent with plan objectives. The preferred camping location is at the southern end of the northern beach on the island. Camping is prohibited elsewhere within the Area.

7(vi) Restrictions on materials and organisms which may be brought into the Area

- No living animals, plant material, microorganisms or soils shall be deliberately introduced into the Area and the precautions listed below shall be taken against accidental introductions;
- To help maintain the ecological and scientific values at Cape Shirreff and San Telmo Island visitors shall take special precautions against introductions. Of concern are pathogenic, microbial, invertebrate or plant introductions sourced from other Antarctic sites, including stations, or from regions outside Antarctica. Visitors shall ensure that sampling equipment and markers brought into the Area are clean. To the

maximum extent practicable, footwear and other equipment used or brought into the area (including backpacks, carry-bags and tents) shall be thoroughly cleaned before entering the Area;

- Dressed poultry should be free of disease or infection before shipment to the Area and, if introduced to the Area for food, all parts and wastes of poultry shall be completely removed from the Area or incinerated or boiled long enough to kill any potentially infective bacteria or viruses;
- No herbicides or pesticides shall be brought into the Area;
- Any other chemicals, including radio-nuclides or stable isotopes, which may be introduced for scientific or management purposes specified in the Permit, shall be removed from the Area at or before the conclusion of the activity for which the Permit was granted;
- Fuel, food, and other materials are not to be stored in the Area, unless required for essential purposes connected with the activities for which a permit has been granted;
- All materials introduced shall be for a stated period only, shall be removed at or before the conclusion of that stated period, and shall be stored and handled so that risk of their introduction into the environment is minimized;
- If release occurs which is likely to compromise the values of the Area, removal is encouraged only where the impact of removal is not likely to be greater than that of leaving the material *in situ*.

7(vii) Taking of, or harmful interference with native flora or fauna

Taking or harmful interference with native flora or fauna is prohibited, except in accordance with a separate permit issued under Article 3 of Annex II by the appropriate national authority specifically for that purpose. CEMP research programs in progress within the Area should be consulted before other Permits for taking or harmful interference with animals are granted.

7(viii) Collection or removal of materials not brought into the Area by the permit holder

- Material may be collected or removed from the Area only in accordance with a Permit and should be limited to the minimum necessary to meet scientific or management needs.
- Material of human origin likely to compromise the values of the Area, which was not brought into the Area by the Permit Holder, and is clearly of no historic value or otherwise authorized, may be removed unless the impact of removal is likely to be greater than leaving the material *in situ*: if this is the case the appropriate authority should be notified.
- Material found that is likely to possess important archaeological, historic or heritage values should not be disturbed, damaged, removed or destroyed. Any such artifacts should be recorded and referred to the appropriate authority for a decision on conservation or removal. Relocation or removal of artifacts for the purposes of preservation, protection, or to re-establish historical accuracy is allowable by permit;
- The appropriate national authority should be notified of any items removed from the Area that were not introduced by the permit holder.

7(ix) Disposal of waste

All wastes shall be removed from the Area, except human wastes and domestic liquid wastes, which may be removed from the Area or disposed of into the sea.

7(x) Measures that may be necessary to continue to meet the aims of the Management Plan

1) Permits may be granted to enter the Area to carry out biological monitoring and site inspection activities, which may involve the collection of limited samples for analysis or review, or for protective measures.
2) Any specific sites of long-term monitoring should be appropriately marked.
3) To avoid interference with long-term research and monitoring activities or possible duplication of effort, persons planning new projects within the Area should consult with established programs working at Cape Shirreff, such as those of Chile and the United States, before initiating the work.
4) In view of the fact that geological sampling is both permanent and of cumulative impact, visitors removing geological samples from the Area shall complete a record describing the geological type,

quantity and location of samples taken, which should, at a minimum, be deposited with their National Antarctic Data Centre or with the Antarctic Master Directory.

7(xi) Requirements for reports

- Parties should ensure that the principal holder for each Permit issued submits to the appropriate authority a report describing the activities undertaken. Such reports should include, as appropriate, the information identified in the visit report form contained in the Guide to the Preparation of Management Plans for Antarctic Specially Protected Areas.

- Parties should maintain a record of such activities and, in the Annual Exchange of Information, should provide summary descriptions of activities conducted by persons subject to their jurisdiction, in sufficient detail to allow evaluation of the effectiveness of the Management Plan. Parties should, wherever possible, deposit originals or copies of such original reports in a publicly accessible archive to maintain a record of usage, to be used both in any review of the Management Plan and in organizing the scientific use of the Area.

- The appropriate authority should be notified of any activities/measures undertaken, and / or of any materials released and not removed, that were not included in the authorized permit.

8. Supporting documentation

Acevedo, J., Vallejos, V., Vargas, R., Torres, J.P. & Torres, D. 2002. Informe científico. ECA XXXVIII (2001/2002). Proyecto INACH 018 "Estudios ecológicos sobre el lobo fino antártico, Arctocephalus gazella", cabo Shirreff, isla Livingston, Shetland del Sur, Antártica. Ministerio de Relaciones Exteriores, Instituto Antártico Chileno. N° Ingreso 642/710, 11.ABR.2002.

Acevedo, J., Aguayo-Lobo, A. & Torres, D. 2009a. Albino Weddell seal at Cape Shirreff, Livingston Island, Antarctica. *Polar Biology* **32** (8):1239–43.

Acevedo, J., Aguayo-Lobo, A. & Torres, D. 2009b. Rare piebald and partially leucistic Antarctic fur seals, Arctocephalus gazella, at Cape Shirreff, Livingston Island, Antarctica. *Polar Biology* **32** (1): 41–45.

Agnew, A.J. 1997. Review: the CCAMLR Ecosystem Monitoring Programme. *Antarctic Science* **9** (3): 235-242.

Aguayo, A. 1978. The present status of the Antarctic fur seal Arctocephalus gazella at the South Shetland Islands. *Polar Record* **19**: 167-176.

Aguayo, A. & Torres, D. 1966. A first census of Pinnipedia in the South Shetland Islands and other observations on marine mammals. In: SCAR / SCOR / IAPO / IUBS Symposium on Antarctic Oceanography, Santiago, Chile, 13-16 September 1966, Section 4: Coastal Waters: 166-168.

Aguayo, A. & Torres, D. 1967. Observaciones sobre mamiferos marinos durante la Vigésima Comisión Antártica Chilena. Primer censo de pinípedos en las Islas Shetland del Sur. *Revta. Biol. Mar.*, **13**(1): 1-57.

Aguayo, A. & Torres, D. 1993. Análisis de los censos de Arctocephalus gazella efectuados en el Sitio de Especial Interés Científico No. 32, isla Livingston, Antártica. *Serie Científica Instituto Antártico Chileno* **43**: 87-91.

Antolos, M., Miller, A.K. & Trivelpiece, W.Z. 2004. Seabird research at Cape Shirreff, Livingston Island, Antarctica 2003-2004. In Lipsky, J. (ed.) AMLR (Antarctic Marine Living Resources) 2003-2004 Field Season Report, Ch. 7. Antarctic Ecosystem Research Division, Southwest Fisheries Science Center, La Jolla, California.

Bengston, J.L., Ferm, L.M., Härkönen, T.J. & Stewart, B.S. 1990. Abundance of Antarctic fur seals in the South Shetland Islands, Antarctica, during the 1986/87 austral summer. In: Kerry, K. and Hempel, G. (Eds). *Antarctic Ecosystems, Proceedings of the Fifth SCAR Symposium on Antarctic Biology*. Springer-Verlag, Berlin: 265-270.

Blank, O., Retamal, P., Torres D. & Abalos, P. 1999. First record of Brucella spp. antibodies in Arctocephalus gazella and Leptonychotes weddelli from Cape Shirreff, Livingston Island, Antarctica. (SC-CAMLR-XVIII/BG/17.) *CCAMLR Scientific Abstracts* 5.

Blank, O., Retamal, P., Abalos P. & Torres, D. 2001a. Additional data on anti-Brucella antibodies in Arctocephalus gazella from Cape Shirreff, Livingston Island, Antarctica. *CCAMLR Science* **8**: 147-154.

Blank, O., Montt, J.M., Celedón M. & Torres, D. 2001b. Herpes virus antibodies in Arctocephalus gazella from Cape Shirreff, Livingston Island, Antarctica. WG-EMM- 01/59.

Bonin, C.A., Goebel, M.E., O'Corry-Crowe, G.M., & Burton, R.S. 2012. Twins or not? Genetic analysis of putative twins in Antarctic fur seals, Arctocephalus gazella, on the South Shetland Islands. *Journal of Experimental Marine Biology and Ecology* **412**: 13–19. doi:10.1016/j.jembe.2011.10.010

Bonin, C.A., Goebel, M.E., Forcada, J., Burton, R.S., & Hoffman, J.I. 2013. Unexpected genetic differentiation between recently recolonized populations of a long-lived and highly vagile marine mammal. *Ecology and Evolution*: 3701–3712. doi:10.1002/ece3.732

Bonner, W.N. & Smith, R.I.L. (eds.) 1985. *Conservation areas in the Antarctic*. SCAR, Cambridge: 59-63.

Carten, T.M., Taft, M., Trivelpiece W.Z. & Holt, R.S. 2001. Seabird research at Cape Shirreff, Livingston Island, Antarctica, 1999/2000. In Lipsky, J. (ed.) AMLR (Antarctic Marine Living Resources) 1999-2000 Field Season Report, Ch. 7. Antarctic Ecosystem Research Division, Southwest Fisheries Science Center, La Jolla, California.

Cattan, P., Yánez, J., Torres, D., Gajardo, M. & Cárdenas, J. 1982. Censo, marcaje y estructura poblacional del lobo fino antártico Arctocephalus gazella (Peters, 1875) en las islas Shetland del Sur, Chile. *Serie Científica Instituto Antártico Chileno* **29**: 31-38.

CCAMLR 1997. Management plan for the protection of Cape Shirreff and the San Telmo Islands, South Shetland Islands, as a site included in the CCAMLR Ecosystem Monitoring Program. In: *Schedule of Conservation Measures in Force 1996/97*: 51-64.

CCAMLR 2010. *CCAMLR Statistical Bulletin* **22** (2000–2009). CCAMLR, Hobart, Australia.

CCAMLR 2015. *CCAMLR Statistical Bulletin* **27**. CCAMLR, Hobart, Australia.

CCAMLR 2015b. Report of the 34th Meeting of the Commission. Hobart, Australia. 19-30 October 2015. CCAMLR, Hobart,

Chisholm, S.E., Pietrzak, K.W., Miller, A.K. & Trivelpiece, W.Z. 2008. Seabird research at Cape Shirreff, Livingston Island, Antarctica 2007-2008. In Van Cise, A.M. (ed.) AMLR (Antarctic Marine Living Resources) 2007-2008 Field Season Report, Ch. 5. Antarctic Ecosystem Research Division, Southwest Fisheries Science Center, La Jolla, California.

Constantinescu, F. & Torres, D. 1995. Análisis bioantropológico de un cráneo humano hallado en cabo Shirreff, isla Livingston, Antártica. Ser. Cient. INACH **45**: 89-99.

Cox, M.J., Demer, D.A., Warren, J.D., Cutter, G.R. & Brierley, A.S. 2009. Multibeam echosounder observations reveal interactions between Antarctic krill and air-breathing predators. *Marine Ecology Progress Series* **378**: 199–209.

Croxall, J.P. & Kirkwood, E.D. 1979. *The distribution of penguins on the Antarctic Peninsula and the islands of the Scotia Sea*. British Antarctic Survey, Cambridge.

Everett, K.R. 1971. Observations on the glacial history of Livingston Island. *Arctic* **24** (1): 41-50.

Felix, N.A. & Raynolds, M.K. 1989. The role of snow cover in limiting surface disturbance caused by winter seismic exploration. *Arctic* **42**(1): 62-68.

Fildes, R. 1821. A journal of a voyage from Liverpool towards New South Shetland on a sealing and sea elephant adventure kept on board Brig Robert of Liverpool, Robert Fildes, 13 August - 26 December 1821. MS 101/1, Scott Polar Research Institute, Cambridge.

Goebel, M.E., Rutishauser, M., Parker, B., Banks, A., Costa, D.P., Gales, N. & Holt, R.S. 2001a. Pinniped research at Cape Shirreff, Livingston Island, Antarctica, 1999/2000. In Lipsky, J. (ed.) AMLR (Antarctic Marine Living Resources) 1999-2000 Field Season Report, Ch. 8. Antarctic Ecosystem Research Division, Southwest Fisheries Science Center, La Jolla, California.

Goebel, M.E., Parker, B., Banks, A., Costa, D.P., Pister, B. & Holt, R.S. 2001b. Pinniped research at Cape Shirreff, Livingston Island, Antarctica, 2000/2001. In Lipsky, J. (ed.) AMLR (Antarctic Marine Living Resources) 2000-01 Field Season Report, Ch. 8. Antarctic Ecosystem Research Division, Southwest Fisheries Science Center, La Jolla, California.

Goebel, M.E., McDonald, B.I., Freeman, S., Haner, R., Spear, N. & Sexton, S. 2008. Pinniped Research at Cape Shirreff, Livingston Island, 2008/09. In AMLR 2007-2008 field season report. Objectives, Accomplishments and Tentative Conclusions. Southwest Fisheries Science Center Antarctic Ecosystem Research Group. La Jolla, California.

Goebel, M.E., Krause, D., Freeman, S., Burner, R., Bonin, C., Vasquez del Mercado, R., Van Cise, A.M. & Gafney, J. 2009. Pinniped Research at Cape Shirreff, Livingston Island, Antarctica, 2008/09. In AMLR 2008-2009 field season report. Objectives, Accomplishments and Tentative Conclusions. Southwest Fisheries Science Center Antarctic Ecosystem Research Group. La Jolla, California.

Goebel, M.E., Burner, R., Buchheit, R., Pussini, N., Krause, D., Bonin, C., Vasquez del Mercado, R. & Van Cise, A.M. 2011. Pinniped Research at Cape Shirreff, Livingston Island, Antarctica. In Van Cise, A.M. (ed.) AMLR (Antarctic Marine Living Resources) 2009-2010 Field Season Report, Ch. 6. Antarctic Ecosystem Research Division, Southwest Fisheries Science Center, La Jolla, California.

Goebel, M.E., Pussini, N., Buchheit, R., Pietrzak, K., Krause, D., Van Cise, A.M. & Walsh, J. 2014. Pinniped Research at Cape Shirreff, Livingston Island, Antarctica. In Walsh, J.G. (ed.) AMLR (Antarctic Marine Living Resources) 2010-2011 Field Season Report, Ch. 8. Antarctic Ecosystem Research Division, Southwest Fisheries Science Center, La Jolla, California.

Goebel, M.E., Perryman, W.L., Hinke, J.T., Krause, D.J., Hann, N.A., Gardner, S., & LeRoi, D.J. 2015. A small unmanned aerial system for estimating abundance and size of Antarctic predators. *Polar Biology* **38**:619–30.

Garcia, M., Aguayo, A. & Torres, D. 1995. Aspectos conductuales de los machos de lobo fino antártico, *Arctocephalus gazella* en cabo Shirreff, isla Livingston, Antártica, durante la fase de apareamiento. *Serie Científica Instituto Antártico Chileno* **45**: 101-112.

Harris, C.M. 2001. Revision of management plans for Antarctic protected areas originally proposed by the United States of America and the United Kingdom: Field visit report. Internal report for the National Science Foundation, US, and the Foreign and Commonwealth Office, UK. *Environmental Research & Assessment*, Cambridge.

Headland, R. 1989. *Chronological list of Antarctic expeditions and related historical events*. Cambridge University Press, Cambridge.

Heap, J. (ed.) 1994. *Handbook of the Antarctic Treaty System*. 8th Edn. U.S. Department of State, Washington.

Hobbs, G.J. 1968. The geology of the South Shetland Islands. IV. The geology of Livingston Island. *British Antarctic Survey Scientific Reports* **47**.

Henadez, J., Prado, V., Torres, D., Waldenström, J., Haemig, P.D. & Olsen, B. 2007. Enteropathogenic *Escherichia coli* (EPEC) in Antarctic fur seals *Arctocephalus gazella*. *Polar Biology* **30** (10):1227–29.

Hewitt, R.P., Kim, S., Naganobu, M., Gutierrez, M., Kang, D., Taka, Y., Quinones, J., Lee Y.-H., Shin, H.-C., Kawaguchi, S., Emery, J.H., Demer, D.A. & Loeb, V.J. 2004. Variation in the biomass density and demography of Antarctic krill in the vicinity of the South Shetland Islands during the 1999/2000 austral summer. *Deep-Sea Research* II **51** 1411–1419.

Hinke, J.T., Salwicka, K., Trivelpiece, S.G., Watters, S.G., & Trivelpiece, W.Z. 2007. Divergent responses of *Pygoscelis* penguins reveal a common environmental driver. *Oecologia* **153**:845–855.

Hucke-Gaete, R., Acevedo, J., Osman, L., Vargas, R., Blank, O. & Torres, D. 2001. Informe científico. ECA XXXVII (2000/2001). Proyecto 018 "Estudios ecológicos sobre el lobo fino antártico, Arctocephalus gazella", cabo Shirreff, isla Livingston, Shetland del Sur, Antártica.

Hucke-Gaete, R., Torres, D., Aguayo, A. & Vallejos, V. 1998. Decline of Arctocephalus gazella population at SSSI No. 32, South Shetlands, Antarctica (1997/98 season): a discussion of possible causes. WG-EMM-98/17. August 1998. Kochin. 10: 16–19

Hucke-Gaete, R, Torres, D. & Vallejos, V. 1997a. Population size and distribution of *Pygoscelis antarctica* and *P. papua* at Cape Shirreff, Livingston Island, Antarctica (1996/97 Season). CCAMLR WG-EMM-97/62.

Hucke-Gaete, R, Torres, D., Vallejos, V. & Aguayo, A. 1997b. Population size and distribution of *Arctocephalus gazella* at SSSI No. 32, Livingston Island, Antarctica (1996/97 Season). CCAMLR WG-EMM-97/62.

Hucke-Gaete, R, Torres, D. & Vallejos, V. 1997c. Entanglement of Antarctic fur seals, *Arctocephalus gazella*, by marine debris at Cape Shirreff and San Telmo Islets, Livingston Island, Antarctica: 1998-1997. *Serie Científica Instituto Antártico Chileno* **47**: 123-135.

Hucke-Gaete, R., Osman, L.P., Moreno, C.A. & Torres, D. 2004. Examining natural population growth from near extinction: the case of the Antarctic fur seal at the South Shetlands, Antarctica. *Polar Biology* **27** (5): 304–311

Huckstadt, L., Costa, D. P., McDonald, B. I., Tremblay, Y., Crocker, D. E., Goebel, M. E. & Fedak, M. E. 2006. Habitat Selection and Foraging Behavior of Southern Elephant Seals in the Western Antarctic Peninsula. American Geophysical Union, Fall Meeting 2006, abstract #OS33A-1684.

INACH (Instituto Antártico Chileno) 2010. Chilean Antarctic Program of Scientific Research 2009-2010. Chilean Antarctic Institute Research Projects Department. Santiago, Chile.

Kawaguchi, S., Nicol, S., Taki, K. & Naganobu, M. 2006. Fishing ground selection in the Antarctic krill fishery: Trends in patterns across years, seasons and nations. *CCAMLR Science*, **13**: 117–141.

Krause, D. J., Goebel, M. E., Marshall, G. J., & Abernathy, K. (2015). Novel foraging strategies observed in a growing leopard seal (*Hydrurga leptonyx*) population at Livingston Island, Antarctic Peninsula. *Animal Biotelemetry*, 3:24.

Krause, D.J., Goebel, M.E., Marshall. G.J. & Abernathy, K. *In Press*. Summer diving and haul-out behavior of leopard seals (*Hydrurga leptonyx*) near mesopredator breeding colonies at Livingston Island, Antarctic Peninsula. *Marine Mammal Science*.Leppe, M., Fernandoy, F., Palma-Heldt, S. & Moisan, P 2004. Flora mesozoica en los depósitos morrénicos de cabo Shirreff, isla Livingston, Shetland del Sur, Península Antártica, in Actas del 10° Congreso Geológico Chileno. CD-ROM. Resumen Expandido, 4pp. Universidad de Concepción. Concepción. Chile.

Leung, E.S.W., Orben, R.A. & Trivelpiece, W.Z. 2006. Seabird research at Cape Shirreff, Livingston Island, Antarctica 2005-2006. In Lipsky, J. (ed.) AMLR (Antarctic Marine Living Resources) 2005-2006 Field Season Report, Ch. 9. Antarctic Ecosystem Research Division, Southwest Fisheries Science Center, La Jolla, California.

McDonald, B.I., Goebel, M.E., Crocker, D.E., & Costa, D.P. 2012a. Dynamic influence of maternal and pup traits on maternal care during lactation in an income breeder, the Antarctic fur seal. *Physiological and Biochemical Zoology* **85**(3):000-000.

McDonald, B.I., Goebel, M.E., Crocker, D.E. & Costa, D.P. 2012. Biological and environmental drivers of energy allocation in a dependent mammal, the Antarctic fur seal. *Physiological and Biochemical Zoology* **85**(2):134-47.

Miller, A.K., Leung, E.S.W. & Trivelpiece, W.Z. 2005. Seabird research at Cape Shirreff, Livingston Island, Antarctica 2004-2005. In Lipsky, J. (ed.) AMLR (Antarctic Marine Living Resources) 2004-2005 Field Season Report, Ch. 7. Antarctic Ecosystem Research Division, Southwest Fisheries Science Center, La Jolla, California.

Miller, A.K. & Trivelpiece, W.Z. 2007. Cycles of *Euphausia superba* recruitment evident in the diet of Pygoscelid penguins and net trawls in the South Shetland Islands, Antarctica. *Polar Biology* 30 (12):1615–1623.

Miller, A.K. & Trivelpiece, W.Z. 2008. Chinstrap penguins alter foraging and diving behavior in response to the size of their principle prey, Antarctic krill. *Marine Biology* **154**: 201-208.

Miller, A.K., Karnovsky, N.J. & Trivelpiece, W.Z. 2008. Flexible foraging strategies of gentoo penguins *Pygoscelis papua* over 5 years in the South Shetland Islands, Antarctica. *Marine Biology* **156**: 2527-2537.

Mudge, M.L., Larned, A., Hinke, J. & Trivelpiece, W.Z. 2014. Seabird research at Cape Shirreff, Livingston Island, Antarctica 2010-2011. In Walsh, J.G. (ed.) AMLR (Antarctic Marine Living Resources) 2010-2011 Field Season Report, Ch. 7. Antarctic Ecosystem Research Division, Southwest Fisheries Science Center, La Jolla, California.

O'Gorman, F.A. 1961. Fur seals breeding in the Falkland Islands Dependencies. *Nature* **192**: 914-16.

O'Gorman, F.A. 1963. The return of the Antarctic fur seal. *New Scientist* **20**: 374-76.

Olavarría, C., Coria, N., Schlatter, R., Hucke-Gaete, R., Vallejos, V., Godoy, C., Torres D. & Aguayo, A. 1999. Cisnes de cuello negro, *Cygnus melanocoripha* (Molina, 1782) en el área de las islas Shetland del Sur y península Antártica. *Serie Científica Instituto Antártico Chileno* **49**: 79-87.

Oliva, D., Durán, R, Gajardo, M. & Torres, D. 1987. Numerical changes in the population of the Antarctic fur seal *Arctocephalus gazella* at two localities of the South Shetland Islands. *Serie Científica Instituto Antártico Chileno* **36**: 135-144.

Oliva, D., Durán, R, Gajardo, M. & Torres, D. 1988. Population structure and harem size groups of the Antarctic fur seal *Arctocephalus gazella* Cape Shirreff, Livingston Island, South Shetland Islands. Meeting of the SCAR Group of Specialists on Seals, Hobart, Tasmania, Australia. *Biomass Report Series* 59: 39.

Orben, R.A., Chisholm, S.E., Miller, S.K. & Trivelpiece, W.Z. 2007. Seabird research at Cape Shirreff, Livingston Island, Antarctica 2006-2007. In Lipsky, J. (ed.) AMLR (Antarctic Marine Living Resources) 2006-2007 Field Season Report, Ch. 7. Antarctic Ecosystem Research Division, Southwest Fisheries Science Center, La Jolla, California.

Osman, L.P., Hucke-Gaete, R., Moreno, C.A., & Torres, D. 2004. Feeding ecology of Antarctic fur seals at Cape Shirreff, South Shetlands, Antarctica. *Polar Biology* **30**(2): 92–98.

Palma-Heldt, S., Fernandoy, F., Quezada, I. & Leppe, M 2004. Registro Palinológico de cabo Shirreff, isla Livingston, nueva localidad para el Mesozoico de Las Shetland del Sur, in V Simposio Argentino y I Latinoamericano sobre Investigaciones Antárticas CD-ROM. Resumen Expandido N° 104GP. Buenos Aires, Argentina.

Palma-Heldt, S., Fernandoy, F., Henríquez, G. & Leppe, M 2007. Palynoflora of Livingston Island, South Shetland Islands: Contribution to the understanding of the evolution of the southern Pacific Gondwana margin. U.S. Geological Survey and The National Academies; USGS OF-2007-1047, Extended Abstract 100.

Pietrzak, K.W., Breeden, J.H, Miller, A.K. & Trivelpiece, W.Z. 2009. Seabird research at Cape Shirreff, Livingston Island, Antarctica 2008-2009. In Van Cise, A.M. (ed.) AMLR (Antarctic Marine Living Resources) 2008-2009 Field Season Report, Ch. 6. Antarctic Ecosystem Research Division, Southwest Fisheries Science Center, La Jolla, California.

Pietrzak, K.W., Mudge, M.L. & Trivelpiece, W.Z. 2011. Seabird research at Cape Shirreff, Livingston Island, Antarctica 2009-2010. In Van Cise, A.M. (ed.) AMLR (Antarctic Marine Living Resources) 2009-2010 Field Season Report, Ch. 5. Antarctic Ecosystem Research Division, Southwest Fisheries Science Center, La Jolla, California.Pinochet de la Barra, O. 1991. El misterio del "San Telmo". ¿Náufragos españoles pisaron por primera vez la Antártida? *Revista Historia* (Madrid), **16** (18): 31-36.

Polito, M.J., Trivelpiece, W.Z., Patterson, W.P., Karnovsky, N.J., Reiss, C.S., & Emslie, S.D. 2015. Contrasting specialist and generalist patterns facilitate foraging niche partitioning in sympatric populations of Pygoscelis penguins. *Marine Ecology Progress Series* **519**: 221–37.

Reid, K., Jessop, M.J., Barrett, M.S., Kawaguchi, S., Siegel, V. & Goebel, M.E. 2004. Widening the net: spatio-temporal variability in the krill population structure across the Scotia Sea. *Deep-Sea Research II* **51**: 1275–1287

Reiss, C. S., Cossio, A. M., Loeb, V. & Demer, D. A. 2008. Variations in the biomass of Antarctic krill (Euphausia superba) around the South Shetland Islands, 1996–2006. *ICES Journal of Marine Science* **65**: 497–508.

Sallaberry, M. & Schlatter, R. 1983. Estimacíon del número de pingüinos en el Archipiélago de las Shetland del Sur. *Serie Científica Instituto Antártico Chileno* **30**: 87-91.

Saxer, I.M., Scheffler, D.A. & Trivelpiece, W.Z. 2003. Seabird research at Cape Shirreff, Livingston Island, Antarctica 2001-2002. In Lipsky, J. (ed.) AMLR (Antarctic Marine Living Resources) 2001-2002 Field Season Report, Ch. 6. Antarctic Ecosystem Research Division, Southwest Fisheries Science Center, La Jolla, California.

Schwarz, L.K., Goebel, M.E., Costa, D.P., & Kilpatrick, A.M. 2013. Top-down and bottom-up influences on demographic rates of Antarctic fur seals Arctocephalus gazella. *Journal of Animal Ecology* 82(4): 903–11.

Shill, L.F., Antolos, M. & Trivelpiece, W.Z. 2003. Seabird research at Cape Shirreff, Livingston Island, Antarctica 2002-2003. In Lipsky, J. (ed.) AMLR (Antarctic Marine Living Resources) 2002-2003 Field Season Report, Ch. 8. Antarctic Ecosystem Research Division, Southwest Fisheries Science Center, La Jolla, California.

Smellie, J.L., Pallàs, R.M., Sàbata, F. & Zheng, X. 1996. Age and correlation of volcanism in central Livingston Island, South Shetland Islands: K-Ar and geochemical constraints. *Journal of South American Earth Sciences* 9 (3/4): 265-272.

Smith, R.I.L. & Simpson, H.W. 1987. Early Nineteenth Century sealers' refuges on Livingston Island, South Shetland Islands. *British Antarctic Survey Bulletin* 74: 49-72.

Stehberg, R. & V. Lucero, 1996. Excavaciones arqueológicas en playa Yámana, cabo Shirreff, isla Livingston, Shetland del Sur, Antártica. *Serie Científica Instituto Antártico Chileno* 46: 59-81.

Taft, M.R., Saxer, I.M. & Trivelpiece W.Z 2001. Seabird research at Cape Shirreff, Livingston Island, Antarctica, 2000/2001. In Lipsky, J. (ed.) AMLR (Antarctic Marine Living Resources) 2000-01 Field Season Report, Ch. 7. Antarctic Ecosystem Research Division, Southwest Fisheries Science Center, La Jolla, California.

Torres, D. 1984. Síntesis de actividades, resultados y proyecciones de las investigaciones chilenas sobre pinípedos antarcticos. *Boletín Antártico Chileno* 4(1): 33-34.

Torres, D. 1990. Collares plásticos en lobos finos antárticos: Otra evidencia de contaminación. *Boletín Antártico Chileno* 10 (1): 20-22.

Torres, D. 1992. ¿Cráneo indígena en cabo Shirreff? Un estudio en desarrollo. *Boletín Antártico Chileno* 11 (2): 2-6.

Torres, D. 1994. Synthesis of CEMP activities carried out at Cape Shirreff. Report to CCAMLR WG-CEMP 94/28.

Torres, D. 1995. Antecedentes y proyecciones científicas de los estudios en el SEIC No. 32 y Sitio CEMP «Cabo Shirreff e islotes San Telmo», isla Livingston, Antártica. *Serie Científica Instituto Antártico Chileno* 45: 143-169.

Torres, D. 1999. Observations on ca. 175-Year Old Human Remains from Antarctica (Cape Shirreff, Livingston Island, South Shetlands). *International Journal of Circumpolar Health* 58: 72-83.

Torres, D. 2007. Evidencias del uso de armas de fuego en cabo Shirreff. *Boletín Antártico Chileno*, 26 (2): 22.

Torres, D. & Aguayo, A. 1993. Impacto antrópico en cabo Shirreff, isla Livingston, Antártica. *Serie Científica Instituto Antártico Chileno* 43: 93-108.

Torres, D. & Gajardo, M. 1985. Información preliminar sobre desechos plásticos hallados en cabo Shirreff, isla Livingston, Shetland del Sur, Chile. *Boletín Antártico Chileno* 5(2): 12-13.

Torres, D. & Jorquera, D. 1992. Analysis of Marine Debris found at Cape Shirreff, Livingston Island, South Shetlands, Antarctica. SC-CAMLR/BG/7, 12 pp. CCAMLR, Hobart, Australia.

Torres, D. & Jorquera, D. 1994. Marine Debris Collected at Cape Shirreff, Livingston Island, during the Antarctic Season 1993/94. CCMALR-XIII/BG/17, 10 pp. 18 October 1994. Hobart, Australia.

Torres, D. & Jorquera, D. 1995. Línea de base para el seguimiento de los desechos marinos en cabo Shirreff, isla Livingston, Antártica. *Serie Científica Instituto Antártico Chileno* 45: 131-141.

Torres, D., Jaña, R., Encina, L. & Vicuña, P. 2001. Cartografía digital de cabo Shirreff, isla Livingston, Antártica: un avance importante. *Boletín Antártico Chileno* 20 (2): 4-6.

Torres, D.E. & Valdenegro V. 2004. Nuevos registros de mortalidad y necropsias de cachorros de lobo fino antártico, Arctocephalus gazella, en cabo Shirreff, Isla Livingston, Antártica. *Boletín Antártico Chileno* 23 (1).

Torres, D., Vallejos, V., Acevedo, J., Hucke-Gaete, R. & Zarate, S. 1998. Registros biologicos atípico en cabo Shirreff, isla Livingston, Antártica. *Boletín Antártico Chileno* 17 (1): 17-19.

Torres, D., Vallejos, V., Acevedo, J., Blank, O., Hucke-Gaete, R. & Tirado, S. 1999. Actividades realizadas en cabo Shirreff, isla Livingston, en temporada 1998/99. *Boletín Antártico Chileno* 18 (1): 29-32.

Torres, T. 1993. Primer hallazgo de madera fósil en cabo Shirreff, isla Livingston, Antártica. *Serie Científica Instituto Antártico Chileno* 43: 31-39.

Torres, D., Acevedo, J., Torres, D.E., Vargas, R., & Aguayo-Lobo, A. 2012. Vagrant Subantarctic fur seal at Cape Shirreff, Livingston Island, Antarctica. *Polar Biology* 35 (3): 469–473.

Tufft, R. 1958. Preliminary biology report Livingston Island summer survey. Unpublished British Antarctic Survey report, BAS Archives Ref. AD6/2D/1957/N2.

U.S. AMLR 2008. AMLR 2007-2008 field season report. Objectives, Accomplishments and Tentative Conclusions. Southwest Fisheries Science Center Antarctic Ecosystem Research Group. October 2008.

U.S. AMLR 2009. AMLR 2008-2009 field season report. Objectives, Accomplishments and Tentative Conclusions. Southwest Fisheries Science Center Antarctic Ecosystem Research Group. May 2009.

Vargas, R., Osman, L.P. & Torres, D. 2009. Inter-sexual differences in Antarctic fur seal pup growth rates: evidence of environmental regulation? *Polar Biology* 32 (8):1177–86

Vallejos, V., Acevedo, J., Blank, O., Osman, L. & Torres, D. 2000. Informe científico - logístico. ECA XXXVI (1999/2000). Proyecto 018 "Estudios ecológicos sobre el lobo fino antártico, Arctocephalus gazella", cabo Shirreff, archipiélago de las Shetland del Sur, Antártica. Ministerio de Relaciones Exteriores, Instituto Antártico Chileno. Nº Ingreso 642/712, 19 ABR.2000.

Vallejos, V., Osman, L., Vargas, R., Vera, C. & Torres, D. 2003. Informe científico. ECA XXXIX (2002/2003). Proyecto INACH 018 "Estudios ecológicos sobre el lobo fino antártico, Arctocephalus gazella", cabo Shirreff, isla Livingston, Shetland del Sur, Antártica. Ministerio de Relaciones Exteriores, Instituto Antártico Chileno.

Vera, C., Vargas, R. & Torres, D. 2004. El impacto de la foca leopardo en la población de cachorros de lobo fino antártico en cabo Shirreff, Antártica, durante la temporada 2003/2004. *Boletín Antártico Chileno* 23 (1).

Warren, J., Sessions, S., Patterson, M. Jenkins, A., Needham, D. & Demer, D. 2005. Nearshore Survey. In AMLR 2004-2005 field season report. Objectives, Accomplishments and Tentative Conclusions. Southwest Fisheries Science Center Antarctic Ecosystem Research Group. La Jolla, California.

Warren, J., Cox, M., Sessions, S. Jenkins, A., Needham, D. & Demer, D. 2006. Nearshore acoustical survey near Cape Shirreff, Livingston Island. In AMLR 2005-2006 field season report. Objectives, Accomplishments and Tentative Conclusions. Southwest Fisheries Science Center Antarctic Ecosystem Research Group. La Jolla, California.

Warren, J., Cox, M., Sessions, S. Jenkins, A., Needham, D. & Demer, D. 2007. Nearshore acoustical survey near Cape Shirreff, Livingston Island. In AMLR 2006-2007 field season report. Objectives, Accomplishments and Tentative Conclusions. Southwest Fisheries Science Center Antarctic Ecosystem Research Group. La Jolla, California.

Woehler, E.J. (ed.) 1993. *The distribution and abundance of Antarctic and sub-Antarctic penguins.* SCAR, Cambridge.

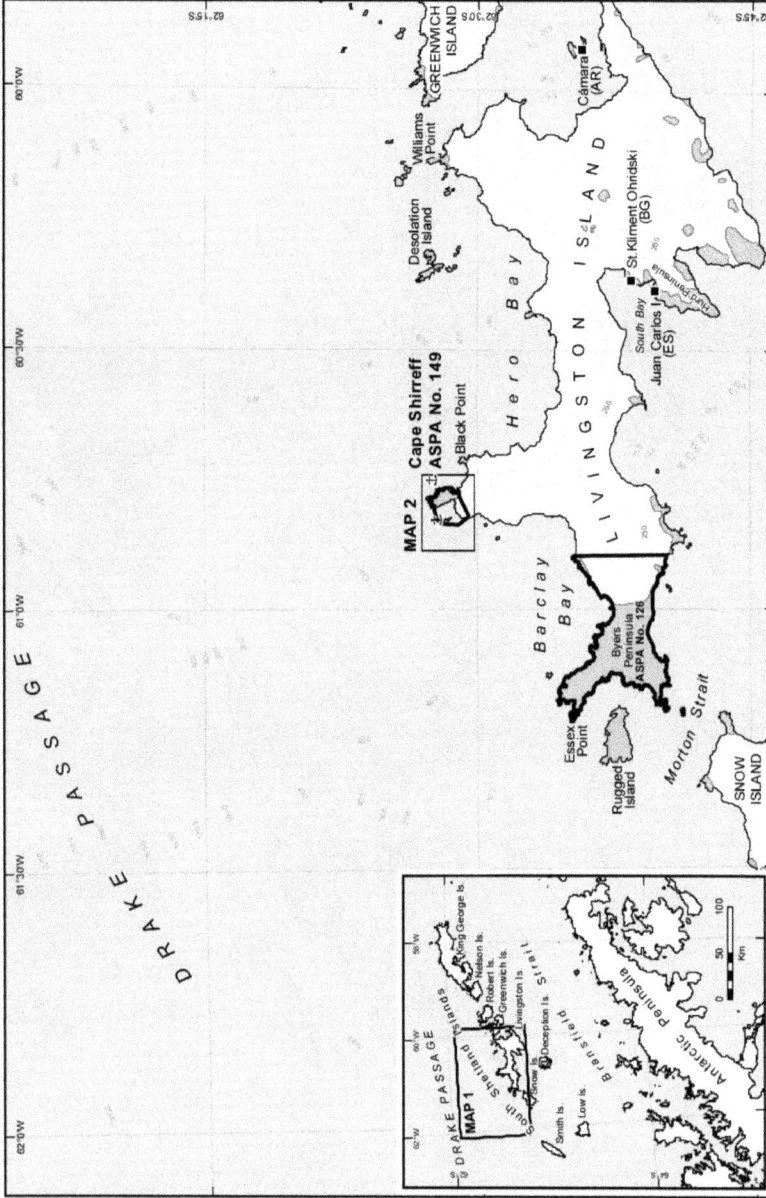

Map 1: ASPA No. 149 - Cape Shirreff & San Telmo Island - Regional overview

04 Mar 2016 (Map ID: 100/9 0003 04)
United States Antarctic Program / INACH
Environmental Research & Assessment

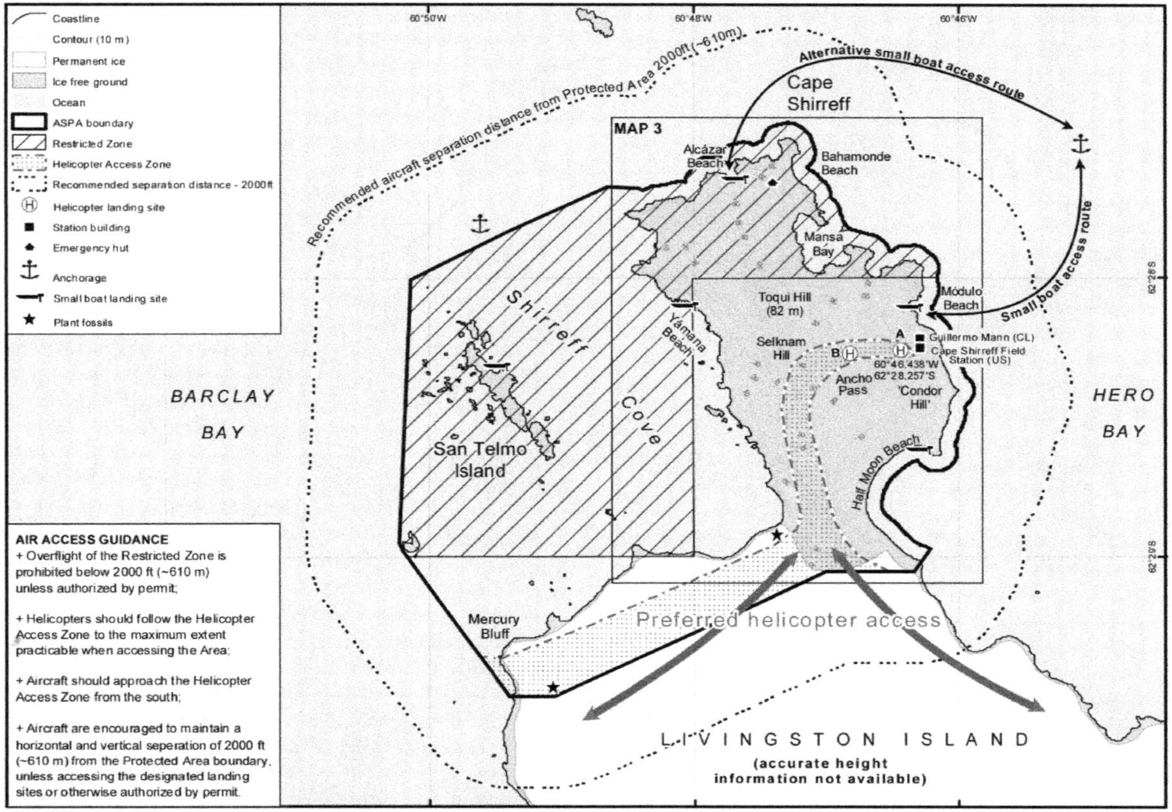
Coastline
Contour (10 m)
Permanent ice
Ice free ground
Ocean
ASPA boundary
Restricted Zone
Helicopter Access Zone
Recommended separation distance - 2000ft
Helicopter landing site
Station building
Emergency hut
Anchorage
Small boat landing site
Plant fossils
AIR ACCESS GUIDANCE
+ Overflight of the Restricted Zone is prohibited below 2000 ft (~610 m) unless authorized by permit;
+ Helicopters should follow the Helicopter Access Zone to the maximum extent practicable when accessing the Area;
+ Aircraft should approach the Helicopter Access Zone from the south;
+ Aircraft are encouraged to maintain a horizontal and vertical seperation of 2000 ft (~610 m) from the Protected Area boundary, unless accessing the designated landing sites or otherwise authorized by permit.
60°50'W
60°48'W
60°46'W
62°28'S
62°29'S
Recommended aircraft separation distance from Protected Area 2000ft (~610m)
Alternative small boat access route
Small boat access route
Cape Shirreff
MAP 3
Alcázar Beach
Bahamonde Beach
Mansa Bay
Módulo Beach
Toqui Hill (82 m)
Selknam Hill
Yámana Beach
A
B
Guillermo Mann (CL)
Cape Shirreff Field Station (US)
60°46.438'W
62°28.257'S
Ancho Pass
'Condor Hill'
Half Moon Beach
Shirreff Cove
San Telmo Island
BARCLAY BAY
HERO BAY
Mercury Bluff
Preferred helicopter access
LIVINGSTON ISLAND
(accurate height information not available)

Map 2: ASPA No. 149 Cape Shirreff & San Telmo Island - boundary and access guidelines

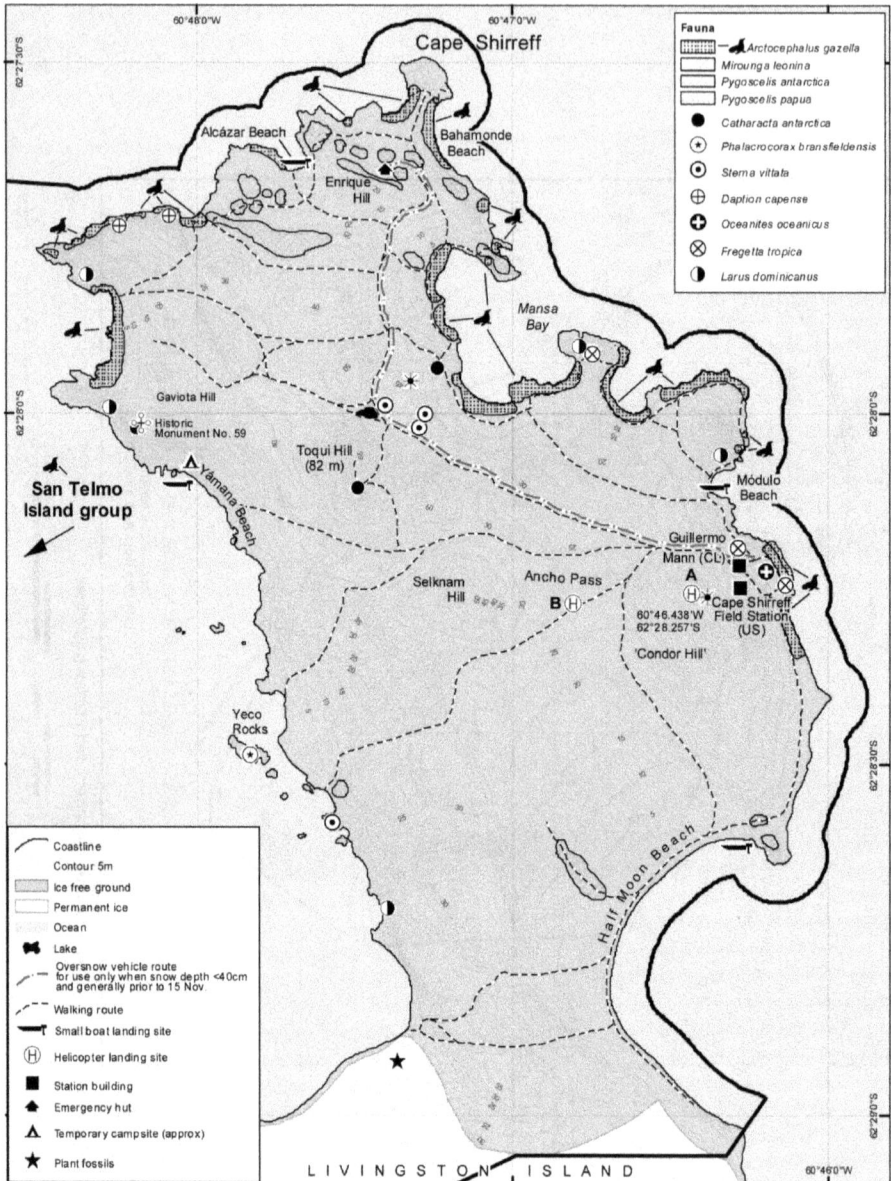

Fauna

	Arctocephalus gazella
	Mirounga leonina
	Pygoscelis antarctica
	Pygoscelis papua
●	*Catharacta antarctica*
⊛	*Phalacrocorax bransfieldensis*
⊙	*Sterna vittata*
⊕	*Daption capense*
✚	*Oceanites oceanicus*
⊗	*Fregetta tropica*
◑	*Larus dominicanus*

Coastline
Contour 5m
Ice free ground
Permanent ice
Ocean
Lake
Oversnow vehicle route for use only when snow depth <40cm and generally prior to 15 Nov.
Walking route
Small boat landing site
Ⓗ Helicopter landing site
■ Station building
♠ Emergency hut
△ Temporary campsite (approx)
★ Plant fossils

Map 3: ASPA No. 149 - Cape Shirreff & San Telmo Island - wildlife & human features

04 Mar 2016 (Map ID: 10069 005 08)
United States Antarctic Program / INACH
Environmental Research & Assessment

Projection: Lambert Conic Conformal
Spheroid and horizontal datum: WGS84
Data sources: Seal tracking station & H&M D. Krause (Dec 2015)
Walking routes: fauna: INACH, updated by M Goebel
D.Krause (2015); All other data: Instituto Antártico Chileno (INACH).

0 100 200 300 400 500
Meters

Management Plan for Antarctic Specially Protected Area No. 167

HAWKER ISLAND, PRINCESS ELIZABETH LAND

Introduction

Hawker Island (68°38'S, 77°51'E, Map A) is located 7 km south-west from Davis station off the Vestfold Hills on the Ingrid Christensen Coast, Princess Elizabeth Land, East Antarctica. The island was designated as Antarctic Specially Protected Area (ASPA) No. 167 under Measure 1 (2006), following a proposal by Australia, primarily to protect the southernmost breeding colony of southern giant petrels (*Macronectes giganteus*) (Map B). A revised management plan for the Area was adopted under Measure 9 (2011). The Area is one of only four known breeding locations for southern giant petrels on the coast of East Antarctica, all of which have been designated as ASPAs: ASPA 102, Rookery Islands, Holme Bay, Mac.Robertson Land (67°36'S, 62°53'E) – near Mawson Station; ASPA 160, Frazier Islands, Wilkes Land (66°13'S, 110°11'E) – near Casey station; and ASPA 120, Pointe Géologie, Terre Adélie (66°40'S, 140°01'E) – near Dumont d'Urville. Hawker Island also supports breeding colonies of Adélie penguins (*Pygocelis adeliae*), south polar skuas (*Catharacta maccormicki*), Cape petrels (*Daption capense*) and occasionally southern elephant seals (*Mirounga leonina*) haul out there.

1. Description of values to be protected

The total population of southern giant petrels in East Antarctica represents less than one per cent of the global breeding population. Estimates of breeding populations are problematic, as birds may be occupying a nest site when monitoring occurs, but not breeding that season. There are currently about 280 occupied nests in East Antarctica, comprising about 40 occupied nests on Hawker Island (2014), 2 occupied nests on Giganteus Island (Rookery Islands group) (2015), about 230 occupied nests on the Frazier Islands (2013) and about 8 occupied nests at Pointe Géologie (2005). Southern giant petrels also breed on islands in the southern Indian and Atlantic oceans and at the Antarctic Peninsula.

The southern giant petrel colony at Hawker Island was discovered in December 1963; at that time there were 40-50 nests present, "some with eggs" but it is unclear how many nests were occupied. From 1963 to 2007, intermittent counts of adults, eggs or chicks were undertaken at various stages of the breeding cycle. Because of the variability in the timing of counts and the inconsistency of count units it is not possible to establish a long term trend for this population. Low numbers were previously reported for this colony because only the numbers of chicks banded in a given year were recorded rather than total chick numbers.

Southern giant petrels are sensitive to disturbance at the nest. Restrictions in activities permitted at breeding sites near Australian stations, including a prohibition of banding, were introduced in the mid-1980s.

At the South Shetland Islands and South Orkney Islands, the incidental bycatch of southern giant petrels in longline fisheries operating in the Southern Ocean is likely to have contributed to observed population decreases. Similar observations have not been made in East Antarctica.

Southern giant petrels are listed as Least Concern by the International Union for Conservation of Nature (IUCN, 2016). However, census data from a number of locations are decades old and the size and trend of the global population is not entirely certain. Hawker Island also supports breeding colonies of Adélie penguins, south polar skuas and Cape petrels. Occasionally southern elephant seals haul out on the southern beaches.

2. Aims and objectives

Management of the Hawker Island ASPA aims to:

- protect the breeding colony of southern giant petrels and other wildlife;

- avoid degradation of, or substantial risk to, the values of the Area by preventing unnecessary human disturbance;
- allow scientific research on the ecosystem, particularly on the avifauna, and physical environment, provided it is for compelling reasons which cannot be served elsewhere;
- minimise the possibility of introduction of pathogens which may cause disease in bird populations within the Area;
- minimise human disturbance to southern giant petrels in the Area;
- allow the Area to be used as a reference area for future comparative studies with other breeding populations of southern giant petrels;
- protect the values of Hawker Island as a reference area for future comparative studies with other breeding populations of southern giant petrels;
- minimise the possibility of the introduction of alien plants, animals and microbes to Hawker Island;
- allow for the gathering of data on the population status and related demography of the bird species on a regular basis; and
- allow visits for management purposes in support of the aims of the management plan.

3. Management activities

The following management activities will be undertaken to protect the values of the Area:

- research visits to assess population status and trends of the southern giant petrel colony and/or other wildlife shall be permitted. Wherever feasible, preference shall be given to activities and methodologies which minimise disturbance to the breeding colony (e.g. use of automated cameras);
- visits shall be made to the Area as necessary (preferably not less than once every five years) to assess whether the Area continues to serve the purposes for which it was designated and to ensure that management activities are adequate;
- if practicable the Area shall be visited outside the breeding season of southern giant petrels (i.e. during the period mid-April to mid-September), to assess whether it continues to serve the purposes for which it was designated and to ensure that management activities are adequate;
- information on the location of Hawker Island ASPA (stating the restrictions that apply) shall be produced and copies of this management plan shall be available at nearby stations. Informative material and the management plan should be provided to ships visiting the vicinity; and
- the management plan shall be reviewed at least every five years.

4. Period of designation

Designation is for an indefinite period.

5. Maps

Map A: Antarctic Specially Protected Area No 167, Hawker Island Vestfold Hills, Ingrid Christensen Coast, East Antarctica.

Map B: Antarctic Specially Protected Area No 167, Hawker Island Vestfold Hills, Ingrid Christensen Coast, East Antarctica, Topography and Fauna Distribution.

Specifications for maps:

> Projection: UTM Zone 49
> Horizontal Datum: WGS84

6. Description of the Area

6(i) Geographical co-ordinates, boundary markers and natural features

Hawker Island is located at 68°38'S, 77°51'E, approximately 300 m offshore from the Vestfold Hills. The Vestfold Hills are a roughly triangular ice-free area of approximately 512 km² of bedrock, glacial debris, lakes and ponds. The Vestfold Hills are bound by the ice plateau to the east, the Sørsdal Glacier to the south, and Prydz Bay to the west. They contain low hills (maximum height 158 m at Boulder Hill) and valleys, and are penetrated deeply by fjords and lakes. Numerous islands fringe the coast of the Vestfold Hills, and Hawker Island lies in the south-west, between Mule Island and Mule Peninsula.

Hawker Island is an irregularly shaped island of low elevation (maximum elevation of nearly 40 m), with two parallel ranges running in a north south direction terminating in two small southern peninsulas. A third peninsula lies directly west and terminates with a 40 m hill with steep cliffs to the sea on the western and southerly aspects. A number of small freshwater lakes lie between the ranges of hills on the northern part of the island, with a number of small lakes lying on the flatter terrain on the eastern sector of the island. At its maximum extent the island is 2 km north to south and 1.7 km east to west.

The Hawker Island ASPA comprises the entire terrestrial area of Hawker Island, with the seaward boundary at the low water mark (Map B). The total area of the Hawker Island ASPA is approximately 1.9 km². There are no boundary markers.

Environmental Domains and Antarctic Conservation Biogeographic Regions

Based on the Environmental Domains Analysis for Antarctica (Resolution 3 (2008)) Hawker Island is located within Environment T *Inland continental geologic.*

Based on the Antarctic Conservation Biogeographic Regions (Resolution 6 (2012)), Hawker Island is located within Biogeographic Region 7 *East Antarctica.*

Human History

The first recorded sighting of the Vestfold Hills was on 9 February 1931 by Douglas Mawson on the BANZARE voyage of the *'Discovery'*. Four years later, on 20 February 1935, Captain Klarius Mikkelsen of the tanker *Thorshavn* (Lars Christensen Company), sighted the hills and landed in the area. He named many features in the area and in the Vestfold Hills after his home province in Norway. The Vestfold Hills were again visited by Mikkelsen in early 1937, while undertaking an aerial survey of the coast.

In January 1939, the American explorer, Lincoln Ellsworth, and his Australian adviser, Sir Hubert Wilkins were the next recorded visitors to the area in the motor ship *Wyatt Earp*. Ellsworth flew some 400 km inland. In early 1947, the *USS Currituck* visited the Ingrid Christensen Coast as part of Operation Highjump. Photographic flights were conducted to survey the coastline.

The first Australian National Antarctic Research Expedition (ANARE) to the area was led by Dr Phillip Law on *Kista Dan* and reached the Vestfold Hills on 1 March 1954. During January 1956, members of the Soviet Antarctic Expedition landed on the Ingrid Christensen Coast in preparation for the International Geophysical Year and established Mirny Station 595 km to the east. Australia established Davis station in the Vestfold Hills in 1957. Hawker Island was named for A.C. Hawker, radio supervisor at Davis station in 1957.

Climate

Meteorological data for the Area are confined almost entirely to observations at Davis station, 7 km northwest of Hawker Island. The Vestfold Hills area has a polar maritime climate that is cold, dry and windy. In summer, average temperatures range from -1°C to +3 °C and from -14°C to -21°C in winter. From 1957 to 2015, the maximum temperature recorded at Davis station was +13°C, while the lowest temperature was -41.8°C recorded on 27 April 1998. Long periods of relatively calm, fine conditions occur throughout the year. Winds are generally light. The yearly average is around 20 km/h. Violent winds and blizzards can commence with little warning at any time of the year, and gusts of over 200 km/h were recorded in 1972. Snowfall averages 78 mm/yr, with the greater proportion of annual accumulation resulting from windblown drift. Apart from several permanent ice banks, the Vestfold Hills are virtually snow free in summer and lightly covered in winter. The highest rainfall recorded at Davis was 55.6 mm in 2013. The record illustrates the seasonal climate expected for high latitudes, but on average Davis station is warmer than other Antarctic stations at similar latitudes. This has been attributed to the "rocky oasis" which results from the lower albedo of rock surfaces compared to ice, hence more solar energy is absorbed and re-radiated.

Geology

The Vestfold Hills consist of Archaean gneiss, upon which thin and often fossiliferous Pliocene and Quaternary sediments occupy depressions. The oldest known Cenozoic strata in the Vestfold Hills are the mid-Pliocene Sørsdal Formation, which contains a diverse marine fossil flora and fauna. Other younger Cenozoic strata attest to repeated glaciation, and several marine transgressions and regressions. The three major lithologies forming the Vestfold Hills are (in order of age) Chelnock Paragneiss, Mossel Gneiss and Crooked Lake Gneiss. This is repeated in units from east-north-east to west-south-west. Intruded into these, are groups of mafic dykes in a rough north-south orientation. The dykes are a major feature of the Vestfold Hills. Hawker Island comprises an extension of the Crooked Lake Gneiss of the northern portion of Mule Peninsula above Laternula Inlet. In common with the Archaean gneisses in the Vestfold Hills, the Hawker Island Crooked Lake Gneiss is cut by very distinctive, middle to early Proterozoic dolerite dykes.

Southern Giant Petrels

At Hawker Island, the colony of southern giant petrels is situated on slightly sloping ground about 20 m above sea-level at the northern end of the island (Map B). The same area has been used for breeding since its discovery in 1963/64.

The breeding season for southern giant petrels on Hawker Island commences in late September/early October and eggs are laid during the second half of October. Following an incubation period of about 60 days, hatching starts in the second half of December. Hatching continues over a period of three to four weeks until mid-January. About 14 – 16 weeks after hatching, the fledglings leave the colony from late March to early May. Images taken year round by automated cameras show that a small number of birds are present outside the breeding season; hence the requirement that visits to the Area at any time of the year be conducted in a manner that ensures minimal disturbance.

In the mid 1980s, a management strategy was implemented for all three southern giant petrels breeding localities in the vicinity of the Australian stations, to minimise human disturbance. Previously the Australian Antarctic Division restricted visits to one in every three to five year period and implemented tight administrative controls over all other visits. At this time, this level of visitation was considered an appropriate compromise between the risk of disturbing the birds and the need to obtain meaningful population data. However, this management regime impacted on the level of visitation needed to assess population status and trends and did not appear to significantly benefit the breeding success of the southern giant petrels. With the development of new technology (automated cameras), some detailed information can now be obtained with little or no human presence during the breeding period.

During the 2013/14 breeding season, 43 nests were occupied at some stage but not all adults attending them attempted to breed. In February 2014, at least 23 well advanced chicks were present. Some nests are not in the field of view of the automated cameras so the number of chicks may have been slightly higher.

Other Birds

Adélie penguins breed along the Vestfold Hills coastline and on 27 offshore islands, including Hawker Island. The total number of Adélie penguins in the Vestfold Hills coast and offshore islands was most recently estimated to be 330 000 pairs in 2009/10. The Hawker Island Adélie penguin colony is currently located in the vicinity of a small hill midway on the western side of the island and was estimated to be 5000 pairs in 2009/10. There has been an historical shift in the occupation of sub-colony areas. Some areas which were previously occupied are no longer occupied. This is common at Adélie penguin populations in the Davis region. As with other breeding sites in the Davis region, the first Adélie penguins usually appear in the area by the middle of October and eggs are laid about four weeks later. The laying interval between the first and second egg is 2 to 4 days, and the incubation period ranges from 32 to 35 days. The last moulted adults usually depart Hawker Island by the end of March.

A small colony of Cape petrels has been recorded on Hawker Island on the southern tip of the south western peninsula. Cape petrels are absent from the Area in winter; they return to their nesting sites during October, lay eggs from late November to early December and chicks fledge in late February and early March.

Seals

Weddell seals breed in the fjords of the Vestfold Hills and occasionally near the south-east part of Hawker Island. The seals start to appear in late September and early October, and pupping occurs from mid-October until late November. Throughout summer, moulting Weddell seals continue to frequent firm sea-ice and occasionally haul out onto land. Most of the local population remains in the sea ice region close to the Vestfold Hills throughout the summer. Non-breeding groups of southern elephant seals (*Mirounga leonina*) haul out during the summer months in the vicinity of the south-western peninsula on Hawker Island. Their moulting areas contain deposits of hair and excrement that have accumulated over several thousand years, and could be considered as sensitive areas.

Vegetation

The flora of the Vestfold Hills comprises at least 82 species of terrestrial algae, six moss species and at least 23 lichen species. The lichens and mosses are distributed chiefly in the eastern or inland sector and their distribution patterns reflect the availability of drift snow, time since exposure of the substrate from the ice plateau, time since the last glaciation, elevation and proximity to saline waters. Very few occurrences of lichens or mosses have been noted towards the salt-affected coastal margin including Hawker Island where the low terrain is densely covered with extensive sand and moraine deposits.

Terrestrial algae are widespread and are major primary producers in the Vestfold Hills. Sublithic (or hypolithic) algae have been reported from Hawker Island, developing on the undersurfaces of translucent quartz stones that are partially buried in soil. The dominant algae, Cyanobacteria, particularly oscillatoriacean species, *Chroococidiopsis sp.*, and *Aphanothece sp.* occur with the greatest frequency together with the Chlorophyta species, *cf. Desmococcus sp. A* and *Prasiococcus calcarius*. The endaphic alga *Prasiola crispa* occurs as green crumpled sheet-like strands at melt flushes, usually associated with the diatom *Navicula muticopsis* and oscillatoriacean algae. The ornithocophilous lichen *Candelariella flava* has been reported from Hawker Island, associated with seabird nesting sites.

Invertebrates

An extensive survey of terrestrial tardigrades (water dwelling, eight legged, segmented invertebrates) was undertaken in the Vestfold Hills in 1981 from which four genera and four species of tardigrade were recovered. Although no tardigrades were recovered from the Hawker Island sample site it has been suggested that, as two species of tardigrade, *Hypsibius allisonii* and *Macrobiotus fuciger (?)* were recovered from Walkabout Rocks, they may be found in other coastal areas of similar ecology, associated with *Prasiola crispa*. The mite, *Tydeus erebus* is associated with breeding sites of Adélie penguins on the island.

6(ii) Access to the Area

Depending on sea ice conditions, the Area can be approached by vehicle, small boat or aircraft, all of which must remain outside the Area. There are no designated landing sites within the Area.

Access by small boat should be via a site that exceeds minimum wildlife separation distance and that, as far as possible, is separated by a geographic feature such as a low ridge line to minimise disturbance on approach.

6(iii) Location of structures within and adjacent to the Area

There are no permanent structures within or adjacent to the Area. Three automated cameras are temporarily located in close proximity to the southern giant petrel colony, for the purposes of ongoing population monitoring.

6(iv) Location of other protected areas in the vicinity

Antarctic Specially Protected Area No. 143 Marine Plain (68°36'S, 78°07'E) is located approximately 8 km to the east.

6(v) Special zones within the Area

There are no special zones within the Area.

7. Terms and conditions for entry permits

7(i)   General conditions

Entry into the Area is prohibited except in accordance with a permit issued by an appropriate national authority. Conditions for issuing a permit to enter the Area are that:-

- it is issued only for compelling scientific reasons that cannot be served elsewhere, in particular for scientific study of the avifauna and ecosystem of the Area, or for essential management purposes consistent with plan objectives, such as inspection, management or review;

- the actions permitted will not jeopardise the values of the Area;

- the actions permitted are in accordance with the management plan;

- the permit, or an authorised copy, shall be carried within the Area;

- a visit report shall be supplied to the authority named in the permit;

- permits shall be issued for a finite period; and

- the appropriate national authority shall be notified of any activities or measures undertaken that were not included in the authorised permit.

7(ii) Access to, and movement within or over the Area

- Vehicles are prohibited within the Area. Movement within the Area is by foot only.

- Access to the Hawker Island ASPA boundary may be by watercraft or vehicle depending upon seasonal conditions. Boats used to visit the islands must be left at the shoreline. Only personnel who are required to carry out scientific/management work in the Area are to leave the landing/parking site. Quad-bikes or other land vehicles used to reach the Area shall not be taken into the Area. Vehicles shall remain on the sea-ice at least 200 m from the edge of the southern giant petrel colony (see Table 1);

- The minimum (closest) approach distances to wildlife are set out in Table 1. If disturbance of wildlife is observed, separation distance should be increased or the activity modified until there is no visible disturbance. Exceptions to this are only allowed when a closer approach distance is authorised in a permit.

- Persons authorised in a permit to approach southern giant petrels to obtain census data or biological data, should maintain the greatest practical separation distance. Persons shall not approach closer than is necessary to obtain census data or biological data from any nesting southern giant petrels, and in no case closer than 20m;

- Disturbance can be minimised by leaving vehicles as far from the site as possible, approaching slowly and quietly, and using topography to screen your approach.

- To reduce disturbance to wildlife, noise levels, including verbal communication are to be kept to a minimum. The use of motor-driven tools and any other activity likely to generate significant noise (thereby risking disturbance to nesting southern giant petrels and other nesting birds) is prohibited within the Area during the breeding period for southern giant petrels (mid-September to mid-April);

- Overflights of the island during the southern giant petrel breeding season are prohibited, except where essential for scientific or management purposes and authorised in a permit. Such overflights are to be at an altitude of no less than 930 m (3050 ft) for single-engine helicopters and fixed-wing aircraft, and no less than 1500 m (5000 ft) for twin-engine helicopters;

- Landing of aircraft within 930 m of a wildlife concentration for single-engine helicopters and fixed-wing aircraft, and within 1500 m (5000 ft) of a wildlife concentration for twin-engine helicopters is prohibited;

- Overflight of the Area, including by unmanned aerial vehicles, is prohibited (except where essential for scientific or management purposes as authorised in a Permit).

- Clothing (particularly all footwear and outer clothing) and field equipment shall be thoroughly cleaned before entering the Area.

Table 1: Minimum distances to maintain when approaching wildlife at Hawker Island

Species	Distances (m)		
	People on foot / ski (unless a closer approach distance is authorised in a permit)	**All vehicles** **Quad/ Skidoo** **Hagglunds, etc.**	**Small watercraft**
Giant petrels	100 m	Not permitted inside the Area. Parking shall be on the sea-ice and no closer than 200 m from wildlife colonies.	Watercraft should maintain 200 m from wildlife during transit and should not be landed within 50 m of wildlife; in particular, the Adélie penguin colony on the eastern shore. Care shall be taken when in close proximity to the island.
Breeding/moulting emperor penguin	50 m		
All other breeding animals and birds	15 m		
Non-breeding seal or bird	5 m		

7(iii) Activities which are or may be conducted within the Area, including restrictions on time and place

Activities undertaken within the breeding period of the southern giant petrel (16 September to 14 April) shall only be permitted if the activity is non-invasive and cannot reasonably be undertaken during the non-breeding period. Where practical, activities not relating to southern giant petrels shall be restricted to areas outside the visual catchment of the southern giant petrel breeding site.

The following activities may be conducted within the Area as authorised in a permit:

- scientific research consistent with the provisions of this management plan which cannot be undertaken elsewhere;

- essential management activities, including monitoring; and

- sampling which should be the minimum required for approved research programs.

7(iv) Installation, modification, or removal of structures

- Permanent structures or installations are prohibited.

- Temporary structures or equipment, including cameras, shall only be erected within the Area in accordance with in a permit.

- Small temporary refuges, hides, blinds or screens may be constructed for the purpose of scientific study.

- Installation (including site selection), removal, modification or maintenance of structures or equipment shall be undertaken in a manner that minimises disturbance to breeding birds and the surrounding environment.

- All scientific equipment or markers installed within the Area must be clearly identified by country, name of the principal investigator or national agency, year of installation and date of expected removal.

- Markers, signs or other structures erected within the Area for scientific or management purposes shall be secured and maintained in good condition and removed under permit when no longer required. All such items should be made of materials that pose minimal risk of harm to wildlife or of contamination of the Area.

7(v) Location of field camps

- Camping is prohibited within the Area except in an emergency. Any emergency camp should avoid areas of wildlife concentrations, if feasible.

7(vi) Restrictions on materials and organisms that may be brought into the Area

- Fuel is not to be stored in the Area. Boat refuelling is permitted at landing sites. A small amount of fuel may be taken into the Area for an emergency stove and must be handled in a way that minimises the risk of accidental introduction into the environment.

- No depots of food or other supplies are to be left within the Area beyond the season for which they are required.

- No poultry products, including dried food containing egg powder, are to be taken into the Area.

- No herbicides or pesticides are to be brought into the Area.

- Any chemical which may be introduced for compelling scientific purposes as authorised in a permit shall be removed from the Area, at or before the conclusion of the activity for which the permit was granted. The use of radio-nuclides or stable isotopes is prohibited.

- No animals, plant material or microorganisms shall be deliberately introduced into the Area and precautions shall be taken against accidental introductions; all equipment and clothing (particularly footwear) should be thoroughly cleaned before entering the Area.

- All material introduced shall be for a stated period only, shall be removed at or before the conclusion of that stated period, and shall be stored and handled so as to minimise the risk of environmental impact.

7(vii) Taking of or harmful interference with native flora and fauna

- Taking of, or harmful interference with, native flora and fauna is prohibited unless specifically authorised by permit. Any such permit shall clearly state the limits and conditions for such activities which, except in an emergency, shall only occur following approval by an appropriate animal ethics committee. Where taking or harmful interference with animals is involved this should, as a minimum standard, be in accordance with the SCAR Code of Conduct for the Use of Animals for Scientific Purposes in Antarctica.

- Ornithological research shall be limited to activities that are non-invasive and non-disruptive to the breeding seabirds present within the Area. Surveys, including aerial photographs for the purposes of population census, shall have a high priority.

- Disturbance of southern giant petrels or other wildlife shall be avoided at all times. Visitors should be alert to changes in wildlife behaviour, especially changes in posture or vocalisation. If birds are showing signs of wanting to leave the nest, all persons shall retreat immediately. .

7(viii) Collection or removal of anything not brought into the Area by the permit holder

- Material may only be collected or removed from the Area as authorised in a permit and should be limited to the minimum necessary to meet scientific or management needs.

- Material of human origin likely to compromise the values of the Area, which was not brought into the Area by the permit holder or otherwise authorised, may be removed unless the impact of the removal is likely to be greater than leaving the material *in situ*. If such material is found, the appropriate national authority must be notified and approval obtained prior to removal.

7(ix) Disposal of Waste

All wastes, including human wastes, shall be removed from the Area.

7(x) Measures that may be necessary to continue to meet the aims of the management plan

- GPS data shall be obtained for specific sites of long-term monitoring for lodgement with the Australian Antarctic Data Centre or the Antarctic Data Directory System through the appropriate national authority.

- Permits may be granted to enter the Area to carry out biological monitoring, Area inspection and management activities, which may involve the collection of samples for analysis or review; the erection or maintenance of temporary scientific equipment and structures, and signposts; or for other protective measures.

- Where practical, a census of southern giant petrels in the Area shall be conducted at least once in every five year period. Censuses of other species may be undertaken provided no additional disturbance is caused to the southern giant petrels.

- Where practical, activities not relating to southern giant petrels shall be restricted to areas outside the visual catchment of the southern giant petrel breeding site.

- Visitors shall take special precautions against introductions of non-indigenous organisms. Of particular concern are pathogenic, microbial or vegetation introductions sourced from soils, flora and fauna at other Antarctic sites, including research stations, or from regions outside Antarctica. To minimise the risk of introductions, before entering the Area visitors shall thoroughly clean footwear and any equipment, particularly sampling equipment and markers to be used in the Area.

7(xi) Requirement for reports

Visit reports shall provide detailed information on all census data; locations of any new colonies or nests not previously recorded, as texts and maps, a brief summary of research findings; copies of relevant photographs taken of the Area; and comments indicating measures taken to ensure compliance with permit conditions.

The report may make recommendations relevant to the management of the Area, in particular as to whether the values for which the Area was designated are being adequately protected and whether management measures are effective.

The report shall be submitted as soon as practicable after the visit to the ASPA has been completed to the appropriate national permitting authority who issue the permit, but no later than six months after the visit has occurred. A copy of the report shall be made available to the permit issuing authority and the Party responsible for development of the Management Plan (Australia - Australian Antarctic Division) (if different) for the purposes of reviewing the management plan. Such reports should include, as appropriate, the information identified in the Visit Report form contained in the Guide to the Preparation of Management

Plans for Antarctic Specially Protected Areas. Parties should maintain a record of such activities and, in the Annual Exchange of Information, should provide summary descriptions of activities conducted by persons subject to their jurisdiction, which should be in sufficient detail to allow evaluation of the effectiveness of the Management Plan.

8. Supporting documentation

Some or all of the data used within this paper were obtained from the **Australian Antarctic Data Centre (IDN Node AMD/AU)**, a part of the Australian Antarctic Division (Commonwealth of Australia).

Adamson, D.A. and Pickard, J. (1986): Cainozoic history of the Vestfold Hills, In Pickard, J., ed. *Antarctic Oasis, Terrestrial environments and history of the Vestfold Hills.* Sydney, Academic Press, 63–97.

Adamson, D.A. and Pickard, J. (1986): Physiology and geomorphology of the Vestfold Hills, In Pickard, J., ed. *Antarctic oasis: terrestrial environments and history of the Vestfold Hills.* Sydney, Academic Press, 99–139.

ACAP (Agreement on the Conservation of Albatrosses and Petrels) (2012) *Species assessments: southern giant petrel Macronectes giganteus.* <www.acap.aq/en/acap-species/288-southern-giant-petrel/file>, downloaded 19 September 2012.

ANARE (1968): Unpublished data.

Australian Antarctic Division (2010): Environmental Code of Conduct for Australian Field Activities, Territories, Environment and Treaties Section, Australian Antarctic Division.

Birdlife International (2000): *Threatened birds of the world.* Barcelona and Cambridge U. K, Lynx Edicions and Birdlife International.

BirdLife International (2011): *Macronectes giganteus,* In: IUCN 2011, 2011 IUCN Red List of Threatened Species, <http://www.iucnredlist.org/>, Downloaded on 17 January2011.

BirdLife International (2011): Species fact sheet: *Macronectes giganteus,* <http://www.birdlife.org/> Downloaded on 17 January 2011.

Cooper, J., Woehler, E., Belbin, L. (2000): Guest editorial, Selecting Antarctic Specially Protected Areas: Important Bird Areas can help, *Antarctic Science* 12: 129.

DSEWPC (Department of Sustainability, Environment, Water, Population and Communities) (2011a): *Background Paper: Population status and threats to albatrosses and giant petrels listed as threatened under Environment Protection and Biodiversity Conservation Act 1999*<http://www.environment.gov.au/resource/national-recovery-plan-threatened-albatrosses-and-giant-petrels-2011%E2%80%942016> Downloaded on 10 February 2016.

DSEWPC (Department of Sustainability, Environment, Water, Population and Communities) (2011b): *National recovery plan for threatened albatrosses and giant petrels: 2011-2016,* <http://www.environment.gov.au/biodiversity/threatened/publications/recovery/albatrosses-and-giant-petrels.html>, Downloaded on 10 February 2016.

Fabel, D., Stone, J., Fifield, L.K. and Cresswell, R.G. (1997): Deglaciation of the Vestfold Hills, East Antarctica; preliminary evidence from exposure dating of three subglacial erratics. In RICCI, C.A., ed. *The Antarctic region: geological evolution and processes,* Siena: Museo Nazionale dell'Antartide, 829–834.

Garnett ST, Szabo JK and Dutson G (2011). *The action plan for Australian birds 2010.* CSIRO Publishing.

Gore, D.B. (1997): Last glaciation of Vestfold Hills; extension of the East Antarctic ice sheet or lateral expansion of Sørsdal Glacier. *Polar Record,* 33: 5–12.

Hirvas, H., Nenonen, K. and Quilty, P. (1993): Till stratigraphy and glacial history of the Vestfold Hills area, East Antarctica, *Quaternary International,* 18: 81–95.

IUCN (International Union for Conservation of Nature) (2001): *IUCN Red List Categories: Version 3.1,* IUCN Species Survival Commission, <www.iucnredlist.org>. Downloaded on 25 January 2016.

IUCN (International Union for Conservation of Nature) (2015): *IUCN Red List of Threatened Species.* Version 2015.4<www.iucnredlist.org>. Downloaded on 25 January 2016.

Jouventin, P., Weimerskirch, H. (1991): Changes in the population size and demography of southern seabirds: management implications, in: Perrins, C.M., Lebreton, J.D. and Hirons, G.J.M. *Bird population studies: Relevance to conservation and management.* Oxford University Press: 297-314.

Johnstone, Gavin W.; Lugg, Desmond J., and Brown, D.A. (1973): The biology of the Vestfold Hills, Antarctica. Melbourne, Department of Science, Antarctic Division, *ANARE Scientific Reports*, Series B(1) Zoology, Publication No. 123.

Law P. (1958): Australian Coastal Exploration in Antarctica, *The Geographical Journal CXXIV*, 151-162.

Leishman, M.R. and Wild, C. (2001): Vegetation abundance and diversity in relation to soil nutrients and soil water content in Vestfold Hills, East, *Antarctic Science*, 13(2): 126-134

Micol, T., Jouventin, P. (2001): Long-term population trends in seven Antarctic seabirds at Point Géologie (Terre Adélie), Human impact compared with environmental change, *Polar Biology* 24: 175-185.

Miller, J.D. et al. (1984): A survey of the terrestrial Tardigrada of the Vestfold Hills, Antarctica, In Pickard, J., ed. *Antarctic Oasis, Terrestrial environments and history of the Vestfold Hills.* Sydney, Academic Press, 197-208.

Orton, M.N. (1963): Movements of young Giant Petrels bred in Antarctica, *Emu* 63: 260.

Patterson D.L., Woehler, E.J., Croxall, J.P., Cooper, J., Poncet, S., Fraser, W.R. (2008): Breeding distribution and population status of the Northern Giant Petrel *Macronectes halli* and the southern giant petrel *M. Giganteus, Marine Ornithology* 36: 115-124.

Pickard, J. ed., (1986): *Antarctic oasis: terrestrial environments and history of the Vestfold Hills.* Sydney, Academic Press.

Puddicombe, R.A.; and Johnstone, G.W. (1988): Breeding season diet of Adélie penguins at Vestfold Hills, East Antarctica, In *Biology of the Vestfold Hills*, Antarctica, edited by J.M. Ferris, H.R. Burton, G.W. Johnstone, and I.A.E. Bayly.

Rounsevell, D.E., and Horne, P.A. (1986): Terrestrial, parasitic and introduced invertebrates of the Vestfold Hills. *Antarctic oasis; terrestrial environments and history of the Vestfold Hills*, Sydney: Academic Press, 309-331.

Southwell C., Emmerson L., McKinlay J., Newberry K., Takahashi A., Kato A., Barbraud C., DeLord K., Weimerskirch H. (2015) Spatially extensive standardized surveys reveal widespread, multi-decadal increase in East Antarctic Adélie penguin populations. PLoS ONE 10(10): e0139877. doi:10.1371/journal.pone.0139877

Stattersfield, A.J., Capper, D.R. (eds.) (2000): Threatened Birds of the World. Lynx Editions, Barcelona.

Terauds, A., Chown, S.L., Morgan, F., Peat, H.J., Watts, D.J., Keys, H., Convey, P., and Bergstrom, D.M. (2012): Conservation biogeography of the Antarctic, *Diversity and Distributions* Vol. 18. 726-741.

Wienecke, B., Leaper, R., Hay, I., van den Hoff, J. (2009): Retrofitting historical data in population studies: southern giant petrels in the Australian Antarctic Territory, *Endangered Species Research* Vol. 8: 157-164.

Woehler, E.J., Cooper, J., Croxall, J.P., Fraser, W.R., Kooyman, G.L., Miller, G.D., Nel, D.C., Patterson, D.L., Peter, H-U, Ribic, C.A., Salwicka, K., Trivelpiece, W.Z., Wiemerskirch, H. (2001): *A Statistical Assessment of the Status and Trends of Antarctic and Subantarctic Seabirds,* SCAR/CCAMLR/NSF, 43 pp.

Map A: Antarctic Specially Protected Area No 167, Hawker Island
Vestfold Hills, Ingrid Christensen Coast, East Antarctica

Australian Government
Department of the Environment
Australian Antarctic Division

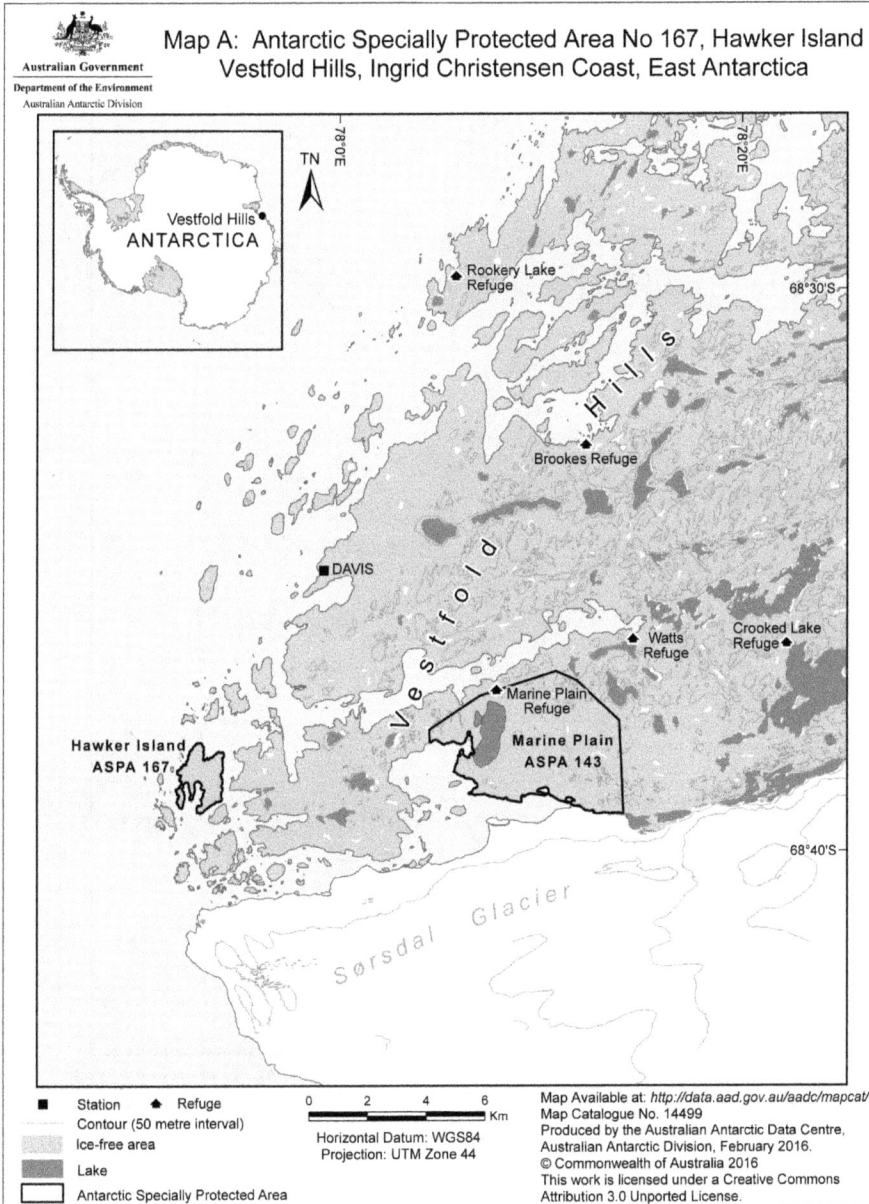

■ Station	♦ Refuge	
Contour (50 metre interval)		
Ice-free area		
Lake		
Antarctic Specially Protected Area		

0   2   4   6
▬▬▬ Km

Horizontal Datum: WGS84
Projection: UTM Zone 44

Map Available at: *http://data.aad.gov.au/aadc/mapcat/*
Map Catalogue No. 14499
Produced by the Australian Antarctic Data Centre,
Australian Antarctic Division, February 2016.
© Commonwealth of Australia 2016
This work is licensed under a Creative Commons
Attribution 3.0 Unported License.

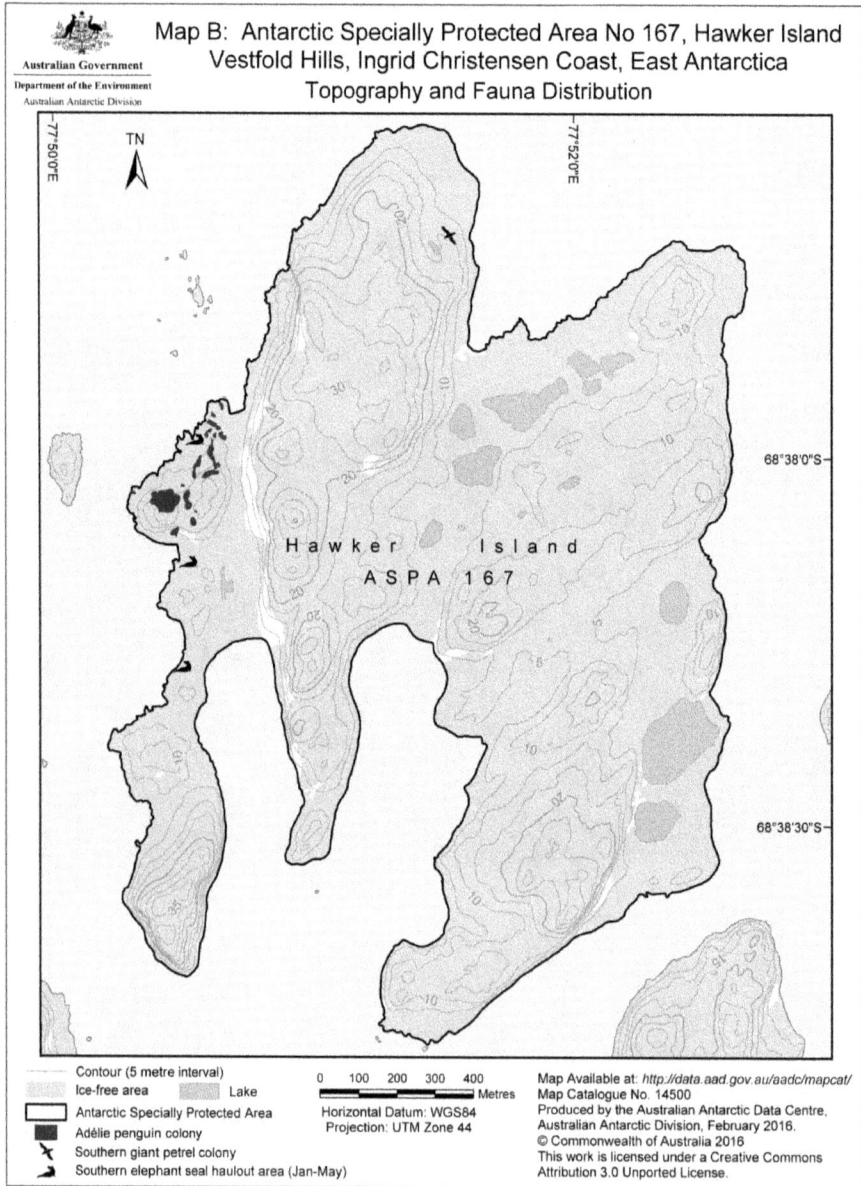

Map B: Antarctic Specially Protected Area No 167, Hawker Island Vestfold Hills, Ingrid Christensen Coast, East Antarctica Topography and Fauna Distribution

PART III

Opening and Closing Addresses and Reports

1. Opening and Closing Addresses

Welcoming Address by the Minister of Foreign Affairs, Heraldo Muñoz Valenzuela, at the Opening Ceremony of the XXXIX Antarctic Treaty Consultative Meeting

Santiago, 23 May 2016

(Vocatives)

First, I would like to welcome the representatives of the international Antarctic community on the occasion of this Thirty-ninth Antarctic Treaty Consultative Meeting (ATCM) and the nineteenth Meeting of the Committee for Environmental Protection.

These meetings take place exactly 50 years after the last regular consultative meeting held in Santiago – in 1966 -, and 55 years after the entry into force of the Antarctic Treaty. In just over half a century, the Antarctic Treaty System has become established as a successful model of international cooperation protecting this continent from international disagreements and conflicts present in other regions of our planet. This is a heritage we must value and protect, avoiding eventual differences that may negatively affect the work of this multilateral forum.

This international regime has considerably evolved since its creation. Every step we have taken, whether in the conservation of its marine and terrestrial resources, or by establishing instruments for the protection of the environment, has been done using creativity, and moved by the collective belief that the purposes and principles of the Antarctic Treaty System have an extraordinary value and deserve to be protected.

I wish to take this opportunity to share some short reflections that we, as a country, have embraced and that I believe may be of interest in the deliberations that will take place over the next eight days of the meeting:

Effective international cooperation for the current major challenges

International cooperation on the Antarctic Continent, particularly in the scientific field, has a long history dating back long before the Antarctic Treaty was signed. This Treaty provided a legal framework to what was already being done in practice, with the International Geophysical Year 1957- 1958 being the best example of this. The entry into force of the Treaty establishes a framework that requires the exchange of scientific information. The *Declaration on Antarctic Cooperation* on the occasion of the fiftieth anniversary of the entry into force of the Antarctic Treaty in 2011 was a clear recent manifestation of the will of the Parties to further develop this cooperation.

But the challenges, as well as the number of acceding countries and Consultative Parties of the Treaty, have grown and we believe that interaction among us remains inadequate. There is a large concentration of stations that support science in the Antarctic Peninsula area, but this installed capacity is underused and the coordination among the national programs is still partial. We believe it is necessary that the Parties seek ways to encourage further cooperation in science, but also in the use of the existing logistics.

Undoubtedly, greater coordination could bring significant benefits: an increased number of scientific projects through the reduction of the operational costs of the national programs, greater synergy across the different research projects and, additionally, a reduction of the human footprint on the continent, ultimately avoiding the construction or new facilities.

In this sense, Chile is making a great effort to support the development of science in Western Antarctica. One of the signature projects of our national program is the construction of the **International Antarctic Centre** in the city of Punta Arenas. With an investment of almost 40 million dollars, the building will include offices, laboratories and logistics facilities, just a two-hour flight from the Antarctic Continent.

Soon, an international tender process will be launched and we expect to have it operational by 2019. This project is not only intended to provide an infrastructure of excellence to the national scientific community. We also want to open up these facilities to our international partners, making the most of the privileged geographic position of our country and its proximity to the White Continent.

In addition to this, our country makes a significant annual effort to serve both the significant logistics platform of the Antarctic Peninsula and the 21 national Antarctic programmes that we received in Punta Arenas in the last season. Our logistics is, in one way or the other, an effective cooperation to the international Antarctic community.

We also recognise that the Antarctic is a privileged place for monitoring different phenomena of global interest and concern, including climate change. Temperature in the Antarctic Peninsula has increased by 3 degrees in the last 50 years. This may seem slight, but represents 5 times the average for the planet. The changes caused by the greenhouse effect that are seen in this region have a direct impact on the continental climate in Chile and the world, thus studying this is vital for the whole planet.

No country on its own can effectively study these phenomena that are of global significance and impact us all. Strengthened international cooperation is required, and Chile is willing to cooperate and make its scientific platform available for this purpose.

A clean Antarctica, but useful for Humankind

The conservation and protection of both terrestrial and marine Antarctic ecosystems are and will remain a priority for Chile. Our country was particularly active in the negotiation of the Protocol on Environmental Protection to the Antarctic Treaty signed in Madrid in 1991. It is no coincidence that our National Antarctic Policy —a document setting forth the major guidelines of our Antarctic work— was drafted just one year after the protocol entered into force. At that time, we considered that it was necessary to adapt our action to the evolution of the Antarctic Treaty System, including environmental protection in our national priorities.

Sixteen years have passed since our National Antarctic Policy was approved and the Antarctic Treaty System has continued to evolve. For this reason, the main national body for Antarctic affairs, the Antarctic Policy Council, which I have the honour to preside, adopted a mandate to update this national policy. This new formulation must necessarily strengthen the aspects of environmental protection taking into account the evolution of this matter since the Protocol on Environmental Protection entered into force. This updating process must be concluded by the end of this year.

This decision results from a detailed analysis of the strengths, weaknesses and opportunities provided by the Chilean Antarctic work. From this analysis conducted among institutions, we present the document *"Chile in Antarctica: Strategic Vision towards 2035"* that lays out more than 100 action proposals seeking to strengthen our position as a country with polar projection. Environmental issues have a special place in that strategy.

Environmental protection and climate change and ocean acidification measuring require being proactive and creative. One of Chile's priorities for the Southern Ocean is the creation of a representative system of Marine Protected Areas (MPAs) around the Antarctic Continent. To this end, our country is working, together with Argentina, on a proposal for MPA for the Antarctic Peninsula and the south of the Scotia Sea. Furthermore, Chile supports the two proposals that are currently being discussed by the Commission for the Conservation of Antarctic Marine Living Resources: one submitted by the United Stated and New Zealand for the Ross Sea region, and the other put forward by Australia, the European Union and France for the East Antarctica region. We also support the process led by Germany to create a proposal for MPA in the Weddell Sea region.

Our national Antarctic Policy on environmental issues can be summarized in the following motto, coined by Ambassador Oscar Pinochet de la Barra when he was Head of the Chilean Antarctic Institute: "*A clean, but useful Antarctica.*" Environmental protection and conservation must go hand in hand with activities for the benefit of humankind. It is not an easy balance to create, but we must unflaggingly aspire to achieve this.

Preservation of the historical heritage

When we talk about cooperation towards the major challenges that our planet is facing today and the need to minimise the impact of man on the Antarctic ecosystems, we are drafting an agenda for the future. However, we must remember that our countries are also united by a shared history, rich in achievements, where due to the inclement weather and geography, the best of man was required to conquer these cold and distant lands.

An example that we remember today was the brave feat when Chile, headed by pilot Luis Pardo, rescued the crew of the Endurance Expedition, exactly 100 years ago. We wanted to offer you a new exhibition at the venue of this conference, which is the result of the hard work undertaken jointly by the Department of Libraries, Archives and Museums (DIBAM), the National Maritime Museum, the Chilean Navy and the Ministry of Foreign Affairs. There you can follow day by day the development of this expedition, conducted in 1916 in conditions that are difficult to imagine nowadays.

Remembering our shared history is important. For this reason, protecting the historical sites in the Antarctica is a work that requires our attention. We are glad that this year through a joint proposal from the United Kingdom, Chile and the *International Association of Antarctica Tour Operators* (IAATO) new guidelines for visitors to Point Wild on Elephant Island, where the Endurance sank, are being addressed. Proposals such as this one seek to care for places of historical importance. It is also in this context that we value the information provided this year by France regarding the reinstatement of a plaque commemorating the journey of *Pourquoi Pas* on Petermann Island. These actions, with a strong historical content, are relevant in the context of the presence of man in the Antarctic Continent.

Final words

Next Monday we will have the opportunity to meet again to celebrate the 25th anniversary of the signing of the Protocol on Environmental Protection to the Antarctic Treaty. That occasion will be appropriate to refer more at length to this international instrument, the negotiation of which began here in Chile at two Special Meetings of the Treaty, held in November and December 1990, in Viña del Mar. We are pleased to celebrate this important anniversary in our country.

For this reason, next Monday we will have a Special Working Group of the Antarctic Treaty Consultative Meeting in the form of a Symposium. It will take stock of what has been achieved since the entry into force of this Protocol and will analyse the current and future environmental challenges to the Antarctic continent as a whole.

I wish you every success in your deliberations and work, as well as a fruitful and pleasant stay in our country. Let's take care of our Antarctica.

Thank you very much.

2. Reports by Depositaries and Observers

Report of the Depositary Government of the Antarctic Treaty and its Protocol in accordance with Recommendation XIII-2

Information Paper submitted by the United States

This report covers events with respect to the Antarctic Treaty and the Protocol on Environmental Protection to the Antarctic Treaty.

In the past year, there haves been one accession to the Treaty. Iceland deposited its instrument of accession to the Treaty on October 13, 2015. There were no accessions to the Protocol in the past year. There are fifty-three (53) Parties to the Treaty and thirty-seven (37) Parties to the Protocol.

The following countries have provided notification that they have designated the persons so noted as Arbitrators in accordance with Article 2(1) of the Schedule to the Protocol:

Bulgaria	Mrs. Guenka Beleva	30 July 2004
Chile	Amb. María Teresa Infante	June 2005
	Amb. Jorge Berguño	June 2005
	Dr. Francisco Orrego	June 2005
Finland	Amb. Holger Bertil Rotkirch	14 June 2006
India	Prof. Upendra Baxi	6 October 2004
	Mr. Ajai Saxena	6 October 2004
	Dr. N. Khare	6 October 2004
Japan	Judge Shunji Yanai	18 July 2008
Rep. of Korea	Prof. Park Ki Gab	21 October 2008
United States	Prof. Daniel Bodansky	1 May 2008
	Mr. David Colson	1 May 2008

Lists of Parties to the Treaty, to the Protocol, and of Recommendations/Measures and their approvals are attached.

Date of most recent action: October 13, 2015

The Antarctic Treaty

Done: Washington; December 1, 1959

Entry into force: June 23, 1961
In accordance with Article XIII, the Treaty was subject to ratification by the signatory States and is open for accession by any State which is a Member of the United Nations, or by any other State which may be invited to accede to the Treaty with the consent of all the Contracting Parties whose representatives are entitled to participate in the meetings provided for under Article IX of the Treaty; instruments of ratification and instruments of accession shall be deposited with the Government of the United States of America. Upon the deposit of instruments of ratification by all the signatory States, the Treaty entered into force for those States and for States which had deposited instruments of accession to the Treaty. Thereafter, the Treaty enters into force for any acceding State upon deposit of its instrument of accession.

Legend: (no mark) = ratification; a = accession; d = succession; w = withdrawal or equivalent action

Participant	Signature	Consent to be bound		Other Action	Notes
Argentina	December 1, 1959	June 23, 1961			
Australia	December 1, 1959	June 23, 1961			
Austria		August 25, 1987	a		
Belarus		December 27, 2006	a		
Belgium	December 1, 1959	July 26, 1960			
Brazil		May 16, 1975	a		
Bulgaria		September 11, 1978	a		
Canada		May 4, 1988	a		
Chile	December 1, 1959	June 23, 1961			
China		June 8, 1983	a		
Colombia		January 31, 1989	a		
Cuba		August 16, 1984	a		
Czech Republic		January 1, 1993	d		1
Denmark		May 20, 1965	a		
Ecuador		September 15, 1987	a		
Estonia		May 17, 2001	a		
Finland		May 15, 1984	a		
France	December 1, 1959	September 16, 1960			
Germany		February 5, 1979	a		2

---

[1] Effective date of succession by the Czech Republic. Czechoslovakia deposited an instrument of accession to the Treaty on June 14, 1962. On December 31, 1992, at midnight, Czechoslovakia ceased to exist and was succeeded by two separate and independent states, the Czech Republic and the Slovak Republic.

Greece		January 8, 1987	a		
Guatemala		July 31, 1991	a		
Hungary		January 27, 1984	a		
Iceland		October 13, 2015	a		
India		August 19, 1983	a		
Italy		March 18, 1981	a		
Japan	December 1, 1959	August 4, 1960			
Kazakhstan		January 27, 2015	a		
Korea (DPRK)		January 21, 1987	a		
Korea (ROK)		November 28, 1986	a		
Malaysia		October 31, 2011	a		
Monaco		May 31, 2008	a		

---

[2] The Embassy of the Federal Republic of Germany in Washington transmitted to the Department of State a diplomatic note, dated October 2, 1990, which reads as follows:

"The Embassy of the Federal Republic of Germany presents its compliments to the Department of State and has the honor to inform the Government of the United States of America as the depositary Government of the Antarctic Treaty that, t[h]rough the accession of the German Democratic Republic to the Federal Republic of Germany with effect from October 3, 1990, the two German states will unite to form one sovereign state which, as a contracting party to the Antarctic Treaty, will remain bound by the provisions of the Treaty and subject to those recommendations adopted at the 15 consultative meetings which the Federal Republic of Germany has approved. From the date of German unity, the Federal Republic of Germany will act under the designation of "Germany" within the framework of the [A]ntarctic system.
"The Embassy would be grateful if the Government of the United States of America could inform all contracting parties to the Antarctic Treaty of the contents of this note.
"The Embassy of the Federal Republic of Germany avails itself of this opportunity to renew to the Department of State the assurances of its highest consideration."

Prior to unification, on November 19, 1974, the German Democratic Republic deposited an instrument of accession to the Treaty, accompanied by a declaration, a Department of State English translation of which reads as follows:

"The German Democratic Republic takes the view that Article XIII, paragraph 1, of the Treaty is inconsistent with the principle that all States which are guided in their policies by the purposes and principles of the United Nations Charter have the right to become parties to treaties which affect the interest of all States."

Subsequently, on February 5, 1979, the Federal Republic of Germany deposited an instrument of accession to the Treaty accompanied by a statement, an English translation of which, provided by the Embassy of the Federal Republic of Germany, reads as follows:

"My dear Mr. Secretary,
"In connection with the deposit today of the instrument of accession to the Antarctic Treaty signed in Washington December 1, 1959, I have the honor to state on behalf of the Federal Republic of Germany that with effect from the day on which the treaty enters into force for the Federal Republic of Germany it will also apply to Berlin (West) subject to the rights and responsibilities of the French Republic, the United Kingdom of Great Britain and Northern Ireland and the United States of America including those relating to disarmament and demilitarization.
"Accept, Excellency, the expression of my highest consideration."

Mongolia		March 23, 2015	a		
Netherlands		March 30, 1967	a		3

[3] The instrument of accession to the Treaty by the Netherlands states that the accession is for the Kingdom in Europe, Suriname and the Netherlands Antilles.

Suriname became an independent state on November 25, 1975.

The Royal Netherlands Embassy in Washington transmitted to the Department of State a diplomatic note, dated January 9, 1986, which reads as follows:

"The Royal Netherlands Embassy presents its compliments to the Department of State and has the honor to request the Department's attention for the following with respect to the Department's capacity of depositary of [the Antarctic Treaty].
"Effective January 1, 1986 the island of Aruba – formerly part of the Netherlands Antilles – obtained internal autonomy as a country within the Kingdom of The Netherlands. Consequently the Kingdom of The Netherlands as of January 1, 1986 consists of three countries, to wit: the Netherlands proper, the Netherlands Antilles and Aruba.
"Since the abovementioned event concerns only a change in internal constitutional relations within the Kingdom of The Netherlands, and as the Kingdom as such, under international law, will remain the subject with which treaties are concluded, the aforementioned change will have no consequences in international law with regard to treaties concluded by the Kingdom, the application of which (treaties) were extended to the Netherlands Antilles, including Aruba.
"These treaties, thus, will remain applicable for Aruba in its new status as autonomous country within the Kingdom of The Netherlands effective January 1, 1986.
"Consequently the [Antarctic Treaty] to which the Kingdom of the Netherlands is a Party, and which [has] been extended to the Netherlands Antilles will as of January 1, 1986 apply to all three countries of the Kingdom of The Netherlands.
"The Embassy would appreciate if the other Parties concerned would be notified of the above.
"The Royal Netherlands Embassy avails itself of this opportunity to renew to the Department of State the assurance of its highest consideration."

The Royal Netherlands Embassy in Washington transmitted to the Department of State a diplomatic note, dated October 6, 2010, which reads in pertinent part as follows:

"The Kingdom of the Netherlands currently consists of three parts: the Netherlands, the Netherlands Antilles and Aruba. The Netherlands Antilles consists of the islands of Curaçao, Sint Maarten, Bonaire, Sint Eustatius and Saba.
"With effect from 10 October 2010, the Netherlands Antilles will cease to exist as a part of the Kingdom of the Netherlands. From that date onwards, the Kingdom will consist of four parts: the Netherlands, Aruba, Curaçao and Sint Maarten. Curaçao and Sint Maarten will enjoy internal self-government within the Kingdom, as Aruba and, up to 10 October 2010, the Netherlands Antilles do.
"These changes constitute a modification of the internal constitutional relations within the Kingdom of the Netherlands. The Kingdom of the Netherlands will accordingly remain the subject of international law with which agreements are concluded. The modification of the structure of the Kingdom will therefore not affect the validity of the international agreements ratified by the Kingdom for the Netherlands Antilles; these agreements will continue to apply to Curaçao and Sint Maarten.
"The other islands that have until now formed part of the Netherlands Antilles – Bonaire, Sint Eustatius and Saba – will become part of the Netherlands, thus constituting 'the Caribbean part of the Netherlands'. The agreements that now apply to the Netherlands Antilles will also continue to apply to these islands; however, the Government of the Netherlands will now be responsible for implementing these agreements."

New Zealand	December 1, 1959	November 1, 1960			
Norway	December 1, 1959	August 24, 1960			
Pakistan		March 1, 2012	a		
Papua New Guinea		March 16, 1981	d		4
Peru		April 10, 1981	a		
Poland		June 8, 1961	a		
Portugal		January 29, 2010	a		
Romania		September 15, 1971	a		5
Russian Federation	December 1, 1959	November 2, 1960			6
Slovak Republic		January 1, 1993	d		7
South Africa	December 1, 1959	June 21, 1960			
Spain		March 31, 1982	a		
Sweden		April 24, 1984	a		
Switzerland		November 15, 1990	a		
Turkey		January 24, 1996	a		
Ukraine		October 28, 1992	a		

---

[4] Date of deposit of notification of succession by Papua New Guinea; effective September 16, 1975, the date of its independence.

[5] The instrument of accession to the Treaty by Romania was accompanied by a note of the Ambassador of the Socialist Republic of Romania to the United States of America, dated September 15, 1971, which reads as follows:
"Dear Mr. Secretary:
"Submitting the instrument of adhesion of the Socialist Republic of Romania to the Antarctic Treaty, signed at Washington on December 1, 1959, I have the honor to inform you of the following:
'The Council of State of the Socialist Republic of Romania states that the provisions of the first paragraph of the article XIII of the Antarctic Treaty are not in accordance with the principle according to which the multilateral treaties whose object and purposes are concerning the international community, as a whole, should be opened for universal participation.'
"I am kindly requesting you, Mr. Secretary, to forward to all parties concerned the text of the Romanian instrument of adhesion to the Antarctic Treaty, as well as the text of this letter containing the above mentioned statement of the Romanian Government.
"I avail myself of this opportunity to renew to you, Mr. Secretary, the assurances of my highest consideration."

Copies of the Ambassador's letter and the Romanian instrument of accession to the Treaty were transmitted to the Antarctic Treaty parties by the Secretary of State's circular note dated October 1, 1971.

[6] The Treaty was signed and ratified by the former Union of Soviet Socialist Republics. By a note dated January 13, 1992, the Russian Federation informed the United States Government that it "continues to perform the rights and fulfil the obligations following from the international agreements signed by the Union of Soviet Socialist Republics."

[7] Effective date of succession by the Slovak Republic. Czechoslovakia deposited an instrument of accession to the Treaty on June 14, 1962. On December 31, 1992, at midnight, Czechoslovakia ceased to exist and was succeeded by two separate and independent states, the Czech Republic and the Slovak Republic.

United Kingdom	December 1, 1959	May 31, 1960			
United States	December 1, 1959	August 18, 1960			
Uruguay		January 11, 1980	a		8
Venezuela		March 24, 1999	a		

---

[8] The instrument of accession to the Treaty by Uruguay was accompanied by a declaration, a Department of State English translation of which reads as follows:

"The Government of the Oriental Republic of Uruguay considers that, through its accession to the Antarctic Treaty signed at Washington (United States of America) on December 1, 1959, it helps to affirm the principles of using Antarctica exclusively for peaceful purposes, of prohibiting any nuclear explosion or radioactive waste disposal in this area, of freedom of scientific research in Antarctica in the service of mankind, and of international cooperation to achieve these objectives, which are established in said Treaty.

"Within the context of these principles Uruguay proposes, through a procedure based on the principle of legal equality, the establishment of a general and definitive statute on Antarctica in which, respecting the rights of States as recognized in international law, the interests of all States involved and of the international community as a whole would be considered equitably.

"The decision of the Uruguayan Government to accede to the Antarctic Treaty is based not only on the interest which, like all members of the international community, Uruguay has in Antarctica, but also on a special, direct, and substantial interest which arises from its geographic location, from the fact that its Atlantic coastline faces the continent of Antarctica, from the resultant influence upon its climate, ecology, and marine biology, from the historic bonds which date back to the first expeditions which ventured to explore that continent and its waters, and also from the obligations assumed in conformity with the Inter-American Treaty of Reciprocal Assistance which includes a portion of Antarctic territory in the zone described in Article 4, by virtue of which Uruguay shares the responsibility of defending the region.

"In communicating its decision to accede to the Antarctic Treaty, the Government of the Oriental Republic of Uruguay declares that it reserves its rights in Antarctica in accordance with international law."

PROTOCOL ON ENVIRONMENTAL PROTECTION TO THE ANTARCTIC TREATY

Signed at Madrid on October 4, 1991*

State	Date of Signature	Date deposit of Ratification, Acceptance (A) or Approval (AA)	Date deposit of Accession	Date of entry into force	Date Acceptance ANNEX V**	Date of entry into force of Annex V
CONSULTATIVE PARTIES						
Argentina	Oct. 4, 1991	Oct. 28, 1993 [3]		Jan. 14, 1998	Sept. 8, 2000 (A) / Aug. 4, 1995 (B)	May 24, 2002
Australia	Oct. 4, 1991	Apr. 6, 1994		Jan. 14, 1998	Apr. 6, 1994 (A) / June 7, 1995 (B)	May 24, 2002
Belgium	Oct. 4, 1991	Apr. 26, 1996		Jan. 14, 1998	Apr. 26, 1996 (A) / Oct. 23, 2000 (B)	May 24, 2002
Brazil	Oct. 4, 1991	Aug. 15, 1995		Jan. 14, 1998	May 20, 1998 (B)	May 24, 2002
Bulgaria			April 21, 1998	May 21, 1998	May 5, 1999 (AB)	May 24, 2002
Chile	Oct. 4, 1991	Jan. 11, 1995		Jan. 14, 1998	Mar. 25, 1998 (B)	May 24, 2002
China	Oct. 4, 1991	Aug. 2, 1994		Jan. 14, 1998	Jan. 26, 1995 (AB)	May 24, 2002
Czech Rep. [1,2]	Jan. 1, 1993	Aug. 25, 2004 [4]		Sept. 24, 2004	Apr. 23, 2014 (B)	May 24, 2002
Ecuador	Oct. 4, 1991	Jan. 4, 1993		Jan. 14, 1998	May 11, 2001 (A) / Nov. 15, 2001 (B)	May 24, 2002
Finland	Oct. 4, 1991	Nov. 1, 1996 (A)		Jan. 14, 1998	Nov. 1, 1996 (A) / Apr. 2, 1997 (B)	May 24, 2002
France	Oct. 4, 1991	Feb. 5, 1993 (AA)		Jan. 14, 1998	Apr. 26, 1995 (B) / Nov. 18, 1998 (A)	May 24, 2002
Germany	Oct. 4, 1991	Nov. 25, 1994		Jan. 14, 1998	Nov. 25, 1994 (A) / Sept. 1, 1998 (B)	May 24, 2002
India	July 2, 1992	Apr. 26, 1996		Jan. 14, 1998	May 24, 2002 (B)	May 24, 2002
Italy	Oct. 4, 1991	Mar. 31, 1995		Jan. 14, 1998	May 31, 1995 (A) / Feb. 11, 1998 (B)	May 24, 2002
Japan	Sept. 29, 1992	Dec. 15, 1997 (A)		Jan. 14, 1998	Dec. 15, 1997 (AB)	May 24, 2002
Korea, Rep. of	July 2, 1992	Jan. 2, 1996		Jan. 14, 1998	June 5, 1996 (B)	May 24, 2002
Netherlands	Oct. 4, 1991	Apr. 14, 1994 (A) [6]		Jan. 14, 1998	Mar. 18, 1998 (B)	May 24, 2002
New Zealand	Oct. 4, 1991	Dec. 22, 1994		Jan. 14, 1998	Oct. 21, 1992 (B)	May 24, 2002
Norway	Oct. 4, 1991	June 16, 1993		Jan. 14, 1998	Oct. 13, 1993 (B)	May 24, 2002
Peru	Oct. 4, 1991	Mar. 8, 1993		Jan. 14, 1998	Mar. 8, 1993 (A) / Mar. 17, 1999 (B)	May 24, 2002
Poland	Oct. 4, 1991	Nov. 1, 1995		Jan. 14, 1998	Sept. 20, 1995 (B)	May 24, 2002
Russian Federation	Oct. 4, 1991	Aug. 6, 1997		Jan. 14, 1998	June 19, 2001 (B)	May 24, 2002
South Africa	Oct. 4, 1991	Aug. 3, 1995		Jan. 14, 1998	June 14, 1995 (B)	May 24, 2002
Spain	Oct. 4, 1991	July 1, 1992		Jan. 14, 1998	Dec. 8, 1993 (A) / Feb. 18, 2000 (B)	May 24, 2002
Sweden	Oct. 4, 1991	Mar. 30, 1994		Jan. 14, 1998	Mar. 30, 1994 (A)	May 24, 2002

Ukraine			May 25, 2001	June 24, 2001	Apr. 7, 1994 (B)	May 24, 2002
United Kingdom	Oct. 4, 1991	Apr. 25, 1995 [5]		Jan. 14, 1998	May 25, 2001 (A) May 21, 1996 (B)	May 24, 2002
United States	Oct. 4, 1991	Apr. 17, 1997		Jan. 14, 1998	Apr. 17, 1997 (A) May 6, 1998 (B)	May 24, 2002
Uruguay	Oct. 4, 1991	Jan. 11, 1995		Jan. 14, 1998	May 15, 1995 (B)	May 24, 2002

** The following denotes date relating either
to acceptance of Annex V or approval of Recommendation XVI-10
(A) Acceptance of Annex V   (B) Approval of Recommendation XVI-10

-2-

State	Date of Signature	Ratification Acceptance or Approval	Date deposit of Accession	Date of entry into force	Date Acceptance ANNEX V**	Date of entry into force of Annex V
NON-CONSULTATIVE PARTIES						
Austria	Oct. 4, 1991					
Belarus			July 16, 2008	Aug. 15, 2008		
Canada	Oct. 4, 1991	Nov. 13, 2003		Dec. 13, 2003		
Colombia	Oct. 4, 1991					
Cuba	July 2, 1992					
Denmark						
Estonia						
Greece	Oct. 4, 1991	May 23, 1995		Jan. 14, 1998		
Guatemala						
Hungary	Oct. 4, 1991					
Korea, DPR of	Oct. 4, 1991					
Malaysia						
Monaco			July 1, 2009	July 31, 2009		
Pakistan			Mar. 1, 2012	Mar. 31, 2012		
Papua New Guinea						
Portugal			Sept. 10, 2014	Oct. 10, 2014		
Romania	Oct. 4, 1991	Feb. 3, 2003		Mar. 5, 2003	Feb. 3, 2003	Mar. 5, 2003
Slovak Rep.[1,2]	Jan. 1, 1993					
Switzerland	Oct. 4, 1991					
Turkey			Aug. 1, 2014	Aug. 31, 2014		
Venezuela						

* Signed at Madrid on October 4, 1991; thereafter at Washington until October 3, 1992.
The Protocol will enter into force initially on the thirtieth day following the date of deposit of instruments of ratification, acceptance, approval or accession by all States which were Antarctic Treaty Consultative Parties at the date on which this Protocol was adopted. (Article 23)

** Adopted at Bonn on October 17, 1991 at XVIth Antarctic Consultative Meeting.

1. Signed for Czech & Slovak Federal Republic on Oct. 2, 1992 - Czechoslovakia accepts the jurisdiction of the International Court of Justice and Arbitral Tribunal for the settlement of disputes according to Article 19, paragraph 1. On December 31, 1992, at midnight, Czechoslovakia ceased to exist and was succeeded by two separate and independent states, the Czech Republic and the Slovak Republic.

2. Effective date of succession in respect of signature by Czechoslovakia which is subject to ratification by the Czech Republic and the Slovak Republic.

3. Accompanied by declaration, with informal translation provided by the Embassy of Argentina, which reads as follows: "The Argentine Republic declares that in as much as the Protocol to the Antarctic Treaty on the Protection of the Environment is a Complementary Agreement of the Antarctic Treaty and that its Article 4 fully respects what has been stated in Article IV, Subsection 1, Paragraph A) of said Treaty, none of its stipulations should be interpreted or be applied as affecting its rights, based on legal titles, acts of possession, contiguity and geological continuity in the region South of parallel 60, in which it has proclaimed and maintained its sovereignty."

4. Accompanied by declaration, with informal translation provided by the Embassy of the Czech Republic, which reads as follows: "The Czech Republic accepts the jurisdiction of the International Court of Justice and of the Arbitral Tribunal under Article 19, paragraph 1, of the Protocol on Environmental Protection to the Antarctic Treaty, done at Madrid on October 4, 1991."

161

5. Ratification on behalf of the United Kingdom of Great Britain and Northern Ireland, the Bailiwick of Jersey, the Bailiwick of Guernsey, the Isle of Man, Anguilla, Bermuda, the British Antarctic Territory, Cayman Islands, Falkland Islands, Montserrat, St. Helena and Dependencies, South Georgia and the South Sandwich Islands, Turks and Caicos Islands and British Virgin Islands.

6. Acceptance is for the Kingdom in Europe. At the time of its acceptance, the Kingdom of the Netherlands stated that it chooses both means for the settlement of disputes mentioned in Article 19, paragraph 1 of the Protocol, i.e. the International Court of Justice and the Arbitral Tribunal.

On October 27, 2004, the Kingdom of the Netherlands deposited an instrument, dated October 15, 2004, declaring that the Kingdom of the Netherlands accepts the Protocol for the Netherlands Antilles with a statement confirming that it chooses both means for the settlement of disputes mentioned in Article 19, paragraph 1 of the Protocol.

The Royal Netherlands Embassy in Washington transmitted to the Department of State a diplomatic note, dated October 6, 2010, which reads in pertinent part as follows:

"The Kingdom of the Netherlands currently consists of three parts: the Netherlands, the Netherlands Antilles and Aruba. The Netherlands Antilles consists of the islands of Curaçao, Sint Maarten, Bonaire, Sint Eustatius and Saba.

"With effect from 10 October 2010, the Netherlands Antilles will cease to exist as a part of the Kingdom of the Netherlands. From that date onwards, the Kingdom will consist of four parts: the Netherlands, Aruba, Curaçao and Sint Maarten. Curaçao and Sint Maarten will enjoy internal self-government within the Kingdom, as Aruba and, up to 10 October 2010, the Netherlands Antilles do.

"These changes constitute a modification of the internal constitutional relations within the Kingdom of the Netherlands. The Kingdom of the Netherlands will accordingly remain the subject of international law with which agreements are concluded. The modification of the structure of the Kingdom will therefore not affect the validity of the international agreements ratified by the Kingdom for the Netherlands Antilles; these agreements will continue to apply to Curaçao and Sint Maarten.

"The other islands that have until now formed part of the Netherlands Antilles – Bonaire, Sint Eustatius and Saba – will become part of the Netherlands, thus constituting 'the Caribbean part of the Netherlands'. The agreements that now apply to the Netherlands Antilles will also continue to apply to these islands; however, the Government of the Netherlands will now be responsible for implementing these agreements."

On October 16, 2014, the Kingdom of the Netherlands deposited an instrument, dated September 3, 2014, declaring that the Kingdom of the Netherlands approves Annex V to the Protocol for the Caribbean part of the Netherlands (the islands of Bonaire, Sint Eustatius and Saba).

Department of State,

Washington, April 21, 2016.

162

Approval, as notified to the Government of the United States of America, of measures
relating to the furtherance of the principles and objectives of the Antarctic Treaty

| | 16 Recommendations adopted at First Meeting (Canberra 1961) | 10 Recommendations adopted at Second Meeting (Buenos Aires 1962) | 11 Recommendations adopted at Third Meeting (Brussels 1964) | 28 Recommendations adopted at Fourth Meeting (Santiago 1966) | 9 Recommendations adopted at Fifth Meeting (Paris 1968) | 15 Recommendations adopted at Sixth Meeting (Tokyo 1970) |
	Approved	Approved	Approved	Approved	Approved	Approved
Argentina	ALL	ALL	ALL	ALL	ALL	ALL
Australia	ALL	ALL	ALL	ALL	ALL	ALL
Belgium	ALL	ALL	ALL	ALL	ALL	ALL
Brazil (1983)+	ALL	ALL	ALL	ALL	ALL	ALL except 10
Bulgaria (1998)+						
Chile	ALL	ALL	ALL	ALL	ALL	ALL
China (1985)+	ALL	ALL	ALL	ALL	ALL	ALL except 10
Czech Rep. (2014)+	1-7, 10 & 12-14	1, 4, 6-7 & 9	1-2, 7 & 11	14-15, 18, 21-24 & 27	2-3 & 6-7	1, 3, 5-7 & 10-13
Ecuador (1990)+						
Finland (1989)+						
France	ALL	ALL	ALL	ALL	ALL	ALL
Germany (1981)+	ALL	ALL	ALL except 8	ALL except 16-19	ALL except 6	ALL except 9
India (1983)+	ALL	ALL	ALL except 8***	ALL except 18	ALL	ALL except 9 & 10
Italy (1987)+	ALL	ALL	ALL	ALL	ALL	ALL
Japan	ALL	ALL	ALL	ALL	ALL	ALL
Korea, Rep. (1989)+	ALL	ALL	ALL	ALL	ALL	ALL
Netherlands (1990)+	ALL except 11 & 15	ALL except 3, 5, 8 & 10	ALL except 3, 4, 6 & 9	ALL except 20, 25, 26 & 28	ALL except 1, 8 & 9	ALL except 15
New Zealand	ALL	ALL	ALL	ALL	ALL	ALL
Norway	ALL	ALL	ALL	ALL	ALL	ALL
Peru (1989)+	ALL	ALL	ALL	ALL	ALL	ALL
Poland (1977)+	ALL	ALL	ALL	ALL	ALL	ALL
Russia	ALL	ALL	ALL	ALL	ALL	ALL
South Africa	ALL	ALL	ALL	ALL	ALL	ALL
Spain (1988)+	ALL	ALL	ALL	ALL	ALL	ALL
Sweden (1988)+						
U.K.	ALL	ALL	ALL	ALL	ALL	ALL
Uruguay (1985)+	ALL	ALL	ALL	ALL	ALL	ALL
U.S.A.	ALL	ALL	ALL	ALL	ALL	ALL

* IV-6, IV-10, IV-12, and V-5 terminated by VIII-2

*** Accepted as interim guideline

+ Year attained Consultative Status. Acceptance by that State required to bring into force Recommendations or Measures of meetings from that year forward.

Approval, as notified to the Government of the United States of America, of measures relating to the furtherance of the principles and objectives of the Antarctic Treaty

	9 Recommendations adopted at Seventh Meeting (Wellington 1972) Approved	14 Recommendations adopted at Eighth Meeting (Oslo 1975) Approved	6 Recommendations adopted at Ninth Meeting (London 1977) Approved	9 Recommendations adopted at Tenth Meeting (Washington 1979) Approved	3 Recommendations adopted at Eleventh Meeting (Buenos Aires 1981) Approved	8 Recommendations adopted at Twelfth Meeting (Canberra 1983) Approved
Argentina	ALL	ALL	ALL	ALL	ALL	ALL
Australia	ALL	ALL	ALL	ALL	ALL	ALL
Belgium	ALL	ALL	ALL	ALL	ALL	ALL
Brazil (1983)+	ALL except 5	ALL	ALL	ALL	ALL	ALL
Bulgaria (1998)+						
Chile	ALL	ALL	ALL	ALL	ALL	ALL
China (1985)+	ALL except 5	ALL	ALL	ALL	ALL	ALL
Czech Rep. (2014)+	4 & 6-8	1, 4, 6-10, 12 & 14	1 & 2	1-3 & 8	ALL except 2	ALL except 3-5
Ecuador (1990)+						
Finland (1989)+						
France	ALL	ALL	ALL	ALL	ALL	ALL
Germany (1981)+	ALL except 5	ALL except 2 & 5	ALL	ALL	ALL	ALL
India (1983)+	ALL	ALL	ALL	ALL except 1 & 9	ALL	ALL
Italy (1987)+	ALL except 5	ALL	ALL	ALL except 1 & 9	ALL	ALL
Japan	ALL	ALL	ALL	ALL	ALL	ALL
Korea, Rep. (1989)+	ALL	ALL	ALL except 3	ALL	ALL	ALL
Netherlands (1990)+	ALL	ALL	ALL	ALL except 9	ALL except 2	ALL
New Zealand	ALL	ALL	ALL	ALL	ALL	ALL
Norway	ALL	ALL	ALL	ALL	ALL	ALL
Peru (1989)+	ALL	ALL	ALL	ALL	ALL	ALL
Poland (1977)+	ALL	ALL	ALL	ALL	ALL	ALL
Russia	ALL	ALL	ALL	ALL	ALL	ALL
South Africa	ALL	ALL	ALL	ALL	ALL	ALL
Spain (1988)+	ALL	ALL	ALL	ALL except 1 & 9	ALL except 1	ALL
Sweden (1988)+						
U.K.	ALL	ALL	ALL	ALL	ALL	ALL
Uruguay (1985)+	ALL	ALL	ALL	ALL	ALL	ALL
U.S.A	ALL	ALL	ALL	ALL	ALL	ALL

---

* IV-6, IV-10, IV-12; and V-5 terminated by VIII-2

*** Accepted as interim guideline

+ Year attained Consultative Status. Acceptance by that State required to bring into force Recommendations or Measures of meetings from that year forward.

Approval, as notified to the Government of the United States of America, of measures relating to the furtherance of the principles and objectives of the Antarctic Treaty

	16 Recommendations adopted at Thirteenth Meeting (Brussels 1985)	10 Recommendations adopted at Fourteenth Meeting (Rio de Janeiro 1987)	22 Recommendations adopted at Fifteenth Meeting (Paris 1989)	13 Recommendations adopted at Sixteenth Meeting (Bonn 1991)	4 Recommendations adopted at Seventeenth Meeting (Venice 1992)	1 Recommendation adopted at Eighteenth Meeting (Kyoto 1994)
	Approved	Approved	Approved	Approved	Approved	Approved
Argentina	ALL	ALL	ALL	ALL	ALL	ALL
Australia	ALL	ALL	ALL	ALL	ALL	ALL
Belgium	ALL	ALL	ALL	ALL	ALL	ALL
Brazil (1983)+	ALL	ALL	ALL	ALL	ALL	ALL
Bulgaria (1998)+				XVI-10	ALL	ALL
Chile	ALL	ALL	ALL	ALL	ALL	ALL
China (1985)+	ALL	ALL	ALL	ALL	ALL	ALL
Czech Rep. (2014)+	1-3, 5-6, 8, 11 & 15-16	1, 3, 5, 7-8 & 10	2, 5, 12-19 & 21	1, 2, 5-6 & 10-12	ALL except 2	ALL
Ecuador (1990)+				XVI-10	ALL	ALL
Finland (1989)+			ALL	ALL	ALL	ALL
France	ALL	ALL	ALL	ALL	ALL	ALL
Germany (1981)+	ALL	ALL	ALL except 3, 8, 10, 11 & 22	ALL	ALL	ALL
India (1983)+	ALL	ALL	ALL	ALL	ALL	ALL
Italy (1987)+		ALL	ALL	ALL	ALL	ALL
Japan	ALL	ALL	ALL except 1-11, 16, 18 & 19	ALL except 1, 3-9, 12 & 13	ALL except 1-2 & 4	ALL
Korea, Rep. (1989)+	ALL	ALL	ALL except 22	ALL except 12	ALL except 1	ALL
Netherlands (1990)+	ALL except 9	ALL	ALL except 22	ALL	ALL	ALL
New Zealand	ALL	ALL	ALL	ALL	ALL	ALL
Norway	ALL	ALL	ALL	ALL	ALL	ALL
Peru (1989)+			ALL except 22	ALL except 13	ALL	ALL
Poland (1977)+	ALL	ALL	ALL	ALL	ALL	ALL
Russia	ALL	ALL	ALL	ALL	ALL	ALL
South Africa	ALL	ALL	ALL	ALL	ALL	ALL
Spain (1988)+	ALL	ALL	ALL	ALL	ALL	ALL
Sweden (1988)+			ALL	ALL	ALL	ALL
U.K.	ALL except 2	ALL	ALL except 3, 4, 8, 10 & 11	ALL except 4, 6, 8 & 9	ALL	ALL
Uruguay (1985)+	ALL	ALL	ALL	ALL	ALL	ALL
U.S.A	ALL	ALL	ALL except 1-4, 10 & 11	ALL	ALL	ALL

---

* IV-6, IV-10, IV-12, and V-5 terminated by VIII-2

*** Accepted as interim guideline

+ Year attained Consultative Status. Acceptance by that State required to bring into force Recommendations or Measures of meetings from that year forward.

ATCM XXXIX Final Report

relating to the furtherance of the principles and objectives of the Antarctic Treaty

	5 Measures adopted at Nineteenth Meeting (Seoul 1995)	2 Measures adopted at Twentieth Meeting (Utrecht 1996)	5 Measures adopted at Twenty-First Meeting (Christchurch 1997)	2 Measures adopted at Twenty-Second Meeting (Tromsø 1998)	1 Measure adopted at Twenty-Third Meeting (Lima 1999)
	Approved	Approved	Approved	Approved	Approved
Argentina	ALL	ALL	ALL	ALL	ALL
Australia	ALL	ALL	ALL	ALL	ALL
Belgium	ALL	ALL	ALL	ALL	ALL
Brazil (1983)+	ALL	ALL	ALL	ALL	ALL
Bulgaria (1998)+					
Chile	ALL	ALL	ALL	ALL	ALL
China (1985)+	ALL	ALL	ALL	ALL	ALL
Czech Rep. (2014)+	ALL except 1 & 2	ALL except 1	ALL except 1 & 2	ALL except 1	
Ecuador (1990)+	ALL	ALL	ALL	ALL	ALL
Finland (1989)+	ALL	ALL	ALL	ALL	ALL
France	ALL	ALL	ALL	ALL	ALL
Germany (1981)+	ALL	ALL	ALL	ALL	ALL
India (1983)+	ALL	ALL	ALL	ALL	ALL
Italy (1987)+	ALL	ALL			
Japan	ALL (except 2&5)	ALL (except 1)	All (except 1-2 & 5)	ALL	
Korea, Rep. (1989)+	ALL	ALL	ALL	ALL	ALL
Netherlands (1990)+	ALL	ALL	ALL	ALL	ALL
New Zealand	ALL	ALL	ALL	ALL	ALL
Norway	ALL	ALL	ALL	ALL	ALL
Peru (1989)+	ALL	ALL	ALL	ALL	ALL
Poland (1977)+	ALL	ALL	ALL	ALL	ALL
Russia	ALL	ALL	ALL	ALL	ALL
South Africa	ALL	ALL	ALL	ALL	ALL
Spain (1988)+	ALL	ALL	ALL	ALL	ALL
Sweden (1988)+	ALL	ALL	ALL	ALL	ALL
U.K.	ALL	ALL	ALL	ALL	ALL
Uruguay (1985)+	ALL	ALL	ALL	ALL	ALL
U.S.A.	ALL	ALL	ALL	ALL	ALL

"+ Year attained Consultative Status. Acceptance by that state required to bring into force Recommendations or Measures of meetings from that Year forward."

166

Approval, as notified to the Government of the United States of America, of measures relating to the furtherance of the principles and objectives of the Antarctic Treaty

	2 Measures adopted at Twelfth Special Meeting (The Hague 2000) Approved	3 Measures adopted at Twenty-Fourth Meeting (St. Petersburg 2001) Approved	1 Measure adopted at Twenty-Fifth Meeting (Warsaw 2002) Approved	3 Measures adopted at Twenty-Sixth Meeting (Madrid 2003) Approved	4 Measures adopted at Twenty-Seventh Meeting (Cape Town 2004) Approved
Argentina			*	XXVI-1, XXVI-2 *, XXVI-3 **	XXVII-1 *, XXVII-2 *, XXVII-3 **, XXVII-4
Australia	ALL	ALL	ALL	XXVI-1, XXVI-2 *, XXVI-3 **	XXVII-1 *, XXVII-2 *, XXVII-3 **, XXVII-4
Belgium	ALL	ALL	ALL	ALL	ALL
Brazil (1983)+	ALL	ALL	ALL	ALL	XXVII-1, XXVII-2, XXVII-3
Bulgaria (1998)+			*	XXVI-1, XXVI-2 *, XXVI-3 **	XXVII-1 *, XXVII-2 *, XXVII-3 **
Chile	ALL	ALL	ALL	ALL	ALL
China (1985)+	ALL	ALL	ALL	ALL	XXVII-1 *, XXVII-2 *, XXVII-3 **
Czech Rep. (2014)+	ALL	ALL	ALL	ALL	ALL
Ecuador (1990)+			*	XXVI-1, XXVI-2 *, XXVI-3 **	XXVII-1 *, XXVII-2 *, XXVII-3 **
Finland (1989)+	ALL	ALL	*	XXVI-1, XXVI-2 *, XXVI-3 **	XXVII-1, XXVII-2 *, XXVII-3 **, XXVII-4
France	ALL (except SATCM XII-2)	ALL	*	XXVI-1, XXVI-2 *, XXVI-3 **	XXVII-1, XXVII-2 *, XXVII-3, XXVII-4
Germany (1981)+	ALL	ALL	ALL	ALL	XXVII-1 *, XXVII-2 *, XXVII-3 **
India (1983)+	ALL	ALL	ALL	ALL	XXVII-1 *, XXVII-2 *, XXVII-3 **
Italy (1987)+		ALL	ALL	XXVI-1, XXVI-2 *, XXVI-3 **	XXVII-1 *, XXVII-2 *, XXVII-3 **
Japan	ALL	ALL	*	ALL	XXVII-1 *, XXVII-2 *, XXVII-3 **, XXVII-4
Korea, Rep. (1989)+	ALL	ALL	*	XXVI-1, XXVI-2 *, XXVI-3 **	XXVII-1 *, XXVII-2 *, XXVII-3 **
Netherlands (1990)+	ALL	ALL	ALL	XXVI-1, XXVI-2 *, XXVI-3 **	ALL
New Zealand	ALL	ALL	ALL	ALL	XXVII-1 *, XXVII-2 *, XXVII-3 **, XXVII-4
Norway		ALL	*	XXVI-1, XXVI-2 *, XXVI-3 **	XXVII-1 *, XXVII-2 *, XXVII-3 **
Peru (1989)+	ALL	ALL	ALL	XXVI-1, XXVI-2 *, XXVI-3 **	XXVII-1 *, XXVII-2 *, XXVII-3 **
Poland (1977)+		ALL	ALL	ALL	ALL
Russia	ALL	ALL	ALL	XXVI-1, XXVI-2, XXVI-3 **	XXVII-1 *, XXVII-2 *, XXVII-3 **
South Africa	ALL	ALL	ALL	ALL	ALL
Spain (1988)+			*	XXVI-1, XXVI-2 *, XXVI-3 **	XXVII-1 *, XXVII-2 *, XXVII-3 **
Sweden (1988)+	ALL	ALL	ALL	ALL	XXVII-1 *, XXVII-2 *, XXVII-3 **
Ukraine (2004)+					XXVII-1 *, XXVII-2 *, XXVII-3 **
U.K.	ALL (except SATCM XII-2)	ALL (except XXIV-3)	ALL	ALL	XXVII-1 *, XXVII-2 *, XXVII-3 **, XXVII-4
Uruguay (1985)+	ALL	ALL	*	XXVI-1, XXVI-2 *, XXVI-3	XXVII-1 *, XXVII-2 *, XXVII-3 **, XXVII-4
U.S.A.	ALL	ALL	*	XXVI-1, XXVI-2 *, XXVI-3 **	XXVII-1 *, XXVII-2 *, XXVII-3 **

* +Year attained Consultative Status. Acceptance by that state required to bring into force Recommendations or Measures of meetings from that Year forward."

* Management Plans annexed to this Measure were deemed to have been approved in accordance with Article 6(1) of Annex V to the Protocol on Environmental Protection to the Antarctic Treaty and the Measure not specifying a different approval method.

** Revised and updated List of Historic Sites and Monuments annexed to this Measure was deemed to have been approved in accordance with Article 8(2) of Annex V to the Protocol on Environmental Protection to the Antarctic Treaty and the Measure not specifying a different approval method.

Approval, as notified to the Government of the United States of America, of measures relating to the furtherance of the principles and objectives of the Antarctic Treaty

	5 Measures adopted at Twenty-Eighth Meeting (Stockholm 2005) Approved	4 Measures adopted at Twenty-Ninth Meeting (Edinburgh 2006) Approved	3 Measures adopted at Thirtieth Meeting (New Delhi 2007) Approved	14 Measures adopted at Thirty-first Meeting (Kyiv 2008) Approved
Argentina	XXVIII-2 *, XXVIII-3 *, XXVIII-4 *, XXVIII-5 **	XXIX-1 *, XXIX-2 *, XXIX-3 **, XXIX-4 ***	XXX-1 *, XXX-2 *, XXX-3 **	XXXI-1 - XXXI-14 *
Australia	XXVIII-1, XXVIII-2 *, XXVIII-3 *, XXVIII-4 *, XXVIII-5 **	XXIX-1 *, XXIX-2 *, XXIX-3 **, XXIX-4 ***	XXX-1 *, XXX-2 *, XXX-3 **	XXXI-1 - XXXI-14 *
Belgium	ALL except Measure 1	ALL	ALL	XXXI-1 - XXXI-14 *
Brazil (1983)+	ALL except Measure 1	XXIX-1 *, XXIX-2 *, XXIX-3 **, XXIX-4 ***	XXX-1 *, XXX-2 *, XXX-3 **	XXXI-1 - XXXI-14 *
Bulgaria (1998)+	XXVIII-2 *, XXVIII-3 *, XXVIII-4 *, XXVIII-5 **	XXIX-1 *, XXIX-2 *, XXIX-3 **, XXIX-4 ***	XXX-1 *, XXX-2 *, XXX-3 **	XXXI-1 - XXXI-14 *
Chile	ALL except Measure 1	XXIX-1 *, XXIX-2 *, XXIX-3 **, XXIX-4 ***	XXX-1 *, XXX-2 *, XXX-3 **	XXXI-1 - XXXI-14 *
China (1985)+	XXVIII-2 *, XXVIII-3 *, XXVIII-4 *, XXVIII-5 **	XXIX-1 *, XXIX-2 *, XXIX-3 **, XXIX-4 ***	XXX-1 *, XXX-2 *, XXX-3 **	XXXI-1 - XXXI-14 *
Czech Rep. (2014)+	ALL except Measure 1	ALL	ALL	ALL except Measure 8
Ecuador (1990)+	XXVIII-2 *, XXVIII-3 *, XXVIII-4 *, XXVIII-5 **	XXIX-1 *, XXIX-2 *, XXIX-3 **, XXIX-4 ***	XXX-1 *, XXX-2 *, XXX-3 **	XXXI-1 - XXXI-14 *
Finland (1989)+	XXVIII-1, XXVIII-2 *, XXVIII-3 *, XXVIII-4 *, XXVIII-5 **	XXIX-1 *, XXIX-2 *, XXIX-3 **, XXIX-4 ***	XXX-1 *, XXX-2 *, XXX-3 **	XXXI-1 - XXXI-14 *
France	XXVIII-2 *, XXVIII-3 *, XXVIII-4 *, XXVIII-5 **	XXIX-1 *, XXIX-2 *, XXIX-3 **, XXIX-4 ***	XXX-1 *, XXX-2 *, XXX-3 **	XXXI-1 - XXXI-14 *
Germany (1981)+	XXVIII-2 *, XXVIII-3 *, XXVIII-4 *, XXVIII-5 **	XXIX-1 *, XXIX-2 *, XXIX-3 **, XXIX-4 ***	XXX-1 *, XXX-2 *, XXX-3 **	XXXI-1 - XXXI-14 *
India (1983)+	XXVIII-2 *, XXVIII-3 *, XXVIII-4 *, XXVIII-5 **	XXIX-1 *, XXIX-2 *, XXIX-3 **, XXIX-4 ***	XXX-1 *, XXX-2 *, XXX-3 **	XXXI-1 - XXXI-14 *
Italy (1987)+	XXVIII-1, XXVIII-2 *, XXVIII-3 *, XXVIII-4 *, XXVIII-5 **	XXIX-1 *, XXIX-2 *, XXIX-3 **, XXIX-4 ***	XXX-1 *, XXX-2 *, XXX-3 **	XXXI-1 - XXXI-14 *
Japan	XXVIII-2 *, XXVIII-3 *, XXVIII-4 *, XXVIII-5 **	XXIX-1 *, XXIX-2 *, XXIX-3 **, XXIX-4 ***	XXX-1 *, XXX-2 *, XXX-3 **	XXXI-1 - XXXI-14 *
Korea, Rep. (1989)+	XXVIII-2 *, XXVIII-3 *, XXVIII-4 *, XXVIII-5 **	XXIX-1 *, XXIX-2 *, XXIX-3 **, XXIX-4 ***	XXX-1 *, XXX-2 *, XXX-3 **	XXXI-1 - XXXI-14 *
Netherlands (1990)+	ALL	ALL	ALL	ALL
New Zealand	XXVIII-1, XXVIII-2 *, XXVIII-3 *, XXVIII-4 *, XXVIII-5 **	XXIX-1 *, XXIX-2 *, XXIX-3 **, XXIX-4 ***	XXX-1 *, XXX-2 *, XXX-3 **	XXXI-1 - XXXI-14 *
Norway	XXVIII-1, XXVIII-2 *, XXVIII-3 *, XXVIII-4 *, XXVIII-5 **	XXIX-1 *, XXIX-2 *, XXIX-3 **, XXIX-4 ***	XXX-1 *, XXX-2 *, XXX-3 **	XXXI-1 - XXXI-14 *
Peru (1989)+	XXVIII-1, XXVIII-2 *, XXVIII-3 *, XXVIII-4 *, XXVIII-5 **	XXIX-1 *, XXIX-2 *, XXIX-3 **, XXIX-4 ***	XXX-1 *, XXX-2 *, XXX-3 **	XXXI-1 - XXXI-14 *
Poland (1977)+	ALL	ALL	ALL	XXXI-1 - XXXI-14 *
Russia	XXVIII-2 *, XXVIII-3 *, XXVIII-4 *, XXVIII-5 **	XXIX-1 *, XXIX-2 *, XXIX-3 **, XXIX-4 ***	XXX-1 *, XXX-2 *, XXX-3 **	XXXI-1 - XXXI-14 *
South Africa	XXVIII-1, XXVIII-2 *, XXVIII-3 *, XXVIII-4 *, XXVIII-5 **	ALL	XXX-1 *, XXX-2 *, XXX-3 **	XXXI-1 - XXXI-14 *
Spain (1988)+	XXVIII-1, XXVIII-2 *, XXVIII-3 *, XXVIII-4 *, XXVIII-5 **	XXIX-1 *, XXIX-2 *, XXIX-3 **, XXIX-4 ***	XXX-1 *, XXX-2 *, XXX-3 **	XXXI-1 - XXXI-14 *
Sweden (1988)+	XXVIII-1, XXVIII-2 *, XXVIII-3 *, XXVIII-4 *, XXVIII-5 **	XXIX-1 *, XXIX-2 *, XXIX-3 **, XXIX-4 ***	XXX-1 *, XXX-2 *, XXX-3 **	XXXI-1 - XXXI-14 *
Ukraine (2004)+	XXVIII-2 *, XXVIII-3 *, XXVIII-4 *, XXVIII-5 **	XXIX-1 *, XXIX-2 *, XXIX-3 **, XXIX-4 ***	XXX-1 *, XXX-2 *, XXX-3 **	XXXI-1 - XXXI-14 *
U.K.	XXVIII-1, XXVIII-2 *, XXVIII-3 *, XXVIII-4 *, XXVIII-5 **	XXIX-1 *, XXIX-2 *, XXIX-3 **, XXIX-4 ***	XXX-1 *, XXX-2 *, XXX-3 **	XXXI-1 - XXXI-14 *
Uruguay (1985)+	XXVIII-2 *, XXVIII-3 *, XXVIII-4 *, XXVIII-5 **	XXIX-1 *, XXIX-2 *, XXIX-3 **, XXIX-4 ***	XXX-1 *, XXX-2 *, XXX-3 **	XXXI-1 - XXXI-14 *
U.S.A.	XXVIII-2 *, XXVIII-3 *, XXVIII-4 *, XXVIII-5 **	XXIX-1 *, XXIX-2 *, XXIX-3 **, XXIX-4 ***	XXX-1 *, XXX-2 *, XXX-3 **	XXXI-1 - XXXI-14 *

*+Year attained Consultative Status. Acceptance by that state required to bring into force Recommendations or Measures of meetings from that Year forward."

* Management Plans annexed to this Measure deemed to have been approved in accordance with Article 6(1) of Annex V to the Protocol on Environmental Protection to the Antarctic Treaty and the Measure not specifying a different approval method.

** Revised and updated List of Historic Sites and Monuments annexed to this Measure deemed to have been approved in accordance with Article 8(2) of Annex V to the Protocol on Environmental Protection to the Antarctic Treaty and the Measure not specifying a different approval method.

*** Modification of Appendix A to Annex II to the Protocol on Environmental Protection to the Antarctic Treaty deemed to have been approved in accordance with Article 9(1) of Annex II to the Protocol on Environmental Protection to the Antarctic Treaty and the Measure not specifying a different approval method.

Approval, as notified to the Government of the United States of America, of measures relating to the furtherance of the principles and objectives of the Antarctic Treaty

	16 Measures adopted at Thirty-second Meeting (Baltimore 2009) — Approved	15 Measures adopted at Thirty-third Meeting (Punta del Este 2010) — Approved	12 Measures adopted at Thirty-fourth Meeting (Buenos Aires 2011) — Approved	11 Measures adopted at Thirty-fifth Meeting (Hobart 2012) — Approved	21 Measures adopted at Thirty-sixth Meeting (Brussels 2013) — Approved
Argentina	XXXII-1 - XXXII-13* and XXXII-14**	XXXIII-1 - XXXIII-14* and XXXIII-15**	XXXIV-1 - XXXIV-10* and XXXIV-11 - XXXIV-12**	XXXV-1 - XXXV-10* and XXXV-11***	XXXVI-1 - XXXVI-17* and XXXVI-18 - XXXVI-21**
Australia	XXXII-1 - XXXII-13* and XXXII-14**, XXXII-15	XXXIII-1 - XXXIII-14* and XXXIII-15**	XXXIV-1 - XXXIV-10* and XXXIV-11 - XXXIV-12**	XXXV-1 - XXXV-10* and XXXV-11***	XXXVI-1 - XXXVI-17* and XXXVI-18 - XXXVI-21**
Belgium	XXXII-1 - XXXII-14* and XXXII-15**	XXXIII-1 - XXXIII-14* and XXXIII-15**	XXXIV-1 - XXXIV-10* and XXXIV-11 - XXXIV-12**	XXXV-1 - XXXV-10* and XXXV-11***	XXXVI-1 - XXXVI-17* and XXXVI-18 - XXXVI-21**
Brazil (1983)+	XXXII-1 - XXXII-13* and XXXII-14**	XXXIII-1 - XXXIII-14* and XXXIII-15**	XXXIV-1 - XXXIV-10* and XXXIV-11 - XXXIV-12**	XXXV-1 - XXXV-10* and XXXV-11***	XXXVI-1 - XXXVI-17* and XXXVI-18 - XXXVI-21**
Bulgaria (1998)+	XXXII-1 - XXXII-13* and XXXII-14**	XXXIII-1 - XXXIII-14* and XXXIII-15**	XXXIV-1 - XXXIV-10* and XXXIV-11 - XXXIV-12**	XXXV-1 - XXXV-10* and XXXV-11***	XXXVI-1 - XXXVI-17* and XXXVI-18 - XXXVI-21**
Chile	XXXII-1 - XXXII-13* and XXXII-14**	XXXIII-1 - XXXIII-14* and XXXIII-15**	XXXIV-1 - XXXIV-10* and XXXIV-11 - XXXIV-12**	XXXV-1 - XXXV-10* and XXXV-11***	XXXVI-1 - XXXVI-17* and XXXVI-18 - XXXVI-21**
China (1985)+	XXXII-1 - XXXII-13* and XXXII-14**	XXXIII-1 - XXXIII-14* and XXXIII-15**	XXXIV-1 - XXXIV-10* and XXXIV-11 - XXXIV-12**	XXXV-1 - XXXV-10* and XXXV-11***	XXXVI-1 - XXXVI-17* and XXXVI-18 - XXXVI-21**
Czech Rep. (2014)+	ALL except 2 and 16	ALL	ALL	ALL	ALL
Ecuador (1990)+	XXXII-1 - XXXII-13* and XXXII-14**	XXXIII-1 - XXXIII-14* and XXXIII-15**	XXXIV-1 - XXXIV-10* and XXXIV-11 - XXXIV-12**	XXXV-1 - XXXV-10* and XXXV-11***	XXXVI-1 - XXXVI-17* and XXXVI-18 - XXXVI-21**
Finland (1989)+	XXXII-1 - XXXII-13* and XXXII-14**, XXXII-16	XXXIII-1 - XXXIII-14* and XXXIII-15**	XXXIV-1 - XXXIV-10* and XXXIV-11 - XXXIV-12**	XXXV-1 - XXXV-10* and XXXV-11***	XXXVI-1 - XXXVI-17* and XXXVI-18 - XXXVI-21**
France	XXXII-1 - XXXII-13* and XXXII-14**, XXXII-15	XXXIII-1 - XXXIII-14* and XXXIII-15**	XXXIV-1 - XXXIV-10* and XXXIV-11 - XXXIV-12**	XXXV-1 - XXXV-10* and XXXV-11***	XXXVI-1 - XXXVI-17* and XXXVI-18 - XXXVI-21**
Germany (1981)+	XXXII-1 - XXXII-13* and XXXII-14**	XXXIII-1 - XXXIII-14* and XXXIII-15**	XXXIV-1 - XXXIV-10* and XXXIV-11 - XXXIV-12**	XXXV-1 - XXXV-10* and XXXV-11***	XXXVI-1 - XXXVI-17* and XXXVI-18 - XXXVI-21**
India (1983)+	XXXII-1 - XXXII-13* and XXXII-14**	XXXIII-1 - XXXIII-14* and XXXIII-15**	XXXIV-1 - XXXIV-10* and XXXIV-11 - XXXIV-12**	XXXV-1 - XXXV-10* and XXXV-11***	XXXVI-1 - XXXVI-17* and XXXVI-18 - XXXVI-21**
Italy (1987)+	XXXII-1 - XXXII-13* and XXXII-14**	XXXIII-1 - XXXIII-14* and XXXIII-15**	XXXIV-1 - XXXIV-10* and XXXIV-11 - XXXIV-12**	XXXV-1 - XXXV-10* and XXXV-11***	XXXVI-1 - XXXVI-17* and XXXVI-18 - XXXVI-21**
Japan	XXXII-1 - XXXII-13* and XXXII-14**, XXXII-15	XXXIII-1 - XXXIII-14* and XXXIII-15**	XXXIV-1 - XXXIV-10* and XXXIV-11 - XXXIV-12**	XXXV-1 - XXXV-10* and XXXV-11***	XXXVI-1 - XXXVI-17* and XXXVI-18 - XXXVI-21**
Korea, Rep. (1989)+	XXXII-1 - XXXII-13* and XXXII-14**	XXXIII-1 - XXXIII-14* and XXXIII-15**	XXXIV-1 - XXXIV-10* and XXXIV-11 - XXXIV-12**	XXXV-1 - XXXV-10* and XXXV-11***	XXXVI-1 - XXXVI-17* and XXXVI-18 - XXXVI-21**
Netherlands (1990)+	XXXII-1 - XXXII-13 and XXXII-14; XXXII-15 - XXXII-16	ALL	ALL	ALL	XXXVI-1 - XXXVI-17* and XXXVI-18 - XXXVI-21**
New Zealand	XXXII-1 - XXXII-13* and XXXII-14**	XXXIII-1 - XXXIII-14* and XXXIII-15**	XXXIV-1 - XXXIV-10* and XXXIV-11 - XXXIV-12**	XXXV-1 - XXXV-10* and XXXV-11***	XXXVI-1 - XXXVI-17* and XXXVI-18 - XXXVI-21**
Norway	XXXII-1 - XXXII-13* and XXXII-14**	XXXIII-1 - XXXIII-14* and XXXIII-15**	XXXIV-1 - XXXIV-10* and XXXIV-11 - XXXIV-12**	XXXV-1 - XXXV-10* and XXXV-11***	XXXVI-1 - XXXVI-17* and XXXVI-18 - XXXVI-21**
Peru (1969)+	XXXII-1 - XXXII-13* and XXXII-14**	XXXIII-1 - XXXIII-14* and XXXIII-15**	XXXIV-1 - XXXIV-10* and XXXIV-11 - XXXIV-12**	XXXV-1 - XXXV-10* and XXXV-11***	XXXVI-1 - XXXVI-17* and XXXVI-18 - XXXVI-21**
Poland (1977)+	XXXII-1 - XXXII-13* and XXXII-14**	XXXIII-1 - XXXIII-14* and XXXIII-15**	XXXIV-1 - XXXIV-10* and XXXIV-11 - XXXIV-12**	XXXV-1 - XXXV-10* and XXXV-11***	XXXVI-1 - XXXVI-17* and XXXVI-18 - XXXVI-21**
Russia	XXXII-1 - XXXII-13* and XXXII-14**	XXXIII-1 - XXXIII-14* and XXXIII-15**	XXXIV-1 - XXXIV-10* and XXXIV-11 - XXXIV-12**	XXXV-1 - XXXV-10* and XXXV-11***	XXXVI-1 - XXXVI-17* and XXXVI-18 - XXXVI-21**
South Africa	XXXII-1 - XXXII-13* and XXXII-14**	XXXIII-1 - XXXIII-14* and XXXIII-15**	XXXIV-1 - XXXIV-10* and XXXIV-11 - XXXIV-12**	XXXV-1 - XXXV-10* and XXXV-11***	XXXVI-1 - XXXVI-17* and XXXVI-18 - XXXVI-21**
Spain (1988)+	XXXII-1 - XXXII-13* and XXXII-14**	XXXIII-1 - XXXIII-14* and XXXIII-15**	XXXIV-1 - XXXIV-10* and XXXIV-11 - XXXIV-12**	XXXV-1 - XXXV-10* and XXXV-11***	XXXVI-1 - XXXVI-17* and XXXVI-18 - XXXVI-21**
Sweden (1988)+	XXXII-1 - XXXII-13* and XXXII-14**	XXXIII-1 - XXXIII-14* and XXXIII-15**	XXXIV-1 - XXXIV-10* and XXXIV-11 - XXXIV-12**	XXXV-1 - XXXV-10* and XXXV-11***	XXXVI-1 - XXXVI-17* and XXXVI-18 - XXXVI-21**
Ukraine (2004)+	XXXII-1 - XXXII-13* and XXXII-14**	XXXIII-1 - XXXIII-14* and XXXIII-15**	XXXIV-1 - XXXIV-10* and XXXIV-11 - XXXIV-12**	XXXV-1 - XXXV-10* and XXXV-11***	XXXVI-1 - XXXVI-17* and XXXVI-18 - XXXVI-21**
U.K.	XXXII-1 - XXXII-13* and XXXII-14**, XXXII-15 - XXXII-16	XXXIII-1 - XXXIII-14* and XXXIII-15**	XXXIV-1 - XXXIV-10* and XXXIV-11 - XXXIV-12**	XXXV-1 - XXXV-10* and XXXV-11***	XXXVI-1 - XXXVI-17* and XXXVI-18 - XXXVI-21**
Uruguay (1985)+	XXXII-1 - XXXII-13* and XXXII-14**, XXXII-15	XXXIII-1 - XXXIII-14* and XXXIII-15**	XXXIV-1 - XXXIV-10* and XXXIV-11 - XXXIV-12**	XXXV-1 - XXXV-10* and XXXV-11***	XXXVI-1 - XXXVI-17* and XXXVI-18 - XXXVI-21**
U.S.A.	XXXII-1 - XXXII-13* and XXXII-14**	XXXIII-1 - XXXIII-14* and XXXIII-15**	XXXIV-1 - XXXIV-10* and XXXIV-11 - XXXIV-12**	XXXV-1 - XXXV-10* and XXXV-11***	XXXVI-1 - XXXVI-17* and XXXVI-18 - XXXVI-21**

"+Year attained Consultative Status.   Acceptance by that state required to bring into force Recommendations or Measures of meetings from that 'Year forward.'"

* Management Plans annexed to these Measures deemed to have been approved in accordance with Article 6(1) of Annex V to the Protocol on Environmental Protection to the Antarctic Treaty and the Measure not specifying a different approval method.

** Modifications and/or additions to List of Historic Sites and Monuments deemed to have been approved in accordance with Article 8(2) of Annex V to the Protocol on Environmental Protection to the Antarctic Treaty and the Measure not specifying a different approval method.

	16 Measures adopted at Thirty-seventh Meeting (Brasilia 2014) Approved	19 Measures adopted at Thirty-eighth Meeting (Sofia 2015) Approved
Argentina	XXXVII-1 - XXXVII-16*	XXXVIII-1 - XXXVIII-18* and XXXVIII-19**
Australia	XXXVII-1 - XXXVII-16*	XXXVIII-1 - XXXVIII-18* and XXXVIII-19**
Belgium	XXXVII-1 - XXXVII-16*	XXXVIII-1 - XXXVIII-18* and XXXVIII-19**
Brazil (1983)+	XXXVII-1 - XXXVII-16*	XXXVIII-1 - XXXVIII-18* and XXXVIII-19**
Bulgaria (1998)+	XXXVII-1 - XXXVII-16*	XXXVIII-1 - XXXVIII-18* and XXXVIII-19**
Chile	XXXVII-1 - XXXVII-16*	XXXVIII-1 - XXXVIII-18* and XXXVIII-19**
China (1985)+	XXXVII-1 - XXXVII-16*	XXXVIII-1 - XXXVIII-18* and XXXVIII-19**
Czech Rep. (2014)+	XXXVII-1 - XXXVII-16*	XXXVIII-1 - XXXVIII-18* and XXXVIII-19**
Ecuador (1990)+	XXXVII-1 - XXXVII-16*	XXXVIII-1 - XXXVIII-18* and XXXVIII-19**
Finland (1989)+	XXXVII-1 - XXXVII-16*	XXXVIII-1 - XXXVIII-18* and XXXVIII-19**
France	XXXVII-1 - XXXVII-16*	XXXVIII-1 - XXXVIII-18* and XXXVIII-19**
Germany (1981)+	XXXVII-1 - XXXVII-16*	XXXVIII-1 - XXXVIII-18* and XXXVIII-19**
India (1983)+	XXXVII-1 - XXXVII-16*	XXXVIII-1 - XXXVIII-18* and XXXVIII-19**
Italy (1987)+	XXXVII-1 - XXXVII-16*	XXXVIII-1 - XXXVIII-18* and XXXVIII-19**
Japan	XXXVII-1 - XXXVII-16*	XXXVIII-1 - XXXVIII-18* and XXXVIII-19**
Korea, Rep. (1989)+	XXXVII-1 - XXXVII-16*	XXXVIII-1 - XXXVIII-18* and XXXVIII-19**
Netherlands (1990)+	XXXVII-1 - XXXVII-16*	XXXVIII-1 - XXXVIII-18* and XXXVIII-19**
New Zealand	XXXVII-1 - XXXVII-16*	XXXVIII-1 - XXXVIII-18* and XXXVIII-19**
Norway	XXXVII-1 - XXXVII-16*	XXXVIII-1 - XXXVIII-18* and XXXVIII-19**
Peru (1989)+	XXXVII-1 - XXXVII-16*	XXXVIII-1 - XXXVIII-18* and XXXVIII-19**
Poland (1977)+	XXXVII-1 - XXXVII-16*	XXXVIII-1 - XXXVIII-18* and XXXVIII-19**
Russia	XXXVII-1 - XXXVII-16*	XXXVIII-1 - XXXVIII-18* and XXXVIII-19**
South Africa	XXXVII-1 - XXXVII-16*	XXXVIII-1 - XXXVIII-18* and XXXVIII-19**
Spain (1988)+	XXXVII-1 - XXXVII-16*	XXXVIII-1 - XXXVIII-18* and XXXVIII-19**
Sweden (1988)+	XXXVII-1 - XXXVII-16*	XXXVIII-1 - XXXVIII-18* and XXXVIII-19**
Ukraine (2004)+	XXXVII-1 - XXXVII-16*	XXXVIII-1 - XXXVIII-18* and XXXVIII-19**
U.K.	XXXVII-1 - XXXVII-16*	XXXVIII-1 - XXXVIII-18* and XXXVIII-19**
Uruguay (1985)+	XXXVII-1 - XXXVII-16*	XXXVIII-1 - XXXVIII-18* and XXXVIII-19**
U.S.A.	XXXVII-1 - XXXVII-16*	XXXVIII-1 - XXXVIII-18* and XXXVIII-19**

*,+Year attained Consultative Status. Acceptance by that state required to bring into force Recommendations or Measures of meetings from that Year forward."

* Management Plans annexed to these Measures deemed to have been approved in accordance with Article 6(1) of Annex V to the Protocol on Environmental Protection to the Antarctic Treaty and the Measure not specifying a different approval method.

** Modifications and/or additions to List of Historic Sites and Monuments deemed to have been approved in accordance with Article 8(2) of Annex V to the Protocol on Environmental Protection to the Antarctic Treaty and the Measure not specifying a different approval method.

Office of the Assistant Legal Adviser for Treaty Affairs
Department of State
Washington, April 21, 2016.

Report of the Depositary Government for the Convention on the Conservation of Antarctic Marine Living Resources (CAMLR)

Information paper submitted by Australia

Abstract

A report is provided by Australia as Depositary of the Convention on the Conservation of Antarctic Marine Living Resources 1980.

Background

Australia, as Depositary of the *Convention on the Conservation of Antarctic Marine Living Resources* 1980 ('the Convention') is pleased to report to the Thirty-ninth Antarctic Treaty Consultative Meeting (ATCM XXXIX) on the status of the Convention.

Australia advises Antarctic Treaty Parties that, since the Thirty-eighth Antarctic Treaty Consultative Meeting (ATCM XXXVIII), there has been no depositary activity.

A copy of the status list for the Convention is available via the internet on the Australian Treaties Database at the following address:

http://www.austlii.edu.au/au/other/dfat/treaty_list/depository/CCAMLR.html

The status list is also available on request to the Treaties Secretariat of the Australian Government Department of Foreign Affairs and Trade. Requests can be conveyed through Australian diplomatic missions.

Report of the Depositary Government for the Agreement on the Conservation of Albatrosses and Petrels (ACAP)

Information paper submitted by Australia

Abstract

A report is provided by Australia as Depositary of the *Agreement on the Conservation of Albatrosses and Petrels* 2001.

Background

Australia, as Depositary of the *Agreement on the Conservation of Albatrosses and Petrels* 2001 ('the Agreement') is pleased to report to the Thirty-ninth Antarctic Treaty Consultative Meeting (ATCM XXXIX) on the status of the Agreement.

Australia advises Antarctic Treaty Parties that, since the Thirty-eighth Antarctic Treaty Consultative Meeting (ATCM XXXVIII), no States have acceded to the Agreement.

A copy of the status list for the Agreement is available, via the internet, on the Australian Treaties Database at the following address:

http://www.austlii.edu.au/au/other/dfat/treaty_list/depository/consalbnpet.html

The status list is also available on request to the Treaties Secretariat of the Australian Government Department of Foreign Affairs and Trade. Requests can be conveyed through Australian diplomatic missions.

Report by the United Kingdom as Depositary Government for the Convention for the Conservation of Antarctic Seals (CCAS) in Accordance with Recommendation XIII-2, Paragraph 2(D)

Parties to the Convention and new accessions

The United Kingdom, as Depositary Government for the Convention for the Conservation of Antarctic Seals (CCAS), has not received any requests to accede to the Convention, or any instruments of accession, since the previous report (ATCM XXXVIII/IP5).

The full list of countries which were original signatories to the Convention, and countries which have subsequently acceded is attached to this report (Annex A).

CCAS Annual Return 2014/2015

Annex B lists all capturing and killing of Antarctic seals by Contracting Parties to CCAS for the reporting year 1 March 2014 to 28 February 2015. All reported captures were for scientific research.

Next CCAS Annual Return

The United Kingdom would like to remind Contracting Parties to CCAS that the Exchange of Information, referred to in Paragraph 6(a) in the Annex to the Convention, for the reporting period of 1 March 2015 to 29 February 2016 is due by **30 June 2016.** CCAS Parties should submit their returns, including nil returns, to both the United Kingdom and SCAR. The UK would like to encourage all Contracting Parties to CCAS to submit their returns on time.

The CCAS report for the reporting period 2015/2016 will be submitted to ATCM XL, once the June 2016 deadline for exchange of information has passed.

Parties to the Convention for the Conservation of Antarctic Seals (CCAS)

London, 1 June-31 December 1972; the Convention entered into force on 11 March 1978.

State	Date of Signature	Date of Deposit (Ratification or Acceptance)
Argentina*	9 June 1972	7 March 1978
Australia	5 October 1972	1 July 1987
Belgium	9 June 1972	9 February 1978
Chile*	28 December 1972	7 February 1980
France**	19 December 1972	19 February 1975
Japan	28 December 1972	28 August 1980
Norway	9 June 1972	10 December 1973
Russia****	9 June 1972	8 February 1978
South Africa	9 June 1972	15 August 1972
United Kingdom**	9 June 1972	10 September 1974***
United States of America	28 June 1972	19 January 1977

Accessions

State	Date of deposit of Instrument of Accession
Brazil	11 February 1991
Canada	4 October 1990
Germany	30 September 1987
Italy	2 April 1992
Poland	15 August 1980
Pakistan	25 March 2013

*   Declaration or Reservation
**   Objection
*** The instrument of ratification included the Channel Islands and the Isle of Man
**** Former USSR

Annual CCAS Report 2014/2015

Synopsis of reporting in accordance with Article 5 and the Annex of the Convention: Capturing and killing of seals during the period 1 March 2014 to 28 February 2015.

Contracting Party	Antarctic Seals Captured	Antarctic Seals Killed
Argentina	248 (a)	2 (b)
Australia	0	0
Belgium	0	0
Brazil	0	0
Canada	0	0
Chile	0	0
France	87 (c)	0
Germany	0	0
Italy	0	0
Japan	0	0
Norway	0	0
Pakistan	No return received	No return received
Poland	0	0
Russia	No return received	No return received
South Africa	0	0
United Kingdom	0	0
United States of America	2926 (d)	9 (e)

All reported capturing was for scientific research.

(a) **Southern Elephant Seals:** 8 juveniles, 56 juveniles and adults, 15 recaptured juveniles and adults, 100 pups. **Leopard Seals:** 14 adults. **Weddell Seals:** 32 adults. **Crabeater Seals:** 23 adults.
(b) 1 adult **Leopard Seal** and 1 adult **Crabeater Seal** died accidentally in captivity owing to a particular physiological problem relating to their reaction to the anaesthetic.
(c) **Weddell Seals:** 2 male adults, 35 female adults, 25 male pups, 25 female pups.
(d) **Antarctic Fur Seals:** 90 adults/juveniles, 592 pups (sex unknown). **Leopard Seals:** 18 adults/juveniles. **Southern Elephant Seals:** 14 adults/juveniles, 10 pups (sex unknown). **Weddell Seals:** 20 adults/juveniles, 26 pups (sex unknown), 289 adult females, 86 adult males, 1176 adults/juveniles observation only, 5 adults (sex unknown) observation only, 2 female juveniles, 1 male juvenile, 278 female pups and 313 male pups. **Crabeater Seals:** 4 adult/juveniles; 2 adults/juveniles observation only.
(e) **Antarctic Fur Seals:** 2 adult males and 2 adult females. **Southern Elephant Seals:** 4 pups (sex unknown). **Weddell Seal:** 1 adult female. All found dead on shore, not previously handled.

Report by the CCAMLR Observer

Report of the Thirty-fourth Meeting of the Commission

(Hobart, Australia, 19 to 30 October 2015)

Opening of the meeting

1.   The Thirty-fourth Annual Meeting of CCAMLR, which was held in Hobart, Australia, 19-30 October 2015, was chaired by Mr Dmitry Gonchar (Russian Federation).

2.   Twenty three Members, two Acceding States and twelve Observers from non-government including industry organisations participated.

Organisation of the meeting

Status of the Convention

3.   Australia, as Depository, reported that the status of the Convention had not changed during the last intersessional period.

Implementation and compliance

4.   The Commission approved the CCAMLR Compliance Report for 2015 – the third year of implementation of the CCAMLR Compliance Evaluation Procedure.

5.   Other issues considered included:

- The successful implementation of a vessel monitoring system in 2015 including the adoption of minimum standards for VMS units and an increase in the reporting frequency to hourly intervals to be implemented across all fisheries by 2019

- An outreach strategy to encourage non-Contracting Parties to cooperate with CCAMLR in the implementation of CCAMLR's Catch Document Scheme for toothfish and CCAMLR's on-going efforts to address illegal, unreported and unregulated (IUU) fishing activities in the Convention Area

- Agreement to provide details of ice classification of vessels with licence notifications

- The successful implementation of an Arrangement for the release CCAMLR VMS data to all 5 MRCCs responsible for SAR in the Southern Ocean to support search and rescue (SAR) efforts in the CAMLR Convention Area (refer to previous discussions regarding SAR at ATCMXXXVI and ATCMXXXVII).

- That there was no CP-IUU Vessel List for 2015/16 and that no new vessels had been proposed for inclusion on the NCP-IUU Vessel List for 2015/16

- The adoption of a Resolution concerning the operations of vessels without nationality in the Convention Area

Administration and Finance

6.   The Commission supported further work to examine revenue generating opportunities and further reduce costs to secure sustainable funding. It was noted that assessed contributions are expected to be maintained at zero real-growth for the period 2014-2018 subject to no unforeseen circumstances.

Report of the Scientific Committee (*a more detailed report that focuses on the five issues of common interest to the CEP and SC-CAMLR, as identified in 2009 at the joint CEP/SC-CAMLR workshop in Baltimore, will be presented to the CEP-XIX by the CCAMLR Scientific Committee Chair, Dr Mark Belchier (United Kingdom)). The CEP will also discuss the outcomes of the second CEP-SC-CAMLR*

Workshop which was convened in Punta Arenas immediately prior to ATCM-XXXVIII (19-20 May 2016).
Additional general matters considered by the Scientific Committee at its last meeting included:

Krill resources

7.   In relation to catches in the 2014/15 season, the preliminary total catch from Subarea 48.1, which was closed on 28 May 2015, was 154 001 tonnes (99% of the 155 000 tonne limit), from Subarea 48.2 it was 17 100 tonnes, and the catch from Subarea 48.3 was 54 364 tonnes. The catches in Subareas 48.2 and 48.3 were 6% and 19% of the respective catch limits for those subareas.

8.   Seven Members notified for 18 vessels to fish for krill in 2015/16 season.

9.   The Commission endorsed the advice from the Scientific Committee that the available indices of krill biomass in Area 48 show no evidence of a systematic change in krill biomass since 2000. The Scientific Committee advised that, as the trigger level is less than 2% of krill biomass estimated in any year between 2000 and 2011, the current trigger level is appropriate for achieving the Convention's Article II objectives for the krill stock at the area scale but is not intended to manage localised fishery impacts on krill predators.

10.   The Commission endorsed the Scientific Committee's advice on the importance of facilitating fisheries-based research that contributes towards the development of feedback management (FBM), including fishery acoustics to help monitoring seasonal and monthly cycles in krill biomass. The Commission also endorsed the advice of the Scientific Committee on the importance of the use of CCAMLR Ecosystem Monitoring Program (CEMP) indices, fishery performance indices and data collected as part of the CCAMLR Scheme of International Scientific Observation (SISO) in the development FBM.

Fish resources

11.   In 2014/15, 13 Members fished for toothfish (Patagonian toothfish (*Dissostichus eleginoides*) and/or Antarctic toothfish (*D. mawsoni*)) in Subareas 48.3, 48.4, 48.6, 58.6, 58.7, 88.1 and 88.2 and Divisions 58.4.1, 58.4.2, 58.4.3a, 58.5.1 and 58.5.2; Members also conducted research fishing for *Dissostichus* spp. in the closed area of Subarea 48.2 and Division 58.4.4b. The reported total catch of *Dissostichus* spp. was 15 795 tonnes. In comparison, the total reported catch of toothfish in 2013/14 was 15 232 tonnes.

12.   In 2015, as catch limits were reached, the Secretariat closed the fisheries for *Dissostichus* spp. in Subarea 48.4 on 22 April, Subarea 48.6 on 10 March, Subarea 88.1 on 1 February and Subarea 88.2 on 14 February 2015. There were also closures at the small-scale research unit (SSRU) level in Subareas 88.1 and 88.2.

13.   The UK targeted mackerel icefish (*Champsocephalus gunnari*) in Subarea 48.3 (277t), Australia fished for this species in Division 58.5.2 (10t) and France fished for this species in Division 58.5.1 (178t).

New and exploratory finfish fisheries

14.   Notifications for exploratory fisheries for Dissostichus spp. in 2015/16 were submitted by nine Members for a total of 18 vessels. These notifications, catch limits (including for by-catch with associated move-on rules), and associated research and survey plans were endorsed by the Commission on the basis of advice provided by the Scientific Committee.

Assessment and avoidance of incidental mortality

15.   Following an analysis of bycatch data that revealed inconsistencies in reporting of non-target catch the Commission agreed that accurate by-catch data are fundamental to the Scientific Committee and the Commission in achieving the objectives of Article II of the Convention.

16.   The Commission welcomed the advice that the number of seabird by-catch mortalities in 2014/15 was the lowest recorded since the beginning of seabird by-catch observations in the Convention Area.

Marine protected areas

17.   The Commission welcomed the update on the preparatory work for the spatial planning of marine protected areas in (i) the Western Antarctic Peninsula–South Scotia Arc, (ii) the Weddell Sea, (iii) the East Antarctic Representative System of MPAs, and (iv) the Ross Sea Region.

Climate change

18.   The Commission endorsed the Scientific Committee's advice that it is vital to factor climate change considerations into its work to ensure that scientific studies are designed, and a time series built, to serve a scientific basis for long-term analysis supporting the implementation of CCAMLR management approaches, including FBM for krill.

19.   The Commission agreed to Terms of Reference for an ICG to consider approaches for appropriately integrating climate change into the work of CCAMLR.

Capacity building

20.   The Commission endorsed the advice of the Scientific Committee in relation to capacity building, including through the CCAMLR Scientific Scholarship Scheme and the invitation of observers and experts to the meetings of the Scientific Committee and its working groups. Six Scholarships have now been awarded since the inception of the Scheme in 2010 – to recipients from Argentina, Chile, China, EU, Poland and Russia (although the Russian awardee has been unable to take up his scholarship at this time).

Conservation measures

21.   Conservation measures and resolutions adopted at CCAMLR-XXXIV have been published on the CCAMLR website (Schedule of Conservation Measures in Force 2015/16).

Marine protected areas

22.   New Zealand and the USA introduced a revised proposal for the establishment of a Ross Sea Region MPA. Australia, France and the EU introduced a revised proposal to establish an East Antarctic Representative System of MPAs and the EU and Germany provided a status report on progress with the development of a proposal for a Weddell Sea MPA. The Commission also considered a proposal tabled by the EU and the UK to adopt a conservation measure to promote and facilitate scientific research in newly exposed marine areas following ice-shelf retreat or collapse around the Antarctic Peninsula. The Commission looked forward to further consideration of these proposals at future meetings of the Commission.

Implementation of Convention objectives

CCAMLR Symposium

23.   At CCAMLR-XXXIII the Commission endorsed a proposal to hold a second CCAMLR Symposium to mark the 35th anniversary of the signing of the Convention. CCAMLR-XXXIV considered the outcomes of the symposium which was held 5- 8 May 2015 in Santiago, Chile. CCAMLR-XXXIV discussed outcomes relating to climate change, the relationship between the Commission and Scientific Committee, strategic priorities for the next five years, the relationship between conservation and rational use, maritime safety and the relationship between CCAMLR and other organisations with related interests, noting that CCAMLR is an integral part of the Antarctic Treaty System, with associated obligations to cooperate.

Cooperation with Antarctic Treaty Consultative Parties

24.   The Commission received reports relating to the outcomes of the 38th Antarctic Treaty Consultative Meeting.

25.   The Commission noted opportunities for engagement with COMNAP in 2016 in relation to the workshop on search and rescue which is scheduled to be held in association with ATCM XXXIX and the with the CEP in relation to the second CEP–SC-CAMLR Workshop which will take place 19-20 May 2016 at Punta Arenas, Chile.

Next meeting

Election of officers

26..   The Commission elected Germany as Vice-Chair of the Commission meetings in 2016 and 2017.

Next meeting

27.   The Commission agreed that its Thirty-fifth Meeting will be held in Hobart from 17 to 28 October 2016. The Thirty-fifth Meeting of the Scientific Committee will be held in the first week of the Commission's Meeting, 17 to 21 October 2016.

The Scientific Committee on Antarctic Research (SCAR) Annual Report 2015/16 to the Antarctic Treaty System

1. Background

The Scientific Committee on Antarctic Research (SCAR) is a non-governmental, Interdisciplinary Scientific Body of the International Council for Science (ICSU), and Observer to the Antarctic Treaty and the UNFCCC.

SCAR's Mission is (i) to be the leading, independent, non-governmental facilitator, coordinator, and advocate of excellence in Antarctic and Southern Ocean science and research and (ii) to provide independent, sound, scientifically-based advice to the Antarctic Treaty System and other policy makers including the use of science to identify emerging trends and bring these issues to the attention of policy makers.

2. Introduction

SCAR's scientific research adds value to national efforts by enabling researchers to collaborate on large-scale scientific programmes to accomplish objectives not easily obtainable by any single country. SCAR's Members currently include 39 countries and 9 ICSU Scientific Unions.

SCAR's success depends on the quality and timeliness of its scientific outputs and the volunteer time of world's leading researchers. Descriptions of SCAR's activities and scientific outputs are available at: *http://www.scar.org/*. This paper should be read in conjunction with a separate Background Paper (BP002) that highlights recent scientific publications by the SCAR research community since the last Antarctic Treaty Meeting.

3. SCAR Highlights (2015/16)

SCAR has a number of subsidiary bodies and programmes that focus on science or science-related activities in the Antarctic region. Here we highlight and provide updates on SCAR activities that we believe to be of particular interest to Treaty Parties.

Standing Committee on the Antarctic Treaty System (SCATS)
(http://www.scar.org/antarctic-treaty-system/scats)

SCATS is the body tasked with developing SCAR's scientific advice to the Antarctic Treaty. In addition to providing and co-ordinating scientific advice for SCAR, SCATS members are also actively involved in research. SCAR supports the Antarctic Environments Portal where the SCATS Chief Officer sits on the Editorial Board, and SCAR's Executive Director sits on the Management Board. SCAR, in collaboration with several partners, continued its development of the Antarctic Conservation for the 21st Century Strategy.

The Monaco Assessment *(http://www.scar.org/monaco-assessment/document)*

In 2015, SCAR was represented at the meeting of global biodiversity and Antarctic experts entitled 'Antarctica and the Strategic Plan for Biodiversity 2011-2020: The Monaco Assessment'. The central purpose of the meeting was to examine the extent to which conservation of the biodiversity of Antarctica and the Southern Ocean is realizing the set of ambitions agreed for the world as part of the Strategic Plan for Biodiversity 2011-2020. The meeting also aimed to provide guidance for action that can effectively help deliver further conservation successes for Antarctica and the Southern Ocean. See IP038 submitted by SCAR and Monaco summarizing the workshop.

Southern Ocean Acidification *(http://www.scar.org/ssg/physical-sciences/acidification)*

SCAR has undertaken a synthesis of the scientific understanding of Southern Ocean acidification. This landmark report was highlighted at the ATCM XXXVIII - CEP XVIII and was the topic the Treaty Lecture (See 2015 BP001). The report will be launched at the SCAR Open Science Conference in Kuala Lumpur, Malaysia 22-26 August 2016.

Follow Up to The SCAR Science Horizon Scan (http://www.scar.org/horizonscanning/)

In 2014, the 1st SCAR Antarctic and Southern Ocean Science Horizon Scan identified the most important scientific questions that should be addressed over the next two decades and beyond (See 2015 IP020). With SCAR's assistance, COMNAP has lead a second stage in the process with the Antarctic Research Challenges (ARC) Project in order to assist national Antarctic programmes to understand, and develop ways to address the challenges, and share any innovation or access to technology (See IP051, submitted by COMNAP). The topic of this year's SCAR Lecture will address both the science priorities from the SCAR Horizon Scan and results from the ARC project and discuss the steps needed to address those science priorities (See BP003).

Antarctic Climate Change and the Environment (http://www.scar.org/ssg/physical-sciences/acce)

The climatic, physical and biological properties of Antarctica and the Southern Ocean are closely coupled to other parts of the global environment by the oceans and the atmosphere. In 2009 SCAR published the landmark Antarctic Climate Change and the Environment (ACCE) Report and since then has provided annual updates. See IP035.

Recommendations for activity within terrestrial geothermal areas

After a broad and extensive consultation, including the SCAR relevant subsidiary bodies and COMNAP, the SCAR Code of Conduct for Activity within Terrestrial Geothermal Environments in Antarctica has been developed (See WP023).

Geoheritage and Geoconservation (http://www.scar.org/ssg/geosciences/geoconservation)

The SCAR Geological Heritage and Geoconservation Action Group was created to consider emerging concerns on the recognition, protection and ongoing management of geological and geomorphological sites of significance within the Antarctic, including fossils. Among the goals is to develop a paper for submission to the CEP in 2018. Advances in this matter are shown in IP031.

SCAR at the UNFCCC COP21 (http://www.scar.org/srp/ant-era#COP21)

SCAR played an active role at the historic 2015 UNFCCC COP21 held in Paris, highlighting changes in the Antarctic that have global ramifications and promoting Antarctic science in general. SCAR partnered with the International Cryosphere Climate Initiative (ICCI) for two official events on Antarctica Day (December 1st) and promoted the 2015 ACCE update presented to ATCM XXXVIII (See 2015 IP092) and information on the Antarctic Environments Portal.

SCAR Data and Products (http://www.scar.org/data-products)

SCAR promotes free and unrestricted access to Antarctic data and information through open and accessible archives, managed by its Standing Committees on Antarctic Data Management (SCADM) and Antarctic Geographic Information (SCAGI). SCAR also has several products of relevance to the Antarctic community, such as Quantarctica, the Antarctic Map Catalogue, and the Biogeographic Atlas of the Southern Ocean among others.

Antarctic Sea Ice Underway Observation Platform v2 (http://aspect.antarctica.gov.au/)

The Antarctic Sea Ice Process and Climate (ASPeCt) digital underway ice observation method, v.2, has been launched. Voyages from October 2015 - March 2016 have uploaded near-real time data, pending networking from vessel to central server, and automatic cameras were implemented on some research cruises to take images that currently supplement ASPeCt visual observations. Ships going to the Antarctic are encouraged to participate in data collection.

SCAR Strategic Plan 2017-2022 (http://www.scar.org/about/futureplans)

SCAR's current Strategic Plan expires at the end of 2016 and efforts are underway for the development of a new plan to meet future needs. SCAR is consulting widely in its development and welcomes comments from all interested in the future direction of the organization and its activities. The new plan will be discussed at the XXXIV SCAR Delegates Meeting in Kuala Lumpur, Malaysia, on 29-30 August 2016, and finalized later this year.

Celebrating Women in Antarctic Research (http://www.scar.org/outreach/women)

In the 1950s most countries did not allow women to work in Antarctica and there were few female Antarctic scientists. Today females are playing leading and influential roles in Antarctic research. To help acknowledge this, SCAR is hosting a Wikibomb event to promote and celebrate the achievements of female Antarctic scientists by increasing their presence in Wikipedia at the next Open Science Conference. The aim is to increase the visibility of models for younger female researchers and to stimulate girls around the world to pursue science careers.

4. SCAR Fellowships and Prizes

In order to expand capacity within all its Members, SCAR runs several Fellowship and Prize Schemes (*http://www.scar.org/awards*):

- *SCAR/COMNAP Fellowships* focus on early career researchers and aim to build new connections and further strengthen international capacity and cooperation in Antarctic research. The fellowships are advertised in tandem with the CCAMLR Scholarships. In 2015 four SCAR fellowships, including the new Prince Albert II of Monaco Biodiversity Fellowship and one SCAR/COMNAP fellowship were awarded. A mini-symposium to highlight the SCAR/COMNAP fellowships will be held during the 2016 SCAR Open Science Conference. *http://www.scar.org/awards/fellowships*

- *SCAR Visiting Professor Scheme* provides mid- to late-career scientists the opportunity to undertake short-term visits to a facility in, or operated by, SCAR member countries, to provide training and mentoring. Two Visiting Professorships were awarded in 2015. *http://www.scar.org/awards/visitingprofs*

  - *Tinker-Muse Prize for Science and Policy in Antarctica*, facilitated by SCAR, is a USD $100,000 unrestricted award presented to an individual in the fields of Antarctic science or policy. Dr. Valérie Masson-Delmotte was awarded the 2015 Tinker-Muse Prize for her work on the characterization, quantification and understanding of past changes in climate and water cycle, translating the isotopic data to paleo-temperature records. *www.museprize.org*

5. Other News

In an effort to continue to improve, a structural review was conducted last year resulting in several recommendations for streaming the SCAR organisational structure and meetings. This year 5 of the 6 SCAR Scientific Research Programmes are also undergoing external review, as is the Southern Ocean Observing System (See IP032 for SOOS update). SCAR itself is also being reviewed by ICSU this year. For more information, see *http://www.scar.org/about/reviews*.

In July 2015, Dr. Jenny Baeseman was appointed as the new SCAR Executive Director, replacing Dr. Mike Sparrow.

6. Major SCAR Meetings

- *XII International Symposium on Antarctic Earth Sciences (ISAES) 2015*. 13-17th July 2015, Goa, India. *http://www.isaes2015goa.in*

- *XXXIV SCAR Meetings and Open Science Conference*. 20-30 August 2016, Kuala Lumpur, Malaysia. *http://scar2016.com*

- *XII SCAR Biology Symposium.* 3-9 July 2017, Brussels, Belgium.

- *The XXXV SCAR Meetings and Open Science Conference*, 15-27 June 2018 in Davos, Switzerland. The Open Science Conference will cover both polar regions, being organized jointly with the International Arctic Science Committee (IASC). *http://www.polar2018.org/*

Annual Report for 2015/16 of the Council of Managers of National Antarctic Programs (COMNAP)

COMNAP is the organisation of National Antarctic Programs which brings together, in particular, the national officials responsible for planning, conducting and managing support to science in Antarctica on behalf of their respective governments.

COMNAP is an international association, established in September 1988, whose Members are the 30 National Antarctic Programs from the countries of Argentina, Australia, Belarus (welcomed to membership in August 2015), Belgium, Brazil, Bulgaria, Chile, China, Czech Republic, Ecuador, Finland, France, Germany, India, Italy, Japan, Republic of Korea, Netherlands, New Zealand, Norway, Peru, Poland, Russian Federation, South Africa, Spain, Sweden, Ukraine, United Kingdom, United States and Uruguay. The National Antarctic Programs of Portugal and Venezuela were welcomed (August 2015) to a three-year term as COMNAP Observer organisations.

COMNAP's purpose is to develop and promote best practice in managing the support of scientific research in the Antarctic. As an organisation, COMNAP acts to add value to National Antarctic Program's efforts by serving as a forum to develop practices that improve effectiveness of activities in an environmentally responsible manner, by facilitating and promoting international partnerships, and by providing opportunities and systems for information exchange.

COMNAP strives to provide the Antarctic Treaty System with objective, practical, technical and non-political advice drawn from the National Antarctic Programs' extensive pool of expertise and their first-hand Antarctic knowledge. Since 1988, COMNAP has been an active contributor to ATCM and CEP discussion, with the presentation of 31 Working Papers and 102 Information Papers to date.

COMNAP continues to have a close working relationship with other Antarctic organisations, in particular with SCAR. A joint COMNAP/SCAR Executive Committee Meeting was held in Tromsø in August 2015. COMNAP was an invited observer to the IAATO meeting and presented reports to the Forum of Arctic Research Operators (FARO) and the International Ice Charting Working Group (IICWG) meetings.

The COMNAP Annual General Meeting (AGM) was held in August 2015 in Tromsø, Norway, hosted by the Norwegian Polar Institute. Break-out sessions on energy & technology, education & outreach, and safety were convened. Professor Kazuyuki Shiraishi of Japan's NIPR continues in his three-year term as the COMNAP Chair to AGM 2017. Michelle Rogan-Finnemore continues as Executive Secretary. The University of Canterbury, Christchurch, New Zealand, continues to host the COMNAP Secretariat.

COMNAP Highlights and Achievements for 2015/16

COMNAP Antarctic Roadmap Challenges (ARC) Project - *complete*

The COMNAP ARC project, a follow-on project from the SCAR Antarctic Science Horizon Scan, explored the technology, logistics, operations, funding and international collaboration challenges that will likely be encountered by the national Antarctic programs in the delivery of Antarctic science in the mid- to long-term. Over 1000 experts participated in the ARC project either by: responding to on-line surveys, participating in a workshop, contributing topical white papers and/or by providing expert review of the writing group reports or the ARC outcomes publication. It was a community effort and all involved are thanked, but, in particular, Mahlon C. Kennicutt II (Emeritus Professor, Texas A & M University) and Yeadong Kim (President, KOPRI) for co-convening the ARC project. ARC outcomes have now been published (see COMNAP Information Paper) and see: www.comnap.aq/Projects/SitePages/ARC.aspx.

Sea Ice Challenges Workshop Report - *published*

COMNAP convened the Sea Ice Challenges Workshop on 12–13 May 2015, co-hosted by AAD and the ACE CRC in Hobart, Tasmania, Australia. It provided an opportunity for the science and operations communities to discuss regional Antarctic sea ice trends and to propose technical and practical ways to address the challenging conditions. The report (published December 2015) can be downloaded from: www.comnap.aq/Publications/SitePages/Home.aspx.

Telemedicine Workshop - *convened*

The Joint Expert Group on Human Biology and Medicine (JEGHBM) convened the Telehealth Workshop on 27 August 2016, Tromsø, Norway. The workshop aim was for national Antarctic programs to view a range of telehealth remote services and to allow them to consider what may be appropriate to their own Antarctic operations. See: www.comnap.aq/Groups/medical/SitePages/Home.aspx.

Unmanned Aerial Systems Working Group (UAS-WG) - *established*

Formed as a sub-group of the COMNAP Air Expert Group, the UAS-WGs purpose is to "…reduce risk to people, infrastructure and environment in the Antarctic Treaty area, while enabling…UAS use in the area for scientific applications and science support purposes." Experts from fourteen COMNAP Member national Antarctic programs are part of the group. The UAS-WG terms of reference include development of COMNAP guidelines; (See also COMNAP Working Paper) and support to Member national Antarctic programs to prepare their program's UAS Operating Procedures which are specific to their own Antarctic operations , exchange of information, and to communicate, in a collaborative manner with other members of the Antarctic community, information on UAS use in the area.

Station Infrastructure Catalogue - *started*

The EU-PolarNet project, conducted in collaboration with INTERACT and COMNAP, includes development of a catalogue, focusing on European Arctic and Antarctic infrastructures. This project already included all the European COMNAP Members. COMNAP decided to use this opportunity to extend the exercise to all its Members. The COMNAP Infrastructure Catalogue will provide for the first time comprehensive and exhaustive information on the national Antarctic program facilities which will be useful to promote future collaboration, exchange of scientists and sharing of infrastructures, in the spirit of the Antarctic Treaty.

COMNAP Antarctic Research Fellowship - *application round open*

COMNAP established the Antarctic Research Fellowship in 2011 and since that time has awarded six fellowships, plus three jointly with SCAR. The Fellowship aims to assist early career researchers, technicians and engineers. The 2015 Fellowship was awarded to Alejandro Velasco Castrillon (University of Adelaide, Australia) to undertake travel to Antarctica in support of research on "A re-evaluation of the first discovery of limno-terrestrial microfauna of the McMurdo Sound region". Also, a joint COMNAP/SCAR fellowship was awarded to Inka Koch (University of Otago, New Zealand) to undertake research on "Detecting marine ice internal layers and thickness in an Antarctic ice shelf with airborne ice penetrating radar". The 2016 Fellowship round closes on 1 June 2016. Both SCAR and COMNAP are also working with CCAMLR to promote their scholarships. See https://www.comnap.aq/SitePages/fellowships.aspx.

Middle Managers Scheme - *trial underway*

The scheme aims to assist national Antarctic program managers with development in the areas of international collaboration, training programmes or sharing of best practice at another national Antarctic program office or Antarctic research station. Applications from personnel of COMNAP Member national Antarctic programs for the scheme can be submitted at any time of the year and will be evaluated by the COMNAP EXCOM.

Search and Rescue (SAR) Workshop III - *upcoming*

In support of safe operations in the Antarctic Treaty region, and as agreed by COMNAP in response to ATCM Resolution 4 (2013), to regularly convene workshops to discuss SAR and emergency response in the region, COMNAP will convene the SAR Workshop III. The workshop will take place on 1-2 June 2016, co-hosted by INACH and DIRECTEMAR. Experts from IAATO, CCAMLR (COLTO and ARK), and from COSPAS-SARSAT have also been invited to attend. The workshop report will be submitted to the ATCM when available. Further information see: https://www.comnap.aq/SitePages/SARWorkshopIII.aspx.

COMNAP Products and Tools

Search and Rescue (SAR) Webpage   www.comnap.aq/membersonly/SitePages/SAR.aspx

As requested in ATCM Resolution 4 (2013), COMNAP has established a SAR webpage in consultation with RCCs which is regularly updated. It will be reviewed during SAR Workshop III.

Accident, Incident & Near-Miss Reporting (AINMR) www.comnap.aq/membersonly/AINMR/SitePages/Home.aspx

The AINMR System was developed to assist in information exchange and is available on the members-only area of the COMNAP website. The AINMR's primary objective is: to capture information about events that had, or could have had, serious consequences; and/or reveal lessons; and/or for novel or very unusual events. Full reports on accidents can also be posted and shared on the site and can be discussed and reviewed. National Antarctic Programs can learn from each other to reduce the risk of serious consequences occurring in the course of their Antarctic activities.

Ship Position Reporting System (SPRS) www.comnap.aq/sprs/SitePages/Home.aspx

The SPRS is an optional, voluntary system for exchange of information about National Antarctic Program ship operations. Its primary purpose is to facilitate collaboration. It can also, however, make a very useful contribution to safety with all SPRS information made available to the RCCs as an additional source of information complementing all other national and international systems in place. Position information is delivered via email and can be graphically displayed in Google Earth. A review of the SPRS is underway.

Antarctic Flight Information Manual (AFIM)

AFIM is a handbook of aeronautical information published as a tool towards safe air operations in Antarctica as per Resolution 1 (2013). COMNAP continues to transform the paper-based AFIM into an electronic product. The AFIM continues to be updated via information from National Antarctic Programs.

Antarctic Telecommunications Operators Manual (ATOM) www.comnap.aq/membersonly/SitePages/ATOM.aspx

ATOM is an evolution of the handbook of telecommunications practices to which ATCM Recommendation X-3 *Improvement of Telecommunications in Antarctica and the Collection and Distribution of Antarctic Meteorological Data* refers. COMNAP Members and SAR authorities have access to the latest version (January 2016) via the COMNAP website.

———————

For more information see www.comnap.aq.

Attachment 1: COMNAP officers, projects, expert groups and meetings

Executive Committee (EXCOM)

The COMNAP Chair and Vice-Chairs are elected officers of COMNAP. The elected officers plus the Executive Secretary, compose the COMNAP Executive Committee as follows:

Position	Officer	Term expires
Chair	Kazuyuki Shiraishi (NIPR) kshiraishi@nipr.ac.jp	AGM 2017
Vice-Chairs	Hyoung Chul Shin (KOPRI) hcshin@kopri.re.kr	AGM 2016
	John Hall (BAS) jhal@bas.ac.uk	AGM 2016
	José Retamales (INACH) jretamales@inach.cl	AGM 2017
	Rob Wooding (AAD) rob.wooding@aad.gov.au	AGM 2017
	Yves Frenot (IPEV) yves.frenot@ipev.fr	AGM 2017
Executive Secretary	Michelle Rogan-Finnemore michelle.finnemore@comnap.aq	

Table 1 – COMNAP Executive Committee.

Projects

Project	Project Manager	EXCOM officer (oversight)
Antarctic Flight Information Manual (AFIM) – Electronic Format Implementation	Paul Morin & Brian Stone	John Hall
Antarctic Roadmap Challenges (ARC)	Michelle Rogan-Finnemore	Kazuyuki Shiraishi
Ship Position Reporting System (SPRS) Review	Robb Clifton	Hyoung Chul Shin
Station Infrastructure Catalogue	Michelle Rogan-Finnemore	Yves Frenot
Suppliers Database	Simon Trotter	John Hall
Telemedicine Workshop	Jeff Ayton	John Hall

Table 2 – COMNAP projects currently in progress.

Expert Groups

Expert Group (topic)	Expert Group leader	EXCOM officer (oversight)
Air (includes the UAS-WG)	Giuseppe Di Rossi & Brian Stone	John Hall
Energy & Technology	Felix Bartsch & Pavel Kapler	Rob Wooding
Environment	Anoop Tiwari	Hyoung Chul Shin
Medical	Jeff Ayton	John Hall
Outreach/Education	Dragomir Mateev	Yves Frenot
Safety	Henrik Törnberg (until 31 Jan 2016) Simon Trotter (from 1 Feb 2016)	Kazuyuki Shiraishi
Science (includes the SOOS "Think Tank")	Robb Clifton	José Retamales
Shipping	Miguel Ojeda	José Retamales
Training	Veronica Vlasich	Yves Frenot

Table 3 – COMNAP Expert Groups.

Meetings

Previous 12 months

22–24 August 2015, Antarctic Roadmap Challenges Workshop, Norwegian Polar Institute (NPI), Tromsø, Norway.

25 August 2015, COMNAP/SCAR Joint Executive Committee Meeting, Norwegian Polar Institute (NPI), Tromsø, Norway.

26–28 August 2015, COMNAP Annual General Meeting (COMNAP AGM XXVII), hosted by the Norwegian Polar Institute (NPI), Tromsø, Norway (includes Safety session, Energy & Technology session and Education & Outreach session and the Joint Expert Group on Human Biology and Medicine Telemedicine Workshop).

29 August 2015, COMNAP EXCOM Meeting, hosted by the Norwegian Polar Institute (NPI), Tromsø, Norway.

29 August 2015, Joint COMNAP/SCAR EXCOM Meeting, hosted by the Norwegian Polar Institute (NPI), Tromsø, Norway.

Upcoming 12 months

1–2 June 2016, Search and Rescue (SAR) Workshop III, co-hosted by Instituto Antartico Chileno (INACH) and DIRECTEMAR, Valparaiso, Chile.

16–18 August 2016, COMNAP Annual General Meeting (AGM) XXVIII (2016), hosted by the National Centre for Antarctic and Oceans Research (NCAOR), Goa, India.

19–20 August 2016, COMNAP Symposium 2016 "Wintering-over Challenges", hosted by the National Centre for Antarctic and Oceans Research (NCAOR), Goa, India.

21 August 2016, Joint SCAR/COMNAP EXCOM Meeting, Kuala Lumpur, Malaysia.

21–22August 2016, Joint Expert Group on Human Biology and Medicine (JEGHBM) Meeting, Kuala Lumpur, Malaysia.

3. Reports by Experts

Report by the International Hydrographic Organization (IHO)

Limitations in hydrographic knowledge in Antarctica and the consequent risks to scientific and maritime operations

Introduction

The International Hydrographic Organization (IHO) is an intergovernmental consultative and technical organization. It comprises 85 Member States. Each State is normally represented by its national Hydrographer.

The IHO coordinates on a worldwide basis the setting of standards for hydrographic data and the provision of hydrographic services in support of safety of navigation and the protection and sustainable use of the marine environment. The principal aim of the IHO is to ensure that all the world's seas, oceans and navigable waters are surveyed and charted.

What is Hydrography?

Hydrography deals with the measurement and description of the physical features of oceans, seas, coastal areas, lakes and rivers. Hydrographic surveying identifies the shape and nature of the seafloor and the hazards that lie upon it, together with an understanding of the impact of tides on the depth and water movement. This knowledge supports all marine activities, including transport, economic development, security and defence, scientific studies, and environmental protection.

Importance of Hydrography in Antarctica

Hydrographic information is a fundamental pre-requisite for the development of successful and environmentally sustainable human activities in the seas and oceans. Unfortunately, there is little or no hydrographic information for a number of parts of the world, especially in Antarctica.

In this particular region, where vessels may face the most severe weather conditions, any grounding due to a lack of adequate surveying or nautical charting may have serious consequences. Unfortunately, the grounding of vessels operating outside previously navigated routes in Antarctica is not uncommon.

The Polar Code, adopted by the International Maritime Organization (IMO) in 2014, includes significant cautions concerning hydrography and nautical charting.

As stated, the Polar Code

> ... *"considers hazards which may lead to elevated levels of risk due to increased probability of occurrence, more severe consequences, or both (...)*

and notes in particular:

> *...remoteness and possible lack of accurate and complete* **hydrographic data and information**, *reduced availability of navigational aids and seamarks with increased potential for groundings compounded by remoteness, limited readily deployable Search and Rescue (SAR) facilities, delays in emergency response and limited communications capability, with the potential to affect incident response ..."*

Most scientific studies and an understanding of the marine environment benefit significantly from a knowledge of the nature and shape of the seafloor and the movement of the water caused by tides. Therefore the lack of such hydrographic knowledge in most Antarctic waters, particularly in the coastal and shallower regions, must compromise many scientific endeavours being undertaken under the auspices of ATCM and individual Member States.

Status of Hydrography and Charting in Antarctica

The state of hydrographic surveying and nautical charting in Antarctica poses serious risks for the safety of navigation as well as impeding the conduct of most activities taking place in the surrounding seas and oceans.

Over 90% of Antarctic waters remain unsurveyed. Large areas are uncharted and where charts do exist, they have limited utility because of a lack of reliable or comprehensive depth information.

Hydrographic surveying in Antarctic waters is expensive and problematic. This is because of hostile and unpredictable sea conditions, short seasons for surveying and the long logistic train involved in supporting ships and equipment.

According to IMO international requirements (Safety of Life at Sea - SOLAS), Electronic Nautical Charts (ENCs) are now required for navigation in all passenger vessels and an increasing number of vessels of other types - all of which are operating in Antarctic waters. So far, only half of about 170 ENCs that have been identified by the IHO Hydrographic Commission on Antarctica (IHO HCA) as being required for navigation in the region have been published.

The production of ENCs for Antarctica is severely hampered by the lack of data, the poor state of the corresponding paper charts that they are intended to replace and the production and financial priorities of those States that have volunteered to make the ENCs; only 10 ENCs were produced in 2014, and only five[9] in 2015.

The status of hydrography and nautical charting is available on the IHO website as a GIS web service (www.iho.int > Committees&WG > Hydrographic Commission on Antarctica > Miscellaneous > IHO GIS for Antarctica).

IHO Hydrographic Commission on Antarctica (HCA)

The IHO HCA is dedicated to improving the quality, coverage and availability of nautical charting and other hydrographic information and services covering the region. The HCA comprises 23 IHO Member States (Argentina, Australia, Brazil, Chile, China, Ecuador, France, Germany, Greece, India, Italy, Japan, Republic of Korea, New Zealand, Norway, Peru, Russian Federation, South Africa, Spain, United Kingdom, Uruguay, USA, Venezuela), all of which have acceded to the Antarctic Treaty and are therefore also directly represented in the ATCM. Colombia has recently indicated its intention to seek to become a full member of the IHO HCA.

The IHO HCA attempts to work closely with stakeholder organizations such as COMNAP, IAATO, SCAR, IMO and IOC, However, with the exception of successful work with IAATO, no co-operative programmes or packages using ships of opportunity or other resources have been achieved in order to improve hydrographic data in critical shipping areas.

It was reported to ATCM last year that the 14th meeting of the IHO HCA had been postponed, due to the low level of registrations from Member States and from Observer Organizations. This is a sad evidence of the low priority that governments have been placing on improving hydrographic and bathymetric knowledge in the region. An invitation letter to participate in the 14th meeting of the IHO HCA which will take place in Ecuador, from 30 June to 2 July 2016, was issued on 18 Feb. We take this opportunity to remind IHO HCA Members and stakeholder organizations that registrations for participants were expected before 15 April 2016, therefore, those interest parties that have not done so, are invited to register right away.

Ways and Means to Improve Hydrography and Nautical Charting in Antarctica

The IHO has reported regularly on the unsatisfactory level of hydrographic knowledge in Antarctica since ATCM XXXI (Kiev, 2008) and the inherent risks involved for all seaborne activities taking place around the continent. The IHO has consistently indicated the requirement to obtain support at the highest political levels if things are to improve significantly.

---

[9] Argentina (1), Chile (1), UK (3).

It is pleasing that ATCM XXXVII adopted Resolution 5 (2014) on strengthening cooperation in hydrographic surveying and charting of Antarctic waters. However, with the exception of the significant surveys carried out in the Gerlache Strait in 2015, there has been little noticeable impact or improvement on the previously reported situation. It can only be hoped that this will improve after the IHO-HCA meets in mid-year in Ecuador where it is expected that a whole of continent risk-assessment analysis will be finalised. All interested ATCM Parties are invited to participate in the meeting as a means of identifying priorities and risks and coordinating their hydrographic surveying and charting activities.

Recommendation for Consideration by ATCM

The IHO invites ATCM to encourage Parties to participate in the next meeting of the HCA in Ecuador 30 June to 2 July and to contribute effectively to its activities in accordance with Resolution 5 (2014).

WMO Annual Report 2015-2016

The World Meteorological Organization[10] (WMO) is a specialized agency of the United Nations and includes 191 Member States and Territories. It is the UN system's authoritative voice on the state and behaviour of the Earth's atmosphere, its interaction with the oceans, the climate it produces and the resulting distribution of water resources.

The WMO Polar and High Mountain Observations, Research and Services activities promote and coordinate relevant programmes that are carried out in the Antarctic, Arctic and high mountain regions by nations and by groups of nations. It interfaces with all WMO programmes, including the World Weather Watch (WWW), and other related programmes throughout the world, meeting global needs and requirements for meteorological observations, research and services in the polar and high mountain regions[11].

In May 2015, the World Meteorological Congress approved Polar and High Mountain activities as one of the seven WMO priorities for 2016 - 2019. These activities, including interactions with the Antarctic Treaty System, are steered by the WMO Executive Council Panel of Experts on Polar and High Mountain Observations, Research and Services (EC-PHORS).

In January 2016, Dr. Petteri Taalas became the new Secretary General of WMO. Originating from the Finnish Meteorological Institute and a member of the PHORS Panel, he has been a champion of cryospheric sciences for many years.

The Global Cryosphere Watch (GCW) is foundational to WMO's Polar initiatives and its observing component is one of the four essential observing systems under WMO Integrated Global Observing Systems. CryoNet is the core observing component of the GCW. There are a number of stations in the Antarctic Observing Network identified as CryoNet sites. In recognition of the importance of GCW, WMO is establishing a GCW Project Office in the Secretariat. The GCW will also be the topic of a future paper to the Treaty.

With various partners WMO are implementing the Global Integrated Polar Prediction System (GIPPS) an initiative that will dramatically improve our predictive capability on all timescales and advance our understanding of polar weather and climate.

The associated Year of Polar Prediction (YOPP) is an initiative covering the period 2017 – 2019 centred on 2018, which aims to improve environmental prediction capabilities by coordinating a period of intensive observing, modelling, prediction, verification, and user-engagement and education activities. See associated IP 15.

Since its inception in 2009, EC-PHORS has based its activities on the desire to create "fit-for-purpose" information services to a broad range of Polar interests. WMO are investigating the development of centres of excellence that operationally generate climate products; these centres are referred to as Polar Regional Climate Centres (see associated IP 14).

WMO is pleased to submit several additional papers on its activities to inform and engage the ATCM in its activities, including *WMO Climate-related Activities in the Antarctic Region, The Antarctic Observing Network, The Polar Challenge, Polar Regional Climate Centres and Polar Climate Outlook Fora, and the Year of Polar Prediction.*

WMO is committed to a positive, mutually beneficial engagement with Treaty Parties in Antarctic weather and climate services and research.

---

[10] www.wmo.int

[11] https://www.wmo.int/pages/prog/www/polar/index_en.html

Recent Findings of IPCC on Antarctic Climate Change and Relevant Upcoming Activities

Summary

The Contribution of Working Group I to the Fifth Assessment Report (AR5) of IPCC concluded with high confidence that the Antarctic ice sheet is losing mass, with the average rate of ice loss higher over the 2002-2011 period than earlier. This recent Antarctic ice loss is estimated to be equivalent to sea level rise of about 0.2 to 0.61 mm/year. It was also found that floating ice shelves around the Antarctic Peninsula continue a long-term trend of retreat and partial collapse in response to changing atmospheric temperatures. Thinning of ice shelves is also reported in the Amundsen Sea region of West Antarctica. Albeit with some regional inhomogeneities, annual sea ice extent around the Antarctic increased by about 0.13 to 0.2 million km^2 per decade between 1979 and 2012, which implies less open water in later years.

The Upcoming Sixth Assessment Report (AR6) Products of IPCC which include Special Reports are described.

Some Key AR5 Findings

The IPCC in its regular assessments pays particular attention to the cryosphere because of the major role it plays in the Earth's climate system through its impact on the surface energy budget, the water cycle, surface gas exchange and sea level. Working Group I of the AR5 assessed recent changes which have occurred in components of the cryosphere across different regions including Antarctica and the surrounding ocean areas[12], attribution of these changes[13], and projection of future changes in the cryosphere[14] and their expected contribution to sea level change[15].

Losses in Antarctic ice sheet mass are reported. Largest ice losses, which outbalance increases in precipitation, were reported along the northern tip of the Antarctic Peninsula where a collapse of several ice shelves in recent decades triggered acceleration of outlet glaciers, and in the Amundsen Sea in West Antarctica[1]. Changes around the Amundsen sea are associated with

---

[12] Vaughan, D.G., J.C. Comiso, I. Allison, J. Carrasco, G. Kaser, R. Kwok, P. Mote, T. Murray, F. Paul, J. Ren, E. Rignot, O. Solomina, K. Steffen and T. Zhang, 2013: Observations: Cryosphere. In: Climate Change 2013: The Physical Science Basis. Contribution of Working Group I to the Fifth Assessment Report of the Intergovernmental Panel on Climate Change [Stocker, T.F., D. Qin, G.-K. Plattner, M. Tignor, S.K. Allen, J. Boschung, A. Nauels, Y. Xia, V. Bex and P.M. Midgley (eds.)]. Cambridge University Press, Cambridge, United Kingdom and New York, NY, USA.

[13] Bindoff, N.L., P.A. Stott, K.M. AchutaRao, M.R. Allen, N. Gillett, D. Gutzler, K. Hansingo, G. Hegerl, Y. Hu, S. Jain, I.I. Mokhov, J. Overland, J. Perlwitz, R. Sebbari and X. Zhang, 2013: Detection and Attribution of Climate Change: from Global to Regional. In: Climate Change 2013: The Physical Science Basis. Contribution of Working Group I to the Fifth Assessment Report of the Intergovernmental Panel on Climate Change [Stocker, T.F., D. Qin, G.-K. Plattner, M. Tignor, S.K. Allen, J. Boschung, A. Nauels, Y. Xia, V. Bex and P.M. Midgley (eds.)]. Cambridge University Press, Cambridge, United Kingdom and New York, NY, USA.

[14] Collins, M., R. Knutti, J. Arblaster, J.-L. Dufresne, T. Fichefet, P. Friedlingstein, X. Gao, W.J. Gutowski, T. Johns, G. Krinner, M. Shongwe, C. Tebaldi, A.J. Weaver and M. Wehner, 2013: Long-term Climate Change: Projections, Commitments and Irreversibility. In: Climate Change 2013: The Physical Science Basis. Contribution of Working Group I to the Fifth Assessment Report of the Intergovernmental Panel on Climate Change [Stocker, T.F., D. Qin, G.-K. Plattner, M. Tignor, S.K. Allen, J. Boschung, A. Nauels, Y. Xia, V. Bex and P.M. Midgley (eds.)]. Cambridge University Press, Cambridge, United Kingdom and New York, NY, USA.

[15] Church, J.A., P.U. Clark, A. Cazenave, J.M. Gregory, S. Jevrejeva, A. Levermann, M.A. Merrifield, G.A. Milne, R.S. Nerem, P.D. Nunn, A.J. Payne, W.T. Pfeffer, D. Stammer and A.S. Unnikrishnan, 2013: Sea Level Change. In: Climate Change 2013: The Physical Science Basis. Contribution of Working Group I to the Fifth Assessment Report of the Intergovernmental Panel on Climate Change [Stocker, T.F., D. Qin, G.-K. Plattner, M. Tignor, S.K. Allen, J. Boschung, A. Nauels, Y. Xia, V. Bex and P.M. Midgley (eds.)]. Cambridge University Press, Cambridge, United Kingdom and New York, NY, USA.

thinning of ice shelves and high ocean heat flux which result in glacier thinning. The seasonal sea ice concentration trends displayed in Figure 1 (adopted from Figure 4.7 of WGI AR5[1]) show significant trends of different signs close to ice margins. Strong upward trends are found around the date line in the Ross Sea in all seasons, and around the Greenwich meridian extending west towards the Weddell Sea in summer and autumn (Figures 1 d,e). Negative trends are found around the Amundsen and Bellingshausen seas in summer and autumn.

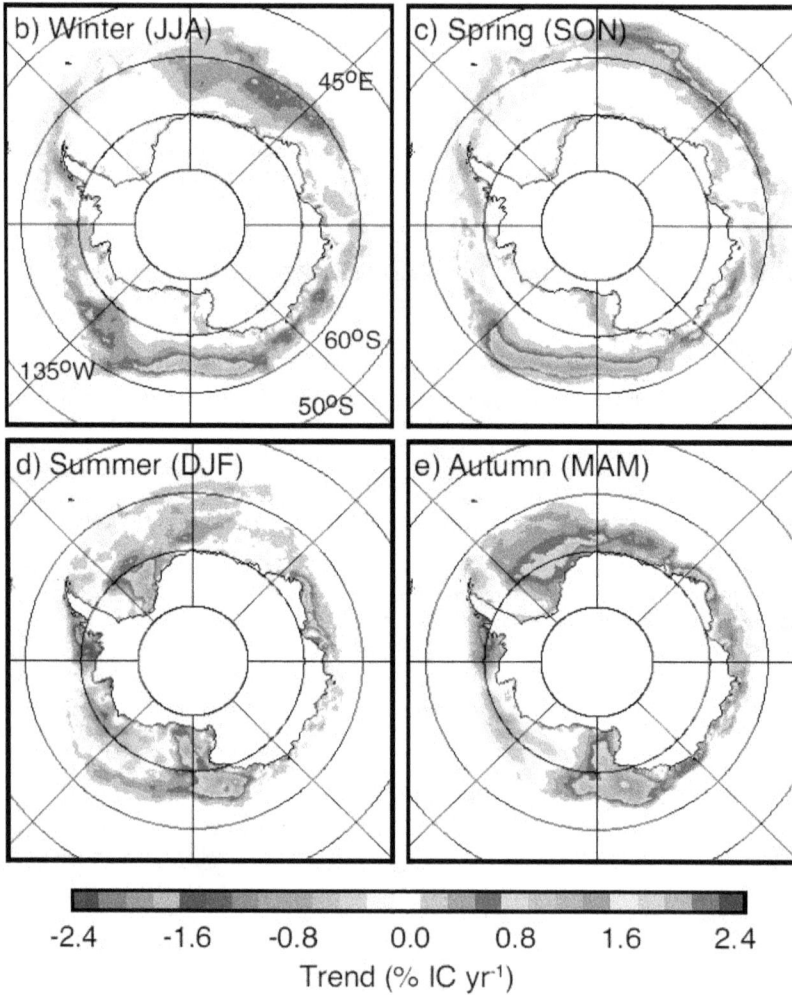

Figure 1: Seasonal trends (1979–2012) in ice concentration during austral (b) winter, (c) spring, (d) summer, and (e) autumn. *Source: IPCC Working Group I Fifth Assessment Report.*

Towards the end of the 21st century (2081-2100), CMIP5[16] models project a decrease in sea ice extent in the Southern Ocean, the highest decrease projected under RCP8.5 in February[3].

Upcoming Sixth Assessment Report (AR6) Products

Special Report on Impacts of Global Warming of 1.5 °C

The Conference of Parties (COP) to the United Nations Framework Convention on Climate Change (UNFCCC) at its 21st Session in Paris, France (30 November to 11 December 2015), invited the IPCC to provide a Special Report (SR) in 2018 on the impacts of global warming of 1.5°C above pre-industrial levels and related global greenhouse gas emission pathways. At its 43rd Session (Nairobi, Kenya, 11 – 13 April 2016), the IPCC Panel decided to accept the invitation from the UNFCCC and to prepare an SR on this topic in the context of strengthening the global response to the threat of climate change, sustainable development and efforts to eradicate poverty. The scoping meeting for this SR will be held in Geneva from 15 to 17 August 2016.

Other Special Reports

The IPCC Panel at its 43rd Session also approved the preparation of two additional SRs:

1) A Special Report on climate change, desertification, land degradation, sustainable land management, food security, and greenhouse gas fluxes in terrestrial ecosystems; and

2) A Special Report on climate change and oceans and the cryosphere.

The scoping meetings for these SRs will be held early in 2017.

AR6 Working Group (WG) Co-Chairs in their commentary on the SR on climate change and oceans and the cryosphere remarked that while many aspects of climate change and oceans, and climate change and cryosphere (with sea level as a joint issue) were addressed in some depth in AR5, there was lack of integrated cross-WG approaches in addressing relevant questions ranging from sea level rise, extreme events, ecosystem impacts, socioeconomic consequences, the ocean's role in mitigation strategies to regional specificities and implications (such as rapid coastal zone urbanisation). The SR, which will provide a platform to integrate all WGs, is expected to cover various sea/ocean basins of the globe and, together with the cryosphere, and will address the largest component in the earth's climate system, the largest living space on earth, with a wide range of societal and socioeconomic implications.

---

[16] Coupled Model Intercomparison Project Phase 5

Report of the Antarctic and Southern Ocean Coalition

1. Introduction

ASOC is pleased to be in Santiago for the XXXIX Antarctic Treaty Consultative Meeting. This report briefly describes ASOC's work over the past year, and outlines some key issues for this ATCM.

ASOC's Secretariat is in Washington DC, USA and its website is http://www.asoc.org. ASOC has 24 full member groups in 10 countries and supporting groups in those and several other countries. ASOC campaigns are carried out by teams of experts in many Antarctic Treaty countries.

2. Intersessional activities

Since XXXVIII ATCM ASOC and its member groups' representatives participated actively in intersessional discussions in the ATCM and CEP fora, including ICGs on 'outstanding values' in the Antarctic marine environment, a review of the guidelines for environmental impact assessment in Antarctica, a review of a draft CEE, the planning for the symposium in celebration of the 25th Anniversary of the Environment Protocol, and developing a strategic approach to tourism.

ASOC and member group representatives attended a range of meetings relevant to Antarctic environmental protection including the XXXIV CCAMLR Meeting, International Maritime Organization meetings relating to the Polar Code, the IAATO meeting, and others.

ASOC is also a member of the Antarctic Wildlife Research Fund (AWR), which provided $250,000 to fund three scientific research projects on Antarctic marine ecosystems.

3. Papers for XXXIX ATCM

ASOC has submitted six Information Papers, and co-sponsored one additional paper, to the XXXIX ATCM. These papers address key environmental issues, and contain recommendations for the ATCM and CEP that will help achieve more effective environmental protection and conservation of Antarctica.

The Future of Antarctica Forum (IP 41) ASOC, along with a number of other Antarctic stakeholders, participated in the Future of Antarctica Forum, which provided a unique opportunity to discuss collaborative ways in which the protection and conservation of Antarctica could be secured into the future.

Antarctic Climate Change, Ice Sheet Dynamics and Irreversible Thresholds: ATCM Contributions to the IPCC and Policy Understanding (IP 78)
In this paper, ASOC suggests the CEP, together with SCAR, may wish to examine the optimal strategy for contributing to the planned Intergovernmental Panel on Climate Change (IPCC) Special Report on Oceans and Cryosphere, perhaps through a summary study of Antarctic ice sheet dynamics and projections in response to climate change. Parties may also wish to consider cooperative efforts with Arctic research bodies, and encourage national research teams to make emerging findings available in time for inclusion in the Special Report.

An Unprecedented Achievement: 25 Years of the Environmental Protocol (IP 79)
On the 25th anniversary of the Madrid Protocol on Environmental Protection, ASOC encourages ATCPs to reflect on the value of the Protocol as a whole, and the enormous benefits, including the mining ban, that the Protocol has had for the continent and for peaceful Antarctic governance. The paper also suggests ways to continue implementation of the Protocol, including expanding the network of protected areas, strengthening the environmental impact assessment process to include consideration of cumulative impacts, and planning for developments in human activities on the continent.

A Systematic Approach to Designating ASPAs and ASMAs (IP 80)
In this paper, ASOC provides preliminary suggestions, based on systematic conservation planning processes,

on how to expand the protected areas system under the Protocol in order to comply with the requirements of Annex V, Arts. 3 and 4. It also discusses how this system might have benefits for progressing discussions on the management of tourism, a topic that has been under discussion by the ATCM for a number of years without significant changes.

Antarctic Climate Change Report Card (IP 81)
In this paper, ASOC presents its Climate Change Report Card, which summarizes scientific breakthroughs and climate events related to anthropogenic climate change in the Antarctic and provides policy recommendations for the ATCM, including that ATCPs make clear commitments to fund research on climate change and ocean acidification.

Progress on the Polar Code (IP 82)
ASOC provides a brief update on progress to protect the Southern Ocean from the risks associated with vessels operating in the region. It also identifies a number of issues that still must be addressed, including extending the Code to cover non-SOLAS vessels such as fishing vessels and private yachts. ASOC recommends that the ATCM further protect the Antarctic environment by developing additional measures on oil spill response and the introduction of non-native species.

ASOC's update on Marine Protected Areas in the Southern Ocean (IP 83)
In this document ASOC provides its perspectives on recent CCAMLR MPA discussions primarily for the benefit of ATCM/CEP Members, stakeholders and individuals not participating in those discussions.

4. *Concluding Remarks*

Over the past year, ASOC has engaged with many and varied partners, including IAATO, SCAR, CCAMLR, the Coalition of Legal Toothfish Operators (COLTO), and the Antarctic Wildlife Research Fund (AWR), to work broadly to identify strengths and weaknesses existing in the Antarctic Treaty System procedures and practices, while suggesting solutions to these gaps. We value our engagement with these groups, as well as with Antarctic Treaty Parties.

Report of the International Association of Antarctica Tour Operators 2015-16

Under Article III (2) of the Antarctic Treaty

Introduction

The International Association of Antarctica Tour Operators (IAATO) is pleased to report its activities to ATCM XXXIX, under Article III (2) of the Antarctic Treaty.

IAATO continues to focus activities in support of its mission statement to advocate and promote the practice of safe and environmentally responsible private sector travel to Antarctica by ensuring:
- Effective day-to-day management of member activities in Antarctica;
- Educational outreach, including scientific collaboration; and
- Development and promotion of Antarctic tourism best practices.

A detailed description of IAATO, its mission statement, primary activities and recent developments can be found in the *2016-17 Fact Sheet*, and on the IAATO website: www.iaato.org.

IAATO Membership and Visitor Levels during 2015-16

IAATO comprises 116 Members, Associates and Affiliates, representing businesses from 66% of the Antarctic Treaty Consultative Party countries. IAATO member operators carry nationals from nearly all Treaty Parties annually to Antarctica. Since 2010, IAATO has represented all passenger vessels operating in Antarctic waters under the International Convention for the Safety of Life at Sea (SOLAS). However during the 2015-16 season, one non-IAATO 'cruise only' vessel, ASUKA II, flagged to Japan cruised the Peninsula late January 2016

During the 2015-16 Antarctic tourism season the total number of visitors travelling with IAATO member companies was 38,478, representing an increase of just under 5% compared to the previous season. IAATO numbers have not reached the peak of the 2007–8 season (46,265), although the trend has been a slowly increase in recent years.

Details on tourism statistics including activities and nationalities can be found in ATCM XXXIX IP112 *IAATO Overview of Antarctic Tourism: 2015-16 Season and Preliminary Estimates for 2016-17*. The Membership Directory and additional statistics on IAATO member activities can be found at www.iaato.org.

Recent Work and Activities

A number of initiatives were undertaken during the year:

- The Dockside Observer program for IAATO yachts is now an established component of the association's Enhanced Observer Scheme, which involves making field observations of member operations to promote best practice. During the 2015-16 season IAATO revised and updated its Yacht Outreach Campaign, aimed at commercial and private non-IAATO yacht operators intending to visit Antarctica. Details can be found at www.iaato.org/yachts.

- 663 field staff passed the IAATO online Field Staff Assessment and Certification Programme for the 2015–16 season. Certification is a mandatory for many IAATO operators and 920 field staff have passed since 2012–13. The Assessment continues to evolve, testing staff's knowledge of IAATO's

Field Operations Manual that is updated annually and incorporates relevant outcomes from ATCM and CEP

- In September 2015, IAATO, in conjunction with its sister organization in the Arctic, the Association of Arctic Expedition Cruise Operators (AECO), held its inaugural Field Staff Conference in Toronto, Canada and welcomed the participation of a number of Treaty Party representatives at the conference.

- Educating members, their field staff and clients about Antarctic science and conservation issues is an important component of IAATO's work. During the 2015/16 season IAATO has augmented its key documents including guidelines, standard operating procedures and briefings with the introduction of three animation films designed to support the mandatory briefing. These are available in ten different languages.

- IAATO receives many enquiries on an annual basis from individuals, yachts and private groups who are at various stages of planning expeditions to Antarctica. IAATO explains the Antarctic Treaty System and permitting process to all of these and passes any relevant information onto a Competent Authority that may be involved.

- Improving hydrographic information on a trial and opportunistic basis by a number of IAATO vessel operators continues. Initiatives include Crowd Sourcing trials in conjunction with Hydrographic Offices and AECO. Additionally the crowd sourcing scheme that enables IAATO and AECO operators to share accumulated historic depth sounding data from the Polar Regions continues to grow within the industry.

- In preparation for the expected entry into force of the Polar Code on 1 January 2017, IAATO held a Vessel Operators Meeting in conjunction with Lloyds Register, *'Towards Polar Code Ready'*, in London, June, 2015. Additionally, IAATO is now contributing to the development of tools for implementing the Code's requirements, such as a database of ice and temperature information to support operator's risk assessments

- In April 2016, IAATO attended an Arctic Search and Rescue Workshop and table top exercise in Iceland in April 2016 coordinated by IAATO's northern counterpart, AECO and the Icelandic Coast Guard. Combining knowledge from both poles enables an exchange of experience, strengthening safety and relationships across the polar tourism industry

IAATO Meeting and Participation at Other Meetings during 2015-16

IAATO's 2016 Annual Meeting will take place May 2-5, 2016 in Newport, Rhode Island, USA. This report was written in advance of IAATO 2016 meeting to meet the Information Paper deadline but, in addition to the above-mentioned initiatives, the meeting will include discussions on:

- A restructuring of the membership into two streamlined categories: "Operators" those who organise and are legally responsible for the expedition and "Associates" those who sell, or provide supporting services to "Operators" and a review of the financing of the Association;

- Revision and updating of a number of IAATO guidelines including wildlife watching, small boat operation in the vicinity of ice and shore stranding equipment;

- A review of IAATO's draft Unmanned Aerial Vehicle (UAV) policies following feedback from the previous season;
- Proposed guidelines including activity guidelines and new site guidelines for Yalour Island and Point Wild.

Treaty Party representatives are always invited to join any of the open sessions during IAATO's Annual Meeting and any subsequent workshops.

IAATO Secretariat staff and member representatives participated in internal and external meetings, liaising with National Antarctic Programs, governmental, scientific, environmental and industry organisations. In addition to individual government meetings, IAATO took part in:

- **Council of Managers of National Antarctic Programs (COMNAP) 27th Annual Meeting**, Tromsø, Norway, August 2015. IAATO places great merit in good cooperation and collaboration between its Membership and National Antarctic Programs.
- **Association of Arctic Expedition Cruise Operators Conference & Annual Meeting,** October 2015, Copenhagen, Denmark.
- **Future of Antarctica Forum**, onboard IAATO Member vessel, One Ocean Expeditions *Akademik Ioffe* March, 2016.
- IAATO continues to be active in the development of the **International Maritime Organization**'s (IMO) mandatory Polar Code as an advisor to Cruise Lines International Association (CLIA), participating in various IMO meetings.

Environmental Monitoring

IAATO continues to provide ATCM and CEP with detailed information on member activities in Antarctica and works collaboratively with scientific institutions particularly on long term environmental monitoring and educational outreach. This includes the Antarctic Site Inventory, the Lynch Lab at Stony Brook University and the Zoological Society of London/Oxford University. Additionally, IAATO operators note sightings of fishing vessels for subsequent reporting to CCAMLR in support of the work against IUU fishing.

IAATO welcomes opportunities for collaboration with other organisations.

Tourism Incidents 2015-16

IAATO continues to follow a policy of disclosing incidents to ensure risks are understood and appropriate lessons are learned for all Antarctic operators. Incidents involving IAATO Operators that have been reported to date during the 2015-16 season include:

- On 15 November 2015, Ocean Endeavour struck ice causing some damage to the hull during the night near the South Shetland Islands. The vessel did not require any assistance and with the agreement of the both Flag State and Classification Society proceeded back to the port of Ushuaia to undertake full repair.

- On 14 December 2015, 10 Zodiacs were temporarily stranded at Port Lockroy during a zodiac cruise for 8 hours due to shifting pack ice. IAATO is grateful to the support afforded by the UK Antarctic Heritage Trust during this time, which in addition to the mandatory safety equipment carried ensured that passengers were safe and comfortable during the stranding.

- On 22 January 2016 Henry Worsley, a UK national attempting an unsupported, solo crossing of Antarctica, requested a pick-up because he was running out of time to complete his expedition. On arrival at Union Glacier camp and following examination by Antarctic Logistics and Expeditions medical staff, Worsley agreed to be flown to Punta Arenas, Chile, on a scheduled flight later that day. Further investigation by Clinica Magallanes, Punta Arenas, identified peritonitis. Worsley subsequently died of complications due to the infection.

- During the 2015-2016 season, there were several incidents involving non-IAATO yachts where IAATO operators assisted with the response. These included two groundings: one off Cuverville Island from yacht Tarka and the second near Vernadsky Station of a yacht Angelique II.

- A fuel spill was reported at in proximity to a National Antarctic Program Station and reported to the relevant authorities who facilitated repairs and a clean up.

- At time of writing (22 April), eight successful medevacs had been reported with clients being evacuated either by other IAATO operators, of via a commercial airlink from King George Island.

Scientific and Conservation Support

During the 2015-16 season, IAATO Members cost-effectively or freely transported over 50 scientific, support and conservation staff, and their equipment and supplies between stations, field sites and gateway ports. This included:

- Transfers of scientists between stations;
- Non-urgent medical evacuations;
- Field support of research projects
- Collection of scientific samples and other data collection for research programs (all permitted);
- Transport of scientific equipment to/from stations.
- Citizen science projects, such as HappyWhale.com

Initial reports indicate that IAATO operators and their passengers also contributed more than US$500,000 to scientific and conservation organisations active in Antarctica and the sub-Antarctic during 2015-2016.

Over the past decade, these donations have totalled over US $4 million.

With Thanks

IAATO appreciates the opportunity to work cooperatively with Antarctic Treaty Parties, COMNAP, SCAR, CCAMLR, IHO/HCA, ASOC and others toward the long-term protection of Antarctica.

PART IV

Additional Documents from ATCM XXXIX

1. Additional Documents

Abstract of SCAR Lecture

Abstract of the SCAR Lecture:
Exploring the future of scientific research in Antarctica

Jerónimo López-Martínez, President of the Scientific Committee on Antarctic Research (SCAR).
Universidad Autónoma de Madrid, Spain.

Scientific research in Antarctica provides critical knowledge about global processes and is recognised by the Antarctic Treaty System as playing a fundamental role in the management of the region. Antarctic research also offers significant opportunities for international cooperation and for communicating and emphasising the importance of Antarctica and the Southern Ocean to both the general public and decision makers.

To support SCAR's leadership and international cooperation in Antarctic and Southern Ocean research and assist in achieving its mission of excellence in science and scientific advice to policy makers, in 2014 SCAR organized the first SCAR Antarctic and Southern Ocean Science Horizon Scan, with support from the Tinker Foundation and others. This initiative assembled world leading Antarctic scientists, policy makers, leaders, and visionaries to identify the most important scientific questions that will or should be addressed by research over the next two decades and beyond. This was the first time that the international Antarctic community has formulated a collective vision, through discussions, debate and voting. The outcome was an agreement on 80 of the most important Antarctic research questions, laying out an ambitious scientific "roadmap" for the next 20 years and beyond.

Answering these many questions will require sustained and stable funding; access to all of Antarctica throughout the year; application of emerging technologies; strengthened protection of the region; growth in international cooperation; and improved communication among all interested parties. At the same time, many Antarctic programmes are suffering budget pressures and uncertainties.

The Council of Managers of National Antarctic Programs (COMNAP) led a second stage of the process, with the Antarctic Roadmap Challenges (ARC) project, focused on answering the question: "How will national Antarctic programmes meet the challenges of delivering Antarctic science identified in the Horizon Scan?"

The 2016 SCAR Science Lecture to the ATCM will present an overview of this process and its main conclusions to the Delegates based on the published outputs of the SCAR Horizon Scan[1,2] and the ARC project[3]. This presentation will describe how actions will be implemented to explore and achieve future scientific priorities and discuss the associated challenges. We will reinforce that wider international partnerships, more coordination of science and infrastructure funding and expanded knowledge-sharing are essential. We will also reinforce to the Delegates the importance of using scientific evidence in decision-making and the development of conservation measures. These processes have been a collective effort of the Antarctic community, based on broad international cooperation, involving many hundreds of scientists, managers and technicians from dozens of countries, with a close cooperation between SCAR and COMNAP, carried out in a framework inspired by the Antarctic Treaty.

[1] Kennicutt, M.C. *et al.* 2014. Polar research: Six priorities for Antarctic science. *Nature* 512 (7512), 23-25.
[2] Kennicutt, M.C. *et al.* 2015. A roadmap for Antarctic and Southern Ocean science for the next two decades and beyond. *Antarctic Science,* 27(1), 3-18.
[3] Kennicutt, M., Kim, Y., Rogan-Finnemore, M. (Eds). 2016. *Antarctic Roadmap Challenges.* Christchurch, COMNAP. ISBN 978-0-473-35672-9.

Presentations at the Special Working Group on the 25th Anniversary of the Protocol on Environmental protection

The Hon Bob Hawke AC address to ATCM XXXIX

I am delighted to join you all today to celebrate the Madrid Protocol's 25th anniversary and to have the opportunity to join my good friend and fellow collaborator, Michel Rocard, to deliver this message.

The ratification of the Madrid Protocol in 1991 was a remarkable achievement of planet changing magnitude. After all, the previous decade had been spent working on an agreement to allow drilling for oil and mining in Antarctica.

It would have been an act of sheer vandalism for the pristine wilderness of this untamed continent to be exploited in this way.

Working together, Antarctic Treaty parties embarked on a new course - one where protecting Antarctica's unique environment was paramount.

At the heart of the Protocol was the overwhelming immediacy and desire to establish Antarctica as a natural reserve, devoted to peace and to science; with a permanent ban on mining at its core.

Despite mounting pressure and demand on the planet's natural energy resources, for me, it was an easy decision to make, and the right one. It took a number of years to work this through, but we succeeded in protecting this unique and fragile continent.

As we should. After all, Antarctica is extraordinary.

It is the highest, driest, windiest and coldest continent in the world. It is one of the planet's greatest natural wonders and we should never challenge or lose the magical mystique of that wonder, but seek to learn from it.

It is home to unique creatures which have adapted to Antarctica's extremes and cannot be found anywhere else on earth.

The scientific treasures contained within its ice, atmosphere and ocean will unlock climate records – expanding our understanding of global climate change – one of the biggest challenges to our survival.

It is indisputable that Antarctica deserves the highest protection from human's desire to conquer and exploit.

As parties to the Antarctic Treaty, we have a collective duty to ensure that this happens. It should be an iron-clad guarantee.

With the Madrid Protocol we have the means to do so.

I am very pleased that 37 Antarctic Treaty parties have signed on to the Protocol. But the Protocol's promise will never be complete until all Antarctic Treaty parties join.

This will signify an unwavering commitment by all countries with a presence in Antarctica that they are at one – working together to ensure its everlasting protection.

Sometimes it is suggested that the mining ban 'sunsets' in 2048. We know better. The ban has no 'expiry date'.

Today, as we reflect on the Principles of the Protocol, we must reaffirm our commitment to Antarctica and in particular to the permanent mining ban. Future generations should be left in no doubt in regard to this generation's fierce and forceful unquestionable commitment and legacy to protecting this extraordinary continent.

Finally, I wish to thank Chile for hosting this important symposium. I also thank and applaud all delegates at the meeting for your hard work and dedication to protecting Antarctica.

I wish you all the very best for this year's meeting.

Remarks on the history, vision behind and impact of the Protocol on Environmental Protection

Evan T. Bloom

I am honored to have been invited to kick-off today's Symposium celebrating the 25th Anniversary of the Protocol on Environmental Protection, otherwise known as the Madrid Protocol. We come together today to take stock of what the Protocol has accomplished and to consider its future as part of the larger issue of how to advance environmental protection in Antarctica, which is one of the most important current priorities of all the Treaty Parties.

Today, I would like to address the history of the development of the Madrid Protocol, discuss its overwhelming positive impact, and review the role the Protocol and its Annexes play in preserving the Antarctic environment.

Those here know rather well that Antarctica's environment is unique and extraordinary. It is a wilderness of vast proportions that is home to a wealth of flora and fauna. Of particular importance is that Antarctica's ice sheet stores an estimated 90 percent of our world's surface fresh water. The United States and other countries have long recognized Antarctica as a world premier scientific laboratory that has yielded, and continues, to yield, insights into some of the more fundamental questions facing mankind today. To give just one example, the world understands climate change better than any time in our history, thanks in large part to the record of changing climate conditions observed in the Antarctic and preserved in Antarctica's ice and sediment layers. There is little question that the scientific value of Antarctica is tied directly to the pristine nature of its environment. It is that environment that the Madrid Protocol has served to protect and preserve for the benefit of all.

My sense is that all of us would agree that the Antarctic Treaty Parties made a wise decision when they decided to negotiate and ultimately adopt the Environmental Protocol. This took an act of political courage, requiring the abandonment of an approach that had been under negotiation for years, namely the establishment of a regulatory regime related to mining, in favor of taking a quite different direction. My government had initially supported the prior approach under the Convention on the Regulation of Antarctic Mineral Resource Activities (CRAMRA). But the daring – perhaps heroic – decision by leaders of countries like Australia and France, we must admit, led to something better. With the benefit of hindsight, the wisdom of that change of course is now quite evident.

It was clear at that point in time that there was a need for the Antarctic legal regime to focus more on environmental concerns. The Antarctic Treaty, as important a milestone as it was, was never intended as an environmental protection instrument. It was the world's first modern arms control treaty, and it did address a series of important geopolitical and science policy issues. But it wasn't about environmental protection. The Antarctic Treaty established a process for meetings of Consultative parties, the very same process that brings us here today. Those meetings, in turn, produced a number of important steps related to environmental regulations, such as the Agreed Measures for the Conservation of Antarctic Fauna and Flora. But more was clearly needed.

In a sense, the Convention for the Conservation of Antarctic Marine Living Resources (CCAMLR) was (and is) an environmental instrument. It was one of the first treaties touching on fisheries to enshrine the ecosystem-based approach to fisheries management, and today we see that CCAMLR is the basis for establishing marine protected areas, which of course have an important relationship to environmental protection. But if we wanted to protect the Antarctic and its dependent and associated ecosystems, more was going to be needed beyond CCAMLR as well, and the Treaty Parties had to act.

In 1991, a mere two years after setting-aside CRAMRA, this body agreed to the Protocol on Environmental Protection, an achievement that we celebrate today. The cornerstone of the Madrid Protocol is of course Article 7, which banned all mineral resource activities in Antarctica, other than scientific research. This was a decisive step for the protection of the Antarctic environment. Given its importance, my delegation proposed at this meeting, together with many co-sponsors, a resolution whereby the Consultative Parties would re-commit themselves to this essential element of the Protocol. The resolution received strong support, it has been agreed by the ATCM's Working Group 1, and will be brought forward for adoption at Wednesday's plenary.

Of course, Article 7 is just one part, albeit a very important and well-known part, of the Madrid Protocol. The Protocol itself provides a framework for the comprehensive protection of the Antarctic environment and dependent and associated ecosystems, while designating Antarctica as a natural reserve, devoted to peace and science. Through 27 separate Articles and six different Annexes, the Protocol addresses marine pollution, protection of fauna and flora, the requirements for environmental impact assessments, waste management, and establishment of protected areas.

We are all very familiar with the Protocol's existing annexes. Annex I requires an environmental impact assessment before activities are undertaken. Annex II provides for the protection of Antarctic animals and plants as well as restrictions on non-native species. Annex III encourages parties to reduce the amount of wastes and imposes requirements for waste clean- up, wastes management plans and strategies. And Annex IV prohibits the discharge of oil and any substances including plastics and sewage into the sea by Treaty Party ships operating in Antarctica. These all have contributed significantly to the preservation of Antarctica's environment.

Annex V provides for the protection and management of the Antarctic Specially Protected Areas or ASPAs, Antarctic Specially Managed Areas or ASMAs, and Historic Sites and Monuments. The existing system of ASPAs and ASMAs has been one of the most important elements of the Protocol. The United States has been proud to promote and support these tools through its Antarctic Program and its contributions to the development of a checklist for inspections of ASPAs and ASMAs. These Annex V mechanisms have proved to be some of our most effective environmental preservation tools and the United States sees them as critical to the future protection of Antarctica.

I turn now to Annex VI, commonly referred to as the Liability Annex. Although it has not yet entered into force, it is a key element of the Protocol and a major undertaking by the Treaty Parties in their efforts to protect the environment. Annex VI has its origin in Articles 15 and 16 of the Protocol, and was designed to establish liability by both governmental and nongovernmental operators that have failed to respond to an environmental emergency. It represents a unique approach to liability, different from other liability treaties, and reflects a practical means to protecting the Antarctic environment where there is little or no baseline data that would permit evaluation of the degree of environmental harm at sea or on land. It serves as an important development in international law, and particularly international environmental law. Ratification by the Consultative Parties remains an important priority for the Antarctic Treaty system.

I also wish to take note of the significant role that the Committee for Environmental Protection (CEP) plays in the Treaty system. The creation of the CEP by the Protocol signaled the importance all of us place on the management of the environment under the Madrid Protocol. The CEP provides advice and formulates recommendations to the Parties in connection with the implementation of this Protocol, and it has done an outstanding job. It has produced key processes and guidelines that form a central part of the Treaty Parties' environmental efforts.

This includes groundbreaking work on assessing environmental impacts, on the protection of flora and fauna, on establishing procedures for area protection and management, and much more.

Lastly, we must all take this opportunity to look to the future and think of innovative ways to maintain the highest standards of environmental protection and stewardship. The pressures on the Antarctic environment will only increase in the future. The challenges are many - climate change, non-native species, impacts of both governmental and non-governmental activities.

Threats to the marine environment are also growing and need attention; whether via the Protocol or through CCAMLR. (Indeed, we are greatly encouraged by the cooperation that exists between the CEP and CCAMLR's Scientific Committee.)

The United States remains committed to continue to work collaboratively with all State Parties to respond to emerging and priority issues such as cumulative impacts, the appropriate regulation of tourism, the implementation of the Polar Code, the establishment of Marine Protected Areas, and climate change. In this regard, the work of the CEP remains critical to the success of the goals of the Protocol, and the need for CEP advice will continue to grow as impacts on Antarctica and its dependent and associated ecosystems increase. We need to explore better ways of working together to allow for more time focused, topical discussions on priority topics during the CEP meetings so the advice provided to the ATCM is the best it can be.

The Madrid Protocol is an extraordinary achievement in international diplomacy. It is a regime that has delivered on its promises, despite the challenges that still remain. We can all take great pride in the anniversary of this unique agreement that has and will continue to serve the high ideals, which it ushered it into existence in 1991.

We, the United States, offer our congratulations and appreciation to all of those who have worked so hard to attain this significant achievement and we look forward to promoting the continued protection of Antarctica for peaceful and scientific purposes into the foreseeable future.

Thank you.

The Protocol in comparison to other global and regional environmental framework agreements

Therese Johansen

Introduction

First of all, it is clear that the Protocol and Antarctica as such, is absolutely unique and in many ways cannot be compared to any other frameworks or areas in the world. Nevertheless, as a second point I will try to draw some comparisons to other regions and the value of a regional and ecosystem-based approach to environmental protection. Thirdly, I will attempt to draw some conclusions on how the Protocol can continue to serve as a model and inspiration for other regions as well

The unique characteristics of the Environmental Protocol

The Protocol and Antarctica as such is unique. A fundamental issue is the agreement to disagree on the territorial claims as long as the Antarctic Treaty is in force, and the designation of an entire continent as a natural reserve devoted to peace and science.

The Protocol serves as the environmental pillar of the ATS, and from a Norwegian perspective, listing the attributes of the Protocol is ticking all the boxes, where all the elements that Norway values the most are present – such as its comprehensiveness – covering all human activities, science- and knowledge based management and the role of the CEP to provide sound scientific advice, a truly ecosystem-based approach where both terrestrial and marine areas can be dealt with as a whole, how it sets out a framework for cooperation and coordination across sectors, with the Antarctic Treaty providing the overarching principles.

Also, the working relationship between the ATCM, CEP, CCAMLR, etc. within their respective mandates and areas of expertise but with a common goal of achieving the highest level of protection of Antarctica as a whole.

I would also highlight the role of the Consultative Parties which ensure that the decision making is in the hands of States with real interest and knowledge about the region. Membership rules that require proof of commitment to Antarctica and the importance of regional governance by actors with the best knowledge of the specific region. This brings me to the next slide on the regional approach to environmental protection and how other regions are addressing these same issues, sometimes being directly inspired by the lessons learned within the ATS

The regional approach – a comparison to the North East Atlantic Ocean

Under this section, the idea was to present how cooperation and coordination across sectors is being achieved in the North East Atlantic and how it compares to the ATS.

The institutional architecture of the North East Atlantic consist of OSPAR as the environmental pillar, NEAFC as the fisheries pillar, IMO for shipping, ISA for seabed mining and the coastal states to address issues with regard to areas under national jurisdiction, such as land based pollution. The overarching framework for all of this is of course the UN Convention on the Law of the Sea.

The objective of the OSPAR Convention is to protect the marine environment of the North East Atlantic through enhanced cooperation between its Parties.

NEAFC on the other hand, manages all fishing within its convention area. When adopting management measures, NEAFC has to apply the precautionary approach, take due account of the impact of fisheries on other species and marine ecosystems and biodiversity.

Together, OSPAR and NEAFC serve as the regional vehicles to implement global obligations, goals and commitments from UNCLOS, and instruments such as UNFSA, UNGA, CBD etc.

OSPAR and NEAFC cooperate closely on issues of joint concern. With regard to human activities already covered by other organisations, OSPAR's role is to keep the overall environmental status and adverse impacts under review, having regard to all human activities and their cumulative impacts. If OSPAR identifies threats and adverse impacts of human activities falling within the competence of other organisations, this information is forwarded to the relevant organisations to form the basis for the design and adoption of management measures. This way, OSPAR can initiate decisions and measures on activities not within its own mandate.

One example of the cooperation between OSPAR and NEAFC, is the establishment of closed areas by NEAFC, followed by the establishment of MPAs by OSPAR in almost the same area – complementing each other and that way enhancing the protection of these areas.

Achieving this has not been easy, and something that we have been working on for several years on how to find the right balance and practical ways of working together. I can only speak for Norway of course, but at least for us, the Antarctic Treaty system served as an inspiration on how to set up the right institutional framework.

In our view, enhanced global oceans management is dependent on this kind of cooperation and coordination across sectors. Thus OSPAR and NEAFC are also seeking to cooperate with regional organisations in other parts of the world.

In 2013 OSPAR signed a MoU with the Convention for Cooperation on the Protection and Development of the Marine and Coastal Environment of the West and Central African Region (Abidjan Convention) focusing on fisheries and environmental cooperation between OSPAR/NEAFC and the Abidjan Secretariat/the West African regional fisheries organisation (SRFC).

Conclusions

What conclusions can be drawn from this – At least from a Norwegian perspective, and putting the unique characteristics and the special status of Antarctica aside, the Environmental Protocol and the institutional architecture in Antarctica is the gold standard and has been an inspiration for our approach to managing our own backwaters so to speak, such as in the North East Atlantic.

There are many lessons to be learned, not least with regard to cooperation and coordination across sectors. In this area, the relationship between ATCM, CEP, CCAMLR, IMO and national competent authorities etc. has been tried and tested over these last 25 years.

Granted, this is a field where there is always room for improvement, but I would argue that in Antarctica much has been achieved and we have the framework in place to continue to represent cutting edge environmental protection as we move forward in our efforts to protect this unique continent.

Address by Mr Michel Rocard

Distinguished Ministers, ladies and gentlemen, dear delegates,

I regret not being with you for the 39th Antarctic Treaty Consultative Meeting; I had grown used to this important yearly event, but I am growing older. I am with you in spirit, and more importantly, France is well represented at the meeting by a solid delegation.

I regret my absence this year even more as our Chilean host for the 39th ATCM has taken the brilliant initiative of commemorating the 25th anniversary of the Madrid Protocol, Protocol on Environmental Protection to the Antarctic Treaty, which has become a -if not THE- centrepiece of the Antarctic Treaty System, which Robert Hawke, Australia's former Prime Minister, and myself, as Prime Minister of France at the time, promoted and pioneered between 1989 and 1991.

I thank the Chilean presidency for this initiative and take this opportunity to pay my respects to our Australian colleagues, who will, I hope, convey my best wishes to my friend Bob.

I have something to confess: I have never been a great fan of commemorations or anniversaries, or even of my own birthdays, which I tend to forget. When you are keen on driving things forward and on political action, ritualized, the over-indulgent staging of past victorious battles contrasts too sharply with hulking tasks and urgent battles waiting to be launched.

Unless, of course, the commemoration is an incentive or a call for concerted action. And this, dear colleagues, is precisely what I wish to touch upon today in my short address.

Five years ago, in 2011, as I reviewed the Antarctic Treaty System panel, I discovered that out of 20 non-Consultative Parties at the time, 14 had not ratified the Madrid Protocol. This situation meant that certain nations, who, through their Washington Treaty membership, had expressed their interest for the region, did not fall under the collective responsibilities which founded the Antarctic community. It also created serious problems for controlling the scientific or tourist activities in the Treaty area of citizens of States that were non party to the Protocol.

I picked up my phone and called my old friend Robert Hawke, explained the situation to him, and together, we decided to take advantage of the symbolic 20th anniversary of the Madrid Protocol, to propose that the 34th ATCM re-launch the ratification process of the Antarctic Treaty's second protocol. We all remember what happened: twenty delegations began lobbying the governments concerned, ultimately resulting in concrete action. Thanks to the Antarctic community's joint initiative, the 20th anniversary commemorations for the Madrid Protocol took on real significance, even if it must be said that the ratification process has since slowed down somewhat...

But such is the function of a commemorative event: to periodically launch again, to tirelessly reactivate, to raise awareness as soon as complacency takes hold, to re-awaken the fundamental, founding values of a community.

How does this apply to the 25th anniversary of the Madrid Protocol? What does it aspire to shed light upon? When I first heard of this celebration, I told myself that in the frenzy which has us slipping from a ten-year cycle of commemorations to a five-year cycle of commemorations of the signing of the Madrid Protocol; the next step could only be an International Antarctic Day.

It is a good idea, which would deserve to be institutionalised. It would no doubt contribute to increasing Antarctica's importance for public opinions, which may one day weigh on the destiny of this area and on its unique legal status.

Above all, I felt that this frenzy for commemoration hid something, no doubt the Antarctic community's concerns for "international harmony" instituted by the 1959 Treaty and consolidated by the Madrid Protocol, which declared Antarctica to be a land devoted to peace and science, and which forbids any activity related to mineral resources aside from scientific research.

From a legal point of view, international harmony in Antarctica is protected by the Antarctic Treaty System. Amendment procedures in both the 1959 Antarctic Treaty and the 1991 Madrid Protocol involve assembling difficult majorities and thereby guarantee the continuity of these legal instruments.

Of course, the prohibition of mining activities may be revised beyond a period of 50 years from the effective date of the Madrid Protocol, but we have no reason to fear a legal tool which we forged together through consensus, and whose solidity was conceived to resist the hazards and uncertainties of international life.

If any concerns are to be voiced, they should not be aimed at the Antarctic Treaty's legal system. Rather, there is concern for the values driving the Antarctic community: fundamental values which ensure community cohesion; shared values which contribute to preserving international harmony in this lost part of our planet, beyond the differences that divide the world.

Remember, twenty-five years ago: the Antarctic community had reached a consensus on a mining moratorium amendable after 50 years, I quote:

"to ensure the effective protection of Antarctica without compromising the options of future generations." You see, we have only ourselves to fear for, and for our children, who learn from us. It is a heavy responsibility; we are the guardians of the Antarctic international order and this order shall continue for as long as the majority of the Antarctic legal community continues to recognise itself in the fundamental values of Antarctica.

It so happens, dear colleagues, that in disregard of historical chronology, the Madrid Protocol of 1991 has imposed itself over the years as the centrepiece of international harmony instigated by the 1959 Treaty, and that the mining moratorium now represents a fundamental value of the Antarctic regime.

The United States were right in proposing to capitalize on the symbolic 25th anniversary of the Madrid Protocol to reinforce and unite the Antarctic community around a declaration of commitment in favour of the mining moratorium. France very quickly joined the initiative, as did the vast majority of Treaty parties.

I encourage all Treaty Parties to support the American initiative which confers meaning to this fifty-year commemoration and reminds us of our collective responsibility:

From a legal and political point of view, the existence of a majority of Treaty parties, united around the fundamental values of the Treaty System, constitutes the best protection against external or internal pressures which would want to suggest an amendment to Antarctica's exceptional status.

Long live Antarctica!

Thank you for your attention. I wish you all a fruitful conference.

--- END ---

Analysis of the Protocol on Environmental Protection to the Antarctic Treaty and its annexes

José Retamales

The well-known Argentine expert Miryam Colacrai, Dr. in Social Sciences and author of many books on the Arctic and the Antarctic described the "Protocol on Environmental Protection to the Antarctic Treaty as a vital commitment towards consolidating the Antarctic system" 20 years ago in the Chilean Antarctic Newsletter dated May 1996.

She started by reminding, in the context of a global political analysis, how the safety issues caught the highest attention and concern in the world agenda throughout the post-war and the containment period. Then, how economic aspects posed a great challenge during the seventies and eighties, and how this would shift the focus to environmental aspects during the nineties.

The execution of the Antarctic Treaty in 1959 was aimed at addressing "safety" in the region and at reaching a balance among the Parties. It further ensured the non-militarisation and denuclearisation on a twofold basis: from the standpoint of safety and from the standpoint of environmental protection.

A second stage, over the seventies and eighties, paid special attention to the regulations on the exploitation of some resources, by means of special Conventions such as the Convention for the Conservation of Antarctic Seals (CCAS), the Commission for the Conservation of Antarctic Marine Living Resources (CCAMLR),and the Convention on the Regulation of Antarctic Mineral Resources Activities, its wording being the result of hard negotiations, but which failed to be ratified by all the Parties in order for it to become effective.

This led to the drafting of the final Protocol after holding several meetings such as the Consultative Meeting held in Paris in 1989, the Special Consultative Meetings held in Viña del Mar in 1990, and the meetings held in the months of April, June, and October 1991 in the city of Madrid. Out of the different proposals submitted, the successful one was the one supporting this kind of instrument, which supplements the Antarctic Treaty instead of the Conventions formula -somehow autonomous- which had characterized the dynamics of previous agreements.

Therefore, in accordance with the world agenda, the implementation of the Protocol on Environmental Protection in 1991 placed this issue in the very centre of the concern and the debate on the Antarctic Treaty System.

It is clear that the integration of the "Protocol" did not mean the integration of any subject unconnected to the Antarctic Treaty. From the first Consultative Meetings held, and for the purpose of regulating such general standards and principles set forth in the Treaty, the fragile nature of the Antarctic environment was taken into account, and a significant number of recommendations were drafted.

The pioneering basis towards the "protection and conservation of the Antarctic resources" can be found on the measures agreed in furtherance of the Conservation of Antarctic Fauna and Flora in 1964. Probably, the most significant aspect of these measures consists in that they declared the territory of the Antarctic Treaty a "special conservation area".

It is worth remembering that scientific contributions on the assessment of the environmental impact started during the seventies, and the debate around it was the central theme of a significant number of reports and seminars by international experts.

However, there is no doubt that the positioning of this matter as the priority issue in the agenda is the consequence of the negotiations which led to the drafting of the "Protocol on Environmental Protection to the Antarctic Treaty".

The Protocol states the need to obtain international cooperation, on the grounds of environmental matters, highlighting that the Parties should consult each other with regard to the selection of locations of potential bases, in order to mitigate, to the highest possible extent, the cumulative impact which may be caused by an excessive amount of facilities.

It also fosters the conduction of joint expeditions and the possibility of sharing the use of scientific bases, with the subsequent optimization of resources by means of the shared use of logistical means as well as a mitigation of the environmental impact caused to a greater or lesser extent by any activity.

The policies developed in the Antarctic Treaty on the basis of the topics discussed over the 19 years of work of the Committee for Environmental Protection have definitely made it possible to accurately specify any environmentally-relevant actions.

Nevertheless, to what extent are we protecting or to what extent are we able to protect that **which we do not see** in the Antarctic? This is just an example of the broad Antarctic biodiversity: *Limacina rangii*, a tiny snail living in the Southern ocean, pictured in the waters of Fildes Bay. It is a helical-shell gastropod, also known as "sea butterfly".

One of its features is that the animal develops fleshy, pale, semitransparent growths, which grow from its foot to both sides of its body making it possible for the animal to "fly" in the water. Its soft parts are deep purple, its hard shell is very thin and fragile, and an adult specimen is hardly 6 mm long. Its "wings" produce the typical mucus of snails with which they wrap their prey before eating it.

In turn, this Limacina rangii is consumed by pelagic gastropods pertaining to the so called "sea angels" group, as the Clione antarctica which may be up to 30 mm long forming one of the many food webs of the animal kingdom.

This pelagic "angel" feeds exclusively from this "butterfly" in the Antarctic. Without a protecting shell, which is lost in embryonic form, it synthesises a chemical product -the pteroenone- which makes it hardly tempting. Unlike "butterflies", these "sea angels" may also be found in sub-Antarctic waters, in large quantities.

Therefore, it is our opinion that it is highly important that the hidden secrets of the southern ocean, i.e., sea life, are communicated to the public at large. Science will make it possible for us to develop an increasingly deeper understanding of what we ought to protect.

The well known and very abundant Antarctic krill has proved to be able to sustain life in the Antarctic, since it constitutes the very basis of the southern trophic chain, from small penguins to big whales. Krill further sustains an increasing fishing industry.

However, will Krill be able to survive the acidification of the southern ocean?

As we all know, the Protocol was mainly outlined to protect the Antarctic environment from the environmental pressure generated by the presence and the activity of human beings in the continent. The Five-Year Work Plan of the Committee for Environmental Protection considers the environmental pressures derived from the introduction of non-native species, tourism, management of specially protected and managed Antarctic areas, of marine spatial protection, and historical sites, among others. The Committee has also created a working group especially focused on climate change.

However, the highest future challenges posed on the protection of the Antarctic environment will most likely not derive from human activity in that continent but from the global activities carried out in the world, which is evidenced in that sort of lighthouse which is the white continent.

Article 4 of the United Nations Framework Convention on Climate Change, defines 9 conditions which render countries vulnerable to the impact of climate change. Chile fulfils 7 out of such 9 conditions, and in this regard, in its issue from 6 December last year, a local newspaper published the figure shown on screen.

Consequently, I would like to venture that the interest by new countries in knowing and studying the Antarctic will continue to increase, as a result of the concern shown by the public opinion about the effects of climate change. This should entail new challenges for the Committee for Environmental Protection and for the protection of the Antarctic System in general.

The impact of the Protocol on protection of the Antarctic environment from a scientist's perspective

Aleks Terauds

Science objectives

There are a range of perspectives across the scientific community on the primary reasons they undertake their work. However, there are also some common broad themes, which I have tried to capture here. Understanding the environment, then using the knowledge obtained to inform management is common path. These management decisions can then be implemented to protect the environment and from this protection flows conservation.

Not every scientist is trying to achieve every one of these objectives, but broadly speaking they cover in some way shape or form, what scientists are trying to achieve

Protection from...?

I think its worthwhile next touching on what we are trying to protect the Antarctic environment from. If we take a step back, prior to the Protocol being adopted in 1991, there were a number of potential threats facing Antarctica. Most of these are linked to human activity.

There is no doubt that the presence of people in Antarctica has the potential to impact on the Antarctic environment. In terms of direct impacts, there is significant human presence, and this presence is increasing. We know that one of the potential threats, mining has been addressed by the explicit mining ban in Article 7 of the Protocol, and that provides a very important broad layer of protection. We also know that climate change has the potential to interact and potential magnify a whole range of threats, with potentially massive impacts on the Antarctic environment. And there are other specific issues, like non-native species that are also known to have far reaching impacts.

In the context of these threats, both potential and realized, the importance of the protection provided by the Protocol becomes very clear.

'..a natural reserve, devoted to peace and science'

The words "a reserve dedicated to peace and science" in Article 2, are one of the best known parts of the Protocol on Environmental Protection to the Antarctic Treaty. These words capture the spirit and essence of the protection afforded to Antarctica through the Protocol. More importantly, these words in Article 2 makes it very clear that environmental protection is a continent wide commitment. They provide a very strong foundation for the protection of the Antarctic environment, on which the Protocol builds on through its subsequent Articles and Annexes.

The high profile of these words also means that there is a high public perception of environmental protection, or probably more important, the intention to protect Antarctica, and, as a scientist this is also important. It's also important to note the inclusion of the word science, and it use here inextricably ties the ideas of Antarctic science and environmental protection together.

These close ties can be seen in the evolution of the SCAR groups, over the last 30 years. A few years prior to the Protocol being adopted, the SCAR Group of Specialists on Environmental Affairs and Conservation was formed. This group was actively involved in helping to inform Antarctic policy and management of the environment for many years until it eventually morphed into the SCAR Standing Committee on the Antarctic Treaty System, who I represent here today.

Professors David Walton and Steven Chown played a very important role in these groups, and SCATS remains the responsible group for providing scientific advice to the Antarctic Treaty on behalf of SCAR, with a strong focus on issues that are related to environmental protection

Environmental principles

Article 3 is one of the most powerful Articles from the perspective of a scientist. It means that all activities in Antarctica must consider the potential environmental impacts. In this regard it provides a very strong level of base protection. In conjunction with the provisions of Annex 1, it is a very effective tool for the management and protection of the Antarctic environment.

From a scientific perspective, this focus on environmental principles in the Protocol provides the opportunity to use science to guide activities. SCAR's Codes of conduct are a good example of this. Using the best scientific knowledge available, SCAR has developed several codes of conduct to guide activities and assist with the protection of the Environment. SCAR also has focus on geoconservation, and this represents another important avenue for protecting the environment in line with the environmental principles specified in the Protocol

Protection of flora and fauna

Annex 2, which deals with the protection of flora and fauna, has some also extremely important elements to do with protecting the Antarctic Environment. These include the regulation and oversight of scientific activities through a requirement for permits, and also the provision to designate specially protected species.

From a scientist's perspective, again I'll point to a couple of SCAR examples where science has been used, in conjunction with the requirements of the Protocol as outlined in this Annex, to improve environmental protection. SCAR science has helped to inform the development of wildlife watching guidelines, and more recently, pointed to research that shows further work is required to not only understand traditional issues around wildlife disturbance, but also the potential impact of emerging technologies like Unmanned Aerial Vehicles (UAVs). Even though UAVs were not an issue when the Protocol came into effect, today it still provides an excellent foundation for informing and guiding their use.

Non-native species

Non-native species are also specified as a threat in Annex 2. Their deliberate introduction is prohibited under this Annex. However, as we have seen through an extensive body of work over the last decade or more, unintended introductions have been, and remain, an issue. This issue can be mitigated somewhat by the use of strict biosecurity practices and SCAR together with a range of collaborators, has used science to inform and develop these practices.

The Aliens in Antarctic project, an initiative associated with the International Polar year of 2007-2008, was an important program in this regard, and we now have a good understanding of pathways of non-native species and a range of biosecurity protocols to minimize the risk.

Therefore, again, through the specification in this Annex, the Protocol has provided the opportunity for science to protect the environment, and contribute to outputs like the COMNAP Supply Chain Checklist, the CEP Non-native species manual and the biosecurity protocols of National Antarctic programs.

Provision for extra protection

The provision of extra protection in Annex 5 to the Protocol is also a key component of Environmental Protection. Antarctic Specially Protected Areas and Antarctic Specially Managed Areas provide for a range of specific values to be protected and these have been shown to be a very effective tool for protecting biodiversity, geodiversity and other important environmental elements. It also provides a very clear framework for the delivery of science into area protection.

SCAR has a focus on ongoing work to inform the development of an evidence-based and systematic Protected Area Network in Antarctica.

Committee for Environmental Protection

I'd like to reiterate the importance of the Committee for Environmental Protection. The formation of this committee was a key part of the Protocol coming into force in 1998, and since this time it has proved to be the powerhouse of the protocol, and very effective at driving change.

The direct relationship that the CEP has with science, whether it be through Parties or through Observers like SCAR, is one of the fundamental elements behind this success

Future Directions

SCAR will continue to advise the CEP on priority issues in line with the requirements of the Protocol and will be guided by SCAR Antarctic and Southern Ocean Horizon Scan and CEP priorities.

SCAR will also continue to provide scientific input that is aligned with the principles in the Protocol and maximize the opportunities for protecting the Antarctic environment.

Implementation of the Environmental Protocol: An operator's perspective on its impact on science support

Yves Frenot, Director IPEV, COMNAP Vice Chairman

Kazuyuki Shiraishi, Director-General NIPR, COMNAP Chairman

Michelle Rogan-Finnemore, COMNAP Executive Secretary

COMNAP is the international association of National Antarctic Programs. It currently includes 30 members and 2 observers. These 32 programs are responsible for supporting governmental activities in over 80 Antarctic research facilities.

COMNAP's mission is to develop and promote best practices that support scientific research in Antarctica. It is an official ATCM and CEP observer. Recognising the importance of its status, COMNAP has committed to supporting the Antarctic Treaty System by offering practical, technical, and apolitical advice drawn from the experience and expertise of National Programs which are active in the Treaty area.

National Antarctic Programs are also the executors of the principles set out in the Madrid Protocol. Indeed, all COMNAP members are countries which have endorsed the Protocol and have included it in their national legislations. Yet the protocol has direct implications on Program activities in terms of supporting science, the maintenance of scientific infrastructures, or implementing associated logistics.

This presentation highlights the manner in which COMNAP contributes to developing Protocol requirements in three ways:

1. Defining requirements which directly impact COMNAP;

2. How COMNAP responds to them, carrying out field verifications on the feasibility of adopted measures; and

3. Providing examples of how these orientations are implemented by national programs.

Due to time constraints, this presentation only highlights examples from Annexes I and III of the Protocol.

The first part therefore relates to Annex I, on Environmental Impact Assessments (EIAs) of activities undertaken in Antarctica. I would first like to show how COMNAP has developed concepts listed in Annex I, before giving illustrations of their implementation by national programs.

Before the Protocol was even drafted, SCAR and COMNAP understood the importance of EIAs and of monitoring activities. Through their respective environmental groups (GOSEAC and AEON), they initiated discussions on environmental management. When GOSEAC was created in 1988 within SCAR, managers of national programs were quick to establish links between scientists and governmental organisations that support science.

Understanding and developing best practices for assessing impacts has therefore always been a matter of prime importance for COMNAP. At its first meeting in Cambridge in 1989, COMNAP discussed the "[...] role and responsibilities of national Antarctic program managers for implementing ATCM recommendations relating to environmental protection. A sub-group has been tasked with preparing a workshop aimed at establishing practical guidelines for environmental evaluation processes. "

The workshop was held in June 1991. At the time, COMNAP remarked that "the objective of practical guidelines is to provide managers of national programs with an explicit and concise mechanism for implementing environmental evaluation processes," thereby following ATCM's recommendations. Results of the workshop, associated with other COMNAP endeavours, were presented at ATCM XVI as practical guidelines for procedures relating to EIAs, and as guidelines for Antarctic visitors.

These discussions, and later those held within the network of COMNAP environmental experts, formed in 1999, launched the beginning of essential work, which ultimately led to establishing CEP's intersessional Working Group on EIAs.

Today, countless impact studies have been prepared by national programs for their respective activities.

For example, amongst the 41 CEEs (drafts or final) currently listed in the Secretariat's database for 1988-2015, 11 final CEEs were prepared alongside infrastructures and 8 others with major scientific projects. This illustrates the considerable resources national programs must devote as they establish research infrastructures in Antarctica, and also how they must implement their activities in order to comply with obligations created by these CEEs.

Second part of the presentation, relating to Annex III on waste disposal and waste management.

From the earliest days of man's presence on the 6th continent, generated waste was simply left behind in Antarctica, either buried or discharged into the sea. Thankfully, as these practices have been increasingly considered as unacceptable, attention has become focused on how to handle and dispose of this waste. COMNAP participated in these discussions via yearly meetings, organising several workshops on the issue.

Waste disposal was directly discussed by ATCM VIII, when the first Code of Conduct was annexed to Recommendation 11 in 1975. Several years later, the code was re-examined, leading to Recommendation 3 (1989), "Impacts of Human Activities on the Antarctic Environment: Waste Disposal." COMNAP then began examining issues around waste disposal at its first meeting in 1989, drafting a waste management declaration form presented at ATCM XVI in 1991, which national programs were encouraged to use. Information which was gathered on station practices and shared amongst all operators enabled considerable strides in waste management. This ongoing approach is all the more useful in that it includes new, more effective, more economic, and more importantly, more responsible environmental methods and technologies.

In 2006, a workshop was organised by the COMNAP Environment Expert Group on sharing best practices in waste management and cleaning-up old sites. Another workshop was organised in 2014, devoted to managing waste waters in Antarctic stations.

Today, mentalities for national programs have changed radically, and it is no longer conceivable to throw something away anywhere, or even in any bin; selective sorting has become universal.

Now, household waste generated in the Treaty area fits within treatment channels or handling which make recycling a priority. Many national programs depend on sophisticated processes aimed at reducing packaging material before being transported to Antarctica, and sorting waste before it is evacuated from the Treaty area.

The importance of managing or cleaning up sites that present old waste is highlighted in Article 1, Annex III of the Protocol, which stipulates that "old and current land disposal sites and abandoned Antarctic work sites shall be cleaned by waste producers and site users."

This aspect was also considered by COMNAP. WP 062, presented at ATCM XXXV in 2012, lists 31 examples of cleaning, waste removal or of remediation led by 16 nations between 1999 and 2011.

The requirement to repair or restore leads the way to a number of important questions for national program leaders, as it applies retrospectively to waste inherited from previous eras.

It comes with high costs, logistic difficulties, environmental risks, security and political issues associated with this type of cleaning, and the removal of old waste always entails transportation and elimination, which require fossil fuels and stocking removed materials elsewhere in the world, unless new uses are found or new processes developed for their removal. This is a genuine challenge for national programs.

We believe that unwavering support of the principles of the Environmental Protocol is the very basis of the fundamental principal of international cooperation in Antarctica. The importance of international partnerships must not be overestimated, but while the ultimate example of international cooperation in Antarctica may be jointly running a research station, there are many other ways for national programs to work together.

Results of the recent survey amongst national programs are the subject of IP 47, presented in 2014 at ATCM XXXVII. They demonstrate, if proof were needed, the incredibly high level of logistic collaboration and exchange which define national program relationships, in keeping with the Antarctic Treaty spirit. As for specifically protecting the Antarctic environment, effective international collaboration may turn out to be our best mechanism to support the principles and ideas of the Antarctic Treaty and its Environmental Protocol.

Managers of Antarctic programs can now call on an array of practical guidelines in scientific stations to help them design and implement environmentally-friendly practices in their activities. Many of them were developed within COMNAP.

As an organisation, COMNAP is focused on the future, as demonstrated by recent actions: long-term conservation challenges were examined in a joint workshop with SCAR in Cambridge in 2013, and the "Antarctic Roadmap Challenges" (ARC) project was just completed, which studied the technical and practical challenges of future research priorities identified by SCAR's Horizon Scan.

Those of us who are lucky to work in Antarctica are passionate about it; everything we undertake in this region must not only be considered in the context of human safety, but also of environmental protection.

As we celebrate the Protocol's 25th anniversary, we should look especially to the future, as much as we draw lessons from the past. As managers of National Antarctic Programs, we are certain that we must shape Antarctica's future. Those of us who have the privilege of working in the Treaty area must ensure that we share our message. We must continue to uphold the fundamental principles of the environmental Protocol which has transformed Antarctica into a natural reserve forever committed to peace and science.

And we must all strive to ensure that these fundamental principles last.

ENGO perspectives on the Antarctic environmental Protocol

Dr. Ricardo Roura & Claire Christian

Overview

Good morning. In this presentation, prepared together with my colleague Claire Christian, I will address the perspectives of environmental non-governmental organizations (ENGOs) on the Protocol of Environmental Protection to the Antarctic Treaty (the Protocol).

First of all I would like to thank Chile, our ATCM host, and also Norway for coordinating the preparatory work on this symposium celebrating the 25th anniversary of the Protocol.

This presentation will cover three distinct periods: The period before the signature Protocol (prior to 1991) reflecting early involvement of ENGOs in Antarctica and the "World Park Antarctica" concept. For the first 25 (1991-2016) I will highlight what we regard as the greatest achievements and ongoing challenges of the Protocol. Finally, I will refer to the next 25 years, for which I see two distinct and complementary models for the Protocol.

"World Park Antarctica" and the Protocol

In the late 1970s and through the 1980s ENGOs promoted "World Park Antarctica", a loosely defined concept based on four principles:[1]

Wilderness values are paramount;

Full protection of flora, fauna and the environment;

Antarctica devoted to scientific research which encourages international co-operation; and

Antarctica as an area of peace, free of nuclear and other weapons and all military activities

It is apparent that the Protocol objectives, designation and principles met - in varying degrees - some of these principles. Art. 2 designates Antarctica as "…a natural reserve, devoted to peace and science". Art. 3 establishes that "The protection of the Antarctic environment and dependent and associated ecosystems and the intrinsic value of Antarctica…" shall be fundamental considerations in the planning and conducting of activities.

How was the Protocol received by the environmental community? I have done some archival research and found an edition of ECO, a newspaper produced by ENGOs on the margins of the ATCM, dating from October 1991 coincident with ATCM XVI. The cover article on the issue is titled "Bonn, the day after" and contains the following assessment:

ECO is especially pleased to see that the Protocol will guarantee that Antarctica is not only kept off limits for minerals activities for a long time, but is also given legally binding protection.[2]

Clearly for ENGOs not only the mining ban itself was significant; the legal status given to environmental protection in the Protocol was seen as a major step forward. However, the article also adds a cautionary note:

While appreciating the Protocol's significant progress, much work still needs to be done, both in refining its details and putting it into practice[3]

---

[1] Modified from Greenpeace International (1990): *Greenpeace Antarctic Expedition - Background Information 89/90.* (in file with authors). See also: May, John (1989): *The Greenpeace Book of Antarctica. A New View of the Seventh Continent.* London: Dorling Kindersley. pp. 158-159
[2] ECO LXXXX Number 1. Bonn, Germany, 7-18 October 1991, p. 1.

ENGOs at the time recognised the importance of completing aspects of the Protocol that were yet unresolved - such as Annex V on area protection and management - and also the importance of practically implementing this agreement. Indeed, much of the ATCM-related work of ASOC since then has focused on the ratification and implementation of the Protocol.

1991-2016: Great achievements and ongoing challenges

For the period 1991-2016 we can identify both great achievements of the Protocol, as well as ongoing challenges. These in fact represents both ends of a continuum of the effectiveness of Protocol.

Some great achievements include:

- Protection of the Antarctic environment and the intrinsic value of Antarctica enshrined as "…fundamental considerations in the planning and conduct…" of all applicable activities (Art. 3) including EIA requirements (Art. 8);

- Prohibition of mineral resource activities (Art. 7);

- Establishment of the Committee for Environmental Protection (CEP) (Art. 11) since 1998 and inspections focused on Protocol 's promotion and compliance (Art. 14). Of course, there was an inspection regime in place before then, but with the Protocol they began to include environmental aspects too.

- Annexes on some key issues of Antarctic operations, and environmental protection and management.

At the other end of the implementation continuum there remain some ongoing challenges for this period. These include:

- Protection of wilderness values (Art. 3 (1)) - This remains an afterthought to most operations, resulting on an increase of the human footprint and encroachment of wilderness areas.

- Precautionary principle/approach implied – Activities should be planned and conducted on basis of "…information sufficient to allow prior assessment of…and informed judgment about…" (Art. 3(2)(c)). However, greater precaution could be used more in decision making in the absence of "information sufficient", ahead of gathering new data.

- Cumulative impacts (Arts. 3(2)(c) & 6) – These are increasingly understood and some progress has been made in terms of conceptualising these impacts and including them on EIA guidelines - but not yet really acted upon. This is a consequence of a number of factors, including limited environmental monitoring (Art. 3(2)(b)).

- Compatibility of compliance criteria (Art. 13) and general implementation standards among Parties. While most aspects of the Protocol are generally implemented, there is still a chronic gap between implementation standards among operators.

As a whole, what is the balance of these past 25 years concerning the effectiveness of the Protocol? As noted above, there is a continuum between what has been achieved and what is still lacking, with some aspects of implementation falling somewhere in the middle. However, since 1991 the Antarctic Treaty Consultative Meeting has developed a strong focus on environmental issues, with further impetus since the establishment of the CEP in 1998; and the Protocol's implementation has become a key component of most Antarctic operations. In addition, the concepts and objectives of the Protocol are shared with other Antarctic Treaty System bodies, such as the Commission for the Conservation of Antarctic Marine Living Resources (CCAMLR).

It should be noted that the October 1991 ENGO newspaper article referred to above, while celebrating the signature of the Protocol, had a number of additional requirements:

---

[3] Ibid., p.2.

> *Some vital additions are also necessary for the effective operation of the Protocol, including a system-wide Secretariat, annual Antarctic Treaty Consultative Meetings (ATCMs), the negotiation of liability provisions, and a comprehensive approach to Protected Areas.* [4]

Plainly progress has been made, again in varying degrees, in all of these "vital" additions, although in a different chronological order:

- ATCMs have taken place on annual basis since 1994;

- Annex V entered into force in 1998;

- the Secretariat has been fully operational since 2004; and

- Annex VI on liability was signed in 2005, although it has not yet been ratified.

The next 25 years: Two models of the Protocol

What will the next 25 years and beyond bring? First of all, it is necessary to both maintain successes AND address ongoing challenges.

In addition, there are multiple emerging challenges including - but not limited to - more Antarctic actors and activities; growing environmental pressure on the continent and at sea; and Antarctic climate change. Some new challenges are not necessarily covered in the *letter* of the Protocol, but require application of its principles to be addressed adequately. In this respect, we can describe two complementary models of Protocol implementation: the Protocol as a set of rules on particular issues, and the Protocol as a guiding principle.

The first model - the Protocol as a set of rules - addresses primarily "How?" questions - how to do things, for instance with respect to specific issues covered in the Protocol Annexes such as EIA or waste management. As such the Protocol provides a basic environmental protection regime. However to achieve its environmental protection objectives in the longer term, the Protocol has to be more than the sum of its parts. It needs to be applied in such a way that allows us to not only to assess "traditional" Antarctic issues as well as anticipate emerging issues - what a distinguished delegate from Australia aptly described this morning as the need to "look over the horizon" to identify emerging issues, and to "take action before it happens."

This brings us to the second model: The Protocol as a guiding principle. In contrast to the first model, which provides for specific rules for particular issues, this model addresses "What?" questions - "what do we want to happen, or not to happen?". It allows for more flexibility to address emerging challenges that may not be covered by the letter of the Protocol, but that need to be addressed in order to meet its objectives.

Putting this model in practice requires strategic thinking applied to protecting environmental and other values, with guidance provide by the vision of the Protocol of Antarctica as a natural reserve, devoted to peace and science, where environmental and other values are subject to comprehensive protection. In addition, this model requires greater synergies between different actors, operators, entities, and instruments of the Antarctic Treaty System.

Conclusions

The adoption of the Protocol does not imply that Antarctica is effectively a World Park, but it met to a certain extent several of the early ENGO criteria for Antarctica.

Clearly, 25 years of Protocol implementation have been successful in improving environmental protection in Antarctica. There are still ongoing challenges, which are compounded by emerging issues affecting the environment at present and in the future.

In this context, the Protocol should not be considered solely as a set of rules on particular issues - useful as that may be to address those issues. Rather, it should also be regarded as a guiding principle that Parties to the

---

[4] Ibid., p.2.

Antarctic Treaty can use – individually and collectively – to plan and conduct their activities, and to address emerging issues strategically before they happen.

Finally, I would like to reiterate that to achieve its objectives in the longer term the Protocol has to be applied so that it is more than the sum of its parts.

Thank you.

The impact of the Protocol on protection of the Antarctic environment: a perspective from the International Association of Antarctica Tour Operators (IAATO)

Kim Crosbie

The Environmental Protocol to the Antarctic Treaty (Environmental Protocol), agreed in 1991, is remarkable for many reasons – both in its legacy for Antarctic conservation but also in the wider context of global environmental management.

The International Association of Antarctica Tour Operators (IAATO), a member association dedicated to advocating and promoting the practice of safe and environmentally responsible private sector travel to Antarctica, was founded in the same year as the Environmental Protocol. Consequently IAATO is also celebrating its 25th anniversary this year.

The connection between IAATO and the Environmental Protocol goes further than simply being the same age. The mission and objectives of IAATO are very similar to the intent of the Environmental Protocol. In particular IAATO and its member Operators feel a deep-seated connection to Article 3 Environmental Principles, the ethos of which helped shape IAATO's approach to safe and environmentally responsible private sector travel to the Antarctic. For example, IAATO bylaws use language taken directly from Article 8 of the Environmental Protocol as the cornerstone of the Association's vision, i.e. that "…Antarctic tourism is a sustainable, safe activity that causes *no more than a minor or transitory impact* on the environment and creates a corps of ambassadors for the continued protection of Antarctica."

While there are elements from each of the annexes that directly affect IAATO Operator activities, from the Association's perspective the key element to the over arching success of the Protocol lies in its intent to provide a recipe for all human activities in Antarctica. The Protocol has strived to provide a level platform for all operators by requiring them to take into consideration the consequences of their actions on the Antarctic environment when planning their activities. Specifically, the Environmental Impact Assessment process, outlined in Annex I, has provided useful as a common framework for operators when planning their activities. For tourist operators, this requirement, combined with other agreements of the ATCM, such as Recommendation XVIII-1, has underpinned the fact that IAATO Operator activities are planned, conducted and subsequently monitored (through reporting of activities) in a consistent fashion.

However, another remarkable success of the Protocol, which is apparent to all IAATO operators but perhaps less obvious to ATCM delegates, is the impact that the principles of the Protocol has had on global conservation in terms of public awareness. Each client that travels with an IAATO operator learns about the Environmental Protocol during their mandatory briefing prior to entering the area. Unlike any other continent, these visitors are taught how to conduct themselves while in Antarctica so that they follow the principles of the Environmental Protocol while on the ground. This training – from learning how to avoid disturbing the wildlife, or to prevent inadvertently introducing non-native species (in line with Annex II *Conservation of Antarctic Fauna and Flora*) to not leaving any evidence of their visit (Annex III *Waste Management*) and an understanding that some areas have additional special protection (Annex V *Protected Area Systems*) – is often the most comprehensive environmental management training that these individuals will have encountered.

Since the inception of the Environmental Protocol and IAATO, half-a-million visitors (nationals from all Treaty Parties) have visited the continent and experienced the environmental measures that are enshrined in the Environmental Protocol. For many, those environmental measures have served to inspire them to subsequently become environmental ambassadors both for Antarctica, but also the wider global environment. For that, the ATCM should be rightly very proud.

Discussions and Reflections. What should, in progressively developing the law of the sea regime, be learned from the Antarctic Protocol, in particular Annex VI

Rüdiger Wolfrum

I. Introduction

Ladies and Gentlemen, it is indeed a great privilege for me to give an introduction into the discussion of agenda item 2. It takes me back to the early years of negotiating Annex VI as required under Articles 15 and 16 of the Protocol on Environmental Protection to the Antarctic Treaty (Protocol). The speakers so far have emphasized that the Protocol has had a positive effect on the protection of the environment of Antarctica and its dependent and associated ecosystems. At the same time it provided guidance and legal security for the activities of scientists as well as operators. Finally I might add that the Protocol and its Annexes served as a blueprint for some elements concerning the legal regime on deep seabed mining. In particular the Regulations of the International Seabed Authority have been influenced by the Antarctic Protocol and its Annexes. This was quite understandable. The Antarctic Protocol with its Annexes, including Annex VI, was certainly breaking new ground in respect of the preservation of the environment when adopted.

My task, though, is different from the previous speakers I believe. I am meant to provoke a discussion on whether the Protocol still provides the adequate answer of today's challenges. These challenges have different roots. The knowledge about environmental changes or demands has increased –let me just mention biodiversity, climate change, impact of an import of alien species etc. but so has the intensity of activities in Antarctica and in its dependent and associated ecosystems. The development of international law has reacted thereto. International law, in particular, international environmental law has developed progressively as can be seen from the development of new international instruments as well as international jurisprudence. In that respect I would like to highlight in particular the two advisory opinions by the International Tribunal for the Law of the Sea and its International Seabed Disputes Chamber. Both have shed new light on the responsibility for environmental risks or damages as well as on the applicability and meaning of the precautionary principle. I shall come back to that in a moment.

What are the challenges for the Antarctic legal regime considering it not only from the point of view of the Protocol but also from international law in general? Perhaps the time reserved for discussion could be used for the identification of issues where improvements may be desirable or even mandatory apart from climate change which has already been mentioned and which certainly calls for intensified considerations.

II. Challenges

Scope of Annex VI

As we all know the scope of the Protocol and the one of its Annex VI are not fully coherent. Article 2 of the Protocol strives for the protection of the Antarctic environment and dependent and associated ecosystems whereas Annex VI applies to environmental emergencies in the "Antarctic Treaty area". This means that environmental impacts in such areas which result from environmental emergencies in the Antarctic Treaty area would not be covered by Annex VI but rather by the relevant law of the coastal States concerned and the laws of the flag state in question or the Regulations of the International Seabed Authority if applicable. I wonder whether the applicability of two different sets of rules to the consequences of environmental emergencies (we all hope that they will never occur) is adequate or even meeting the objective and purpose of the Protocol. It is not without reason that the Protocol refers to the commitment of the Parties to 'the comprehensive protection of the Antarctic environment and dependent and associated ecosystem' a commitment which the Santiago Declaration reemphasizes. I am aware of the intricacies of including dependent and associated ecosystems into a regime providing, among others, for environmental responsibility and liability.

Liability regimes – and this is equally true for Annex VI to the Protocol – are meant to secure the implementation of commitments entered into by the parties concerned. Invoking liability is certainly a means of last resort. The possibility of liability serves several interrelated purposes: it has a deterring effect and should ensure that those responsible for the activity concerned take all required precautionary measures. However, liability for environmental damage also has the effect that it may be used to restore the environment as far as possible. To be more specific Annex VI to the Protocol aims to reduce the likelihood of environmental harm caused by accidents and to ensure responsibility is taken for the costs involved in a response action to minimize the effect that any such accident might have on the environment by requiring Parties to adopt laws that impose certain conditions on their operators organizing activities in the Antarctic Treaty area.

There is, however, a further aspect. Any liability regime tailored to a specific situation, such as the one of Annex VI to the Protocol, excludes the applicability of liability regimes with a more extended scope or more stringent standards based upon international customary law. In this respect Articles 15, 16 of the Protocol and Annex VI resemble Article 139 in connection with Article 4 Annex III of the UN Convention on the Law of the Sea. Such a further reaching liability regime exists under general international law as set out in the Draft Articles of the ILC on International Responsibility. As the International Tribunal for the Law of the Sea has stated based upon its earlier jurisprudence that the Draft Articles of the ILC provide that every international wrongful act of a State entails the international responsibility of that State (art. 1) and that the responsible State is under an obligation to make full reparation for the injury caused by the international wrongful act. The Tribunal further stated that several of these Draft articles are considered to reflect customary international law.

What I mean to say is there is a general liability regime in place under customary international which may be abrogated by treaty law. But this has not been achieved as long as Annex VI is not in force.

The traditional arguments against what I have sketched out are a) that international liability requires damage on the side of a State; b) that activities of operators in Antarctica are not attributable to a State; c) that strict liability as envisaged by Annex VI goes beyond international law and d) that environmental damage is impossible to calculate. None of these arguments is sustainable.

The ILC Draft Rules do not require damage on the side of a claiming State to become operative. Damage and its amount is only relevant in respect of calculating liability. Let me come to the second counterargument. Sure the activities of private entities are, as a matter of principle, not attributable to a State. However, is the operation of research stations or of scientific expeditions in Antarctica really private? This is not the decisive point, though. Apart from that the Parties to the Antarctic Treaty are obliged to enact the necessary rules for the implementation of the environmental commitments; the failure to do so constitutes a wrongful act in itself which is clearly attributable to the States concerned. The Seabed Dispute Chamber of ITLOS has in its advisory opinion dealt with this particular aspect. As to the third counterargument it is not correct to say that strict liability is the exception in international law. Finally, as to the las point, damage to the environment can be calculated on the basis of the costs for restoration. National legal regimes have developed such schemes, there even exist isolated international jurisprudence to that extent.

The gist of what I have said is that it will be necessary, considering the development in respect of the international rules on State responsibility as to whether Annex VI to the Protocol is still sufficient to implement the commitments entered into by the Protocol. In particular article 16 of the Protocol has not yet been implemented. This brings to my final point.

In paragraph 4 of the Preamble of the Protocol contains a reference to Article 16 and indicates the willingness of the Parties to undertake "consistent with the objectives of the Protocol for the comprehensive protection of the Antarctic environment and dependent and associated ecosystems to elaborate, in one or more Annexes to the Protocol, rules and procedures relating to liability for damage arising from activities taking place in the Antarctic Treaty area and covered by the Protocol." This commitment has not yet been fulfilled but I take note of the renewed commitment in the Santiago Declaration. So far this legal gap would be filled by the more general rules of customary international law briefly outline above. These standards may exceed the ones which may be envisaged for Antarctica and therefore call for actions to be taken by the Antarctic Treaty Consultative Meeting.

The International Seabed Authority being in a different situation than the Consultative Parties to the Antarctic Treaty is in the process of developing a comprehensive responsibility/ liability regime for the time economic mining (exploitation) will commence. It will set new standards which will reflect the developments in international customary law I have briefly touched upon. This should be an incentive for the Consultative Parties to fulfill the commitments entered into in the Protocol.

I hope I have – as an outsider now – provided some thoughts for discussion.

Thank you for your attention!

The functioning of the Committee for Environmental Protection

Ewan McIvor

I would like to thank Norway for leading the preparations for this special session on the 25th anniversary of the Environmental Protocol, and thank Chile for hosting and chairing the meeting.

I was very pleased to be invited to give a talk on the functioning of the CEP.

Admittedly, the functioning of a committee might not ordinarily be the most engaging of topics.

But it is an important topic, I would suggest, when the committee in question is responsible for advising a community of nations on how best to protect an entire continent.

This talk will outline some of the challenges that influence the functioning of the CEP, and the more notable aspects of its working methods.

It will also highlight some opportunities for the Parties to support the Committee's work.

Challenges

A clear challenge is the steady growth in the Committee's workload.

The purpose of the Protocol was to stimulate a greater emphasis on environmental protection, and the CEP was established to support that objective.

Over the past 25 years the Parties have continually enhanced their commitment to protecting Antarctica. This is demonstrated, among other things, by the growing volume of environment-related proposals submitted to annual CEP meetings.

This is undoubtedly a good thing, but it does place pressure on the Committee.

A further challenge arises from the fact that the environmental management requirements for Antarctica are not static.

To provide timely, relevant and high quality advice to the Parties, the Committee has had to keep pace with a suite of changes, including:

- improvements in understanding of the state of the Antarctic environment, how it is changing, and how it is predicted to change in the future
- changes in the nature, location and scale of human activities
- the need to understand how those activities interact with the environment, and the consequences of those interactions
- an increasing understanding of the environmental implications of pressures arising primarily from outside the Antarctic region
- developments in environmental practices worldwide and in the Antarctic.

The need to find solutions to these challenges has not been lost on the CEP.

Operation of the CEP

The Operation of the CEP has been a standing agenda item since the first meeting, and the Committee has prioritised consideration of ways to improve its effectiveness.

Perhaps the most notable aspect of the Committee's work practices is its regular and extensive intersessional activity.

Since 1998 over forty intersessional contact groups have facilitated detailed and interactive work that could not practically be advanced during annual meetings.

The Committee has also formally established a subsidiary body, which since 2008 has streamlined the review of management plans, and has generated enhanced guidance for applying the area protection and management provisions of the Protocol.

There may be opportunities for further such subsidiary bodies.

The Committee has also convened workshops to advance priority issues such as area protection and area management, and cooperation with the Scientific Committee of CAMLR.

While unquestionably productive, the logistical challenges and costs associated with hosting, and participating in, workshops have placed practical limitations on their use.

The Committee has used strategic planning tools to focus and manage its work.

The most important of these is the prioritised five-year year work plan, which evolved following the 2006 CEP Workshop on Antarctica's Future Environmental Challenges.

The Committee has regularly acknowledged the value of the work plan, as a guide to assist Members and Observers to direct their individual and collective efforts towards shared priorities.

- It also gives the ATCM a clear picture of the Committee's priorities and plans, and an opportunity to consider and provide feedback on those, including to align with priorities in the ATCM's own Multi-Year Strategic Work Plan.

- The CEP has also developed detailed work programs for particular high priority issues, which feed into the five-year plan, such as the Climate Change Response Work Programme, the Non-Native Species Manual and the Clean-Up Manual.

In addition to these planning tools, the Committee continues to develop a suite of procedures and guidelines for conducting important aspects of its work.

Examples include:

- procedures for reviewing draft comprehensive environmental evaluations

- guidelines for reviewing protected and managed area management plans

- guidelines for considering designations of Specially Protected Species

The Secretariat maintains these in the CEP Handbook, and supports the Committee with other useful tools such as the Environmental Impact Assessment database and Antarctic Protected Areas database.

The Committee has recognised the need for an integrated approach to the protection and conservation of the Antarctic region, and has developed effective collaborations with other key organisations.

The official observer bodies – SCAR, SC-CAMLR and COMNAP – each provide valuable input to the CEP's deliberations, and the practice of exchanging observers and reports raises awareness of respective priorities, activities and needs.

It is also important to acknowledge the contributions of expert organisations representing civil society, the tourism industry, and other scientific, environmental and technical organisations, which present a diverse range of expertise and viewpoints that enrich the Committee's deliberations.

Opportunities to support the CEP

In this last part of the presentation, I will touch on some opportunities to ensure the Committee remains well placed to serve the Parties.

People

The work of the CEP is advanced by the people appointed to serve as the representatives of Members and Observers, and their colleagues who provide valuable support.

In the 13 years I have been involved, I have found these people to be incredibly knowledgeable, and passionate about their work to protect Antarctica.

However they often have other important responsibilities that constrain their ability to engage in CEP activities, particularly during the intersessional period.

Increasing the number of active participants in CEP activities would help spread the workload, and expand the pool of skills and expertise available to inform the Committee's recommendations and advice.

Increasing the number of CEP Members, as more States accede to the Protocol, would deliver similar benefits.

Parties may wish to consider opportunities to enhance the level of engagement by their representatives in annual CEP meetings and intersessional activities.

Parties may also wish to consider opportunities to expand the CEP membership by encouraging further accessions to the Protocol.

The CEP is well served by its representatives, many of whom have years of experience in the forum.

To help ensure that past successes are built on as experienced representatives leave the Committee, it would be useful for Parties to consider succession planning for their own national engagement.

Coordination among Parties could also assist, including by supporting initiatives such as mentor programs or fellowships, some of which are used to good effect by other Antarctic organisations.

Parties may wish to consider opportunities to develop the CEP representatives of the future.

Information

As I mentioned, the environmental management requirements for Antarctica are not static, so the Committee needs robust and up-to-date information, in particular policy-relevant scientific information.

SCAR makes a significant contribution to the work of the CEP, routinely providing independent scientific advice on priority issues, including through its important role in the recently established Antarctic Environments Portal.

But its capacity to do so depends on the resources and priorities of its members.

Parties may wish to consider opportunities to promote and support science that is aimed at better understanding and addressing the environmental challenges facing Antarctica.

Priorities

As an advisory body to the ATCM, the CEP's operational practices should be designed to ensure the delivery of timely, relevant, and high quality advice on the issues of greatest importance to the Parties.

Parties may wish to consider providing direction and feedback on the Committee's priorities, including to promote alignment with ATCM deliberations on governing and managing the Antarctic region.

As a related and final point, the CEP has no budget to support its work, which is entirely supported by the generous efforts and contributions of its Members and Observers.

The recent joint workshop of the CEP and the Scientific Committee of CAMLR is a perfect example.

Further such contributions, perhaps in the form of voluntary financial or in-kind support for intersessional meetings, or to support important studies, could help the Committee address matters of particular interest to the Parties.

Parties may wish to consider opportunities to make available financial or other resources to support CEP activities.

Conclusions

To conclude, I note that when the Parties adopted the Protocol on Environmental Protection to the Antarctic Treaty, they foresaw an important role for the Committee for Environmental Protection – to support them to achieve their shared objective of comprehensively protecting the Antarctic environment.

The 25th anniversary is a timely opportunity to consider how the Parties, in turn, can best support the Committee to continue to discharge that important role.

Speaking as the current CEP Chair, and on behalf of the Members of the Committee, my take-home message and encouragement to the Parties is to 'help us help you'.

Thank you.

The Future of the Environmental Management in Antarctica[5]

Rodolfo A. Sánchez

This presentation attempts to outline the main environmental challenges that National Antarctic Programs (NAP) likely will have to face in the future, as a consequence of changing circumstances stemming both from inside and outside of the Antarctic continent.

What Will the Future Bring to Antarctica?

Such changing circumstances are the result of a number of factors that will affect (or continue to affect) current environmental management regimes in the future. Such factors do not work separately: they usually interrelate, and the way a certain factor evolves over time may have a strong influence on others. These include, among others, the following ones:

a) struggle for funding

When compared to basic services, research in Antarctica - a relatively high resource-demanding activity- may not be seen as a top priority issue by politicians. Therefore, some governments may prioritise other areas of public spending at the expense of Antarctic research. However, some others may perceive the other way round, due to the global or strategic significance of Antarctic research.

b) diversification of services provision

Traditionally, Antarctic operations have mostly been a purely national responsibility, with clear national structures and organisations behind them. As more external private interests are becoming involved -and increasingly influential-, the role of NAPs may become gradually more diffuse in the future, and there may be confusion regarding responsibility for conforming to all aspects of the Antarctic Treaty and the Environmental Protocol.

c) new regulation

As a result of a currently observed ongoing trend, more stringent environmental provisions and standards are likely to be put in place for Antarctica in future years. The impact that proposed new regulations may have on the NAPs' future work is, however, hard to assess.

d) new technologies

The introduction of new technologies will certainly have positive implications for the Antarctic environment and would result in lesser human impacts by reducing carbon emissions and the human footprint. However, new technologies also could facilitate easier access over currently pristine areas, leading to more human presence and potentially undesirable impacts on the Antarctic environment.

e) environmental changes

The effects of the predicted climate change over the next century may be extensive. For example, the higher the risk of establishment of non-native species, the higher the focus on preventive and reactive measures required. Therefore, it might be necessary for some NAPs to put more emphasis on preventive and adaptive measures to ensure the necessary level of environmental protection in the changing environmental setting.

f) pressure from science

The scientific community is exerting a growing pressure on NAPs, by demanding more access to Antarctica, due to the obvious importance of this area in understanding global processes. This presents NAPs with the

---

[5] *This presentation is based in an article published by the author jointly with his Norwegian colleague Birgit Njaastad (doi 10.1007/978-94-007-6582-5_1).*

challenge of supporting a wider array of activities within budgetary frameworks that often remain constant, as well as a relatively stringent environmental framework.

g) new Treaty Parties

In recent years, new countries are becoming –or are showing an interest to become- Treaty Parties. This means more human presence in Antarctica –and the resulting likely increase of human impacts-, and the need of more cooperation and more efforts to keep Antarctica free of anthropogenic disturbance.

h) oil price

Future global oil production and cost could also play a dominant role in the conduct of NAPs activities, as most of them still depend heavily on the consumption of fossil fuels, which again will consequently have an influence on the level of environmental impacts they cause.

In the future, as a result of the combination of the factors described, NAPs will have to cope with changing circumstances. One can expect, therefore, to see changes of varying degrees on the way NAPs will manage their resources and their strategic policies in Antarctica. All such changes will gradually have mostly positive consequences on the Antarctic environment. However, the question remains whether these changes will be implemented rapidly enough—or be adequate—to cope with the threats that may face the Antarctic environment over coming years. Larger NAPs will have more resources available to do it, but they will have to overcome the inherent inertia to change. Smaller ones are likely to be flexible and more able to adapt their internal organisations to adjust to new environmental standards, but they would have to deal with the considerable cost of conforming to these new standards in a timely manner.

So, what are the likely options NAPs have in hand?

First, NAPs could consider using strategic approaches such as the implementation of Environmental Management Systems, as framework for the conduct of their activities. This would enable them to allow environmental objectives and targets to be set, achieved and, importantly, to demonstrate that they have been achieved, in a process of ongoing improvement. However, implementing these systems may take considerable manpower and may result in more bureaucracy; and the goals the organisation has set up for the process may not be challenging or ambitious enough.

Then it is international cooperation, through bilateral or multilateral partnerships, which also provides the opportunity to enhance environmental standards, due to the need to standardise procedures and to the natural transfer of knowledge as partnerships evolve. Partnerships often occur among NAPs that already share similar standards, which limits the necessary extent of improvement in environmental performance. Examples of cooperation between NAPs with different standards (including operational, environmental and even cultural differences) are less frequently found.

Antarctic Treaty Parties should also work towards gradually closing the gap between environmental implementation levels of different NAPs. The CEP has elaborated various environmental guidelines for Antarctic activities, so as to standardise procedures and practices. However, this may not always be the best strategy to collectively achieve better environmental standards. As the standards move upward, the resources (e.g. human, technical, economic) needed to implement them tend to vary greatly among NAPs. Consequently, the gap between implementation levels of different NAPs tends to become larger, rather than smaller. Innovative cooperation strategies are needed to ensure a fluent transfer of knowledge and technology so as to collectively reach acceptable environmental performances.

Finally, NAPs should best utilize tools to monitor and control. These mainly include environmental monitoring and inspection programs. Environmental monitoring has not been homogeneously conducted in Antarctica, partly due to the fact that allocating resources for monitoring activities is usually challenging. NAPs should therefore implement simple, long-lasting and cost-effective programmes for their stations and field sites in order to meet the requirements of the Madrid Protocol. Inspections are another tool that can assist in checking and controlling the environmental performance of NAP's facilities and equipment in Antarctica and in ensuring the observance of Treaty and the Environmental Protocol's regulations. Inspections may work like an audit, looking for 'opportunities for change', rather than 'errors'; and should be aimed to achieve mutual learning, both from the inspected side and from the observers' team. Debates on the undertaking of inspections initiated during the XXXIX ATCM are therefore very welcomed.

Conclusions

Collectively, NAPs should commit to promote the implementation of better environmental standards throughout their diverse range of operations, based on the spirit of mutual cooperation present in the ATS. The environmental challenge for NAPs will only be met if environmental progress is made collectively.

Finally, NAPs will also need to keep society informed on—and engaged with—their activities in Antarctica. As the environmental message is much stronger today than in the past, societies should become aware that human presence in Antarctica will allow progress in science and technology, but in a manner that will not compromise the outstanding natural values of the continent.

Presentation by Jillian Dempster

The Environmental Protocol reinforced a strong and ambitious common vision for the future of Antarctica.

The Protocol was intended to be dynamic – that is to say, we as the membership agreed to be vigilant and deliberate in implementing the Protocol. We also envisaged that as new environmental challenges became evident, that we would be equally as vigilant in updating and adding to our toolkit.

The future of Antarctica should hold few surprises for us;
- We know the environment is responding to a changing climate and that this trend will continue and likely accelerate over the coming decades;
- We know that human activity in Antarctica is increasing and will likely continue to grow;
- It is clear that scientific interest in Antarctica will continue to intensify;
- We can also anticipate that new countries will continue to join the Treaty System, which will both enrich our work and add more complexity.

This morning Dr Yves Frenot's made the statement: "We are the creators of the Antarctic future." So – what future will we create?

25 years on from the Protocol, we face many challenges which are increasing in urgency. The question is: what <u>actions</u> are we going to take – now and in coming years – to ensure the system remains effective for the <u>next</u> 25 years?

We see that there are three key areas to attend to:

1. Wise management of the natural Antarctic environment and human activities;
2. Further developing an enduring and resilient Antarctic Treaty System; and,
3. The full realisation of the Treaty System's global responsibilities.

Firstly, **wise management** requires full and effective implementation of the Protocol. After 25 years there are several aspects of the Protocol that have yet to be adequately implemented. We need to do better.

Our goal is the retention of Antarctica's value as a global scientific laboratory and as a natural reserve. If we permit the gradual erosion of the region's intrinsic values, and of its value for research, it will bring into question the effectiveness of the Protocol and the Treaty System more broadly. Our discussions and our consequent policy reactions need to be dynamic and responsive if we are to keep pace with changing Antarctic environments.

To achieve this, we must not shy away from amending and up-dating the Protocol's annexes to ensure that our management tools are fit-for-purpose and take a best practice approach. For example, when do we consider the Marine Pollution Annex in view of the entry into force of the Polar Code on 1 January 2017?

In our view, we should have as a standing agenda item the question of how to bring Annexes into effect, whether updates or revisions to the Protocol's Annexes are required, and whether new instruments are needed.

We need to be prepared to take bold management decisions based on the best available scientific knowledge. Back home, we must work to generate the science programmes we need to inform our work. And it goes without saying, in the absence of certainty, we must take a precautionary approach.

The second major area, **developing an enduring and resilient Antarctic Treaty System** means we must make a more determined commitment. If we consider our support systems, we could be accused of have been running the system on a "low cost" principle. As we face new challenges, that may no longer be appropriate.

Investment is needed in the governance regime to ensure that policy, and decision-making, is keeping pace with the known and emerging pressures.

We will be asking the Secretariat to perform ever more complex tasks to support us. We therefore need to ensure that we keep under review whether the Secretariat is resourced to meet our growing expectations.

Our agenda needs to remain flexible and adaptive.

And we must improve the dialogue between the ATCM and the CEP so that the relationship is meaningful and adds value. We can use better tools, such as five-year work programmes and enhanced dialogue mechanisms, so that we are truly listening to one another.

We need also to look across the system as a whole and to ensure the operative components of it are operating coherently and consistently.

The final major category, **realising the Treaty System's global responsibilities** means recognizing that the world really is watching and that civil society holds expectations of us.

Antarctica is a remote part of the planet, but that does not mean that the governance regime needs to remain remote and disconnected. More needs to be done to connect with other like-minded regimes and the public and to communicate our successes and challenges.

As the collective governors of Antarctica, we must be proactive and forward-thinking. We must not be caught asleep at the wheel with this serious responsibility.

Instead, we need to front-foot initiatives to ensure Antarctica's value as a continent devoted to peace and scientific research is retained long into the future.

Thank you

Protocol stood test of time

Jane Rumble

What do we want in 25 years time....

Protocol establishes reserve for peace & science. I believe we will still want this in 25 years time.

Antarctica changing – faster than we understand it. Changes in the rest of the world will affect Antarctica – and changes in Antarctica will affect the rest of the world.

Protocol can cope with change – but it also needs to adapt and develop. It was always foreseen as living document – Annexes were developed precisely to facilitate updates and extensions.

Need to consider the challenges for the next 25 years – what is over the horizon (AUS).

World is likely to continue to warm. Overall population is predicted to continue to rise. Global diversity will remain under stress. And there will likely be more human activity in Antarctica – more science, more tourism, more fishing.

In my view, we don't have to be daunted by any of this; but we do need to be proactive in our management and forward looking.

Some thoughts on what we need to consider to address these activities – focusing on the Annexes, in no particular order...

- Annex II – flora and fauna. Good news from the US this morning that revised Annex will shortly enter into force; crucial for changing ecosystem; Non-native species – handling the response to any unnatural introductions will be seriously challenging and require multi-national collaboration.

- Annex V – area protection. Another anniversary: 50 years since first 15 areas, as recommended by SCAR, were adopted for special protection, in 1966 here in Santiago. Need effective protected areas for a range of objectives – protecting unique habitats; protecting stressed species; protecting climate resilient areas and refugio areas. Need systematic protected areas to provide a dynamic system and one which is well managed and monitored. Also need to get to a stage where heritage in Antarctica is assessed and managed in just an effective way as we each conserve our domestic heritage.

- Annex I – EIA cornerstone of Protocol. Still seen as international model, but modern domestic EIA procedures have moved on. Need more flexible in-activity monitoring and adjustment; how do we consider "minor or transitory" in such a rapidly changing Antarctic environment. And what about post-activity assessment and monitoring?

- Annex VI – not in force; but have we yet fully implemented the commitment to environmental clean-up and remediation from Antarctic activities?

Excellent to hear today that we all share a very clear sense of environmental objectives – Parties, CCAMLR, SCAR, COMNAP, IAATO, ASOC and others. But we need to ensure that we all continue to come together to make most effective policy, with all relevant constituents around the table. We must be proactive, not reactive. And we are stronger together.

Have we done enough to fully implement all the provisions of the Protocol (cf Russia). And how well is the Protocol integrated across the Treaty System (cf CEP/SC-CCAMLR workshop)? The first Future of Antarctica forum earlier this year bought together all stakeholders, including tourism and fishing representatives at the same table – should we facilitate more of this within the Treaty System?

Protocol deserves to be celebrated – and we should all go back to our respective countries and shout loudly about our common and shared objectives, as enshrined in the Declaration that we adopted this morning. We all have a responsibility to inform and educate our stakeholders and constituents in a way that communicates to their interests.

But we cannot be complacent.   There will be serious challenges ahead. But we have ridden a number of waves together and – to repeat - we are stronger together.

My vision for the next 25 years is that Antarctica remains a natural reserve, dedicated to peace and science – and that we hand it on to the next generation in as good a state as we found it.

2. List of Documents

2. List of Documents

Working Papers								
Number	**Ag. Items**	**Title**	**Submitted By**	**E**	**F**	**R**	**S**	**Attachments**
WP001	CEP 8b	UAV and wildlife minimum distances	Germany					
WP002	CEP 9a	Revised Management Plan for Antarctic Specially Protected Area No. 149 - Cape Shirreff and San Telmo Island, Livingston Island, South Shetland Islands	United States					ASPA 149 Map 1 ASPA 149 Map 2 ASPA 149 Map 3 ASPA 149 Revised Management Plan
WP003	CEP 9a	Revised Management Plan for Antarctic Specially Protected Area No. 122 - Arrival Heights, Hut Point Peninsula, Ross Island	United States					ASPA 122 Map 1 ASPA 122 Map 2 ASPA 122 Revised Management Plan
WP004	CEP 9a	Revised Management Plan for Antarctic Specially Protected Area No. 126 - Byers Peninsula, Livingston Island, South Shetland Islands	United Kingdom Chile Spain					ASPA 126 Revised Management Plan
WP005	ATCM 6 CEP 9e	Revision of the 'Guide to the presentation of Working Papers containing proposals for Antarctic Specially Protected Areas, Antarctic Specially Managed Areas or Historic Sites and Monuments'	United Kingdom					
WP006	CEP 9e	Templates to summarise the prior assessment of a proposed Antarctic Specially Protected Area (ASPA) or Antarctic Specially Managed Area (ASMA) for subsequent consideration by the CEP	United Kingdom Norway					
WP007	ATCM 6	ATCM Rules of Procedure relating to Intersessional Consultations	United Kingdom United States					
WP008	CEP 9d	The concept of "outstanding values" in the Antarctic marine environment	Belgium					
WP009	CEP 9a	The status of Antarctic Specially Protected Area No. 107 Emperor Island, Dion Islands, Marguerite Bay, Antarctic Peninsula	United Kingdom					
WP010	CEP 4	Antarctic Environments Portal	Australia Japan New Zealand Norway SCAR Spain					

Working Papers								
Number	Ag. Items	Title	Submitted By	E	F	R	S	Attachments
			United States					
WP011	ATCM 17	Antarctic Treaty Party nationals engaging with unauthorised non-Governmental expeditions to Antarctica	United Kingdom	🗎	🗎	🗎	🗎	
WP012	CEP 9b	Managing Antarctic Heritage: British Historic Bases in the Antarctic Peninsula	United Kingdom	🗎	🗎	🗎	🗎	
WP013	CEP 10a	Report of the Intersessional Contact Group on Revision of the CEP Non-native Species Manual	United Kingdom	🗎	🗎	🗎	🗎	Revised CEP Non-native Species Manual
WP014	ATCM 13 CEP 8b	The COMNAP Unmanned Aerial Systems-Working Group (UAS-WG)	COMNAP	🗎	🗎	🗎	🗎	COMNAP Antarctic Unmanned Aerial Systems (UAS) Handbook Flowchart (see page 4 of the Handbook)
WP015	CEP 8b	Report of the intersessional contact group established to review the Guidelines for Environmental Impact Assessment in Antarctica	Australia United Kingdom	🗎	🗎	🗎	🗎	Annex: Revised Guidelines for Environmental Impact Assessment in Antarctica
WP016	CEP 11	A methodology to assess the sensitivity of sites used by visitors: prioritising future management attention	Australia New Zealand Norway United States	🗎	🗎	🗎	🗎	
WP017	ATCM 10 CEP 4	Report of the intersessional contact group established to review information exchange requirements	Australia	🗎	🗎	🗎	🗎	
WP018	CEP 9a	Revision of the Management Plan for Antarctic Specially Protected Area (ASPA) No. 167 Hawker Island, Princess Elizabeth Land	Australia	🗎	🗎	🗎	🗎	ASPA 167 Map A ASPA 167 Map B ASPA 167 Revised Management Plan
WP019	ATCM 6	Enhancing awareness of the Antarctic Treaty Parties' work through the earlier public release of the ATCM report	Australia	🗎	🗎	🗎	🗎	
WP020	ATCM 11	Enhancing Antarctic Education and Outreach Visibility	Spain United Kingdom Belgium Bulgaria Chile Italy Portugal	🗎	🗎	🗎	🗎	
WP021	CEP 8a	Report of the intersessional open-ended contact group established to consider the draft CEE for the "Proposed construction	France	🗎	🗎	🗎	🗎	

Working Papers								
Number	Ag. Items	Title	Submitted By	E	F	R	S	Attachments
		and operation of a gravel runway in the area of Mario Zucchelli Station, Terra Nova Bay, Victoria Land, Antarctica"						
WP022	ATCM 14 CEP 12	Inspection undertaken by the People's Republic of China in accordance with Article VII of the Antarctic Treaty and Article XIV of the Protocol on Environmental Protection	China	📄	📄	📄	📄	
WP023	CEP 9e	SCAR Code of Conduct for Activity within Terrestrial Geothermal Environments in Antarctica	SCAR	📄	📄	📄	📄	SCAR Code of Conduct for Activity within Terrestrial Geothermal Environments in Antarctica
WP024	ATCM 11	First report of the Intersessional Contact Group on Education and Outreach	Bulgaria Belgium Brazil Chile Portugal United Kingdom	📄	📄	📄	📄	
WP025	ATCM 17	Benefits of Communication Among Competent Authorities for Tourism and Non-governmental Activities	United States	📄	📄	📄	📄	
WP026	CEP 9a	Revision of the Management Plan for Antarctic Specially Protected Area (ASPA) No. 116: New College Valley, Caughley Beach, Cape Bird, Ross Island	New Zealand	📄	📄	📄	📄	ASPA 116 Revised Management Plan
WP027	CEP 9a	Revision of the Management Plan for Antarctic Specially Protected Area (ASPA) No. 131: Canada Glacier, Lake Fryxell, Taylor Valley, Victoria Land	New Zealand	📄	📄	📄	📄	ASPA 131 Revised Management Plan
WP028	ATCM 17	Report of the Intersessional Contact Group 'Developing a Strategic Approach to Environmentally Managed Tourism and Non-Governmental Activities'	New Zealand India	📄	📄	📄	📄	
WP029	CEP 9a	Report of the 2015/16 Intersessional Informal Discussions on the Proposal for a New Antarctic Specially Managed Area at Chinese Antarctic Kunlun Station, Dome A and the Follow-up Work	China	📄	📄	📄	📄	
WP030	CEP 9b	Consideration of protection approaches for historic heritage in Antarctica	Norway	📄	📄	📄	📄	

Working Papers

Number	Ag. Items	Title	Submitted By	E	F	R	S	Attachments
WP031	CEP 9a CEP 9e	Subsidiary Group on Management Plans – Report on 2015/16 Intersessional Work	Norway					Draft - Guidance for assessing an area for a potential ASMA designation
WP032	CEP 9c	Site Guidelines for the Yalour Islands, Wilhelm Archipelago	Ukraine United Kingdom United States Argentina IAATO					Yalour Islands map
WP033	CEP 9c	Site Guidelines for Point Wild, Elephant Island	United Kingdom Chile IAATO					Point Wild, Elephant Island map
WP034	ATCM 17	Data Collection and Reporting on Yachting Activity in Antarctica in 2015-16	United Kingdom Argentina Chile IAATO					
WP035	ATCM 17	Communication mechanisms: National Competent Authorities	Norway France Netherlands New Zealand United Kingdom					
WP036	CEP 9a	Revised Management Plan for ASPA No. 120, Pointe-Géologie Archipelago, Adélie Land	France					ASPA 120 Revised management plan.
WP037	CEP 9a	Revised Management Plan for ASPA No. 166, Port-Martin, Adélie Land. Extension Proposal for the Existing Plan	France					
WP038	ATCM 6	Confirming Ongoing Commitment to the Prohibition of Mining Activity in Antarctica, other than for Scientific Research. Antarctic Mining Ban	United States Argentina Australia Belgium Chile Czech Republic Finland France Germany Italy Japan Korea (ROK) Netherlands New Zealand Norway Poland South Africa Spain Sweden United Kingdom Uruguay					

Working Papers								
Number	Ag. Items	Title	Submitted By	E	F	R	S	Attachments
WP039 rev.1	ATCM 6	On "openness" of the gateway to the Antarctic	Russian Federation					
WP040	CEP 9a	Revised Management Plan for Antarctic Specially Protected Area No. 127 "Haswell Island" (Haswell Island and Adjacent Emperor Penguin Rookery on Fast Ice)	Russian Federation					ASPA 127 Revised Management Plan
WP041 rev.1	ATCM 17	Consideration for Non-governmental and Tourism Activities Involving Combined Air and Cruise Transportation to Antarctica	United States					
WP042	ATCM 7	Revised Procedure for Selection and Appointment of the Executive Secretary of the Secretariat of the Antarctic Treaty	Argentina Chile United States					Standard Application Form
WP043	CEP 8a	Draft Comprehensive Environmental Evaluation for the construction and operation of a gravel runway in the area of Mario Zucchelli Station, Terra Nova Bay, Victoria Land, Antarctica	Italy					Draft CEE
WP044	ATCM 14 CEP 12	General Recommendations from the Joint Inspections Undertaken by Argentina and Chile under Article VII of the Antarctic Treaty and Article 14 of the Environmental Protocol	Argentina Chile					
WP045	CEP 9c	Assessment of moss communities nearby the tracks of Aitcho Island. Monitoring report	Ecuador Spain					Annex 1. Figures
WP046 rev.1	ATCM 18 CEP 3	Report of the Intersessional Contact Group on the Development of a Publication on the Occasion of the 25th Anniversary of the Madrid Protocol	Argentina					Annex 1: Draft publication Annex 2: Possible means of outreach for the publication on the 25th anniversary of the Madrid Protocol.
WP047 rev.2	CEP 9b	Incorporation of a historic wooden pole to HSM No. 60 (Corvette Uruguay Cairn), in Seymour / Marambio Island, Antarctic Peninsula	Argentina Sweden					
WP048 rev.1	CEP 9b	Notification of the location of historical pre-1958 remains in the vicinity of the Argentine Station Marambio	Argentina Norway Sweden United Kingdom					
WP049	ATCM	Summary of Abstracts -	Norway					

Working Papers								
Number	Ag. Items	Title	Submitted By	E	F	R	S	Attachments
	18	Symposium						
WP050	ATCM 6	Improving interaction between CEP and ATCM	Norway Australia	🗎	🗎	🗎	🗎	
WP051	CEP 9b	Proposal to add Antarctic King Sejong Station History Gallery (Dormitory No.2) at the Antarctic King Sejong Station to the Historic Sites and Monuments	Korea (ROK)	🗎	🗎	🗎	🗎	
WP052	CEP 10a	Non-native flies in sewage treatment plants on King George Island, South Shetland Islands	Korea (ROK) United Kingdom Chile Uruguay	🗎	🗎	🗎	🗎	
WP053	CEP 5	Report of the Joint CEP / SC-CAMLR Workshop on Climate Change and Monitoring, Punta Arenas, Chile, 19-20 May 2016	United Kingdom United States	🗎	🗎	🗎	🗎	Appendices 1 to 4.

Information Papers

Number	Ag. Items	Title	Submitted By	E	F	R	S	Attachments
IP001	ATCM 17 CEP 9b	Reinstalling the memorial plaque of "Le Pourquoi Pas?" on Petermann Island (Charcot's cairn 1909, HSM 27)	France IAATO	📄				
IP002	ATCM 4	Report by the Depositary Government for the Convention for the Conservation of Antarctic Seals (CCAS) in Accordance with Recommendation XIII-2, Paragraph 2(D)	United Kingdom	📄	📄	📄	📄	
IP003	CEP 8b	Application of air dispersion modeling for impact assessment of construction/operation activities in Antarctica	Belarus	📄		📄		
IP004	ATCM 4	Report by the International Hydrographic Organization (IHO)	IHO	📄	📄	📄	📄	
IP005	ATCM 4	Report by the CCAMLR Observer to the Thirty-ninth Antarctic Treaty Consultative Meeting	CCAMLR	📄	📄	📄	📄	
IP006	CEP 5	Report by the SC-CAMLR Observer to the nineteenth meeting of the Committee for Environmental Protection	CCAMLR	📄	📄	📄	📄	
IP007	ATCM 11 CEP 13	POLAR WEEKS: an Education and Outreach activity to promote Antarctic science and the Antarctic Treaty System	Portugal Brazil Bulgaria France United Kingdom	📄				
IP008	ATCM 15 CEP 11	Assessment of trace element contamination within the Antarctic Treaty area	Portugal Chile Germany Russian Federation United Kingdom	📄				
IP009	ATCM 18	25th Anniversary of the Protocol on Environmental Protection to the Antarctic Treaty: South African Accomplishments	South Africa	📄				
IP010	ATCM 4 CEP 5	Annual Report for 2015/16 of the Council of Managers of National Antarctic Programs (COMNAP)	COMNAP	📄	📄	📄	📄	
IP011	ATCM 4	WMO Annual Report 2015-2016	WMO	📄	📄	📄	📄	
IP012	ATCM 16 CEP 7a	WMO Climate-related Activities in the Antarctic Region	WMO	📄				
IP013	ATCM 15	The Polar Challenge: towards a new paradigm	WMO	📄				

Information Papers								
Number	Ag. Items	Title	Submitted By	E	F	R	S	Attachments
		for long-term under-ice observations						
IP014	ATCM 15	Polar Regional Climate Centres and Polar Climate Outlook Fora (PRCC – PCOF)	WMO	📄				
IP015	ATCM 15 CEP 5	The Year of Polar Prediction	WMO	📄				
IP016	ATCM 15	Boletín Antártico Venezolano	Venezuela				📄	
IP017	ATCM 11	Libro Digital: Aprendemos en la Antártida	Venezuela				📄	
IP018	ATCM 15	IX Campaña Venezolana a la Antártida	Venezuela				📄	
IP019	ATCM 11	Video 15 años de Venezuela en la Antártida	Venezuela				📄	
IP020	ATCM 4 CEP 5	The Scientific Committee on Antarctic Research (SCAR) Annual Report 2015/16 to the Antarctic Treaty System	SCAR	📄	📄	📄	📄	
IP021	ATCM 15 ATCM 4	Report from Asian Forum of Polar Sciences to the ATCM XXXIX	Korea (ROK)	📄				
IP022	ATCM 13	Formation of Belarusian Antarctic infrastructure – modern state and prospects	Belarus	📄	📄	📄	📄	
IP023	ATCM 4	Programa Antártico Colombiano – PAC	Colombia				📄	
IP024	ATCM 15	II Expedición Científica de Colombia a la Antártica Verano Austral 2015/2016 "Almirante Lemaitre"	Colombia				📄	Información Pretemprada II Expedición de Colombia a la Antártica "Almirante Lemaitre" Verano Austral 2015-2016 Informe Ejecutivo Avances de la II Expedición Científica de Colombia a la Antártica
IP025	ATCM 11	Campaña Educación Marítima "Todos Somos Antártica" Programa Antártico Colombiano – PAC	Colombia				📄	
IP026	ATCM 15	POLAR.POD: Observatory of the Southern Ocean - An unprecedented international maritime exploration and data exchange	France	📄	📄			
IP027	CEP 10a	Introduction of biofouling organisms to Antarctica on vessel hulls	United Kingdom	📄				Breaking the ice: the introduction of biofouling organisms toAntarctica on vessel hulls. Hughes K. A. and G.V. Ashton.

Information Papers

Number	Ag. Items	Title	Submitted By	E	F	R	S	Attachments
IP028	ATCM 13	Operación de UAV/RPAS en la Antártida: Normativa aplicada por España	Spain				📄	
IP029	ATCM 15	The experience of a joint Ukrainian-Turkish Expedition to the Antarctic Vernadsky Station in 2016	Ukraine Turkey	📄		📄		
IP030	ATCM 13 CEP 8b	Modernisation of GONDWANA-Station, Terra Nova Bay, northern Victoria Land	Germany	📄				
IP031	CEP 9e	Antarctic Geoconservation: a review of current systems and practices	SCAR	📄				Antarctic geoconservation: a review of current systems and practices.
IP032	ATCM 15 CEP 11	Report on the 2015-2016 activities of the Southern Ocean Observing System (SOOS)	SCAR	📄				
IP034	ATCM 15 CEP 5	The Antarctic Observing Network (AntON) to facilitate weather and climate information	SCAR WMO	📄				
IP035	ATCM 16 CEP 7a	Antarctic Climate Change and the Environment 2016 Update	SCAR	📄				
IP036	ATCM 17	Antarctic Tourism Study: Analysis and Enhancement of the Legal Framework	Germany	📄				
IP037	ATCM 13	Search and Rescue (SAR) Initiatives Affecting Antarctica	United States	📄				
IP038	CEP 10c	Antarctica and the Southern Ocean in the context of the Strategic Plan on Biodiversity 2011-2020	Monaco SCAR	📄	📄	📄	📄	Attachment A: Aichi Targets
IP039	CEP 9e	Inspections of Antarctic Specially Protected Areas in the Ross Sea and Antarctic Peninsula Regions by the United States Antarctic Program	United States	📄				
IP040	ATCM 15	United Kingdom's Antarctic Science: Summary of British Antarctic Survey Science Priorities 2016-20	United Kingdom	📄				
IP041	ATCM 16	The Future of Antarctica Forum	United Kingdom Argentina ASOC IAATO	📄				
IP042	ATCM 4	Report of the Depositary Government of the Antarctic Treaty and its Protocol in accordance with Recommendation XIII-2	United States	📄	📄	📄	📄	Antarctic Treaty Status Table List of Recommendations/Measures and their approvals Protocol Status Table

Information Papers

Number	Ag. Items	Title	Submitted By	E	F	R	S	Attachments
IP043	ATCM 4	Report of the Depositary Government for the Agreement on the Conservation of Albatrosses and Petrels (ACAP)	Australia	📄	📄	📄	📄	
IP044	ATCM 4	Report of the Depositary Government for the Convention on the Conservation of Antarctic Marine Living Resources (CAMLR)	Australia	📄	📄	📄	📄	
IP045	CEP 8b	Renovation of the King Sejong Korean Antarctic Station on King George Island, South Shetland Islands	Korea (ROK)	📄				
IP046	ATCM 15	Programa de Investigación en Mamíferos Marinos Antárticos: Con especial atención hacia Cetáceos Migratorios a aguas colombianas	Colombia				📄	
IP047	ATCM 13 CEP 13	Upgrade of the SANAE IV Base Systems	South Africa	📄				
IP048	ATCM 14 CEP 12	Report of the Antarctic Treaty Inspections undertaken by the People's Republic of China in accordance with Article VII of the Antarctic Treaty and Article 14 of the Environmental Protocol: April 2016	China	📄				
IP049	ATCM 15	III Expedición Científica de Colombia a la Antártica Verano Austral 2016/2017 "Almirante Padilla"	Colombia				📄	
IP050	ATCM 13	Contribución de Colombia a la Seguridad Marítima en la Antártica	Colombia				📄	
IP051	ATCM 15	COMNAP Antarctic Roadmap Challenges (ARC) Project Outcomes	COMNAP	📄				
IP052	ATCM 13	COMNAP Search & Rescue (SAR) Workshop III	COMNAP	📄				
IP053	CEP 8b	A tool to support regional-scale environmental management	New Zealand	📄				
IP054	ATCM 15	Australian Antarctic Science Programme: highlights of the 2015/16 season	Australia	📄				
IP055	ATCM 15	Belgian Antarctic Research Expedition BELARE 2015-2016	Belgium	📄	📄			
IP056	ATCM 17 CEP	Developing a blue ice runway at Romnoes in Dronning Maud Land	Belgium	📄				

Information Papers								
Number	Ag. Items	Title	Submitted By	E	F	R	S	Attachments
	8b							
IP057	CEP 10a	Monitoring for the presence of Poa pratensis at Cierva Point after the eradication	Spain United Kingdom Argentina	▣				
IP058	CEP 8a	The Initial Responses to the Comments on the Draft Comprehensive Environmental Evaluation for the construction and operation of a gravel runway in the area of Mario Zucchelli Station, Terra Nova Bay, Antarctica	Italy	▣				
IP059	CEP 8b	UAV remote sensing of environmental changes on King George Island (South Shetland Islands): update on the results of the second field season 2015/2016	Poland	▣				Supporting figures
IP060	CEP 10a	Next step in eradication of non-native grass Poa annua L. from ASPA No 128 Western Shore of Admiralty Bay, King George Island, South Shetland Islands	Poland	▣				
IP061	CEP 8a	Initial Environmental Evaluation for the extension to the Boulder Clay site of the access road to Enigma Lake, Mario Zucchelli Station, Terra Nova Bay, Victoria Land, Antarctica	Italy	▣				
IP062	CEP 9c	National Antarctic Programme use of locations with Visitor Site Guidelines in 2015-16	United Kingdom Argentina Australia United States	▣				
IP063	ATCM 15	Malaysia's Activities and Achievements in Antarctic Research and Diplomacy	Malaysia	▣				
IP064	CEP 7a	Report on the activities of the Integrating Climate and Ecosystem Dynamics in the Southern Ocean (ICED) programme	United Kingdom	▣				
IP065	CEP 9d	The relevance of the MPA designation process in Domain 1 in the current climate change context	Argentina Chile	▣		▣		
IP066	ATCM 15	Solution of the problem of influence of Freon clathrate hydrates in the drilling fluid on lake water purity in the deep borehole at the Russian Vostok station	Russian Federation	▣	▣			

Information Papers

Number	Ag. Items	Title	Submitted By	E	F	R	S	Attachments
IP067	ATCM 11	Russian initiative on declaring 2020 the Year of Antarctica	Russian Federation	📄		📄		
IP068	ATCM 13	Russian hydrographic studies in the Southern Ocean in the season 2015-2016	Russian Federation	📄		📄		
IP069	ATCM 18	Preconditions for adopting the Protocol on Environmental Protection to the Antarctic Treaty	Russian Federation	📄		📄		
IP070	ATCM 15	Current Russian results of studies of climate variability at present and in the past	Russian Federation	📄		📄		
IP071	CEP 9a	Present zoological study at Mirny station area and at ASPA No 127 "Haswell Island" (2011–2015)	Russian Federation	📄		📄		
IP072	ATCM 14 CEP 12	Report of the Joint Inspections' Program undertaken by Argentina and Chile under Article VII of the Antarctic Treaty and Article 14 of the Environmental Protocol	Argentina Chile	📄			📄	Inspection Report
IP073	ATCM 10	XXXIV Antarctic Operation	Brazil	📄				
IP074	ATCM 10	Regulations and procedures for vessels proceeding to Antarctica	Brazil	📄				
IP075	ATCM 10	Reconstruction and Launch of the Foundation Stone of the New Brazilian Station in Antarctica	Brazil	📄				
IP076	CEP 6	Environmental Remediation in Antarctica	Brazil	📄				
IP077	CEP 5	Introduction from Co-Conveners of the Joint CEP/SC-CAMLR Workshop (Punta Arenas, Chile, 19-20 May 2016)	United Kingdom United States	📄				
IP078	ATCM 16 CEP 7a	Antarctic Climate Change, Ice Sheet Dynamics and Irreversible Thresholds: ATCM Contributions to the IPCC and Policy Understanding	ASOC	📄				ICCI: Thresholds and Closing Windows
IP079	ATCM 6	An Unprecedented Achievement: 25 Years of the Environmental Protocol	ASOC	📄				
IP080	CEP 9e	A Systematic Approach to Designating ASPAs and ASMAs	ASOC	📄				
IP081	CEP 7a	Antarctic Climate Change Report Card	ASOC	📄				
IP082	ATCM	Progress on the Polar	ASOC	📄				

Information Papers

Number	Ag. Items	Title	Submitted By	E	F	R	S	Attachments
	13	Code						
IP083	CEP 9d	ASOC's update on Marine Protected Areas in the Southern Ocean	ASOC	📄				
IP084	ATCM 15	Cooperación Científica Chile – Corea (Ciencia KOPR-I-NACH)	Chile				📄	
IP085	ATCM 15	Programa Nacional de Ciencia Antártica de Chile: Análisis crítico 2000-2015	Chile				📄	
IP086	ATCM 15	Seminarios Científicos en Base Escudero: creando espacios para la colaboración científica en Antártica	Chile				📄	
IP087	ATCM 11	Educational Program "Polar Scientist for a Day": opening an Antarctic Laboratory for the children	Chile	📄			📄	
IP088	ATCM 11	Antarctic Dialogues Chile-Bulgaria: Art and Culture	Bulgaria Chile	📄			📄	
IP089	ATCM 11	Antarctic stories: a seed of identity	Chile	📄			📄	
IP090	ATCM 11	New educational map of Antarctica using Augmented Reality	Chile	📄			📄	
IP091	ATCM 15	Ilaia. Information for international collaboration beyond the South	Chile	📄			📄	
IP092	ATCM 17	Taller Nacional de Turismo Antártico, Punta Arenas, 5 de abril 2016.	Chile				📄	Programa Taller de Turismo Antártico, Punta Arenas, Chile.
IP093	ATCM 13	Chilean Aids to Navigation in the Antarctic Peninsula	Chile	📄			📄	
IP094	ATCM 13	Search and Rescue Cases in the Antarctic Peninsula Area Season 2015/2016 Chile	Chile	📄			📄	
IP095	ATCM 13	Guides and Recommendations made by Chile for Diving Activities in the Antarctica	Chile	📄			📄	
IP096	ATCM 15 CEP 11	Monitoreo Ambiental en Bahía Fildes. Programa de Observación del Ambiente Litoral de Chile (P.O.A.L.)	Chile				📄	
IP097	ATCM 13	Cooperation of the Hydrographic and Oceanographic Service of the Chilean Navy (SHOA) in the Manufacturing of Nautical Cartography in the Antarctic Area (Program 2010-2020)	Chile	📄			📄	
IP098	ATCM 11	XV Encuentro de Historiadores Antárticos Latinoamericanos: "Rescatando el pasado	Chile				📄	

Number	Ag. Items	Title	Submitted By	E	F	R	S	Attachments
Information Papers								

Number	Ag. Items	Title	Submitted By	E	F	R	S	Attachments
		para entregarlo a las futuras generaciones"						
IP099	ATCM 11	EAE & JASE Expedición Antártica Escolar / Joint Antarctic School Expedition	Chile United States	⬇				
IP100	ATCM 13	Recuperación de la infraestructura y mejoramiento medioambiental para la Base O'Higgins. Un esfuerzo nacional para mejorar el apoyo a la investigación científica antártica.	Chile				⬇	
IP101	ATCM 17 CEP 9c	Analysis of Management Measures of the Tourism Management Policy for Brown Scientific Station	Argentina	⬇			⬇	
IP102	ATCM 14 CEP 12	Rethinking Antarctic Treaty inspections; patterns, uses and scopes for improvements	Korea (ROK)	⬇				
IP104 rev.1	ATCM 17 CEP 9c	Patterns of Tourism in the Antarctic Peninsula Region: a 20-year analysis	United States IAATO	⬇				
IP105	ATCM 17 CEP 9c	Report on IAATO Operator Use of Antarctic Peninsula Landing Sites and ATCM Visitor Site Guidelines, 2015-16 Season	IAATO	⬇				
IP106	ATCM 17	Towards Developing a Strategic Approach to Environmentally Managed Tourism and Non-governmental Activities: an industry perspective	IAATO	⬇				
IP107	ATCM 17 CEP 10c	How to be a Responsible Antarctic Visitor: IAATO's New Animated Briefings	IAATO	⬇				
IP108	ATCM 17	Report on Antarctic tourist flows and cruise ships operating in Ushuaia during the 2015/2016 Austral summer season	Argentina	⬇			⬇	
IP109	ATCM 13	XVIII Combined Antarctic Naval Patrol 2015-2016	Argentina Chile	⬇			⬇	
IP110	ATCM 13	Incorporation of new units to maritime SAR and protection of the marine environment operations in the Antarctic area	Argentina	⬇			⬇	
IP111	ATCM 15	Australian Antarctic Strategy and 20 Year Action Plan	Australia	⬇				
IP112	ATCM 17	IAATO Overview of Antarctic Tourism: 2015-16 Season and Preliminary Estimates for	IAATO	⬇				

Information Papers

Number	Ag. Items	Title	Submitted By	E	F	R	S	Attachments
		2016-17						
IP113	CEP 9e	Recent findings from monitoring work in ASPA 142 Svarthamaren	Norway	📄				
IP114	ATCM 17	Areas of tourist interest in the Antarctic Peninsula and South Orkney Islands region. 2015/2016 austral summer season	Argentina	📄			📄	
IP115	CEP 4	Committee for Environmental Protection (CEP): summary of activities during the 2015/16 intersessional period	Australia	📄				
IP116	ATCM 16 ATCM 4	Recent Findings of IPCC on Antarctic Climate Change and Relevant Upcoming Activities	IPCC	📄				
IP117	ATCM 15	Japan's Antarctic Research Highlights 2015–16	Japan	📄				
IP118	ATCM 17	IAATO Assessing New Activities Checklist	IAATO	📄				
IP119	CEP 10a	IAATO Procedures Upon the Discovery of a High Mortality Event	IAATO	📄				
IP120	CEP 8b	IAATO Policies on the Use of Unmanned Aerial Vehicles (UAVs) in Antarctica: Update for the 2016/17 Season	IAATO	📄				
IP121	ATCM 17 CEP 10c	IAATO Wildlife Watching Guidelines for Emperor Penguins and Leopard Seals	IAATO	📄				IAATO Emperor Penguin Colony Visitor Guidelines IAATO Leopard Seal Watching Guidelines
IP122	CEP 8b	Licencia Ambiental de la Estación Científica Pedro Vicente Maldonado	Ecuador				📄	
IP123	ATCM 4	Report of the Antarctic and Southern Ocean Coalition	ASOC	📄	📄	📄	📄	
IP124 rev.1	ATCM 15	Proposal for a Cooperation of Romania with Argentina and Australia in Antarctica	Romania	📄				
IP125 rev.1	ATCM 15	Prospectives of Romania cooperation with Australia in Antarctica	Romania	📄				

Secretariat Papers								
Number	Ag. Items	Title	Submitted By	E	F	R	S	Attachments
SP001 rev.1	ATCM 3	ATCM XXXIX Agenda and Schedule	ATS					
SP002	CEP 2 CEP 3 CEP 7b	Preliminary Agenda for CEP XIX - CEP Five-Year Work Plan - Climate Change Response Work Programme	ATS					
SP003 rev.1	ATCM 7	Secretariat Report 2015/16	ATS					Appendix 1 a: Auditor's Report Appendix 1 b: Audited Financial Report 2014/15 Appendix 2: Provisional Financial Report 2015/16 Appendix 3: Contributions Received by the Antarctic Secretariat 2015/16
SP004	ATCM 7	Secretariat Programme 2016/17	ATS					Appendix 1: Provisional Report for the Financial Year 2015/16, Budget for the Financial Year 2016/17, Forecast Budget for the Financial Year 2017/18 Appendix 2: Contribution scale 2017/18 Appendix 3: Salary Scale 2016/17
SP005	ATCM 7	Five Year Forward Budget Profile 2016-2020	ATS					Five Year Forward Budget Profile 2016 - 2020
SP006 rev.1	CEP 8b	Annual list of Initial Environmental Evaluations (IEE) and Comprehensive Environmental Evaluations (CEE) prepared between April 1st 2015 and March 31st 2016	ATS					
SP007	ATCM 16 CEP 7a	Actions taken by the CEP and the ATCM on the ATME recommendations on climate change	ATS					
SP008 rev.1	CEP 2	CEP XIX Schedule, Annotated Agenda and Summary of Papers	ATS					
SP009	ATCM 17	Review of ATCM discussions relating to Antarctic Tourism 2008-2015	ATS					
SP010	ATCM 10 ATCM 11 ATCM 12 ATCM 6 ATCM 7 ATCM 8 ATCM	Working Group 1 - Summary of Papers	ATS					

Secretariat Papers

Number	Ag. Items	Title	Submitted By	E	F	R	S	Attachments
	9							
SP011	ATCM 13 ATCM 14 ATCM 15 ATCM 16 ATCM 17	Working Group 2 - Summary of Papers	ATS	📄				Proposed Schedule for Working Group 2
SP012 rev.1	ATCM 21 CEP 16	Draft Report Comments System - Instructions for Delegates and Contributors	ATS	📄				
SP013	ATCM 18	WG3 for the 25th Anniversary of the Protocol - Oral Presentations	ATS	📄				Effectiveness of the Protocol. A scientist's perspective. Dr Aleks Terauds, SCAR. ENGO perspectives on the Antarctic Environmental Protocol. Dr. Ricardo Roura & Claire Christian, ASOC Implementation of the Environmental Protocol. Yves Frenot and Kazuyuki Shiraishi, COMNAP. Presentation by Dr José Retamales. Chile Remarks on the History, Vision behind and Impact of the Protocol on Environmental Protection. Evan T. Bloom, United States. The functioning of the Committee for Environmental Protection. Ewan McIvor, Australia The Future of the Environmental Management in Antarctica. Rodolfo Sánchez, Argentina. The impact of the Protocol on protection of the Antarctic environment: an IAATO perspective. Dr Kim Crosbie The Protocol in comparison to other global and regional environmental framework agreements. Therese Johansen, Norway.

Background Papers								
Number	Ag. Items	Title	Submitted By	E	F	R	S	Attachments
BP001	ATCM 15	Scientific and Science-related Cooperation with the Consultative Parties and the Wider Antarctic Community	Korea (ROK)	⬇				
BP002	ATCM 4 CEP 5	The Scientific Committee on Antarctic Research (SCAR) - Selected Science Highlights for 2015/16	SCAR	⬇				
BP003 rev.1	ATCM 4 CEP 5	Abstract of the SCAR Lecture: Exploring the future of scientific research in Antarctica	SCAR	⬇	⬇	⬇	⬇	
BP004	ATCM 11	The book Belarus in Antarctic: on the 10th anniversary of the beginning of scientific and expeditional research	Belarus	⬇		⬇		
BP005	ATCM 14	Follow-up to the Recommendations of the Inspection Teams on Maitri Station	India	⬇				
BP006	ATCM 15	Twenty years of Ukraine in Antarctica: main achievements and prospects	Ukraine	⬇				
BP007	ATCM 10	Measures under the Protocol on Environmental Protection to the Antarctic Treaty: Implementing Legislation of the Kingdom of the Netherlands	Netherlands	⬇				
BP008	CEP 13	Installation of a new waste water treatment facility at Australia's Davis station	Australia	⬇				
BP009	ATCM 13	Australia's new Antarctic icebreaker	Australia	⬇				Icebreaker fact sheet
BP010	ATCM 13	Polish sailing yacht accident at King George Island (Antarctic Peninsula) – update on the successful rescue operation	Poland	⬇				
BP011	ATCM 13 CEP 9a	Aplicación del Plan de Manejo Ambiental en la Estación Maldonado	Ecuador				⬇	
BP012	ATCM 13	Seguridad en las operaciones ecuatorianas en la Antártida	Ecuador				⬇	
BP013	ATCM 13	XX Campaña Ecuatoriana a la Antártida	Ecuador				⬇	
BP014	ATCM 13	Uso de drones para la generación de cartografía en la Isla Greenwich - Antártida	Ecuador				⬇	

Background Papers

Number	Ag. Items	Title	Submitted By	E	F	R	S	Attachments
BP015	ATCM 14	Preparación de la Estación Ecuatoriana "Pedro Vicente Maldonado para la Inspección Ambiental	Ecuador				🔻	
BP016	ATCM 13	Generación de cartografía oficial en el sector de la Isla Greenwich-Punta Fort William-Glaciar Quito-Punta Ambato, e Islas Aledañas	Ecuador				🔻	
BP017	ATCM 15	Niveles de concentración de metales pesados y efectos del cambio climático en macrohongos y macrolíquenes, estación Maldonado-Antártida	Ecuador				🔻	
BP018	ATCM 13	Refugio Antártico Ecuatoriano (RAE): Desarrollo y aplicación de eco-materiales en el proyecto y construcción de un prototipo habitable de emergencia	Ecuador				🔻	
BP019	ATCM 15	Desarrollo del Programa Nacional Antártico del Perú	Peru				🔻	
BP020	ATCM 15	Actividades del Programa Nacional Antártico de Perú Periodo 2015 – 2016	Peru				🔻	

3. List of Participants

3. List of Participants

Consultative Parties				
Party	**Name**	**Position**	**Arrival Date**	**Dep.Date**
Argentina	Bordon, Jose Octavio	Delegate	22/05/2016	01/06/2016
Argentina	Capurro, Andrea	Delegate	22/05/2016	02/06/2016
Argentina	Chiffel Figueiredo, Veronica	Delegate	22/05/2016	01/06/2016
Argentina	Gowland, Máximo	Head of Delegation	21/05/2016	03/06/2016
Argentina	Humarán, Adolfo Ernesto	Advisor	22/05/2016	01/06/2016
Argentina	Jimenez Corbalan, Lautaro	Advisor	22/05/2016	01/06/2016
Argentina	Ortúzar, Patricia	CEP Representative	22/05/2016	02/06/2016
Argentina	Sánchez, Rodolfo	CEP Representative	22/05/2016	02/06/2016
Argentina	Sartor, Jorge	Delegate	22/05/2016	02/06/2016
Argentina	Tarapow, Marcelo Cristian	Advisor	22/05/2016	01/06/2016
Argentina	Vereda, Marisol	Advisor	22/05/2016	01/06/2016
Argentina	Videla, Enrique	Advisor	22/05/2016	01/06/2016
Argentina	Vlasich, Verónica	Advisor	22/05/2016	02/06/2016
Argentina	Yanino, Vanina	Alternate	23/05/2016	01/06/2016
Australia	Ault, Tim	Delegate	22/05/2016	01/06/2016
Australia	Clark, Charlton	Delegate	22/05/2016	01/06/2016
Australia	Cooper, Katrina	Head of Delegation	22/05/2016	01/06/2016
Australia	Dainer, Drew	Delegate	22/05/2016	01/06/2016
Australia	Fenton, Gwen	Delegate	20/05/2016	01/06/2016
Australia	Gales, Nicholas	Alternate	22/05/2016	01/06/2016
Australia	Goldsworthy, Lyn	Advisor	21/05/2016	27/05/2016
Australia	Kane, Timothy	Delegate	22/05/2016	01/06/2016
Australia	Lees, Alexandra	Delegate	22/05/2016	01/06/2016
Australia	Mcivor, Ewan	Delegate	16/05/2016	01/06/2016
Australia	Miller, Denzil	Advisor	22/05/2016	31/05/2016
Australia	Tracey, Phillip	CEP Representative	20/05/2016	01/06/2016
Australia	Young, Amy	Delegate	20/05/2016	28/05/2016
Belgium	André, François	CEP Representative	22/05/2016	01/06/2016
Belgium	De Beyter, Patrick	Delegate	22/05/2016	01/06/2016
Belgium	Touzani, Rachid	Delegate	22/05/2016	29/05/2016
Belgium	Vancauwenberghe, Maaike	Head of Delegation	22/05/2016	28/05/2016
Belgium	Vanden Bilcke, Christian	Head of Delegation	22/05/2016	01/06/2016
Belgium	Wilmotte, Annick	Delegate	21/05/2016	28/05/2016
Brazil	Boechat de Almeida, Barbara	Alternate	22/05/2016	02/06/2016
Brazil	Borges Sertã, Marcos	Delegate	22/05/2016	02/06/2016
Brazil	Cardia Simões, Jefferson	Advisor	22/05/2016	25/05/2016
Brazil	Galdino De Souza, Paulo César	Advisor	22/05/2016	02/06/2016
Brazil	Lamazière, Georges	Head of Delegation	22/05/2016	01/06/2016
Brazil	Leite, Marcio Renato	Advisor	22/05/2016	02/06/2016
Brazil	Lessa, Eduardo	Delegate	22/05/2016	01/06/2016
Brazil	Mariz, Hugo	Advisor	22/05/2016	02/06/2016
Bulgaria	Gaytandjiev, Maxim	Head of Delegation	21/05/2016	28/05/2016
Bulgaria	Mateev, Dragomir	Delegate	22/05/2016	01/06/2016
Bulgaria	Pimpirev, Christo	Head of Delegation	22/05/2016	01/06/2016
Chile	Aimone, Gustavo	Advisor	16/05/2016	02/06/2016
Chile	Arias, Germán	Advisor	16/05/2016	02/06/2016
Chile	Barticevic, Elías	Delegate	16/05/2016	02/06/2016
Chile	Berguño, Francisco	Head of Delegation	16/05/2016	02/06/2016
Chile	Blasco, Christian	Delegate	22/05/2016	01/06/2016

Consultative Parties				
Party	Name	Position	Arrival Date	Dep.Date
Chile	Castillo, Rafael	Advisor	16/05/2016	02/06/2016
Chile	Figueroa, Miguel	Advisor	23/05/2016	01/06/2016
Chile	García, Magdalena	Advisor	26/05/2016	27/05/2016
Chile	García, Ángel	Delegate	16/05/2016	02/06/2016
Chile	González, Rodolfo	Advisor	16/05/2016	02/06/2016
Chile	González, Marcelo	Delegate	16/05/2016	02/06/2016
Chile	Herrera, Ricardo	Advisor	23/05/2016	24/05/2016
Chile	Leppe, Marcelo	Delegate	16/05/2016	02/06/2016
Chile	Madrid, Santiago	Advisor	23/05/2016	01/06/2016
Chile	Mancilla, Alejandra	Delegate	16/05/2016	02/06/2016
Chile	Manley, Michelle	Advisor	22/05/2016	01/06/2016
Chile	Pavez , Cassandra	Advisor	21/05/2016	02/06/2016
Chile	Quezada, Macarena	Delegate	16/05/2016	02/06/2016
Chile	Ranson, John	Advisor	22/05/2016	01/06/2016
Chile	Retamales, José	Delegate	16/05/2016	02/06/2016
Chile	Riquelme, José	Advisor	23/05/2016	01/06/2016
Chile	Santibañez, Miguel	Advisor	16/05/2016	02/06/2016
Chile	Sardiña, Jimena	Delegate	16/05/2016	02/06/2016
Chile	Sepúlveda, Víctor	Advisor	22/05/2016	01/06/2016
Chile	Silva, Manuel	Advisor	23/05/2016	01/06/2016
Chile	Tobar, Ángela	Delegate	16/05/2016	02/06/2016
Chile	Uribe, Paola	Delegate	23/05/2016	01/06/2016
Chile	Vallejos, Verónica	Delegate	16/05/2016	02/06/2016
Chile	Vega, Edgardo	Delegate	16/05/2016	02/06/2016
Chile	Velásquez, Ricardo	Advisor	22/05/2016	01/06/2016
Chile	Villanueva, Tamara	HCS Staff	16/05/2016	02/06/2016
China	Ao, Shan	Delegate	22/05/2016	02/06/2016
China	Chen, Danhong	Delegate	22/05/2016	02/06/2016
China	Chen, Li	Delegate	23/05/2016	28/05/2016
China	Fang, Lijun	Delegate	22/05/2016	02/06/2016
China	Guo, Xiaomei	Head of Delegation	22/05/2016	02/06/2016
China	Qin, Weijia	CEP Representative	22/05/2016	02/06/2016
China	Song, Wei	Delegate	22/05/2016	02/06/2016
China	Sun, Wenjie	Delegate	21/05/2016	02/06/2016
China	Yang, Xiaoning	Delegate	22/05/2016	02/06/2016
China	Yang, Lei	Delegate	22/05/2016	28/05/2016
China	Yu, Xinwei	Delegate	22/05/2016	02/06/2016
China	Zheng, Cheng	Delegate	22/05/2016	02/06/2016
Czech Republic	Filippiova, Martina	Alternate	22/05/2016	01/06/2016
Czech Republic	Nyvlt, Daniel	Delegate	22/05/2016	27/05/2016
Czech Republic	Rychtar, Josef	Delegate	22/05/2016	01/06/2016
Czech Republic	Smolek, Martin	Head of Delegation	22/05/2016	25/05/2016
Czech Republic	Štěpánek, Přemysl	Delegate	22/05/2016	02/06/2016
Czech Republic	Venera, Zdenek	CEP Representative	22/05/2016	28/05/2016
Ecuador	Arellano, Jorge	Advisor	22/05/2016	01/06/2016
Ecuador	Egas, Miguel	Advisor	22/05/2016	01/06/2016
Ecuador	Izquierdo, Oscar	Advisor	22/05/2016	01/06/2016
Ecuador	Ortega, Germán	Head of Delegation	26/05/2016	02/06/2016
Ecuador	Proano Vega, Juan Carlos	Delegate	22/05/2016	02/06/2016
Ecuador	Ríofrio, Mónica	Delegate	22/05/2016	28/05/2016
Ecuador	Vela, Jaime	Advisor	23/05/2016	01/06/2016
France	Caroline, Dumas	Delegate	22/05/2016	30/05/2016

Consultative Parties

Party	Name	Position	Arrival Date	Dep.Date
France	Frenot, Yves	CEP Representative	22/05/2016	02/06/2016
France	Guillemain, Anne	Delegate	22/05/2016	01/06/2016
France	Guyonvarch, Olivier	Head of Delegation	22/05/2016	01/06/2016
France	Koubbi, Philippe	CEP Representative	22/05/2016	24/05/2016
France	Lebouvier, Marc	CEP Representative	22/05/2016	02/06/2016
France	Runyo, Fabienne	Alternate	22/05/2016	01/06/2016
France	Semichon, Carole	CEP Representative	18/05/2016	01/06/2016
Germany	Duebner, Walter	Delegate	23/05/2016	27/05/2016
Germany	Gaedicke, Christoph	Delegate	22/05/2016	28/05/2016
Germany	Guretskaya, Anastasia	Delegate	21/05/2016	02/06/2016
Germany	Hain, Stefan	Delegate	20/05/2016	28/05/2016
Germany	Herata, Heike	CEP Representative	20/05/2016	01/06/2016
Germany	Heyn, Andrea	Delegate	23/05/2016	01/06/2016
Germany	Lassig, Rainer	Head of Delegation	21/05/2016	02/06/2016
Germany	Läufer, Andreas	Delegate	24/05/2016	28/05/2016
Germany	Liebschner, Alexander	Delegate	22/05/2016	27/05/2016
Germany	Mißling, Sven	Delegate	21/05/2016	02/06/2016
Germany	Nixdorf, Uwe	Delegate	23/05/2016	31/05/2016
Germany	Schwarzbach, Wiebke	Delegate	20/05/2016	27/05/2016
Germany	Thiede, Felix	Advisor	23/05/2016	01/06/2016
Germany	Vöneky, Silja	Advisor	20/05/2016	02/06/2016
Germany	Winterhoff, Esther	Delegate	23/05/2016	27/05/2016
Germany	Wolfrum, Rüdiger	Advisor	21/05/2016	02/06/2016
India	Chaturvedi, Sanjay	Delegate	22/05/2016	28/05/2016
India	Kumar, Vijay	Head of Delegation	18/05/2016	02/06/2016
India	Ravichandran, M	Head of Delegation	18/05/2016	02/06/2016
India	Reddy, A Sudhakara	Delegate	22/05/2016	28/05/2016
India	Tiwari, Anoop Kumar	CEP Representative	18/05/2016	02/06/2016
India	Vajapayajula, Venkataraman	Delegate	22/05/2016	01/06/2016
Italy	De Rossi, Giuseppe	Advisor	22/05/2016	02/06/2016
Italy	Fioretti, Anna	Delegate	22/05/2016	02/06/2016
Italy	Sgrò, Eugenio	Head of Delegation	21/05/2016	02/06/2016
Italy	Tomaselli, Maria Stefania	Delegate	22/05/2016	02/06/2016
Italy	Torcini, Sandro	CEP Representative	22/05/2016	02/06/2016
Japan	Miyamori, Joji	Head of Delegation	22/05/2016	01/06/2016
Japan	Nakano, Akiko	Advisor	22/05/2016	01/06/2016
Japan	Omori, Ryo	Advisor	22/05/2016	01/06/2016
Japan	Shiraishi, Kazuyuki	Advisor	22/05/2016	31/05/2016
Japan	Takehara, Mari	Advisor	22/05/2016	01/06/2016
Japan	Tanaka, Kenichiro	Advisor	22/05/2016	01/06/2016
Japan	Watanabe, Kentaro	Advisor	22/05/2016	01/06/2016
Japan	Yamaguchi, Shigeru	Advisor	22/05/2016	01/06/2016
Korea (ROK)	Cho, Minjun	Delegate	22/05/2016	01/06/2016
Korea (ROK)	Choi, Hyun-Soo	Delegate	22/05/2016	01/06/2016
Korea (ROK)	Chung, Rae-Kwang	Delegate	22/05/2016	01/06/2016
Korea (ROK)	Kim, Jeong-Hoon	Delegate	22/05/2016	01/06/2016
Korea (ROK)	Park, Jeong-Hak	Delegate	22/05/2016	01/06/2016
Korea (ROK)	Seo, won-sang	Delegate	22/05/2016	01/06/2016
Korea (ROK)	Shin, Hyoung Chul	CEP Representative	22/05/2016	01/06/2016
Korea (ROK)	Yu, Ji-eun	Head of Delegation	22/05/2016	01/06/2016
Netherlands	Bastmeijer, Kees	Advisor	23/05/2016	01/06/2016
Netherlands	De Vries, Janneke	CEP Representative	22/05/2016	01/06/2016

Consultative Parties

Party	Name	Position	Arrival Date	Dep.Date
Netherlands	Elstgeest, Marlynda	Advisor	24/05/2016	01/06/2016
Netherlands	Lefeber, René J.M.	Head of Delegation	21/05/2016	01/06/2016
Netherlands	Peijs, Martijn	Delegate	22/05/2016	02/06/2016
Netherlands	Rossum, van, Edith	Delegate	23/05/2016	01/06/2016
New Zealand	Beggs, Peter	Delegate	20/05/2016	01/06/2016
New Zealand	Dempster, Jillian	Head of Delegation	22/05/2016	01/06/2016
New Zealand	Gilbert, Neil	Advisor	21/05/2016	28/06/2016
New Zealand	Morgan, Fraser	Advisor	21/05/2016	26/05/2016
New Zealand	Newman, Jana	CEP Representative	20/05/2016	01/06/2016
New Zealand	Stent, Danica	Advisor	20/05/2016	01/06/2016
New Zealand	Townend, Andrew	Delegate	20/05/2016	01/06/2016
New Zealand	Trotter, Simon	Delegate	20/05/2016	06/06/2016
New Zealand	Weeber, Barry	Delegate	21/05/2016	01/06/2016
New Zealand	Wilkinson, Kelsie	Delegate	20/05/2016	02/06/2016
New Zealand	Wilson, Gary	Delegate	22/05/2016	27/05/2016
Norway	Araldsen, Hege	Delegate	22/05/2016	01/06/2016
Norway	Eikeland, Else Berit	Head of Delegation	26/05/2016	02/06/2016
Norway	Guldahl, John E.	Delegate	24/05/2016	31/05/2016
Norway	Halvorsen, Svein Tore	Delegate	22/05/2016	28/05/2016
Norway	Heggelund, Kristin	Delegate	24/05/2016	30/05/2016
Norway	Høgestøl, Astrid Charlotte	Delegate	22/05/2016	01/06/2016
Norway	Instefjord, Idar Asmund	Delegate	22/05/2016	01/06/2016
Norway	Johansen, Therese	Delegate	22/05/2016	02/06/2016
Norway	Lowther, Andrew	Advisor	22/05/2016	25/05/2016
Norway	Midthun, Bjørn	Alternate	21/05/2016	27/05/2016
Norway	Njaastad, Birgit	CEP Representative	20/05/2016	01/06/2016
Peru	Chang Boldrini, Luis	Head of Delegation	21/05/2016	01/06/2016
Peru	Tejada, David	Delegate	22/05/2016	01/06/2016
Peru	Villanueva Flores, Rogelio Rolando	Delegate	21/05/2016	01/06/2016
Poland	Bialik, Robert	Alternate	22/05/2016	01/06/2016
Poland	Kidawa, Anna	Delegate	22/05/2016	01/06/2016
Poland	Krawczyk-Grzesiowska, Joanna	Delegate	22/05/2016	01/06/2016
Poland	Misztal, Andrzej	Head of Delegation	22/05/2016	01/06/2016
Poland	Piatkowska, Aleksandra	Advisor	23/05/2016	01/06/2016
Russian Federation	Chernysheva, Larisa	Delegate	22/05/2016	03/06/2016
Russian Federation	Lukin, Valery	CEP Representative	17/05/2016	07/06/2016
Russian Federation	Melnikov, Nikolay	Advisor	22/05/2016	01/06/2016
Russian Federation	Tarasenko, Sergey	Delegate	21/05/2016	02/06/2016
Russian Federation	Titushkin, Vassily	Head of Delegation	22/05/2016	03/06/2016
South Africa	Stemmet, Andreas	Advisor	21/05/2016	02/06/2016
South Africa	Abader, Moegamat Ishaam	CEP Representative	21/05/2016	02/06/2016
South Africa	Bhengu, Thanduxolo	Delegate	22/05/2016	02/06/2016
South Africa	Kingsley, Angela	Alternate	21/05/2016	02/06/2016
South Africa	Mphepya, Jonas	Head of Delegation	21/05/2016	31/05/2016
South Africa	Mthembu, Sibusiso	CEP Representative	21/05/2016	02/06/2016
South Africa	Skinner, Richard	Advisor	21/05/2016	31/05/2016
Spain	Catalan, Manuel	CEP Representative	21/05/2016	02/06/2016
Spain	Gonzalez Ferrera, Eliseo	Delegate	23/05/2016	01/06/2016
Spain	Muñoz de Laborde Bardin, Juan Luis	Head of Delegation	22/05/2016	02/06/2016

Consultative Parties				
Party	Name	Position	Arrival Date	Dep.Date
Spain	Ojeda, Miguel Angel	Delegate	24/05/2016	02/06/2016
Spain	Ramos, Sonia	Delegate	21/05/2016	02/06/2016
Spain	Robles Fraga, Carlos	Alternate	23/05/2016	24/05/2016
Sweden	Karasalo, Mina	Delegate	13/05/2016	07/06/2016
Sweden	Kiefer, Jakob	Head of Delegation	22/05/2016	01/06/2016
Sweden	Selberg, Cecilia	Advisor	21/05/2016	01/06/2016
Sweden	Sjostrand, Rikard	Delegate	22/05/2016	01/06/2016
Ukraine	Fedchuk, Andrii	Alternate	21/05/2016	28/06/2016
United Kingdom	Clouder, Fiona	Delegate	23/05/2016	01/06/2016
United Kingdom	Doubleday, Stuart	CEP Representative	21/05/2016	01/06/2016
United Kingdom	Downie, Rod	Advisor	23/05/2016	27/05/2016
United Kingdom	Francis, Jane	Delegate	22/05/2016	02/06/2016
United Kingdom	Grant, Susie	Delegate	21/05/2016	26/05/2016
United Kingdom	Griffiths, Lowri	Alternate	21/05/2016	02/06/2016
United Kingdom	Hall MBE, John	Delegate	21/05/2016	28/05/2016
United Kingdom	Hughes, Kevin	Delegate	22/05/2016	28/05/2016
United Kingdom	Muñoz, Francisca	Delegate	22/05/2016	01/06/2016
United Kingdom	Nichol, Camilla	Delegate	24/05/2016	27/05/2016
United Kingdom	Rumble, Jane	Head of Delegation	21/05/2016	02/06/2016
United Kingdom	Stockings, Tim	Delegate	29/05/2016	31/05/2016
United Kingdom	Warwick, Paul	Delegate	22/05/2016	01/06/2016
United States	Bergmann, Trisha	Delegate	21/05/2016	31/05/2016
United States	Bloom, Evan T.	Head of Delegation	22/05/2016	02/06/2016
United States	Borg, Scott	Delegate	22/05/2016	27/05/2016
United States	Edwards, David	Delegate	22/05/2016	02/06/2016
United States	Falkner, Kelly	Delegate	22/05/2016	02/06/2016
United States	Ganser, Peter	Alternate	22/05/2016	02/06/2016
United States	Jones, Christopher	Delegate	22/05/2016	02/06/2016
United States	Karentz, Deneb	Advisor	22/05/2016	27/05/2016
United States	Kill, Theodore P.	Delegate	22/05/2016	01/06/2016
United States	Leff, Karin	Delegate	22/05/2016	02/06/2016
United States	McGinn, Nature	Delegate	22/05/2016	02/06/2016
United States	Naveen, Ron	Advisor	22/05/2016	01/06/2016
United States	O'reilly, Jessica	Advisor	22/05/2016	02/06/2016
United States	Penhale, Polly A.	CEP Representative	22/05/2016	01/06/2016
United States	Rudolph, Lawrence	Delegate	22/05/2016	02/06/2016
United States	Rusin, Jeremy	Delegate	22/05/2016	01/06/2016
United States	Wheatley, Victoria	Advisor	24/05/2016	01/06/2016
Uruguay	Nuñez, Daniel	Head of Delegation	22/05/2016	02/06/2016
Uruguay	Fajardo, Alberto	Alternate	22/05/2016	01/06/2016
Uruguay	Lluberas, Albert	Delegate	22/05/2016	02/06/2016
Uruguay	Vignali, Daniel	Advisor	23/05/2016	02/06/2016

Non-Consultative Parties				
Party	**Name**	**Position**	**Arrival Date**	**Dep.Date**
Belarus	Haidashou, Aliaksei	Head of Delegation	22/05/2016	02/06/2016
Canada	File, Susan	Delegate	23/05/2016	28/05/2016
Canada	Scott, David	Alternate	23/05/2016	28/05/2016
Canada	Taillefer, David	Head of Delegation	22/05/2016	02/06/2016
Colombia	Correa Godoy, Leonardo Enrique	Delegate	22/05/2016	01/06/2016
Colombia	Diaz Sanchez, Christian	Delegate	22/05/2016	02/06/2016
Colombia	Echeverry Gutierrez, Alvaro Mauricio	Delegate	22/05/2016	01/06/2016
Colombia	Ferrero Ronquillo, Alex Fernando	Delegate	22/05/2016	31/05/2016
Colombia	Jaimes, Nancy Rocío	Delegate	22/05/2016	01/06/2016
Colombia	Jaimes Parada, Gerson Ricardo	Delegate	22/05/2016	01/06/2016
Colombia	Molano, Mauricio	Delegate	22/05/2016	01/06/2016
Colombia	Monje Pastrana, José Antonio	Delegate	22/05/2016	01/06/2016
Colombia	Montenegro Coral, Ricardo	Head of Delegation	22/05/2016	01/06/2016
Colombia	Sanchez, Dania Lorena	Delegate	22/05/2016	02/06/2016
Colombia	Soltau, Juan Manuel	Delegate	22/05/2016	31/05/2016
Finland	Mähönen, Outi	CEP Representative	20/05/2016	02/06/2016
Finland	Valjento, Liisa	Head of Delegation	20/05/2016	02/06/2016
Malaysia	Abd Rahman, Mohd Nasaruddin	Delegate	22/05/2016	28/05/2016
Malaysia	Mohd Nor, Salleh	Delegate	22/05/2016	31/05/2016
Malaysia	Yahaya, Mohd Azhar	Head of Delegation	21/05/2016	26/05/2016
Monaco	Biancheri, Daniele	Advisor	24/05/2016	01/06/2016
Monaco	Impagliazzo, Céline	Head of Delegation	22/05/2016	27/05/2016
Portugal	Cotrim, António Luís	Delegate	22/05/2016	01/06/2016
Portugal	Podgorny, Rosa	Delegate	22/05/2016	01/06/2016
Portugal	Xavier, José Carlos Caetano	Head of Delegation	20/05/2016	03/06/2016
Romania	Cotta, Mihaela	Advisor	22/05/2016	31/05/2016
Romania	Radu, Camelia	Head of Delegation	25/05/2016	01/06/2016
Switzerland	Dörig, Edgar	Head of Delegation	22/05/2016	05/06/2016
Switzerland	Krebs, Martin	Delegate	26/05/2016	05/06/2016
Switzerland	Schürch, Frank Markus	Delegate	22/05/2016	05/06/2016
Switzerland	Trautweiler, Barbara	Delegate	22/05/2016	30/05/2016
Turkey	Bayar, Eda	Delegate	21/05/2016	28/05/2016
Turkey	Beşiktepe, Şükrü Turan	Delegate	22/05/2016	02/06/2016
Turkey	Celik, Yakup	Advisor	24/05/2016	02/06/2016
Turkey	Durak, Onur Sabri	Delegate	22/05/2016	01/06/2016
Turkey	Evlice, Onur	Delegate	21/05/2016	02/06/2016
Turkey	Gürkaynak, Muharrem	Delegate	22/05/2016	02/06/2016
Turkey	Güven, Mahmut	Delegate	22/05/2016	02/06/2016
Turkey	Hacioğlu, Mr. Ekrem	Delegate	21/05/2016	01/06/2016
Turkey	Halici, Gökhan	Delegate	23/05/2016	31/05/2016
Turkey	Kaya, Naciye Gökçen	Delegate	21/05/2016	02/06/2016
Turkey	Önder, Ali Murat	Delegate	21/05/2016	02/06/2016
Turkey	Özsoy Çiçek, Burcu	Delegate	21/05/2016	27/05/2016
Turkey	Öztürk, Bayram	Delegate	21/05/2016	28/05/2016
Turkey	Şahinkaya, İbrahim Cem	Head of Delegation	21/05/2016	02/06/2016
Turkey	Tabak, Haluk	Delegate	21/05/2016	02/06/2016

Non-Consultative Parties				
Party	**Name**	**Position**	**Arrival Date**	**Dep.Date**
Turkey	Tolun, Leyla Gamze	Delegate	20/05/2016	05/06/2016
Turkey	Türkel, Mehmet Ali	Delegate	21/05/2016	02/06/2016
Turkey	Ural, Hayri Şafak	Delegate	22/05/2016	25/05/2016
Venezuela	Barreto, Guillermo	Delegate	28/05/2016	02/06/2016
Venezuela	Carlos , Castellanos	Delegate	22/05/2016	01/06/2016
Venezuela	Palacios, Sugerlys	Delegate	22/05/2016	01/06/2016
Venezuela	Prieto, Dulce	Delegate	28/05/2016	02/06/2016
Venezuela	Sira, Eloy	Head of Delegation	22/05/2016	02/06/2016

Observers, Experts and Guests				
Party	Name	Position	Arrival Date	Dep.Date
CCAMLR	Belchier, Mark	Advisor	22/05/2016	28/05/2016
CCAMLR	Reid, Keith	Advisor	22/05/2016	28/05/2016
CCAMLR	Wright, Andrew	Head of Delegation	22/05/2016	01/06/2016
COMNAP	Rogan-Finnemore, Michelle	Head of Delegation	22/05/2016	01/06/2016
SCAR	Baeseman, Jenny	Delegate	22/05/2016	01/06/2016
SCAR	Chown, Steven L.	Delegate	22/05/2016	28/05/2016
SCAR	López-Martínez, Jerónimo	Head of Delegation	22/05/2016	02/06/2016
SCAR	Terauds, Aleks	CEP Representative	22/05/2016	02/06/2016
ASOC	Bodin, Svante	Delegate	23/05/2016	01/06/2016
ASOC	Chen, Jiliang	Delegate	21/05/2016	01/06/2016
ASOC	Christian, Claire	Head of Delegation	21/05/2016	02/06/2016
ASOC	Dolan, Ryan	Delegate	22/05/2016	28/05/2016
ASOC	Kavanagh, Andrea	Delegate	23/05/2016	01/06/2016
ASOC	Roura, Ricardo	CEP Representative	23/05/2016	01/06/2016
ASOC	Tamm, Sune	Delegate	23/05/2016	01/06/2016
ASOC	Werner Kinkelin, Rodolfo	Delegate	23/05/2016	27/05/2016
IAATO	Crosbie, Kim	Head of Delegation	21/05/2016	31/05/2016
IAATO	Hohn-Bowen, Ute	Advisor	24/05/2016	01/06/2016
IAATO	Kelley, Lisa	Advisor	21/05/2016	02/06/2016
IAATO	Lynnes, Amanda	CEP Representative	21/05/2016	28/06/2016
IAATO	Prossin, Andrew	Advisor	24/05/2016	31/05/2016
IAATO	Retamales, Mauricio	Advisor	24/05/2016	26/05/2016
IAATO	Rootes, David	Alternate	22/05/2016	01/06/2016
IAATO	Schillat, Monika	Advisor	22/05/2016	02/06/2016
IHO	Gorziglia, Hugo	Alternate	23/05/2016	27/05/2016
IHO	Ward, Robert	Head of Delegation	23/05/2016	27/05/2016
IPCC	Sivakumar, Mannava	Head of Delegation	22/05/2016	01/06/2016
WMO	Sparrow, Mike	Head of Delegation	22/05/2016	31/05/2016

Host Country Secretariat				
Party	**Name**	**Position**	**Arrival Date**	**Dep.Date**
HC Secretariat	Aranda, Rosario	HCS Staff	16/05/2016	02/06/2016
HC Secretariat	Arce, María Josefa	HCS Staff	16/05/2016	02/06/2016
HC Secretariat	Argomedo, Rocío	HCS Staff	16/05/2016	02/06/2016
HC Secretariat	Arriagada, Luis	HCS Staff	16/05/2016	02/06/2016
HC Secretariat	Benev, Boriana	HCS Staff	16/05/2016	02/06/2016
HC Secretariat	Bravo, Pablo	HCS Staff	16/05/2016	02/06/2016
HC Secretariat	Bustamante, Christian	HCS Staff	16/05/2016	02/06/2016
HC Secretariat	Cahue, Karla	HCS Staff	16/05/2016	02/06/2016
HC Secretariat	Castillo, Ismael	HCS Staff	16/05/2016	02/06/2016
HC Secretariat	Cifuentes, María José	HCS Staff	16/05/2016	02/06/2016
HC Secretariat	Cisternas, Giovanni	HCS Staff	16/05/2016	02/06/2016
HC Secretariat	Cofré, Eduardo	HCS Staff	16/05/2016	02/06/2016
HC Secretariat	Contardo, Fernando	HCS Staff	16/05/2016	02/06/2016
HC Secretariat	Echavarría, Paula	HCS Staff	16/05/2016	02/06/2016
HC Secretariat	Escobar, Natalia	HCS Staff	16/05/2016	02/06/2016
HC Secretariat	Estay, Sebastián	HCS Staff	16/05/2016	02/06/2016
HC Secretariat	Estay, Denisse	HCS Staff	16/05/2016	02/06/2016
HC Secretariat	Fuentes, Montserrat	HCS Staff	16/05/2016	02/06/2016
HC Secretariat	Galaz, Marcela	HCS Staff	16/05/2016	02/06/2016
HC Secretariat	Gallardo, María Fernanda	HCS Staff	16/05/2016	02/06/2016
HC Secretariat	González, Oriana	HCS Staff	16/05/2016	02/06/2016
HC Secretariat	González, Karen	HCS Staff	16/05/2016	02/06/2016
HC Secretariat	González, Hugo	HCS Staff	16/05/2016	02/06/2016
HC Secretariat	Guerrero, Néstor	HCS Staff	16/05/2016	02/06/2016
HC Secretariat	Guggisberg, Nadin	HCS Staff	16/05/2016	02/06/2016
HC Secretariat	Gutiérrez, Cristina	HCS Staff	16/05/2016	02/06/2016
HC Secretariat	Henríquez, Lorena	HCS Staff	16/05/2016	02/06/2016
HC Secretariat	Herrera, Claudia	HCS Staff	16/05/2016	02/06/2016
HC Secretariat	Klaassen, Consuelo	HCS Staff	16/05/2016	02/06/2016
HC Secretariat	Koffmann, Mariana	HCS Staff	16/05/2016	02/06/2016
HC Secretariat	Larenas, Alejandra	HCS Staff	16/05/2016	02/06/2016
HC Secretariat	Llanos, Carolina	HCS Staff	16/05/2016	02/06/2016
HC Secretariat	Matamoros, Rodrigo	HCS Staff	16/05/2016	02/06/2016
HC Secretariat	Molina, Carla	HCS Staff	16/05/2016	02/06/2016
HC Secretariat	Montero, Alejandro	HCS Staff	16/05/2016	02/06/2016
HC Secretariat	Murua, Javier	HCS Staff	16/05/2016	02/06/2016
HC Secretariat	Pino, Ana	HCS Staff	16/05/2016	02/06/2016
HC Secretariat	Powell, Patricio	HC Executive Secretary	16/05/2016	02/06/2016
HC Secretariat	Quiñones, Claudio	HCS Staff	16/05/2016	02/06/2016
HC Secretariat	Rivera, Francisca	HCS Staff	16/05/2016	02/06/2016
HC Secretariat	Robinovich, Daniel	HCS Staff	16/05/2016	02/06/2016
HC Secretariat	Rodríguez, Monserrat	HCS Staff	16/05/2016	02/06/2016
HC Secretariat	Rodríguez, Jacqueline	HCS Staff	16/05/2016	02/06/2016
HC Secretariat	Soto, Oriana	HCS Staff	16/05/2016	02/06/2016
HC Secretariat	Tort, Fabián	HCS Staff	16/05/2016	02/06/2016
HC Secretariat	Ureta, Paola	HCS Staff	16/05/2016	02/06/2016
HC Secretariat	Vergara, Isabel	HCS Staff	16/05/2016	02/06/2016
HC Secretariat	Vergara, Alejandro	HCS Staff	16/05/2016	02/06/2016
HC Secretariat	Villegas, Roberto	HCS Staff	16/05/2016	02/06/2016

Antarctic Treaty Secretariat				
Party	**Name**	**Position**	**Arrival Date**	**Dep.Date**
ATS	Acero, José Maria	Alternate	18/05/2016	02/06/2016
ATS	Agraz, José Luis	Staff	15/05/2016	02/06/2016
ATS	Balok, Anna	Staff	18/05/2016	02/06/2016
ATS	Davies, Paul	Staff	19/05/2016	02/06/2016
ATS	Portella Sampaio, Daniela	Staff	19/05/2016	02/06/2016
ATS	Reinke, Manfred	Head of Delegation	15/05/2016	02/06/2016
ATS	Wainschenker, Pablo	Staff	16/05/2016	02/06/2016
ATS	Walton, David W H	Staff	16/05/2016	02/06/2016
ATS	Wydler, Diego	Staff	15/05/2016	02/06/2016
T&I Services	Alal, Cecilia	Head of Delegation	19/05/2016	02/06/2016
T&I Services	Babaev, David	Staff	20/05/2016	02/06/2016
T&I Services	Bouladon, Sabine	Staff	25/05/2016	01/06/2016
T&I Services	Cook, Elena	Staff	22/05/2016	02/06/2016
T&I Services	Coussaert, Joelle	Staff	22/05/2016	02/06/2016
T&I Services	Falaleyev, Andrey	Staff	22/05/2016	02/06/2016
T&I Services	Fernandez, Jimena	Staff	20/05/2016	02/06/2016
T&I Services	Garteiser, Claire	Staff	22/05/2016	01/06/2016
T&I Services	Kasimova, Katya	Staff	22/05/2016	01/06/2016
T&I Services	Malmontet, Benoit	Staff	22/05/2016	01/06/2016
T&I Services	Malofeeva, Elena	Staff	22/05/2016	02/06/2016
T&I Services	Martinez, Silvia	Staff	25/05/2016	01/06/2016
T&I Services	Mullova, Ludmila	Staff	22/05/2016	01/06/2016
T&I Services	Orlando, Marc	Staff	21/05/2016	02/06/2016
T&I Services	Perino, María del Valle	Staff	22/05/2016	01/06/2016
T&I Services	Piccione Thomas, Georgina	Staff	22/05/2016	01/06/2016
T&I Services	Speziali, Maria Laura	Staff	22/05/2016	02/06/2016
T&I Services	Tanguy, Philippe	Staff	21/05/2016	02/06/2016
T&I Services	Wallace, Roslyn	Staff	22/05/2016	02/06/2016

www.ingramcontent.com/pod-product-compliance
Lightning Source LLC
Chambersburg PA
CBHW061616210326
41520CB00041B/7470

9 7 8 9 8 7 4 0 2 4 2 6 8